COLORING INTO EXISTENCE

D1594646

Coloring into Existence

Queer of Color Worldmaking
in Children's Literature

Isabel Millán

NEW YORK UNIVERSITY PRESS
New York, New York

NEW YORK UNIVERSITY PRESS
New York
www.nyupress.org

© 2023 by New York University
All rights reserved

Please contact the Library of Congress for Cataloging-in-Publication data.
ISBN: 9781479816972 (hardback)
ISBN: 9781479816989 (paperback)
ISBN: 9781479817009 (library ebook)
ISBN: 9781479817009 (consumer ebook)

This book is printed on acid-free paper, and its binding materials are chosen for strength and durability. We strive to use environmentally responsible suppliers and materials to the greatest extent possible in publishing our books.

Manufactured in the United States of America

10 9 8 7 6 5 4 3 2 1

Also available as an ebook

To Melissa Cardoza and Margarita Sada,
whose 2004 picture book, Tengo una tía que no es monjita, *inspired my own journey into the wondrous possibilities of LGBTQ+ children's literature.*

CONTENTS

Introduction

Reading in Drag, Coloring in Autofantasia

When each of your colors has space to shine, you light up the whole sky.
—Trinity Neal and DeShanna Neal

Picture books are, often, both much simpler and richer and more complicated than texts for older children, or even for young adults.
—Perry Nodelman

In 2015, drag queens sashayed off runways and into libraries, making Drag Queen Story Hour their new performative platform. While gender performers have entertained adults and children alike for centuries, this contemporary phenomenon is unique in its celebration of drag culture, its didactic emphasis on LGBTQ+ children's literature, and, of course, its target audience: children. Michelle Tea, founder of Radar Productions, began Drag Queen Story Hour (DQSH) at a San Francisco public library to "defy rigid gender restrictions and imagine a world where people can present as they wish."[1] Since then, DQSH events have become increasingly popular worldwide, spreading across Europe, Asia, and Latin America, while attracting criticism across the political spectrum. For example, a *Wall Street Journal* opinion piece denounced DQSH for its "propagandistic reading list," asking, "How many kids really want to hear one more tiresome lesson about 'individuality,' much less same-sex marriage?"[2] Reducing drag to "comic entertainment," what the *Wall Street Journal* missed was the complexity and depth of drag as well as children's picture books. Yet, while story hours provide lively spaces that bring LGBTQ+ themes and people into children's lives, finding queer and trans of color (QTOC) reading material has proven more challenging. Within what might be called the LGBTQ+ children's literary canon, there are fewer children's picture books with central characters who are queer or trans people of color compared to white queer or trans characters.

Coloring into Existence: Queer of Color Worldmaking in Children's Literature is a venture into queer and trans of color children's picture books across North America, but also, and more urgently, it aims to counter forms of marginalization that can lead to real violence against entire communities. An incident in a Houston city library makes this visceral: an armed individual interrupted a DQSH event, shouting queerphobic and transphobic hate speech. Although this threat of violence was eventually de-escalated and ended with the perpetrator being escorted outside, the risk of similar encounters occurring remains persistent.[3]

As this episode reveals, children are unfortunately not exempt from hate crimes against LGBTQ+ and QTOC communities.[4] Outside of DQSH events, children have experienced extreme forms of anti-LGBTQ+ violence. For example, three-year-old Ronnie Antonio Paris was tragically murdered in 2005 by his father, who believed he would grow up to be gay.[5] In August 2010, Pedro Jones murdered his girlfriend's seventeen-month-old toddler for "acting like a girl."[6] In May 2013, eight-year-old Gabriel Fernandez died after being repeatedly beaten and starved by his mother and her boyfriend for allegedly being gay.[7] In June 2018, ten-year-old Anthony Avalos was also tortured to death after coming out to his family.[8] Two months later, nine-year-old Jamel Myles died by suicide after coming out and being bullied at school.[9] These are only a few documented examples of children of color ages ten and under who lost their lives because they were or were perceived as queer, trans, or gender variant.[10] Can we imagine a world without such cruelty?

These examples of horrific violence force us to reckon with the paradox that while children are generally figured as "innocents," not all of them are seen as deserving of life. José Esteban Muñoz powerfully articulates this reality: "The future is only the stuff of some kids. Racialized kids, queer kids, are not the sovereign princes of futurity."[11] Instances of bewildering violence enacted upon queer and trans children of color shadow the perceived innocence of childhood and necessarily shape cultural materials aimed at children and their families. If queer and trans of color children are not meant to survive, their resiliency into adulthood might constitute a triumph.

In contemplating the concept of existence, one might ask, for whom?[12] Who can truly exist under our contemporary understandings of humanity, freedom, rights, and responsibilities? Such triumph is predicated on multiple factors, including the role of individuals, families, communities, and society as a whole. Our recent history demonstrates how quickly our laws, policies, and political climate can change. Within the US, for example, on October 28, 2009, then-president Obama signed the Matthew Shepard and James Byrd, Jr., Hate Crimes Prevention Act into law, which expanded federal protections against hate crimes by including gender, sexual orientation, gender identity, and disability to the prior categories of race, color, religion, and national origin. Despite this law, the 2016 presidential election results that led to the Trump administration erupted into a rolling back of protections and an increase in hate crimes.[13] Across individual US states, it is astonishing how much state-sanctioned curriculum can vary around LGBTQ+ inclusivity. California's FAIR Education Act, which went into effect on January 1, 2012, mandates that the state's public education be LGBTQ-inclusive. Meanwhile, one of many anti-LGBTQ+ pieces of legislation signed into law includes Florida's HB 1557 or "Don't Say Gay" Bill.[14] Book bans, although not at all a recent occurrence, are being enacted at an alarming rate, mobilized into organized efforts to remove LGBTQ-inclusive books from libraries and schools.[15] Embedded within all of these examples are the effects this has on queer and trans of color communities who must also contend with queerphobia, transphobia, xenophobia, classism, sexism, ableism, and racism—including equal efforts against critical race theory. This context informs my critical engagement with children's picture books.

My research documents the emergence of a North American queer of color children's literary archive, focusing on the creation, distribution, and potential impact of picture books by and about queer and trans of color authors. *Coloring into Existence* is a comparative and hemispheric study across Canada, the United States, and Mexico over approximately three decades (1990 to 2020), from the publication of *Asha's Mums* in 1990 to more recent titles like *My Rainbow* in 2020. This project asks the following questions: Under what sociopolitical circumstances does this literature emerge? What does a queer and trans of color aesthetic or theory look like in picture books? Can the acts of imagination and worldmaking that picture books inspire produce a realm of freedom, healing, and transformation for queer and trans children of color, as well as for the books' authors, illustrators, publishers, or additional readers?

This book responds to a growing interest in LGBTQ-themed children's literature on all sides of the political spectrum, albeit for different reasons. Fusing literary criticism and close readings with historical analysis and interviews, I survey an emerging literary archive and begin to delineate the boundaries and characteristics of what I am arguing can be conceptualized as a queer and trans of color children's picture book canon. I also argue that we must understand the rich context in which *Asha's Mums* (1990) and other queer and trans of color picture books were produced, because considering their political and sociohistorical circumstances, along with the national and cultural factors regulating their circulation, is vital to comprehending their impressive transborder reach and potential impact on creators, publishers, and readers.

Throughout *Coloring into Existence*, I engage these picture books through what I coin the hermeneutic of autofantasía, a mode of interpretation and methodology that considers autofantasía as (1) a literary genre of life writing or autofiction, (2) an artistic or illustration technique, (3) a political impetus mobilized by publishers, and (4) a subversive (mis)reading practice. I analyze the curious ways that queer and trans of color narratives overwhelmingly infuse biographical details of sexuality, gender identity, race/ethnicity, language, citizenship, and disability, which otherwise tend to fall outside contemporary understandings of age-appropriate or childnormative content for children. Often unapologetically politically motivated, queer and trans of color picture books can serve as the basis for imagining or fantasizing about potential disruptions to structures of power within and outside literary worlds.

Coloring Inside, Over, and Outside the Lines

"Coloring"

As the title suggests, *Coloring into Existence* takes the act of coloring seriously, exploring its multifaceted significance. Coloring, as in the verb *to color*, may include the acts of coloring inside or over and outside the lines of a coloring book. It may also refer to coloring, drawing, painting, or otherwise illustrating children's picture books. More conceptually, coloring captures the act of coloring in characters and, in doing so, racializing and gendering markings on paper. The term also usefully invokes Frederick Douglass's "The Color Line" (1881), which he used to analyze prejudice and white supremacy as it related to slavery, personhood, and Black Americans.[16] The concept of the color line was rearticulated by W. E. B. Du Bois, Alexander Walters, Henry B. Brown, and H. Sylvester Williams in "To the Nations of the World," an address at the 1900 Pan-African Association Conference in London in which Du Bois declared: "The problem of the twentieth century is the problem of the colour line, the question as to how far differences of race, which show themselves chiefly in the colour of the skin and the texture of the hair, are going to be made, hereafter, the basis of denying to over half the world the right of sharing to their utmost ability the opportunities and privileges of modern civilisation."[17] *Coloring into Existence* recognizes the color line's transborder etymology and its continued relevance to contemporary understandings of Blackness and the racialization of communities of color. To acknowledge these acts of coloring can be transgressive. As Imani Perry articulates: "people live in the zone of nonpersonhood. They may be treated as 'dead' before the law. But their creations have always persisted, and they trouble and haunt the dominant order."[18] Within the creative realm, Perry argues, "Art is both creative and artifactual, and it is artifice to the extent that we get taken up in its worlds."[19] Considering cultural and artistic endeavors alongside the Spanish translation for "of color" ["de color"] also invokes the popular Spanish folk song "De colores." While scholars continue to debate the song's origins, it is often associated with Catholicism, as well as the Chicanx movement, where it was reappropriated as a freedom song by the United Farm Workers (UFW).[20] Within my own autofantastic worldview, I reimagine it or read it queerly, noting its explicit references to the "many colors" of the "lustrous rainbow."[21]

What does a queer and trans of color aesthetic look like within picture books? How does one extract a queer of color critique from children's literature? In response, I am suggesting that queer and trans of color children's authors, illustrators, publishers, and readers color over and outside the lines. For author/illustrator Maya Gonzalez, "art is always an act of courage."[22] The courageous utility of art—in this case, children's picture books—is evident across Gonzalez's repertoire and those of other queer and trans of color authors and illustrators whose picture books intentionally "irritate, alienate, and shock" the mainstream public while also providing a habitable literary home for queer and trans of color children.[23] Often refusing to conform to industry standards, these picture book creators tend to mobilize alternative modes of production and distribution to create a world for themselves and the wider queer and trans of color community.

Blood Orange Press, a small independent press in Oakland, California, asks, "What if every child saw themselves in children's books?"[24] While an aspiring vision, this question reveals the unfortunate reality that some children, and even entire communities, are not reflected in children's literature. It is no secret that whiteness dominates children's literature. Little has changed since Nancy Larrick surveyed US children's publishing in 1965 in "The All-White World of Children's Books."[25] Each year, the Cooperative Children's Book Center (CCBC) collects and releases statistics demonstrating patterns in the publication of children's books in the United States.[26] In 2018, for example, half of the 3,134 picture books published depicted white characters. In contrast, only 10 percent depicted Black or African American characters, 7 percent depicted Asian Pacific Islander/Asian Pacific American characters, 5 percent depicted Latinx characters, and 1 percent depicted American Indian/First Nations characters.[27] Most telling, perhaps, is the fact that after "White," the category of "Animals or Others" was in the second highest percentage of books, at 27 percent.[28] If, in addition to race, ethnicity, and indigeneity, we also consider the LGBTQ+ and disabled communities, the figures are even more devastating. Maya Gonzalez usefully depicts the data as a matter of "missing books," noting that in 2015, at least 498 additional books should have been published to proportionately represent the LGBTQ+ community, and by the same measure, at least 996 books on the disabled community were missing. My analysis of picture books considers not only who is being represented but *how*.

Queer Theory's "Child" and Children's Literature

From its inception, queer theory has not shied away from the concept of the child or childhood, although how they converge is often contested. For example, Gloria E. Anzaldúa's essay "La Prieta" in *This Bridge Called*

My Back (1981) recounted her queer childhood: "In [my mother's] eyes and in the eyes of others I saw myself reflected as 'strange,' 'abnormal,' 'QUEER.' I saw no other reflection."[29] This sense of queer alienation as a child developed into her theorization of El Mundo Zurdo [The Left-Handed World].[30] Ten years later, Eve Kosofsky Sedgwick published "How to Bring Your Kids Up Gay" (1991), a response to suicide rates among LGBTQ+ youth, psychoanalysis, and psychiatry that cautioned against the newly established DSM-III category of "Gender Identity Disorder of Childhood" (GIDC).[31]

Since then, queer theory's fascination with the concept of "the child" has yielded Lee Edelman on the one hand and Kathryn Bond Stockton on the other. Edelman's *No Future: Queer Theory and the Death Drive* (2004) problematized "the cult of the Child" and "Save Our Children" rhetoric by proposing that "the Child as futurity's emblem must die."[32] While one must be critical of "reproductive futurism," I join other queer of color scholars such as José Esteban Muñoz who disagree with Edelman's assertion that queerness can only exist once the child is usurped or that queerness must "choose, instead, *not* to choose the Child, as disciplinary image of the Imaginary past or as site of a projective identification with an always impossible future."[33] Considering the relationality between queerness and children from multiple interlocutors, Steven Bruhm and Natasha Hurley's edited volume, *Curiouser: On the Queerness of Children* (2004), brought together scholars of sexuality studies (Part I. Sexing the Child) with queer theorists (Part II. The Queers We Might Have Been). The collection emphasized "*identifying* and *articulating* queer child life" in order to "imagine where the desire of the adult and the desire of the child might diverge."[34] Therefore, "the figure of the child is not the anti-queer, but its future is one we might do well not to predict."[35] The last chapter, Kathryn Bond Stockton's "Growing Sideways, or Versions of the Queer Child: The Ghost, the Homosexual, the Freudian, the Innocent, and the Interval of Animal," would eventually be expanded into the monograph *The Queer Child: Or Growing Sideways in the Twentieth Century* (2009), detailing the numerous ways children are always already queer or queered. Building on *Curiouser*'s conceptual work of the child and childhood, the 2016 *GLQ: A Journal of Lesbian and Gay Studies* special issue, "The Child Now," edited by Jules Gill-Peterson, Rebekah Sheldon, and Kathryn Bond Stockton, aimed to "confront how race, gender, and sexuality are made to live and grow in children's bodies."[36] Gill-Peterson also advanced a trans of color critique of eugenics, experimental testing, and Western medicine in *Histories of the Transgender Child* (2018). More recent titles such as Hannah Dyer's *The Queer Aesthetics of Childhood: Asymmetries of Innocence and the Cultural Politics of Child Development* (2019) and Anna Fishzon and Emma Lieber's collection, *The Queerness of Childhood: Essays from the Other Side of the Looking Glass* (2021), continue to justify our ongoing preoccupations between queerness and child.[37] As Kenneth Kidd summarizes in "Queer Theory's Child and Children's Literature Studies" (2011), "Children's literature scholars have learned a lot from queer theory, and queer theory, while it has no particular obligation to children's literature, could benefit from greater and more diverse engagement with it."[38]

Thus, for readers outside the field, I humbly present this paragraph as a crash course in the field of children's literature. As a field of study, children's literature became institutionalized in the 1970s. This included the creation of international and national associations such as the International Research Society for Children's Literature (IRSCL) and the Children's Literature Association (ChLA).[39] Among the leading journals in children's literature, we might consider *Children's Literature, Children's Literature Association Quarterly, The Lion and the Unicorn, Journal of Children's Literature, Children's Literature in Education, International Research in Children's Literature,* and *Bookbird: A Journal of International Children's Literature,* to name a few that publish primarily in English. Children's literary criticism takes as its mode of analysis an array of texts that might fall under the larger umbrella of "children's literature." Examples of such primary sources are included in *The Norton Anthology of Children's Literature: The Traditions in English* (2005), namely: alphabets, chapbooks, primers and readers, fairy tales, fables, myths, legends, religious stories, fantasy, science fiction, picture books, comics, verse, plays, books of instruction, and life writing.[40] Each of these can be understood within its unique history and context such that, for example, European print culture directed explicitly at children can be traced back to the fifteenth century through nursery rhymes, but it only fully emerged during the eighteenth and nineteenth centuries, when the rise of childhood as a concept led to the development of children's primers, periodicals, and magazines.[41] Generally, children's literary scholars consider texts that are intentionally directed at children or young adults but, more often than not, authored by adults. Stories written by children might also be considered children's literature, although they tend to be referred to as "children's writings" or "writing by children." Children's literature may also refer to literary works not originally intended for children or work consumed by adults and children alike.[42]

When combining queer studies and children's literature, scholarship on LGBTQ+ young adult (YA) literature has gained more traction within these fields than scholarship on LGBTQ+ picture books until more recently. Notable examples of the former include Michael Cart and Christine A. Jenkins's *The Heart Has Its Reasons: Young Adult Literature with Gay/Lesbian/Queer Content, 1969–2004* (2006); Michelle Anne Abate and Kenneth Kidd's edited volume, *Over the Rainbow: Queer Children's and Young Adult Literature* (2011), which prioritized literary criticism and queer cultural materials such as YA novels, although it did include at least one chapter on picture books; Tison Pugh's *Innocence, Heterosexuality, and the Queerness of Children's Literature* (2011); and Derritt Mason's *Queer Anxieties of Young Adult Literature and Culture* (2021).[43] Meanwhile, scholarship on LGBTQ+ picture books has been more successful as journal articles or book chapters.[44] Only recently are collections or whole monographs being devoted exclusively to LGBTQ+ children's picture books, such as Jennifer Miller's *The Transformative Potential of LGBTQ+ Children's Picture Books* (2022) and her forthcoming co-edited volume with Sara Austin, *Reading LGBTQ+ Children's Picture Books* (expected 2024), as well as this title, *Coloring into Existence*.[45]

Although ancient writing systems such as hieroglyphs incorporated logograms, and manuscripts such as codices and those produced during the medieval period are known for their elaborate illustrations, the picture book as we understand it today is a relatively recent format combining written text with illustrations.[46] Not to be confused with an illustrated story, which might include cover art, an illustrated dust jacket, or limited illustrations scattered throughout, the modern picture book format emerged from toy books and was greatly influenced by illustrators such as Randolph Caldecott.[47] Although exceptions abound, the typical standard for a contemporary children's picture book is thirty-two pages, printed in color, and usually dominated by illustrations, larger fonts, and "age-appropriate" or childnormative vocabulary.[48] Unlike unillustrated or sparingly illustrated middle-grade chapter books or YA novels, contemporary children's picture books are distinct in that each text has the potential to tell at least three stories: one based on the written text, a second based on the illustrations, and a third based on the union between text and illustrations.[49] And although some picture books are created exclusively for adults, my focus on picture books prioritizes a much younger target audience—children in preschool, kindergarten, or early elementary school.

My analysis herein considers the paratextual features of picture books, including peritext and epitext.[50] Taken together, my close readings emphasize the relevance of context, much like Jack Zipes, Julia L. Mickenberg, and Philip Nel. Jack Zipes argues, for example, that "from the very beginning, when books were first explicitly printed for children in the sixteenth century, politics played a 'radical' role in primers, the Bible, and alphabet books."[51] In addition to analytic practices of detailing the sociopolitical and historical contexts of particular works, scholars such as Barnard Dupriez emphasize the relationship between literature and readers or reading practices, positing that "the meaning of every text depends on the decisions made by its author and by its reader," or, in the words of Katharine Jones: "acknowledging the contribution of both reader *and* text."[52] My own engagement with queer and trans of color children's literature similarly takes into account both the context in which it was produced, as well as the question of readership and autofantastic reading practices—or using Meyer Howard Abrams's classifications: a literary analysis that considers the work, the artist, the audience, and the universe.[53]

Deciding which picture books warrant immediate attention and should be included under "LGBTQ+ children's literature" has been, despite my careful attention, an act in creating borders—not only in regard to genre but also in terms of authorship and content. For example, one of the dilemmas in categorizing LGBTQ+ children's picture books lies in how we conceptualize gender and sexuality. Consider, for example, books depicting girls who want to play sports, cut their hair short, or do not like wearing dresses. These characters can be perceived as tomboys, or even as butch, but their gender transgressions, more often than not, are framed as feminist rather than as queer or both.[54] Such picture books are more likely to appear in feminist bibliographies than LGBTQ+ ones.

In contrast, boys who want to wear dresses or play with dolls are often perceived as gay or queer, conflating gender with sexuality. An early example, told through animal characters, is Munro Leaf's *The Story of Ferdinand* (1936), which includes a bull who would rather smell flowers than fight. Decades later, Charlotte Zolotow's *William's Doll* (1972) features a little boy named William, who is ridiculed as a "creep" and a "sissy" for wanting a doll. William's unfathomable gender transgression is resolved in the book through the cisnormativity and heteronormativity of his grandmother's gaze, which equates having a doll with William's future paternal responsibilities. Other titles with similar gender transgressions include Bruce Mack's *Jesse's Dream Skirt* (1977/1979), Tomie dePaola's *Oliver Button Is a Sissy* (1979), and Elizabeth Winthrop's *Tough Eddie* (1985).[55] In contrast, Lois Gould's *X: A Fabulous Child's Story* (1972), published the same year as *William's Doll*, explicitly centers gender-neutral childrearing as its primary theme. The story originally appeared in *Ms.* magazine and then as a picture book illustrated by Jacqueline Chwast in 1978.[56] These titles were mostly published during the 1970s—an era shaped by the American Psychiatric Association's removal of "homosexuality" as a classification of mental illness in 1973.

Titles featuring out or explicit adult lesbian characters also began to be published in the United States during the 1970s. Jane Severance's *When Megan Went Away* (1979) was an early title that included lesbian relationships and breakups.[57] With the ongoing effects of the US Civil Rights, feminist, and LGBTQ+ rights movements, the 1980s ushered in picture books with more robust lesbian representation, such as titles by Jane Severance (*Lots of Mommies*, 1983) and Lesléa Newman (*Heather Has Two Mommies*, 1989; *Belinda's Bouquet*, 1989), whereas the tragedies of the 1980s HIV/AIDS epidemic were introduced by MaryKate Jordan (*Losing Uncle Tim*, 1989).

Though each merits its own analysis, all titles published throughout the 1970s and 1980s—crucially marking the beginning of the LGBTQ+ children's picture book canon within North America—exclusively featured white characters or were written by white authors. Additionally, as would later become an established trend, these LGBTQ-themed children's picture books only depicted adults as queer or emphasized gender transgressions over sexuality for child characters. Where queer desire was concerned, this was restricted to queer desire among adults.

Elizabeth A. Ford clarifies this tendency: "Ultimately, it is the fear of what children might learn about their own sexual identities, not about the sexuality of adults around them, that makes these books controversial."[58] In search of queer and trans of color visuality, *Coloring into Existence* unearths QTOC authors and illustrators, examining how they have reinvigorated gender, sexuality, and racial discourse directed at children between 1990 and 2020.

Childnormativity

Queer and trans of color children's literature exists within a liminal space, at times in opposition to and at other times cloaked beneath what I call "childnormativity," or what society recognizes as childhood's normative culture. First, childnormativity creates subjects categorized by age into socially acceptable groupings like infants and toddlers.[59] All children, in turn, are juxtaposed against those who are not constructed as children, such as tweens, young adults, adults, or elders.[60] Second, childnormativity includes the cultural production of material goods such as literature, television, films, toys, games, and social media that explicitly target child audiences. These materials are often didactic in that they provide some form of instruction or lessons for children. Although presumably for children, they must equally target and appeal to adults, who almost exclusively produce and purchase them. Third, children and their material goods usually circulate in childnormative spaces such as schools, playgrounds, or daycares supervised by adults.[61] These three phenomena work together to socialize children, producing a form of childnormativity that centers an idealized Western, white, middle-class, abled-bodied, heteronormative, and cisnormative sense of what it means to be a child or to experience childhood.[62]

The primary function of childnormativity includes identifying and upholding rubrics for appropriate child development to successfully socialize future citizens. However, if dominance is control exerted over others, and submission is a lack of power, then a child is always already assumed to be submissive to an adult. If not, they are likely to be construed as willful, unruly, or deviant.[63] Since being a child is not automatically or directly tied to power, the privilege of being childnormative is contingent upon being legible to those in power—or why some children are not given the privilege of childhood. Importantly, childnormative is not a synonym for childish; rather, it captures what normative society deems "child-appropriate" during a particular time or space. Children's picture books might be childnormative because of their target audience, but also counter-childnormative depending on their content.

The Transborder Optic

Canada, the United States, and Mexico offer vital comparative contexts not only because of their shared borders but because of their distinct histories of colonization, slavery, war, and migration. This historically specific geopolitical and sociocultural space, better understood as North America or the North American continent, operates as an incohesive amalgamation of heterogeneity encompassing the region's peoples, cultures, traditions, politics, and borders.[64] Meanwhile, economic policies, such as the enactment of NAFTA in 1994, solidified free-market capitalism as the continent's reigning political-economic logic.[65] Its recent iteration, the United States–Mexico–Canada Agreement (USMCA) or "NAFTA 2.0," was signed in 2018 and came into effect in 2020. These international agreements affect not only trade in manufactured goods but also digital trade, intellectual property rights, and shared patterns of production, distribution, and consumption of cultural products across the three countries.

For this reason, I focus on children's picture books in each of the major North American countries, employing an explicitly transborder perspective.[66] Privileging the malleability of borders, I prefer the term *transborder* over *border* to emphasize the constant state of flux that characterizes geographic, identity-based, and discursive borders alike.[67] I also strategically employ *transborder* over *transnational* to distinguish transnational corporations and global economies from the tangible bodies and communities that occupy, trespass, and transgress all types of borders. This approach builds on Gloria Anzaldúa's evocative theorization of "atravesando fronteras" [crossing borders], or the "atravesados" [the border-crossers].[68] In *Coloring into Existence*, we encounter atravesadxs in the form of QTOC characters, along with QTOC children's picture book authors, illustrators, publishers, and readers. However, despite this lens, it should be noted that my comparative and hemispheric approach is necessarily limited by my own position as a US scholar, which entails both conscious and unconscious US-centric biases. For example, my use of "queer of color" not only privileges English and the US spelling of "color" rather than the Canadian "colour" but is also predominantly theoretically rooted in queer and trans of color scholarship emerging from the US.

Defining "Queer of Color" and "Queer and Trans of Color"

The timeframe of my analysis, as noted above, starts with the publication of *Asha's Mums* in 1990, which marked the emergence of a distinctly queer of color children's literature in North America. Yet, it is important to recognize that using "queer of color" as an umbrella term has important limitations. For one, the term is English-centric and does not account for Indigenous, Spanish, or French terminologies—nor does it adequately address the particularities of race/ethnicity, religion, or citizenship within each North American nation-state.[69] The term is also unable to capture all of the theoretical nuances that comprise the vast landscape of gender and sexuality. I intentionally distinguish between LGBTQ+ and either queer of color or queer and trans of color. While I may sometimes use the latter two interchangeably, they are not always synonymous. At times, queer of color serves as an umbrella term that captures trans, nonbinary, and gender nonconforming communities, whereas, in other examples, queer of color and trans of color must be differentiated to account for trans-specificity. I use the phrase "Queer of Color" in the title and throughout these pages to signal Roderick Ferguson's *Aberrations in Black* and queer of color critique as a theoretical intervention in queer theory that honors and builds upon its feminist, women of color, and queer women of color theoretical lineages.[70]

The QTOC picture books I identify throughout *Coloring into Existence* are the political enactment of their creators and readers. These picture books might be understood as ways of circumventing the wider national and transborder contexts in which concepts of childnormativity are produced. Most do not neatly conform to categories of appropriate children's literature but instead effectively push against them or pose an intentional threat to childnormativity. Since QTOC picture books do not always map onto the ideals of childnormativity, their characters can provide critical insights into those structures, as well as offer possibilities for thinking about childhood beyond its normative constraints. In this regard, I do not explicitly prioritize what children make of these picture books, although the intended reader remains important throughout my analysis.[71] Instead, I focus on the potential healing or transformative effects for QTOC communities at large, and the general public more broadly construed.

Children's literature is an underappreciated yet rich archive for theorizing queer and trans of color identities, politics, and futurity.[72] Indeed, this archive has much to offer us because of the way it colors or writes and illustrates queer and trans of color communities into existence, making these embodied subjects visible to children and adults. The mode or hermeneutic through which these acts of cultural conjuring take place is what I call autofantasía.

The Hermeneutic of Autofantasía

How do authors, illustrators, publishers, or readers convey their prior lived experiences or expectations for the future onto picture books? And how do we classify or interpret such cultural products? With the goal of coloring oneself into existence, autofantasía offers a mode through which to do this.[73] While I initially theorized the term as a literary technique, *Coloring into Existence* allows me to reconceptualize the concept into a broader hermeneutic that is useful for understanding QTOC worldmaking through picture books. If Romantic theory is to be believed, "all literature is no more than disguised autobiography (the work *is* the author, and vice versa)," making the degree to which authors reveal themselves essential.[74] Autofantasía accounts for the literary and visual techniques employed by authors and illustrators, as well as the political motivations of publishers, and the subversive reading practices engaged by those who read or listen to picture books. Through the act of fantasizing about oneself—whether as an author, illustrator, publisher, or reader—autofantasías help create new worlds or possibilities for queer and trans of color communities within and outside children's picture books.

In order to understand how picture books function as autofantasías, we might first conceive of the unprivileged category of the child as one that is temporally grounded in the past of all adults, including authors, illustrators, and publishers. Unlike most hierarchical dichotomies, the child/adult dichotomy is unique in that most children eventually enter adulthood (e.g., privilege based on age). Recalling childhood becomes the inspiration or experiential nexus through which marginalized authors, illustrators, and publishers conceive of their imagined child audiences. By centering characters and narratives that contest dominant discourse, these creators of picture books also privilege an imagined child reader who may be dealing with intersectional or compounded experiences such as racism, sexism, ableism, xenophobia, transphobia, or queerphobia. This can yield any combination of these, including children of color who are also undocumented and queer or also disabled and trans.[75]

Authors, illustrators, publishers, and readers of children's literature engage creative literary, visual, publishing, and reading techniques, like autofantasía, to interject a sense of political urgency into narratives for children. As a literary and visual technique, authors and illustrators enact autofantasía by deliberately inserting themselves within the text or illustrations to fantasize about possible responses to hegemonic structures or imagine alternative realities. Meanwhile, publishers mobilize autofantasía when determining what and whom they publish, while readers do so through "misreadings" or autofantastic reading practices.

As the root word *auto* suggests, I am privileging the "self" or an autobiographical perspective, although not in a traditional sense. As a genre of writing, autobiographies (as well as memoirs, journals, diaries, or other forms of life writing) are temporally situated in the past. The genre's assumption that authors may be motivated to write autobiographies or biographies of others after long and meaningful lives suggests that children cannot author or publish their own because they have yet to achieve such greatness. Thus, children's biographies featuring famous figures, including picture books on Shirley Chisholm, Emma Tenayuca, Mary Golda Ross, Malala Yousafzai, Sonia Sotomayor, or Kamala Harris, tend to encompass major achievements across their life trajectories.[76] Children's autobiographies, in contrast, are written by adults reflecting on their childhoods. Ruby Bridges's 1999 memoir, for example, documented her experiences with desegregation at the age of six, intermixing personal photographs and news coverage from that period.[77] One notable exception to the genre's age parameters might be the publication of childhood journals or diaries.[78]

Yet, as literary genres, autobiographies, biographies, memoirs, journals, diaries, or other forms of life writings have their limitations and can also be considered forms of fiction. Sandra K. Soto cautions against the authenticating effect autobiographic writing can have, as well as the danger of applying one author's narrative to all "others" within a given marginalized category.[79] Similarly, authors may purposely omit critical information that could negatively reflect upon them or reveal personal secrets.[80] It is for these reasons that in his introduction to the "Autobiographical Que(e)ries" special issue of *a/b: Auto/Biography Studies*, Thomas C. Spear surmised that autobiographies are at the "margins of both fact and fiction."[81] These challenges to autobiographic writing provide an important basis for identifying the ways in which I am proposing autofantasía within children's literature. Although autofantasía as a literary practice may be regarded as an example of *autoficción* or autofiction, I postulate *autofantasía* over *autoficción* or autofiction in order to stress the intentionality behind fantasizing about alternative pasts or utopic futures. As a hermeneutic, this includes the interpretation and methodology of autofantasía that accounts for how one engages not only authors or illustrators but also publishers and readers.

My articulation of *autofantasía* is also a play on Gloria Anzaldúa's definition of *autohistorias*, or autohistories, where one shares prior experiences through the retelling and rewriting of history to directly challenge what constitutes "valid" history.[82] In Spanish, "historia" means both history and story, suggesting that autohistoria can also encompass or be translated as "autostory" or the telling of one's story. "A story is always a retelling of an older story," explained Anzaldúa.[83] For her, that also meant "writing about one's personal and collective history using fictive elements, a sort of fictionalized autobiography or memoir."[84] She primarily accomplished this by writing as or through a recurring character she named Prieta/Prietita whose stories were "part fiction and part autohistorias" or "autobiography that's fictionalized, . . . parts of [her] life which are true but which [she] embellish[ed] with fiction."[85] Although Anzaldúa's children's books (*Friends from the Other Side/Amigos del otro lado*, 1993; and *Prietita and the Ghost Woman/Prietita y la Llorona*, 1995) may also be read as examples of *autohistorias*, they crucially merge nonfiction and fiction. By writing herself as a child character (Prietita) into her stories for children, Anzaldúa recreates her childhood past in order to demonstrate what could have been, creating an *autofantasía* that is autobiographical in her insertion of self and fantastical in her rewelding of the past. "By redeeming your most painful experiences," explained Anzaldúa, "you transform them into something valuable, algo para compartir, or share with others so they too may be empowered."[86] While both *autohistorias* and *autofantasías* may empower readers, the former is temporally anchored primarily in past events, while the latter more overtly allows for alternative realities or responses to contemporary worldly problems through its temporal flexibility.[87]

Fantasía completes the concept of *autofantasía*, where *fantasía* may signal a form of fiction that engulfs everything that can be imagined or fantasized. Unlike the genre of fantasy fiction, which might be limited to supernatural, magical, or otherwise fantastical themes, I utilize *fantasía* as an umbrella term incorporating elements that seem not only fantastical but unbelievable or utopic within our current world order and context. While literary genres such as magical realism, an aesthetic popularized across Latin America, which "makes no distinction nor discriminates between events that defy the laws of nature (in physics or genetics, for example) and those that conform to the laws of nature," or between what is seemingly unnatural and natural, is usually thought of in opposition to realism, so too, is realism a form of fiction, even if it attempts to present "a reflection of reality."[88] The utility of *autofantasía* as hermeneutic lies in the multifaceted interpretations of that which can be imagined or fantasized not only by authors but also by illustrators, publishers, or readers.[89] Another genealogy of the term is inspired by Afrofuturism and Chicanafuturism. Coined by Mark Dery in 1993, Afrofuturism describes literature that "treats African-American themes and addresses African-American concerns in the context of twentieth-century technoculture—and, more generally, African-American signification that appropriates images of technology and a prosthetically enhanced future."[90] Canonical authors include Octavia Butler and Samuel R. Delany. Working alongside Afrofuturism, Ebony Elizabeth Thomas adds, "The fantastic can intrude upon the world the reader knows, or the reader can choose to remain in the liminal space between the real and the unreal. What unites all of these paths into the fantastic is *belief*: one must *believe* the world that one is entering."[91] Within Chicana/x studies, Catherine S. Ramírez built on Afrofuturism through her concept of Chicanafuturism, which led to the reconceptualization of Anzaldúa's writing as science fiction.[92]

In sum, an autofantastic lens produces autofantasías steeped in personal experience, collective worldviews, political commentary, and utopian idealism. Once these picture books are released into the world, readers engage with them in nuanced and plural ways, regardless of the authors', illustrators', or publishers' intentions. This, then, solidifies autofantasía as a reading practice whereby readers "misread" picture books by inserting themselves or their perceptions of the authors, illustrators, or publishers onto characters.

While prior authors have at least uttered the words separately as "auto fantasía" ("auto fantasy"), or as the combined term "autofantasía," each has done so only in passing. My goal, in contrast, is to reinstate the term as a hermeneutic relevant to the present.[93] Whether a subversive reading practice, a publishing practice, or a visual or literary technique, understanding queer and trans of color children's picture books through the framework of autofantasía is useful in undertaking potentially polemic conversations with children, as well as for comprehending some of the inspirations or motivations behind writing, illustrating, or publishing for children, and the potential impact of this literature on children and adults alike.

* * *

Each chapter of *Coloring into Existence* presents a unique vantage point from queer and trans people of color, focusing on autofantasía in relation to authors, illustrators, publishers, and readers. Chapter 1 delineates the emergence of a new or contemporary literary genre—that of "by and about" queer of color children's literature. I identify "literary firsts" or trailblazers across North America, beginning with Canada, where I read Rosamund Elwin and Michele Paulse's *Asha's Mums* (1990) against the backdrop of *Chamberlain v. Surrey School District No. 36*, a legal case aimed at restricting LGBTQ-themed children's literature in the classroom. In Mexico, the country's first lesbian-themed children's picture book, *Tengo una tía que no es monjita* [I have an aunt who is not a little nun], was published in 2004.[94] In the United

States, two potential contenders compete for the distinction of "literary first": *A Beach Party with Alexis* (1991/1993) and *Antonio's Card/La tarjeta de Antonio* (2005).[95] As evidenced by these four picture books, I ascertain that a common practice in earlier LGBTQ+ children's literature was to limit same-sex desire to adult characters. Throughout the chapter, I extract a queer of color critique from the authors' deployment of autofantasía as a literary and visual technique, demonstrating how they mirror or insert themselves into their texts. Intermixing autobiographical or lived experience with fiction, they each contend with traumas or anxieties over sexuality.

Chapter 2 shifts to consider independent micro publishers of LGBTQ+ children's literature, such as Ediciones Patlatonalli in Mexico, Reflection Press in the United States, and Flamingo Rampant Press in Canada. Each of these grew out of a particular sociopolitical and historical context that has informed the types of authors and titles they choose to publish. Utilizing an autofantastic publishing practice, they each publish picture books informed by their own identities, political frameworks, worldviews, and ideal futures. For example, all of Ediciones Patlatonalli's picture books feature lesbian adults, whereas Reflection Press positions itself as a publisher of radical revolutionary children's books that center a nature-based analysis of gender and queer and trans of color children, and Flamingo Rampant Press prioritizes transgender and queer or trans of color communities. Despite being rooted in their respective countries, each is also informed by and contributes to a more extensive transborder circulation of LGBTQ+ children's picture books.

Chapter 3 notes another trend in LGBTQ+ children's publishing: an emphasis on gender and gender transgressions over expressions of sexuality. I survey picture books starring children of color grappling with gender and divide these into three major categories: (1) gender nonconforming, (2) nonbinary, and (3) transgender characters. Within each, I consider how picture books engage children's gender and gender identities, and how this is informed by the child's racial/ethnic or Indigenous background, traditions, and ancestral knowledge, emphasizing gender as a culturally specific spectrum.

Overall, children's LGBTQ+ picture books, and even queer and trans of color picture books, are more likely to feature child protagonists grappling with their gender rather than their sexuality. Chapter 4 engages with the conundrum that while queer and trans of color authors are more likely to discuss their queer childhood experiences in retrospect, often in YA or adult novels, few incorporate them into children's picture books. Among those who either define or describe queer of color children's sexuality are picture books that use gender as a metaphor for sexuality, such as Myles E. Johnson's autofantasía, *Large Fears* (2015). The chapter crucially advances the premise that children are capable of articulating and experiencing same-sex or same-gender desire. While several of the previously mentioned texts gesture toward queer identities and might be read as capturing the seedlings of queer sexualities, it is essential to include a picture book that does not shy away from depicting desire among two boys of color. Ernesto Javier Martínez's *When We Love Someone We Sing to Them/Cuando amamos cantamos* (2018) beautifully and succinctly conveys such a romance. Reading the text as an autofantasía, I explore Martínez's own childhood alongside the protagonist's, noting how they interestingly deviate from one another.

Chapter 5 shifts from the creators of children's picture books to those reading or being read to, evidencing autofantastic reading. Here, I more explicitly describe the interpretive framework and methodology behind autofantasía when employed as a "misreading" practice by either (1) projecting oneself, or one's political worldviews, onto the story, or (2) projecting the author, illustrator, or publisher onto the story. Throughout the chapter, I apply autofantasía as a reading practice to works by authors Marcela Arévalo Contreras, Gloria Anzaldúa, Jacqueline Woodson, and Syrus Marcus Ware. Whereas my autofantastic reading of the first three prioritizes queerness, Ware also more directly asks us to consider transgender and disability "misreadings." I demonstrate how readers can consciously or unconsciously "misread" or autofantasize a text to see themselves or their politics reflected in it.

I conclude *Coloring into Existence* by considering picture books' aesthetic design and composition, noting how they may bolster childnormativity while presenting unconventional illustrated stories for children that do not adhere to publishing standards. Significant examples include James Baldwin's *Little Man, Little Man: A Story of Childhood* (1976), and Maya Gonzalez's *The Interrupting Chupacabra* (2015). While Baldwin's book is just shy of one hundred pages, the latter is only nine pages and more closely resembles a handout; yet they both provide compelling textual and visual content for children. Heeding Gonzalez's motto to "Write Now! Make Books," the coda ends with a self-reflexive analysis of my personal journey from a children's literary scholar to a writer and illustrator of my own picture book, *Chabelita's Heart/El corazón de Chabelita* (2022). Reflecting on my queer Chicana childhood, I share the inspiration behind my own autofantasía, *Chabelita's Heart*, which centers a crush between two girls, Chabelita and Jimena. Although many of the themes and subthemes incorporated in *Chabelita's Heart*, and across all the other queer and trans of color picture books in *Coloring into Existence*, risk book bans or censorship, they include challenges already being faced by marginalized children, even if too few have access to these counternarratives or autofantasías within national and state-sanctioned curricula.

1

Literary Firsts

Picturing Queer of Color Adulthood in Children's Literature

Writing is a way into the beauty of memory and imagination.
—Rigoberto González

Eight years after the publication of her first children's picture book, *Asha's Mums*, co-author Rosamund Elwin joined kindergarten teacher James Chamberlain in filing a lawsuit against the school district of Surrey, British Columbia, Canada.[1] In *Chamberlain et al. v. The Board of Trustees of School District No. 36 (Surrey)*, the plaintiffs challenged a 1996 policy mandating that anyone teaching the family life component of the district's Career and Personal Planning curriculum had to use previously approved materials.[2] Chamberlain, an openly gay kindergarten teacher in the Surrey School District, approached the school board in December of 1996 seeking permission to use three LGBTQ-themed children's picture books as part of his family-life education unit: Lesléa Newman's *Belinda's Bouquet* (1989), Rosamund Elwin and Michele Paulse's *Asha's Mums* (1990), and Johnny Valentine's *One Dad, Two Dads, Brown Dad, Blue Dads* (1994). None were on the approved lists. Not only was Chamberlain's initial request denied, but in April of 1997, the school's Board of Trustees passed additional resolutions prohibiting the use of any "resources from gay and lesbian groups" throughout the entire district.[3] Such resources included works recommended by the Gay and Lesbian Educators of British Columbia (GALE-BC), of which Chamberlain was a member.[4]

The Supreme Court of Canada eventually heard the case in 2002 as *Chamberlain v. Surrey School District No. 36* (2002 SCC 86), ruling in favor of Chamberlain and the other appellants. Although the ruling denounced the Surrey School Board's actions as unlawful, it was not unanimous.[5] Dissenting statements from Justices Gonthier and Bastarache expressed concern over who decides what is "age-appropriate," echoing objections raised by parents in the initial appeal.[6] Supreme Court Justice Gonthier's dissenting arguments contended that "while the best interests of children includes education about 'tolerance,' 'tolerance' does not require the mandatory approval of the books," adding, "'Tolerance' ought not be employed as a cloak for the means of obliterating disagreement."[7] He also insisted that the "moral status of same-sex relationships is controversial," creating "significant parental concern that these materials may be confusing for these young children."[8] Despite Chamberlain's Supreme Court victory, the dissenting arguments and continued queerphobia led the Surrey School Board to ultimately remove the books from their district. Since they could no longer do so on the basis of their queer content, the board cited faulty grammar as their justification.[9]

Paradoxically, this experience indicates that even legal victories at the Supreme Court level may be unable to circumvent queerphobia. The case was important within Canada because it set a precedent for challenging individual districts on LGBTQ-inclusive curriculum, while upholding both the School Act (R.S.B.C. 1996, c.412) and the Canadian Charter of Rights and Freedoms (Constitution Act, 1982). Combined, legal protections like these promise to give Canadian children better access to LGBTQ+ children's literature in public schools—such as efforts made by the Equity Department within Ontario's Toronto District School Board (TDSB).[10] In the mid-1990s, this unit created the Triangle Program for students experiencing homophobia who had either dropped out of high school or were considered at risk of doing so.[11] Unfortunately, the program's success was severely curtailed by budget cuts from conservative legislatures.[12] Thus, while countries such as the United States and Mexico may look to Canada for successful examples of federal support for institutionalizing queer curricula, such support is not necessarily permanent.

Queerphobic discourse and social anxieties over children's sexuality curtail the publication of LGBTQ-themed children's literature. Whether intentional or not, this often results in a common practice within queer-themed picture books whereby authors have historically introduced queer topics through adult characters, often limiting same-sex desire to homonormative adult couples. In doing so, they attempt to bypass the topic of children's sexuality altogether while simultaneously presenting children as asexual or queer allies (e.g., heterosexual). Yet, queer of color desire, even if limited to adult characters, remains a powerful textual-visual marker of resistance against heteronormative children's literature.

The main goal of this chapter is to identify and contextualize each of the first "by and about" queer of color children's picture books published in Canada, Mexico, and the United States in order to establish the parameters of an emerging literary field. I use "firsts" loosely since, as I will show in chapter 5, other picture books could also fall into this category depending on our autofantastic reading of them. What is important for this chapter, however, is that the picture books discussed here were first in their respective countries to explicitly and unapologetically depict and name queer of color characters, while also being written by queer of color authors. An important caveat is that, within the context of these picture books, "queer" is usually represented as either "lesbian or gay." Another equally important caveat is that I limit my scope to picture books published in each country's predominant (not official) language (English for Canada and the United States and Spanish for Mexico). I do so only because of my own limitations as a bilingual (English/Spanish) speaker. While I cannot account for oral traditions or stories published in French or in any of the hundreds of Indigenous or migrant languages spoken across what is now North America, those stories are equally important, even if they are beyond the scope of this project, and I whole-heartedly encourage future research in these areas.

In my research, with a scope of books created by queer of color authors that feature explicitly queer sexuality, the genealogy begins in Canada with the publication of *Asha's Mums* in 1990 by Women's Press. In Mexico, the lesbian feminist organization Patlatonalli followed suit, publishing *Tengo una tía que no es monjita* [I have an aunt who is not a little nun] in 2004. The question of which queer of color picture book came first in the United States is more difficult. If we decide that certain coloring books count as picture books, then we might recognize Sarita Johnson-Calvo's *A Beach Party with Alexis* (1991/1993, Alyson Wonderland).[13] Otherwise, the honor goes to Rigoberto González's *Antonio's Card/La tarjeta de Antonio* (2005, Children's Book Press). All four picture books provide rich illustrations for deciphering racial or ethnic backgrounds, each of which are distinct and uniquely racially othered within their countries of publication. These queer of color authors across

North America turned to picture books and independent publishers for political meaning-making and community resilience. Each of the authors of these literary "firsts" wields autofantasía as a literary and visual technique, mirroring or inserting themselves into their texts. They intermix autobiographical or lived experience with fiction in order to contend with their own personal experiences or society's anxieties over sexuality, while also presenting an idealized world for queer of color individuals and communities.

Within the publishing industry responsible for the four previously mentioned picture books, and compared to gay or gay of color men, feminists and queer women of color were more successful in establishing independent presses.[14] One might surmise that this likely influenced why all four picture books also engaged sexuality from the perspective of adult lesbian couples regardless of the authors' own genders or sexualities. Although queer parents, often framed as "abusive" or "predatory," were historically more likely to lose custody battles, lesbian and bisexual women were slightly (but not always) more successful than gay or bisexual men because of normative gender roles that framed women as more nurturing.[15] Presently, more LGBTQ+ adults are choosing to raise children, though the legality of their parenthood continues to be challenged, whether within the legal system, through newly proposed legislation, or by adoption agencies that choose not to allow queer adoptions on the basis of religious freedom. Despite these challenges and heteronormative anxieties over queer adults raising children, LGBTQ+ adults are having children, adopting, or finding new ways of creating queer families.[16] Nevertheless, LGBTQ+ adults must also contend with their children's potential exposure to queerphobia and transphobia.

Together, these factors produced what might be described as an imperfect petri dish that sprouted the beginning of a queer of color picture book archive, which I am proposing as a new literary field. While advocating that these books be understood as canonical primary documents of such an area of study, I am aware of the ongoing critiques of "the canon" and canonization. Instead, I am using "canon" here not to mean exemplary of one type of "high culture," but rather a highly valued collection. In other words, I am advocating that we understand these queer of color children's picture books as classics or canonical because of their importance as a type of shared inheritance or material genealogy likely to resonate with queer of color communities. In using the plural of *community*, I am also advocating not for one canon, but rather for multiple canons, overlapping canons, contradicting canons, and ever-expanding canons. For allowing these queer of color literary collections to grow over time is to allow them to reflect future realities, goals, and desires. Anchored within a queer of color critique that "address[es] culture not as the reflection of the social but as an active participant in the construction of the social world," my engagement with the following four picture books considers each of their literary worlds alongside the larger goal of queer of color worldmaking.[17]

Asha's Mums (1990): Black Lesbian Motherhood in Canada

Asha's moms, despite their centrality to the title of the children's picture book, remain elusive. Readers do eventually learn their names, but Alice and Sara exist exclusively as maternal figures, appearing together only thrice. Of these, the first time they appear is on the cover and the second is within a classroom drawing. Their omnipresence throughout exemplifies a hypervisible/invisible dialectic—most noticeably because of their lesbian relationship, which exists both as the source of conflict and its resolution. An autofantastic textual and visual analysis of *Asha's Mums* also suggests that Black Caribbean and South African immigrant identities are subsumed under Canada's multiracial or multiethnic logics. Emerging at the beginning of what we might call Canada's third-wave feminist movement and released by notable Canadian feminist publisher Women's Press, *Asha's Mums* was pivotal in depicting a Black lesbian family and centering queer of color communities within Canadian and North American children's literature.[18]

Picture books are almost always, often absolutely, and unequivocally judged by their covers. Readers and listeners of picture books gravitate toward titles and covers that attract and maintain their attention. Covers provide their audiences with a glimpse into the characters' lives and the forthcoming narrative. The cover of *Asha's Mums* has Asha positioned in the foreground, with her mothers in the background, visually dividing the cover diagonally. All three are drawn with dark black hair and dark brown or black skin. Depicted on the upper righthand corner, one parent reads while the other sits nearby with her legs crossed. Bare feet peek out from underneath Alice's orange dress and Sara's blue jeans, and although their faces are only partially visible, they appear to be at ease, leaning back onto comfortable living room furniture. In contrast, a close-up of Asha gazing solemnly toward them dominates the bottom-left corner. Asha's body is tilted, leaning away from the corner where her mothers sit. One might interpret Asha's position as moving away from or juxtaposing herself against her mothers; however, she appears to be both part of this family and an interlocutor between her family and readers. By moving slightly away from the center of the cover, she provides readers a view into her home, an introduction to her mothers, and an invitation to discover more about her family. The cover's illustration is framed by a thick green border, which could act as a visual boundary between the characters and readers or could offer a window into this home. Analogous earth tones and shades of green saturate the image, calling to mind nature and the natural environment, perhaps to normalize this queer of color family (fig. 1.1).

The story's plot involves Asha's urgency in obtaining validation for her queer family, prompted by her teacher Ms. Samuels not allowing her to participate in a class trip to the Science Center because of what she perceived as an error on Asha's permission slip. "Want[ing] to know which of the names on the form was [Asha's] mum's," Ms. Samuel cannot fathom a scenario where Asha might have two mothers.[19] Once home, Asha's mom Alice reassured her, "Don't worry about it Asha, the form is filled out right. We'll go see your teacher and talk with her."[20] Unable to contain her concern over her family's legitimacy among her teacher and classmates, Asha outs her lesbian mothers in a family drawing during Show and Tell. The implication here is that if only Asha can show off her family—can have others "see" them—will she be able to convince them to acknowledge and accept her queer family structure. Through creative expression, storytelling, and fantasizing—similar to the function of *Asha's Mums* for its authors—Asha visually and verbally shares, "When my turn came to talk about my drawing I said, 'This is my brother Mark and my mummies and me. We're on our way to the Science Centre.'" Serving as Asha's own autofantasía within the picture book, her drawing depicts her family visiting what she desires most at that moment in time. Her two desires—to visit the Science Center and to obtain her classmates' validation of her queer family—intertwine in this illustration

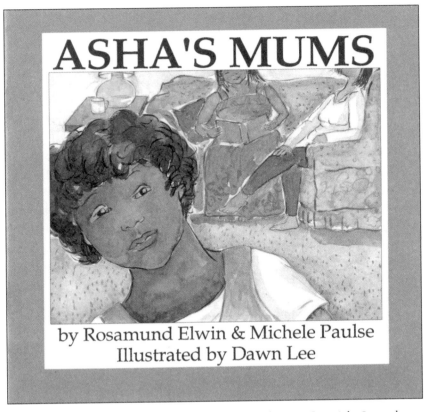

Figure 1.1. Cover of *Asha's Mums*. Published by Women's Press. Copyright © 1990 by Rosamund Elwin, Michele Paulse, and Dawn Lee.

within an illustration. Asha watercolors herself with a huge smile and arms extended outward in excitement next to her brother, with their mothers holding hands next to them.[21] If, as Shannon Jackson states, "the show and tell ritual is . . . always already performance," Asha participates in Show and Tell in order to perform a type of legible homonormativity for her classroom.[22] Aside from the book's cover, this is the first time both parents appear together within the text.

Justices Gonthier and Bastarache used the possibility of a similar activity to Asha's Show and Tell experience in their *Chamberlain v. Surrey School District No. 36* dissenting statement, to argue against *Asha's Mums* being taught in the classroom. They called attention to the Ministry of

Education K-1 "Family Life" curriculum's prescribed learning outcomes, which included "having children draw and write about their own families, and having children talk about each others' families," or, the very activity Asha used in her attempt to validate her family to her class.[23] Demonstrating that this was either completely lost on them or was done intentionally, the Justices added: "In a situation where there is a child in the classroom that has same-sex parents, these activities and others would raise the issue of same-sex parented families and teachers may feel it necessary to discuss it. Even in such a situation it is not necessary that educational resource materials which portray same-sex parents be generally approved for use in all classrooms in a particular school district."[24] Yet, as we saw in the case of Asha's fictional classroom, teachers are not always well-equipped or willing to mediate these discussions. Adding insult to injury, the dissenting Justices also used the fact that the school board had an anti-discrimination policy to declare the school board unbiased.[25] This flawed logic suggests that because anti-discrimination is "on the books," it cannot occur. As is well-documented, these policies exist not only to prevent discrimination but also as legal recourse for those who are discriminated against in institutions such as schools.

As depicted in her illustration, a joyous Asha does eventually emerge—at least within Elwin and Paulse's autofantastic world—once she learns her mothers have resolved her permission slip conundrum. Like Asha, readers are not privy to the manner in which this occurred, only that Sara and Alice intervened:

> "We talked to your teacher while you were at gym," Sara said.
>
> ["]Do I get to go to the Science Centre tomorrow? Do I get to look like a porcupine? Does she believe I have two mummies?" I shouted all at once.

Delighted her mothers were able to convince her teacher of their family's queer structure, Asha cannot contain her excitement, thanking and kissing each mom on the cheek. As readers, we might ask ourselves: What does it mean for Ms. Samuels to believe she has two mummies? The authors spare us this dialogue, which is presumably the climax and resolution to the story's primary conflict. Instead, we are left wondering if Ms. Samuels changed her mind once she realized Alice and Sara were a lesbian couple, or if Asha's mums had to involve the school's principal or threaten legal action.

The lack of dialogue between the lesbian couple and the teacher serves to provide a reflective space for adult readers to imagine what their own responses or actions might be, had they been confronted with similar heteronormative biases. As for heteronormative readers, scholars such as Claudia Mitchell emphasize that "the point is not that a minority group—what Hardiman and Jackson call the 'target group'—needs to read stories about its own members, but that members of the 'agent group' (in this case the heterosexual community) need to become more aware of their own teaching practices."[26] Ultimately, *Asha's Mums* presents queerness as normal and effectively accepted or, at a minimum, tolerated.

Within a queer context, though Asha's family unit initially resembles a two-parent, two-child homonormative nuclear household, the book's queer of color critique against hetero- and homonormativity only becomes clear by engaging with Alice and Sara's embodiment of Black lesbian femininity. While it could be radical to reimagine or autofantasize Asha's mothers as both butch, studs, or gender nonconforming, Alice and Sara's queer femininity is also a radical act that challenges stereotypical portrayals of Black women as incapable of femininity.[27]

Asha's Mums' important racial/ethnic implications are also evident in stylistic choices within the illustrations. For example, illustrator Dawn Lee alternates between full-color and black-and-white drawings. It is unclear if the black-and-white pages were sketches meant to be colored in later, or if all of the illustrations were originally completed in color and then only half were actually printed in color. However, instead of appearing unfinished, there is a sense of intentionality that emerges from the mixed use of color and black-and-white images. This may have been a deliberate creative choice by Lee, or it might have been determined by Women's Press in order to reduce printing costs. Surprisingly, the black-and-white or gray-scale illustrations carefully avoid connoting negativity or associating darker tones of gray or black with conflict.[28] Both full-color and black-and-white images are included at high and low points in the story's narrative.

In terms of race or ethnicity, characters effectively become racialized in black-and-white pages through some combination of shading techniques on skin tone—similar to black-and-white comics—and the outlining of racialized phenotypical characteristics like eyes, noses, mouths, and hair. Lee's technique also appears sketch-like at times, such that Alice might seem Black on one page and Asian or Indigenous on another. The reverse is true for Ms. Samuels, who appears Asian, Pacific Islander, or Indigenous throughout most of the illustrations, while in others she shares Asha's skin tone and could be read as Black. What results is a kind of racial or ethnic ambiguity, which could be seen as transgressive, if also risking appearing inauthentic, misleading, or lacking specificity. From an autofantastic perspective, it allows readers to choose.

Although Lee's illustrations do not overtly link the story with Toronto or Canada, the racial and ethnic heterogeneity suggests the setting is likely a classroom within a major city.[29] Asha's classmates include an array of multiracial children, such as Rita and Diane who are racially or ethnically ambiguous, as well as ideological differences. Two classmates, Coreen and Judi, are particularly troubled by Asha's queer family, and they appear to be racialized as Black and white, visually debunking the stereotype that queerphobia is more prominent within communities of color. Instead, each child symbolizes possible queerphobia across racial or ethnic lines:

> Coreen said "How come you've got two mummies?"
>   "Because I do," I said.
>   "You can't have two mummies," Judi insisted.
>   "Yes she can," Rita said turning around in her seat.
>   "Just like you can have two aunts, and two daddies and two grandmas,"
> yelled Diane from across the room. Diane likes to yell.

Coreen and Judi remain troubled despite Rita and Diane's affirmations. Coreen insists, "My mum and dad said you can't have two mothers living together. My dad says it's bad."[30] Asha defends herself: "It's not bad. My mummies said we're a family because we live together and love each other."[31] Judi remains perplexed. Coreen, meanwhile, appears to have heard queerphobic comments from parents. Lee depicts Coreen with her arms crossed, her back toward Asha, and her eyes tightly closed as if she were extremely upset or unsettled and not wanting to engage further.

Even after explanations, Judi also appears baffled, with her mouth open as she asks, "But how come you have two?"[32] This question remains unresolved for Judi.

Although most of Asha's peers are supportive, she must contend with others who remain resistant to queer families. That said, like Ms. Samuels, Coreen eventually has a change of heart. Once again, readers are not privy to exactly how this occurs, but Coreen joins several of the other children toward the end of *Asha's Mums* as they inquire about which mother is which. Splitting parenting duties, Alice dropped off Asha at school and Sara picked her up. Each time, students asked, "Which mummy are you?" And each parents responds, "Mummy number one." Laughter solidifies the children's approval of Asha's moms, illustrating the possible effects of long-term coalitional practices among queer communities of color and allies. Despite Coreen's initial resistance, she is eventually able to rejoice with Asha and other peers.

Asha's Mums began as a creative endeavor within the Young Readers Manuscript Group, in which the writers and illustrator—all women of color—participated. The group formed as a result of Women's Press's own collaborative process. Founded in 1972, and emerging amid Canada's Women's Liberation era, the Toronto-based independent press "played an integral role in the proliferation of feminist writing in Canada."[33] Part of its feminist praxis included collective editing: "The work is done collectively, skills are developed in a collective sense, and decisions are made collectively, whether it's about distribution or manuscript work we do."[34] Rosamund Elwin and Michele Paulse would later author a second children's picture book with Women's Press titled *The Moonlight Hide and Seek Club* (1992), also published with financial support from the Canada Council for the Arts and the Ontario Arts Council.[35]

Elwin and Paulse's contributions to the independent feminist press extended beyond authorship. Each held staff or volunteer positions in which they published other authors' works and organized events such as Everywoman's Almanac in 1989. They also participated in the Lesbian Writing and Publishing Collective, which edited titles such as *Dykeversions: Lesbian Short Fiction* (1986) and *Dykewords: An Anthology of Lesbian Writing* (1990).[36] Independently, Elwin edited or co-edited a series of lesbian titles including *Tongues on Fire: Caribbean Lesbian Lives and Stories* (1997).[37]

Although one may initially racialize Elwin and Paulse as Black Canadians, as the last title above suggests, their ethnic and immigrant backgrounds provide another possible reading of *Asha's Mums*. Seemingly worlds apart, Elwin was born in the Caribbean island Dominica, while Paulse is South African. Not to be confused with the Dominican Republic, Dominica is a small island southeast of Puerto Rico and north of Martinique colonized by the French in the 1600s and then by the British Empire in the late 1700s, following the Seven Years' War.[38] Elwin left Dominica in 1979 at the age of twenty-one during the transition between Commonwealth and Republic, approximately two years before the election of Eugenia Charles, Dominica's first female prime minister.[39] Also in 1979, Hurricane David raged over the island, its disastrous aftermath forcing many to leave. Among them, Elwin's mother Naomi James migrated to Boston and lived in the United States until her death on March 22, 2018.[40] Elwin's sister Eleanor remains in the United States, while her brother Gregory lives in France.[41]

Reflecting on her youth in Dominica, Elwin recounted, "when I left the Caribbean for Canada, I did not know the word lesbian. I knew the word zami. Women made zami or your zami was your closest friend. Whether the word was used as a noun or a verb, it was understood that a zami was intimate with other women or with another woman."[42] The term was first popularized across North America by Audre Lorde, who, like Elwin, was of Caribbean descent, tracing her family lineage to various Caribbean islands including Grenada and Carriacou.[43] In Lorde's biomythology, *Zami: A New Spelling of My Name* (1982), she defined it as, "A Carriacou name for women who work together as friends and lovers."[44] Anthropologist Michael Garfield Smith documented the term in 1962, noting, "Women who practise such homosexual relations are referred to in the French patois as *madivine* or *zami*."[45] He elaborated, "In effect, Carriacou Lesbianism is a form of deviance stimulated by the island culture and partially institutionalised in it," calling it an "example of the way in which a culture and society may promote abnormalities among normal folk."[46] Although Smith was pathologizing lesbianism, he nevertheless attributed the term "zami" to Carriacou, like Lorde twenty years later. By the time Elwin learned of it, zami had become synonymous with lesbianism throughout multiple islands across the Caribbean.

It would inform her articulation of sexual and racial experiences in Canada as well.

Like Elwin, Michele Paulse migrated to Canada. She was "born and [had] lived in South Africa long enough to know and remember" and "has been living in North America longer than she likes to admit."[47] Paulse attributed her desire to write to her mother: "I credit my mother for my interest in life stories. In our house in Vancouver, Canada, at the kitchen table, as she sewed, prepared a meal or rested between jobs, my mother often spoke of her youth in Swartdam, Athlone. My parents emigrated from Cape Town to Vancouver in 1968."[48] In the early eighties, she moved from Vancouver to Toronto "wanting to face new challenges," and "writing [was] just one of them."[49] The complexity with which Paulse navigated racial logics was contingent upon her geographic location, noting that she was categorized as "Cape Coloured" within apartheid logics of race. Because of histories of colonialism and slavery, her ancestors were not only African but Indian, Malay, German, and Scottish, which gave her an important perspective: "As a woman of racially different ancestors whose family emigrated from South Africa, I am constantly aware of the profound effect that perceptions of differences among people can have. In the social and political climate of Canada, disrespect for those differences will be to the detriment of us all."[50] Though Elwin and Paulse might initially be read as Black, their complex immigrant backgrounds ask us to leave room for greater cultural specificity.

While often read as fiction, *Asha's Mums* is grounded within specific autobiographical truths that warrant an autofantastic analysis. Like the two mothers, Rosamund Elwin and Michele Paulse were in a relationship at the time of the book's publication. The two siblings in the story, Asha and her brother Mark, mirror Paulse's own children, Aziza and Tarik, to whom the book is dedicated. Although the co-authors' relationship is not explicitly mentioned within the dedication or in their biographies, the lesbian anthology *Dykewords* was also published in 1990, and Paulse made their relationship public in that text's biography: "Michele Grace Paulse currently lives in Toronto with Rosamund, her sweetie. They recently published *Asha's Mums*, a children's book about a young girl whose two mums become an issue for Asha's teacher and the curiosity of classmates."[51] Paulse's tender acknowledgment of their relationship may also be inferred by the co-authors' joint photograph on the back cover of *Asha's Mums* and the first line of their joint biography: "Rosamund and Michele currently live in Toronto." The remainder of the biography establishes their individuality and the presumption of them being just friends for readers unfamiliar with their personal relationship: "Rosamund likes attending to her plants and romping around with her kids. Michele likes knitting, sewing and bicycling. They are very excited about having written this book together." For readers "in the know," they did not just "live in Toronto," they lived *together* in Toronto.

Their second children's picture book, *The Moonlight Hide and Seek Club* (1992), though not explicitly queer in content, depicts the couple in a physically close embrace but also bypasses their relationship in the joint biography. Instead, it emphasizes that "Rosamund and Michele have known each other for five years." Throughout that time, they discovered their shared interest in "writing and together had unique ideas for children's stories." The biography concludes by notifying readers that "Rosamund and Michele are currently working on their third children's book."[52] This third picture book remains an unfinished project, suggesting they may have ended their relationship before it could come to fruition (or they did not secure a publisher for it). Either way, their collaborative efforts in publishing for children resulted in a transformative picture book that mirrored their own queer family. Moreover, the co-authors' biographical backgrounds expand and complicate how Asha and her family might be racialized; they not only are Black Canadians but can also be imagined as a queer Black immigrant family in Canada.

Returning to the Chamberlain legal battles, Elwin's involvement is heroic considering all the ways she was targeted, for not only being queer and Black but also an immigrant. She remained active in the case, even consenting to and aiding in drawing attention to it within academic circles. A photograph of Elwin and her daughter, Aziza Elwin Carrington, graced the 1999 cover of the *Journal of the Association for Research on Mothering* special issue on "Lesbian Mothering" (fig. 1.2). Taken by Rachel Epstein, a member of the Guest Editorial Board, the photograph and its accompanying two-page "About the Front Cover" that opened the special issue informed readers of the then-ongoing legal battles in Surrey and highlighted organized efforts against the board's

Figure 1.2. Cover of the *Journal of the Association for Research on Mothering* special issue, "Lesbian Mothering" (1999). Photograph copyright © 1999 by Rachel Epstein.

queerphobic censorship of queer children's picture books. This included a group of parents who had formed Heterosexuals Exposing Paranoia "to counter what they see as sexual hysteria" by arguing that "prejudice, hatred, and discrimination against gay and lesbian people is a serious problem, especially for homosexual students" who do not see themselves represented in school curricula or who must "combat homophobia in our schools and in society at large."[53] The statement also named school board members whose efforts against LGBTQ+ rights included actively participating in the Campaign Life Coalition that proclaimed: "to have become a homosexual is to have acquired a moral disorder."[54]

The statement concluded with a black-and-white image of *Asha's Mums'* picture book cover, visually situating it among these legal battles.

The lasting effects of Elwin's publications on her own daughter are evident in a Mother's Day public post Aziza shared online, titled "Our Moms . . . the original Women of Distinction." She explained why her mother was a woman of distinction, noting, "She is strong, inspiring, knowledgeable, and extremely funny. I can talk to her about anything. Even with a great support system and extended family, all credit goes to my mother for raising me into the strong, independent young woman I am today."[55] Aziza also recounted her mother's migration to Canada and writing contributions, describing her as "a prolific author for Women's Press during the eighties and nineties."[56] Not only did Aziza share her post with her mother, but the online platform allowed Elwin to publicly respond: "Not every parent get[s] to hear what their children think of them and their parenting. [It's] a career that has no evaluation, no raise in pay status, perks or prestige. . . . Thank you."[57] The very bond between mother and daughter that inspired *Asha's Mums* also fueled Elwin's larger queer and feminist of color worldview and publishing priorities.

Those priorities included collaborating alongside Paulse, not only as co-author but as part of editorial and staff teams within Women's Press. Leading up to the publication of *Asha's Mums*, Elwin and Paulse found themselves amidst internal turmoil within feminist publishing. Specifically within Women's press, this conflict manifested around the publication of the anthology *Dykeversions: Lesbian Short Fiction* (1986), in which Michele Paulse participated. Following the introduction and before the creative fiction, a section titled "Notes about Racism in the Process" included two statements: one from the Lesbian of Colour Caucus authored by Michele Paulse and Nila Gupta, and another titled "White Lesbians' Statement" authored by Ellen Quigley and Maureen Fitzgerald.[58] "Our constant struggle as women of colour on this collective has been around racism," began Paulse and Gupta.[59] They continued: "The feminist network in Canada is a white feminist network, and exclusive networking such as this reproduces racism."[60] Prior to the Lesbian of Colour Caucus's involvement in the anthology, all but one of the contributions were from white authors. The caucus's statement referred to this as "racism by exclusion," arguing that "By leaving it to us to do most of the work, white women were saying that racism is not a white women's issue and networking amongst women of colour is not the responsibility of white women."[61] Yet, the caucus members agreed to participate in the anthology in order to "ensure that the power of the voices and visions of lesbians of colour erupt through the racist fabric of feminist publishing."[62]

Although both Paulse and Elwin were actively working within Women's Press to change the organization's culture and power dynamics, the years leading up to *Asha's Mums'* publication proved particularly contentious for Women's Press, even drawing the mainstream media's attention. As author Marlene Nourbese Philip expressed, "the crisis at the Press touched—directly or indirectly—most women writers in Toronto, if not Canada."[63] Newspaper articles such as the *Globe and Mail*'s "Race Issue Splits Women's Press" (1988) emphasized how "stories by white writers [were] rejected" for publication, thus spinning the story into an account of "reverse racism" as opposed to an effort to combat racism within the white lesbian community.[64] The article's accompanying photograph depicted five members of Women's Press, including two women of color: Rosamund Elwin and Michele Paulse.[65] The struggles within Women's Press were emblematic of larger critiques surrounding white feminism, tokenism, and institutionalized multiculturalism.[66] This controversial publishing experience was soon followed by curriculum controversies, well before Chamberlain.

Outside of Canada, *Asha's Mums* sparked controversy in the US. In 1991, Joseph A. Fernandez, then Chancellor of the New York City Board of Education, introduced *Children of the Rainbow*, a teachers' guide to inclusive curriculum that included *Asha's Mums*. It propelled the city into a national debate and ultimately led to Fernandez's firing. Although the proposed curriculum was almost five hundred pages long and focused primarily on racial and ethnic diversity, it also included a handful of references to gender and sexuality, "homosexuals," "children of lesbian/gay parents," "homophobia," and HIV/AIDS—all of which were at the root of the controversy. For example, a proposed project for first graders titled "Families at Home" focused on cultural or religious holidays but also included a bibliography with several queer titles such as *Heather Has Two Mommies*, *Gloria Goes to Gay Pride*, *When Megan Went Away*, *Daddy's Roommate*, and *Asha's Mums*. Despite protests against these books, which led to most of the titles being pulled, *Asha's Mums* remained.[67] In *Disputing the Subject of Sex: Sexuality and Public School Controversies*, Cris Mayo suggests that *Asha's Mums* slipped through the proverbial cracks because its title was not explicitly queer, noting that "perhaps reviewers thought it was about Asha's flowers," referring to chrysanthemums.[68] Certainly, it is very likely a US audience would not automatically read "mums" as "moms." However, a major difference between *Asha's Mums* and the other texts is that *Asha's Mums* depicts a queer Black family (from Canada), while the others depict queer white families (from the US). Though the title's reference to two mothers is explicitly queer, it was perhaps easier to disregard this book's lesbian content because its cover could be perceived as a book about "race" rather than "sexuality."

Asha's Mums has not been given the attention it deserves and is instead often overshadowed by *Heather Has Two Mommies*. As such, it is important to underscore that *Asha's Mums* is the first children's picture book in North America written by queer of color authors to explicitly depict queer of color relationships, albeit between adults. In addition to including Canadian signifiers such as "mum" (mom), "centre" (center), and "colour" (color), *Asha's Mums* reflects Canada's institutionalization of federally-sponsored initiatives and anti-discriminatory laws. As a result, LGBTQ+ children's literature may be more common in Canadian schools (depending on the providence and district) and more likely to have a greater reach across society, as opposed to Mexico and the United States. However, that does not necessarily mean Canada is more inclusive of queer of color communities or that the United States and Mexico have not also published queer of color children's literature. But it does mean we should not always look to the US first.

If Not a Nun, Perhaps a Lesbian? Aunts and Catholicism in Mexico

While co-authors Elwin and Paulse inserted themselves within *Asha's Mums* as the protagonist's mothers, *Tengo una tía que no es monjita* [I have an aunt who is not a little nun] depicts autofantasía through the protagonist's aunt. Author Melissa Cardoza inserts herself into her writing for children as a woman in love with another woman, recalling actual discussions with her niece. As an adult, Cardoza left her home in

Honduras and migrated to Mexico, where she resided for approximately nine years.[69] On a trip to her home country, she was inspired to write *Tengo una tía que no es monjita* after visiting her eight-year-old niece, who told her she must be a nun because she was not married and had no children. Cardoza reflected, "I believe that for her, there were no other options, and it surprised her that I was a nun who did not use traditional religious attire, nor did she ever see me praying."[70] Cardoza clarified to her niece she was not a nun but rather a lesbian and had a novia, or girlfriend, and that like men, women could have girlfriends as well, demonstrating her willingness to be transparent about her sexuality.[71] To Cardoza's disillusionment, her niece did not initially read the published version of *Tengo una tía que no es monjita* since her parents were adamant about shielding their child from its lesbian-themed content.[72] As an autofantasía, the picture book provided a literary space where Cardoza could reimagine an expanded conversation with her niece, even introducing her to her girlfriend, though she could not in real life.[73]

The book's simplistic yet sophisticated aesthetic appeal is evident from its cover. Warm tones of orange in thick brushstrokes emanate a soft and inviting ambiance resembling an intimate, sunny room (fig. 1.3). This backdrop is complemented with a sizable bright-red chair positioned in the center. Instead of the thick brushstrokes that color the background, the chair is loosely outlined with what appears to be a thick black pencil or charcoal, giving the appearance of smeared edges. Imitating a lens brought into focus, thick brush strokes and charcoal edges crystallize into thin, fine lines toward the center of the cover. It is here that we get our first glimpse of the giddy little girl who will soon be introduced to us by the name of Meli. Drawn with precise lines, neat edges, and occupying her place as the protagonist and narrator of this story, she sits gayly in the oversized chair. I was immediately taken in by her wide smile, rosy cheeks, pebble-like eyes, yellow triangular nose, and short curly hair darting outward. Arms crossed, she wears a turquoise-striped summer dress with matching turquoise shoes.

The aunt, invoked in the title, is not initially visible on the cover unless one considers her absence counterintuitively in order to further her presence. Stated differently, the aunt might be signaled and interpellated through subtleties in text and image. In addition to the title, Meli's comfort on the chair suggests it could belong to her loving aunt; it appears

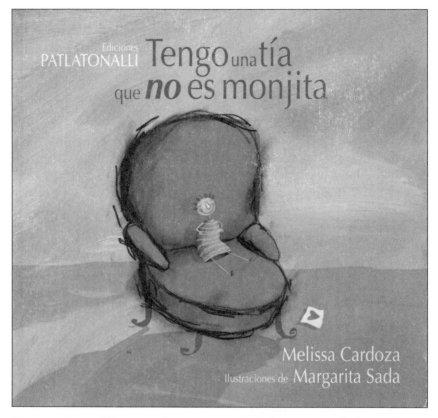

Figure 1.3. Cover of *Tengo una tía que no es monjita* [I have an aunt who is not a little nun]. Published by Ediciones Patlatonalli. Copyright © 2004 by Melissa Cardoza and Margarita Sada.

familiar, intimate, and almost womb-like—alluding to her aunt's maternal qualities. To Meli's left is a crafty little yellow sheet of paper or cloth with a pink heart in the center—yet another indication of the familial and loving feelings evoked by this niece-aunt relationship. Importantly, the "real" queer or lesbian aunt, Melissa Cardoza, represents herself on the cover when she is credited as author in the bottom-right corner, along with the illustrator, Margarita Sada.

Opening the book, the reader is met with a sea of pink hearts—this time serving as a grid-like backdrop to the inner cover (verso). As with the connotations of these hearts, the parallel title page provides additional symbolism; at the center is an illustration of a green houseplant—a small but significant detail that will reappear four additional times throughout the text, as well as on the back covers of all other children's books by the publisher, Ediciones Patlatonalli. A young plant, it comes to represent life and growth, foreshadowed by its own particularly widespread shadow. This growth will manifest in the plot, as both niece and aunt contend with who they are and what they believe about one another and their relationship.

The book's title invokes a second figure, a nun, whose perceived characteristics provide points of comparison for the perceived characteristics of the lesbian aunt. At times, one subject precludes the other so that one can only exist exclusively as a nun or exclusively as a lesbian. At other moments, both subjects overlap, suggesting a potential slippage or possibility in subject formation and identification. We might ask ourselves: What distinguishes the qualities or characteristics that comprise each identity, and what assumptions make these characteristics determine who belongs, or does not, to each?

Both the nun and the lesbian are gendered and assume a female-bodied cisgender identity constrained within heteropatriarchal relations of power—body politics that leave little room for transgender and nonbinary individuals (unless we consider autofantastic reading, such as in chapter 5). A stereotypical nun, and likewise a stereotypical lesbian, must not be married or have desires to marry, as is made evident in the text when Meli comments on her aunt's lack of interest in marriage: "No tiene esposo y no quiere tener" [She does not have a husband and does not want one]. Presumably, nuns and lesbians have no children and do not desire any. Again, Meli interjects with her observations of her aunt's de facto motherhood, which Meli directly benefits from: "Tampoco tiene hijos, mejor para mí, así soy su consentida" [She also does not have children. Better for me; that way I'm her favorite]. This absence of a husband and children puzzles Meli to such an extent that her only explanation is that her aunt must be a nun: "Como no tiene hijos ni quiere casarse, pensé que mi tía era monjita, pero no" [Since she does not have children and does not want to marry, I thought my aunt was a nun, but she isn't]. Unable to come up with another explanation, Meli simply concludes that, no, her aunt is not a nun. It is only later in the story that she discovers her aunt's lesbian identity.

While a queer or lesbian identity may explain her aunt's desire toward other women, the assumption that lesbians are neither married nor have children does not take into consideration the steady rise in same-sex marriages and LGBTQ+ adoptions across North America.[74] Likewise, there are exceptions for nuns, who, like religious sisters, may have been married in the past so long as the marriage has been annulled or they are widowed. Although nuns and sisters take vows of chastity, this does not mean they are virgins or never gave birth. Nuns may have had children—children who are no longer dependent on them once they enter a convent. The homosocial space of a convent is also worth mentioning. Although they are theoretically associated with asexuality (or abstinence), under the guise of sisterhood and homosocial bonding, convents have also allowed for same-sex exploration and desire. Convents, like same-sex Catholic schools, have been widely documented as fostering same-sex or queer desire.[75]

Although the subject of the nun is invoked throughout the picture book, nuns are only illustrated once. This page of *Tengo una tía que no es monjita* highlights possible tensions and contradictions surrounding this figure and what she may represent. Despite Mexico's *laico* designation, or the constitutional divide between the state and religion, Catholicism heavily saturates the nation's history, politics, and society. Nonetheless, aside from explicit religious doctrines such as biblical stories or materials found within private schools, religion is usually avoided in children's literature. Through subtleties in diction and imagery, both the author and illustrator of *Tengo una tía que no es monjita* play with the representation of the nun in a manner that is explicit yet sensitive to the possible implications of including this figure in a children's book. For example, Cardoza chooses the term "monjita" over "monja," privileging the diminutive form of nun and adhering to the common Spanish language use of diminutives as forms of endearment. Cardoza's word choice and word order also employ humor and play.

Juxtaposed cleverly with the text, Margarita Sada's illustration deploys visual techniques such as the illusion of transparency to guide the audience through their reading of the nun's figure. The nun is easily identified based on her attire: a white coif surrounded by a black veil hiding her hair, a long holy habit, stockings covering the bottom of her legs, and modest shoes. Her hands grip a rosary with the symbol of the cross dangling at the bottom. She gazes off to the left, smiling. The yellow "X" carefully drawn over the figure of the nun visually tells us that, despite the similarities between Meli's aunt and nuns, her aunt is not a nun. Although this big and bright yellow "X" crosses over much of the length of the page, it is lightened and appears almost transparent over the nun's body. This subtlety illustrates the point made by the text in a manner that does not represent a full rejection of the individual nun. More likely, this might be a critique of the institution of religion, which is also evident in the aunt's rejection of church hymns. Despite the aunt's critique of organized religion, this illustration presents the possibility of merging lesbian identities with religion or some form of spirituality—or at least, not dismissing such a merger altogether.

In choosing to include a nun in this picture book, the author assumes a common understanding of Catholicism or, at least, a basic recognition of such a figure. The saturation of Catholicism within Mexican society notwithstanding, two panelists at a presentation by Ediciones Patlatonalli shared that while reading *Tengo una tía que no es monjita* aloud to children, they were surprised when a child asked not about the lesbian relationship or to clarify what a lesbian was, but instead asked, "¿Qué es una monjita?" [What is a nun?]. Such events shift possible anxieties over sexuality toward those of religion, placing adults in the position of deciding how to explain Catholicism or religion to the child. Religion may not have been inculcated in them by parents or caregivers, or their religion may not be Catholic. Regardless of the particular circumstances, these examples confront the association commonly made between religion and nation in Mexico and challenge perceptions of normative Mexican cultural identity.

Tengo una tía que no es monjita's narrative arc culminates as Meli, hiding behind one of her aunt's houseplants, spots her aunt kissing one of her female "friends" on the lips. Albeit the most explicit representation of lesbian desire, the entire book pays homage to queer—and more specifically lesbian—families, communities, and loving partnerships. Before her aunt comes out to her, Meli comments on her aunt's friendships, poignantly observing, "Tiene muchas amigas mi tía. Eso sí" [She has many female friends. That's for sure]. These words are coupled with a collage of photographs depicting this tight-knit circle. Many of the photographs include Meli's aunt sharing a glass of wine with a friend or holding a woman in a tight embrace. There are also several individual headshots of other women: one draped in a scarf and knit winter hat, another dressed in a suit while also wearing a hat, and a third wearing glasses and tilting her head toward the camera. Interspersed throughout are several photographs that are presumably of Meli: as a baby sucking on her pacifier, holding a teddy bear, and hugging her classmates. Interestingly, the family resemblance between Meli and her aunt is such that these photos could just as easily be of Meli's aunt as a child. If we decide, however, that the person depicted is Meli, we see yet another example of her integration into her aunt's social and emotional spheres. This collage alludes to the making of family or choosing one's family—a common practice within queer communities, represented in many of the picture books throughout *Coloring into Existence*. Such families may of course include one's partner, and, being a keen observer, Meli notices her aunt's preoccupation with one friend in particular, who she describes as having funny red hair and wearing big shoes similar to those worn for agricultural work. It is only after a visit from her aunt's red-haired friend that Meli discovers her aunt's attraction toward other women.

Notably, this lesbian desire is not pathologized. Even when Meli's father makes the comment about her aunt, "Está loca," or *she is crazy*, he is the one who appears as a caricature. Unlike any of the other characters, Meli's father's eyes are mere dots encircled within exaggerated spirals, his tongue hangs out from the side of his mouth, and his fingers move in a circle resembling the common gesture for suggesting someone is crazy. He is surrounded by a cluster of blurred stars in the background. These elements collectively suggest that he may be the one who is "crazy" or mistaken, not Meli's aunt. Just next to the image of the father, the adjacent page depicts Meli and her aunt in a playful and loving manner, with both smiling and seeming extremely comfortable with each other.

Similar emotions will be revealed toward the end of the book. Initially surprised to see her aunt kiss a woman, Meli gasps, "Huuuuy ¿por qué la besa en la boca, tía . . . ?" [Ohhhh, aunt, why do you kiss her on the mouth?]. Her aunt responds: "Vení, te voy a contar un secretito. Y me dijo bien suavecito en el oído . . . Es que es mi novia" [Come here. I'm going to share a little secret with you. And she whispers softly in my ear . . . It's just that she is my girlfriend]. These phrases are paired with an image of Meli's aunt and her girlfriend side-by-side, enclosed in a big heart and surrounded by additional hearts. The book's final pages depict the niece-aunt duo hugging and smiling—the assumption being that Meli understands and accepts her aunt's relationship with her girlfriend.

This final moment also provides a lesson in adult-child power dynamics. Her aunt's revelation is met with an initial pause, during which Meli observes, "Yo la vi a los ojos y le brillaban mucho como cuando parece que va llorar" [I looked into her eyes which shined brightly, like when she is about to cry]. Unlike the perceived childnormative and hierarchical relationship between niece and aunt, the aunt's pause and teary eyes indicate she is seeking validation, briefly flipping—or queering—the roles of adult and child. Challenging the perceived autonomy of adults, the onus of approval and validation are placed on the child, in this case on Meli. Similarly, the child reader must decide to accept or not accept the lesbian relationship at hand.

The centrality of sexuality in *Tengo una tía que no es monjita* does not take away from the other topics included in this picture book. While the text could have easily been solely a coming-out narrative, the author interweaves a subtext that critiques the United States and neoliberalism. A pivotal moment occurs when Meli bakes a cake for her aunt's birthday. Above the words "Cumplió años hace poco y le hicimos un pastel con muchísimas velas, es que tiene un montón de años. Yo tengo ocho" [It was her birthday recently and we baked her a cake with lots of candles because she is many, many years old. I'm eight], we see a bug-eyed Meli enthralled as she whisks away at an enormous bowl surrounded by a whimsical cloud of flour. This commotion is amplified by additional baking supplies: a spatula, eggs and eggshells, a milk carton with the word "leche" on it, a bag of flour with the word "harina" on it, and butter with (unlike the milk carton and flour) the English word "butter" on it. If the reader does not notice the word in English, the next page points this out: "Se enojó porque hicimos el pastel con mantequilla gringa y ella prefiere la que hace la gente de aquí, la que compra en el mercado" [She was upset because we baked the cake with butter from the US and she prefers the one made by the people here, the one she buys at the local market]. From an economics perspective, her dislike of imported butter also conjures the "guns and butter" model and possible correlations between goods and services (e.g., butter) and militarization (e.g., guns), as they relate to imports and exports, particularly after NAFTA.

By differentiating between local products and imported products, the author challenges Meli and, by extension, readers to consider our roles as consumers, effectively encouraging social responsibility and local economies.

This assessment of imported goods from the United States is paralleled by a similar critique of the imposition of US children's culture and the US entertainment industry on Latin America. For example, Cardoza asks us to reflect on media conglomerate the Walt Disney Company when, after baking her aunt's birthday cake, Meli begins to fantasize about her own birthday: "Para mi cumple you quiero ir a Disneylandia" [For my birthday I want to go to Disneyland]. Her desire to visit Disneyland is met with opposition from her aunt, who prefers to take her to Guatemala since "es más bonito" [it is much prettier]. Meli responds affirmatively, "Le digo que sí" [I agree, yes]. This exchange between niece and aunt speaks to several issues—especially border crossing and Mexico's relationships with the US and Guatemala—as well as the potential difficulties of having this conversation with children. Discussing border crossing and nation-state relationships also implies an understanding of passports, visas, immigration debates, and the role of tourism. By steering her niece away from Disneyland, the aunt may be telling us something about her socioeconomic or immigration status. Disneyland, located in California, would be a challenging destination for someone who could not afford to apply for a US tourist visa or who did not meet visa requirements. Furthermore, the cost of flying to California and the actual theme-park expenses are beyond the reach of many in Latin America. If this were strictly an economic issue, we might say that the aunt chose Guatemala instead because it borders Mexico to the south and would be more economically feasible.

However, the politicized dimensions of *Tengo una tía que no es monjita* suggest the political positionings of author Cardoza, who has publicly advocated against US globalization and in favor of immigrant rights.[76] Thus, it is more likely that Cardoza dismisses Disneyland because of what it represents—US economic and cultural hegemony. In this case, it manifests itself via the mass commodification of children's media and consumer products, making Disney characters recognizable to children around the globe. And although there are currently no Disney amusement parks in Latin America, regular Disney cruise ships like the Disney Magic and Disney Wonder can be seen sailing off from various Mexican coastlines.

Cardoza's deliberate choice of Guatemala over Disneyland, and Meli's subsequent agreement, merit further contemplation, for a potential pitfall in including numerous subplots within a children's book narrative is that each does not receive equal attention. Within this picture book, we see an astute little girl making sense of her aunt's preoccupations with her world order. It is quite possible that Meli may not grasp the entirety of her aunt's disapproval of Disneyland or why this makes her aunt's eyes tear up. Despite this, or perhaps because of it, Meli understands that these things are important for her aunt. They trouble her aunt so much, in fact, that Meli sacrifices her desire to go to Disneyland and trusts her aunt that Guatemala is indeed more beautiful. Other readers may not be as easily convinced to make Meli's sacrifice without an explanation or justification for why they should go to Guatemala over Disneyland.

Disney characters saturate popular culture across Latin America to the point that their dismissal might seem preposterous to a young audience raised to esteem the magical world of Disney. The illusion sold by Disney has been challenged by numerous scholars on the grounds of racism, sexism, ableism, and corporate greed, such that deciding between Guatemala and Disneyland is an opportune place to introduce such critiques in a simple and straightforward manner.[77] Indeed, these could very easily be the main plotline of a book of their own. Without such a context in *Tengo una tía que no es monjita*, it is likely that, if given the choice, more children would choose Disneyland. Such was the case in a play adaptation of this book. In 2007, school children chose to reproduce *Tengo una tía que no es monjita* under the direction of the lesbian organization Hijas de la Luna during the Second Annual Sexual Diversity Cultural Festival of Zacatecas.[78] In the process of assigning roles, the children collectively decided to change the lines of the text so that they would go to Disneyland instead of Guatemala. These children read the original children's book, decided to replicate it, and revised it according to their own needs and worldviews, reflecting a critical engagement with the text. Although I do not seek to discredit their agency, I will problematize it by pointing out that they may have been reacting less critically to the commercialization and marketing strategies of corporations such as Disney.

Afro-Indigeneity and racialization are equally important topics that emerge when analyzing this book through autofantasía. As previously alluded to, notions of race and ethnicity are not homogenous across North America, relying instead on specific cultural and national distinctions. For example, racial hierarchies and stereotyping in US children's literature have been well documented in the work of Donnarae MacCann, who found that whiteness was often positioned in binary opposition to and above anyone considered Black, non-white, or "of color."[79] Unlike the particular racial politics of the US, however, Mexico's colonial history was one of racial "mixing," which created what is more commonly referred to today as a mestizo population.[80] This national discourse of mestizaje, however, aims to boost national morale by valorizing an Indigenous past—one that allegedly belongs to all Mexicans—while refusing to acknowledge the modern nation's own role in slavery and acts of genocide. In demarcating Indigenous and Black populations into an imagined past, Mexico consequently invisibilizes its current Indigenous and Black populations from the national imaginary, invoking these communities only in national discourses of patriotism or tokenism.[81] How, then, are characters racialized within Mexican children's literature? What we can observe is a pattern where characters in children's books are more often than not overtly racialized only in books that are specifically about a particular community. Otherwise, the majority of characters default to light-skinned mestizos.

Keeping with this logic of mestizaje, at first glance all the characters of *Tengo una tía que no es monjita* appear to have the same light brown mestizo skin tone. On closer inspection, however, we can observe the subtle racialization, or racial subversion, of Meli and her aunt through a critical reading of hair and diction. Meli and her aunt share the same short, curly, brown hair that darts upward and around their faces. As Ginetta E. B. Candelario has shown, the politics of hair reveal wider social notions of beauty, representation, and power dynamics.[82] US children's authors, meanwhile, have engaged in projects that validate different types of hair, including *Happy to Be Nappy*, written by bell hooks and illustrated by Chris Raschka, and *Hair/Pelitos*, written by Sandra Cisneros and illustrated by Terry Ybáñez. Although *Tengo una tía que no es monjita* is not explicitly about hair, its visual representation warrants attention. Within the logics of mestizaje, mestizas are usually represented

with straight or wavy hair, whereas tight curly hair is more often reserved for explicitly racialized "others" or Black characters. While these
are arbitrary distinctions, they reveal how a given society perceives racial and ethnic phenotypes and the qualities attributed to them.

Probing further, Meli's aunt is also othered through her use of language. After Meli discovers her aunt and partner, Meli's aunt calls her
over: "Veni, te voy a contar un secreto" [Come here, I'm going to tell you
a secret]. Paying attention to diction, we see the use of "veni" instead of
"ven," with the former commonly used in parts of Central America and
the latter used in Mexico. To consider Central America—and Honduras specifically, given the author's background—also entails the region's
racial politics, with racial formation in Honduras blurring the lines of
inclusion and exclusion among Black and Indigenous groups.[83] Cardoza publicly organizes around and identifies as Afro-Indigenous or as
a "negra lenca" or "GariLenca," of mixed Black and Indigenous heritage
from Garifuna and Lenca populations in Honduras.[84] This also frames
her participation in Honduran resistance political movements, which
she has documented in publications such as *13 colores de la resistencia
hondurena/13 Colors of the Honduran Resistance*.[85] Although *Tengo una
tía que no es monjita* does not explicitly mention race, ethnicity, or Afro-
Indigeneity, these are invoked through subtleties in image and diction
manifested through autofantasía.

The short film adaptation under the same title, *Tengo una tía que no
es monjita*, offers a more overtly racialized version of the original. Produced and directed by Gloria Margarita Larios Ponce in 2008, the film
was publicly screened at the Universidad de Guadalajara and given the
award of Mejor Cortometraje [Overall Best Short Film] by Ruth Padilla
Muñoz, director of the Sistema de Educación Media Superior (SEMS).
As the winning short film, it was also distributed within the SEMS school
system and shown publicly on Televisión de la UDG, the local university
television channel.[86] Just under seven minutes, the short film retells the
story of Meli and her aunt using hand-held puppets.[87] The most notable
differences from the original picture book include subtle variations in
the storyline, as well as the inclusion of audio (voiceovers and music).
Yet, placing the illustrated version of Meli and her aunt side-by-side with
their puppet counterparts reveals striking differences in racialization; in
addition to having dark, curly hair, the puppets are also dark-skinned.

This may have something to do with the puppeteers who created them—a family business invested in representing and giving voice to less visible groups like Mexico's Indigenous communities. In their attempts to localize the narrative, they also revert back to the use of "ven" instead of "veni," and before the credits roll, this message is delivered: "La tolerancia es el respeto con igualdad sin distinción de ningún tipo" [Tolerance is equal respect for everyone without any type of distinction between people]. While this likely refers to sexuality and sexual difference, it could just as easily apply to racial, ethnic, and Indigenous differences. In my comparison of each medium, I am not suggesting that one—either picture book or short film—is necessarily "better" or more accurate. Instead, each version allows its creators to manifest their own autofantasías. As with the group of children who adapted the story into a play, each interpretation presents the possibility of localism or individualized representation, depending on the particular meanings imagined by each version's creators.

Either/Or: Between a Beach Party and Mother's Day Traditions in the United States

One way to answer the question of which queer of color picture book came first in the United States is to also ask whether a coloring book warrants the title of picture book. This question of genre or format determines whether we begin with Sarita Johnson-Calvo's coloring book *A Beach Party with Alexis* (1991/1993), or Rigoberto González's picture book *Antonio's Card/La tarjeta de Antonio* (2005).[88] While my own differentiation between the two might suggest I favor the latter, I want to first make a case for why some coloring books are also picture books and should not be excluded from the larger field of children's literature. Coloring books are usually relegated to the margins of children's literature, in part because they are designed to be ephemeral. Children are meant to color in their pages and, in doing so, "taint" or "ruin" their original form. Given their eventual disposability, they are often printed on thinner or lower-quality paper. Considering the politics of color, it is not lost on me that what we usually consider lower-quality paper is often unbleached, brown or tan, or otherwise not white paper. Unlike other picture books, coloring books rarely circulate (e.g., in libraries), and they often lack words or a consistent and cohesive narrative. For all of these reasons and more, coloring books are rarely mentioned in children's literary criticism.

Some exceptions, however, include scholars Julia A. Mickenberg and Philip Nel, who tangentially mention a coloring book in their introduction to *Tales for Little Rebels: A Collection of Radical Children's Literature* (2008). They do so only to expose what they call "faux children's lit"—a label given not because the title in question was a coloring book, but because it was created by the FBI in order to discredit the Black Panthers.[89] Kenneth Kidd also includes a coloring book in his survey of US 9/11 picture books, although he argues that, like the other books he reviewed, it failed to "grapple with the political contexts of the attacks."[90] Other children's literary scholars have referenced coloring book metafictions within children's picture books, such as *Bad Day at Riverbend*.[91] Meanwhile, Diana Gonzalez Kirby includes several coloring books in a survey of children's literature produced by the US Government during the second half of the 1900s.[92]

While I am inclined to agree that most coloring books might not be considered picture books for the above reasons, certain exceptions exist. *A Beach Party with Alexis*, for example, might be regarded as both a coloring book and a picture book because, unlike a more typical coloring book, it has a unique set of characters and includes a plot or cohesive narrative. In what follows, I present the competing titles for "first" queer of color picture book in the United States that explicitly incorporate queer characters. Both are noteworthy and should be unequivocally considered among the first by and about queer of color children's picture books in the United States.

Remarkably, the covers of *A Beach Party with Alexis* and *Antonio's Card/La tarjeta de Antonio* share visual similarities. Both present a child of color looking over their shoulder and include the child's name within the title. Although one walks and the other sits, both children are engaged in some activity pertaining to the title and plot—namely, a beach party and a card—although we do not yet know why or for whom. Both authors, Sarita Johnson-Calvo (aka Sarita Johnson) and Rigoberto González, also incorporate the physical act of coloring into their creative works. Johnson does so by creating a literal coloring book, whereas González leaves the act of coloring to his protagonist who is depicted coloring on the cover and within the book. Each was published by a small, independent, niche press or imprint—Alyson Wonderland (LGBTQ+ children's literature) and Children's Book Press (children's literature with a focus on communities of color).[93] Johnson both wrote and illustrated *A Beach Party with Alexis*, whereas Cecilia Concepción Álvarez illustrated *Antonio's Card*. The first is colored using markers and the second primarily with acrylic paints (fig. 1.4). While both *A Beach Party with Alexis* and *Antonio's Card* include a child of color and queer parents, the topic of sexuality is a point of contention only in the latter. Each integrates autobiographical details, albeit the first more than the second, since it is also based on a true story.

Embodying the joyous reaction of many students on the last day of the academic school year, Alexis cannot wait to begin summer vacation at the start of *A Beach Party with Alexis*. Surrounded by other students, some dash out of the school building, another waves goodbye, while someone else appears to be shouting. Amidst the commotion, Alexis heads toward a parked car:

> My mother Sarita was waiting for me in the car.
> "Sarita," I said, "since it's going to be summer vacation, I'd like to have a beach party. Don't you think that would be a good idea?"
> "I think that would be a great idea," my mom said.

Child and parent resemble one another phenotypically. Both seem to have similar hair, although Sarita's is worn in dreadlocks while Alexis has cornrows. Large, round glasses frame each face. Once home, Alexis makes a list of guests—Keiko, Ashley, Quise, Izayah, Sean, and Leah—and child and parent make invitations together: "You are invited to a Beach Party. WHERE? Alameda Beach. WHEN? July 21, 11–12." For those familiar with California geography, the beach within the book refers to an actual beach located in the east bay, next to Oakland. The setting where Alexis drops off the invitations across the street from their home is that of a city. Several passengers enter a public bus with an ad running across its length that reads: "Fight AIDS Not People with AIDS." Even though the word "not" is not fully visible, and only part of the letters "o" and "t" can be seen, astute readers would be able to make out all of the words, which, historically, also appeared on ACT UP buttons and stickers.

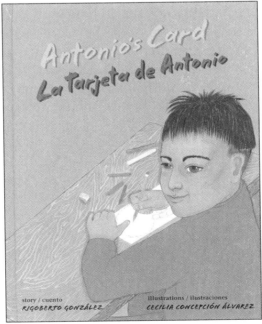

Figure 1.4. Covers of (a) *A Beach Party with Alexis*, self-published in 1991 and published by Alyson Wonderland in 1993, and (b) *Antonio's Card/La tarjeta de Antonio*, published by Children's Book Press in 2005. Copyright © 1991 by Sarita Johnson-Calvo; 2005 by Rigoberto González and Cecilia Concepción Álvarez.

Notably, *A Beach Party with Alexis* was copyrighted in 1991, the same year as New York City's "Children of the Rainbow" curriculum. As mentioned above, this curriculum was targeted not only for listing picture books like *Asha's Mums* that depicted same-sex households but also because of its explicit reference to HIV/AIDS that included a section titled "Facts about HIV Infection."[94] Displaying the ACT UP phrase in such a large font across most of the page within *A Beach Party with Alexis* would likely catch the attention of children, either because they would read it themselves or ask an adult what it said.

Also visible around the postal service drop box and bus stop are people of different ages, sizes, shapes, genders, and racial or ethnic backgrounds—racialized through phenotypical markers such as eyes, noses, lips, and hair. Since only the coloring book's cover was printed in color, the author left those doing the coloring to decide how they might "color" each individual. Gender, too, appears ambiguous. *A Beach Party with Alexis* is narrated in the first person through Alexis. Within the coloring book, Alexis wears everything from t-shirts and a sports jersey to a dress and a one-piece swimsuit. Although readers are not given Alexis's pronouns, advertising materials from the publisher used "she/her," and the character is based on the author's daughter by the same name.[95] In an interview, Johnson shared, "What motivated me to create *A Beach Party with Alexis* was the actual event. It was an incredibly magical day from start to finish. . . . Sandy [Johnson's partner at the time] and I were also motivated to have this party because Alexis, who has autism spectrum disorder, needed a no-pressure context for interacting with peers."[96] In this case, Johnson creates an autofantasía that also serves to document biographical details of her daughter. And as in other chapters (see especially chapters 3 and 5), her daughter's autism challenges assumptions readers may make about visible or invisible disabilities and how these might be incorporated into picture books.

Meanwhile, readers do not learn Alexis has another mother until the day of the beach party. Excited it is finally July 21st, Alexis is the first one up in the morning. The next page depicts her in a grocery store, Sarita pushing a cart and looking off to the side of the aisle in the backdrop. To the reader's surprise, or queer delight, Alexis stands next to another adult whom we have never seen before. The text reads: "After we ate, bathed, and dressed, my mothers and I went to the grocery store. We got hot dogs, buns, pickles, sodas, ice, napkins, ketchup, mustard, salad dressing, and green balloons." The adjacent page mentions Alexis's second mother's name, Sandy: "When we arrived at Alameda Beach, Sandy and I picked out a good spot. Sarita tied green balloons to nearby trees so my guests would know where my beach party was." While readers may be surprised to learn of Alexis's two-mom home, it is not meant to come off as an actual surprise or particularly noteworthy within the storyline, since queer couples and families populate many of the pages. Johnson shares, "It was a celebration with Alexis, but it was also a celebration of our little LGBT community." Phenotypically, Sandy does not share Alexis's physical characteristics and could fall within a range of racial or ethnic identities and skin tones, depending on how one reads her or the color one chooses when coloring her in.[97] As far as the real Sandy is concerned, Johnson described her as "a dedicated teacher of English for middle and high school students, eventually becoming a dean of students before retiring. Being first-generation Costa Rican, Sandy has a strong Latinx identity which made her an invaluable leader and role model at her schools."[98] Even though they are no longer partners, they remain friends and chosen family.

Over a decade would pass in the US before another queer of color author would publish a children's picture book explicitly depicting queer characters. Rigoberto González's *Antonio's Card/La tarjeta de Antonio* (2005) received the American Library Association's Rainbow Project Book List award in 2008 and was a Finalist for the Lambda Literary Award in 2006. *Antonio's Card* is narrated in the third person (limited POV), told from the vantage point of a little boy named Antonio, who has two loving parents at home: Mami and her partner Leslie. Mami has dark-brown eyes and shoulder-length hair, while Leslie has green eyes and short, light-brown or reddish hair. The picture book begins with a glimpse into the family's morning rituals, which culminate with leaving for school: "'Good-bye, Antonio,' a sleepy voice calls out. . . . It is Leslie, his mother's partner. She waves through the bedroom window, as she does every morning." This is followed by a heartwarming gesture: "Antonio runs up to the window and presses his hand against the glass, his small hand against her bigger hand. All the way to school, he feels the press of the window on his palm."[99] Although one might suspect that Leslie did not raise Antonio from birth, since the author refers to her as Antonio's "mother's partner," this good-bye mirroring interaction illuminates their affection for each other, which contrasts sharply with Antonio's feelings for Leslie once he is at school.

Leslie becomes the target of mockery by Antonio's classmates when she picks him up after school dressed in jean overalls splattered with different colors of paint. The children giggle and tease, "'That woman looks like a guy!' 'She looks like a box of crayons exploded all over her.' . . . 'She looks like a rodeo clown.'"[100] Embarrassed his peers will associate him with Leslie, Antonio heads toward her, away from the other children, and pulls her further away from the school as they wait for his mother. Although Antonio has two queer parents, only Leslie (who is white and butch) is read as queer, not his femme Latina mother. The students' comments about Leslie are a response to her queer identity, coded through transgressive gender norms that mark her as visibly butch or gender nonconforming. While Leslie was seen as different or queer because of her gender presentation, Antonio's school—comprised primarily of other Latinx youth—also posed a sharp contrast to Leslie's race. Within this context, the default working-class butch lesbian is racialized as white. This raises the question of whether the students may have responded differently if Leslie were a person of color. What if they had read Antonio's first mother as queer, or if both mothers had shown up at the school together holding hands or otherwise announcing their relationship?[101] As written, the children are teasing Leslie because of her butch aesthetic or gender, even if this is coded within her presumed queer sexuality.

A pillar of childnormativity, schools become primary sites for socializing children through the guise of education, as this text makes evident. Antonio is forced to confront two realities or forms of socialization: one at home and another at school, which has the potential to yield internalized hate or queerphobia toward his mothers over time. For example, just before Mother's Day, Antonio and his classmates draw cards "for the special women in their lives."[102] Antonio's best friend, Carlos, compliments him on the large green tree at the center of his card, beneath which a child and two adults are seated reading a book. Ms. Mendoza asks, "And who is your card for?"[103] Not wanting to reveal too much, Antonio hunched over his card, eventually relieved no one asked about Leslie. Presumably, Antonio had hoped to hide his card from his peers; however, his anxiety returned when his teacher announced that their cards would be displayed in the cafeteria for Mother's Day: "Antonio's hand freezes on his card. The taunting of the kids echoes in his head: *Look, there's that rodeo clown!*"[104]

Over the course of the book, Antonio comes to regard and publicly acknowledge Leslie as part of his family. He confesses his initial hesitation to his mother as he gets ready for bed: "Mami? Sometimes the kids at school make fun of the way Leslie dresses. And of the way she walks."[105] His mother responded with questions: "And how does Leslie dress, Antonio? And how does Leslie walk?' Antonio thinks about it carefully. 'Like Leslie, I guess,' he finally answers."[106] Nodding, his mother elaborates, "Leslie dresses and walks like Leslie, just like Antonio dresses and walks like Antonio. We're all a little different from each other. That's what makes each one of us an individual."[107] By responding to his trepidation with questions, we witness Mami's support of Antonio as he reflects on his feelings toward Leslie and how she is perceived by his peers. Ultimately, she leaves it up to him: "You're old enough now to decide what to do."[108] This statement reiterates the significance of choice since, by definition, members of a chosen family must ultimately be chosen.

Evidently, Mami has chosen Leslie as her partner. At one point, she "leans over to give Antonio and Leslie each a kiss on the cheek."[109] Queer affect, however, need not be restricted solely to queer couples. Throughout *Antonio's Card*, we witness love and joy not only between Antonio's moms but also among queer parents and their children. Leslie proudly showcases her love toward Mami and Antonio by creating a painting of the three of them as a Mother's Day gift for Mami. Eager to know Antonio's response, she asks, "Well, what do you think?"[110] The similarity between Leslie's painting and Antonio's card from school is not lost on him or readers. The text describes Antonio's sense of guilt and potential loss: "Antonio feels a lump in his throat. He can hardly speak. Antonio imagines what his afternoons would be like without Leslie, while his mother is at work. In his mind, he sees a solitary tree, and beneath the leaves he sees a solitary boy. No one to read with, no one to play spelling games with or curl up next to. He doesn't want ever, ever to have to write the word L-O-N-E-L-Y."[111] The accompanying illustration portrays a close-up of a melancholic Antonio contemplating his life without Leslie. In contrast, the final spread depicts Antonio and Leslie walking out of the studio, gazing at one another with their arms wrapped around each other. "Suddenly Antonio feels so lucky that Leslie is part of his family. And that is nothing to be ashamed of." His acceptance of Leslie as his chosen family is cause for celebration:

> "I have a surprise for you too, Leslie," Antonio says.
> "Really?" says Leslie.
> "Absolutely," Antonio answers, thinking about how very glad he is to know such good words.
> "I like surprises," Leslie giggles. "And when do I get to see this surprise?"
> "Today," Antonio says. "As soon as we walk back to school to see the Mother's Day display."[112]

The book concludes without a definitive answer as to how Antonio's peers might react to Leslie. They could very well continue to tease her, but this no longer seems to matter. Instead, the book emphasizes Antonio's sense of pride in his queer family. He unapologetically loves and is loved by his two queer moms.

Both Sarita Johnson and Rigoberto González are recognizable queer of color artists primarily known for other artistic and literary projects. Johnson was mostly known for her illustrations. In 1991, at the time of her initial copyright of *A Beach Party with Alexis*, she was described in *Out/Look: National Lesbian and Gay Quarterly* as "an artist who has been contributing illustrations for progressive causes for almost a decade. She currently teaches a class for school children in connection with the Oakland Museum."[113] In the creation of *A Beach Party with Alexis*, we see a convergence between her political illustrations and her work with children. She was also involved with the *Black Lesbian Newsletter*, which later changed its name to *Onyx: Black Lesbian Newsletter*, in reference to the black crystalline stone, and was active in the Bay Area Black Lesbian Political Caucus and Bay Area African-American Sisters Together (BAST) Cafe.[114] Johnson's illustrations graced the pages of numerous publications, including *Onyx, Sinister Wisdom, Aegis: Magazine on Endling Violence against Women*, and the Alberta Status of Women Action Committee (ASWAC) March 1990 newsletter.[115] She was also the featured artist of *Aché: A Journal for Lesbians of African Descent* in

1990. *A Beach Party with Alexis* served as Sarita Johnson's autofantasía and is autobiographical in terms of what occurred and who was present, choosing to include herself, her former partner Sandy, her daughter, and their queer and POC community. Notably, Johnson, Sandy, and Alexis also appeared in *A Day with Alexis*, a coloring book Johnson created just prior to *A Beach Party with Alexis*.[116] Self-publishing it under the name Sarita Johnson-Hunt, she described this first coloring book as "rough-looking" because she was "just learning how to draw on computer" with a mouse.[117] Since then, Johnson has developed additional skills in digital artmaking. Both Johnson and her current partner (Susan) live in Albany, California, and are retired teachers. All three (including her daughter Alexis) appear in Johnson's most recent graphic artwork collections, *The Donkey in Albany* and *Answer*.[118] The latter further intertwines Johnson's love of drawing and coloring with her career as an elementary school teacher.

Whereas Johnson is primarily known as an artist/illustrator, Rigoberto González is best known for his prose and verse, including *Unpeopled Eden* (2013), which was awarded the 2014 Lambda Literary Award for Gay Poetry and the 2014 Lenore Marshall Poetry Prize. In 2015, he was honored with the Publishing Triangle's Bill Whitehead Award for Lifetime Achievement and was included in the 2009 list "25 Most Influential GLBT Latinos" by *My Latino Voice*. González incorporates autobiographical details into most of his work, even publishing several memoirs, including *Butterfly Boy: Memories of a Chicano Mariposa* (2006), *Autobiography of My Hungers* (2013), and *What Drowns the Flowers in Your Mouth: A Memoir of Brotherhood* (2018). In addition to poetry, novels, memoirs, short stories, and anthologies, González authored another picture book two years before *Antonio's Card*. Titled *Soledad Sigh-Sighs / Soledad suspiros* (2003), it tells the story of a young Puerto Rican girl living in an urban space resembling New York City, who is often alone due to her family's long workdays. Soledad's coping mechanism is an imaginary friend, which eventually leads two of her neighborhood friends to join her as she discovers the perks of being alone such as reading, dancing, finding animal shapes in the clouds, and drawing. González, who taught for two years in a New York City afterschool program, was inspired by his predominantly Puerto Rican and

Dominican students "with their wonderful stories, poems and drawings. Together, [they] confronted a social reality: that many parents work long hours; that there are very few such places where children can explore, dream, and create; and that there are more children than available slots in good programs."[119] Without access to after-school programs or care-givers, children became responsible for themselves at a much younger age, thus challenging the childnormative notion that children constantly be under adult supervision. Labeling children like Soledad "survivors," González admits that he "too was a latchkey kid and [he] knew about feeling lonely."[120]

The lonely child, or more specifically the child left alone at home, queers childhood expectations and parenting guidelines because, from a childnormative perspective, Soledad's parents would be labeled bad parents and might even be reported to Child Protective Services. Instead, González depicts childrearing as a community practice whereby others also watch over Soledad, including her neighbor Mrs. Ahmed who checks in after Soledad arrives home from school and calls her mother to let her know Soledad made it safely. The act of being alone and creating a homosocial space further raises the possibility of queer inclinations among children. For example, as the two girls prepare to leave Soledad's apartment, Nedelsy asks, "Can I come over and play with you when it's too crazy at my house?"[121] "Yes," Soledad responds, "and we can be alone together."[122] This brief moment of possible mischief or queerness is interrupted by her mother's early arrival. Nonetheless, González leaves open the possibility of the two girls spending more time together in the near future.

Girls and women are integral to both of González's picture books. As noted above, the main character in his first picture book is a little girl, and even though Antonio is the protagonist in his second, lesbian figures are vital to the story. Interestingly, Antonio physically resembles González. Although González self-identifies as male and uses male pronouns, his gender vacillates. As a boy, he was teased for not wanting to engage in stereotypically masculine activities like sports and was considered effeminate by those around him, including his family. The loss of his mother at age twelve also affected his desire to learn from women, as he describes: "I believe women are much stronger than men, so what I seek is an association with that strength."[123] Of course, not all of his characters are women, and some of his writings are outwardly autobiographical; however, he is intentional in how and why he prioritizes female characters: "I like to think I'm empathetic enough to write in close proximity to the female perspective. I am not performing ventriloquism or mimicry, I'm simply placing into words what I observe from my limited perspective. In short, all this time I've been listening, paying attention—what many of us males should do more often—so that I don't exclude women from the art I create."[124]

González was initially hesitant to write about himself. Reflecting on completing his first memoir, he shared: "I wasn't sure if anyone would be interested in reading about me; I wasn't sure if my family would be devastated that I was revealing so much about them as well."[125] Summarizing his childhood, youth, and early adult life, González added: "I was born in California, raised in Michoacan, educated in Spanish, and then English when my family returned to the U.S. when I was ten." González's narrative is unique in that his migration from Mexico into the US is one of returning to his place of birth. This provides him with a significant advantage over others who might be undocumented, allowing him and his family to speak out more easily. He notes, "One element that has remained consistent is my identity as a politicized person. My family was always willing to participate in boycotts and labor strikes. The good fight is the single sensibility I have kept sacred all these years."[126]

This sense of political responsibility is also evident in his writing. After his first memoir, his second and third added greater depth to his sense of self and purpose as a writer. While in his forties, he reflected, "Now . . . I understand that my difficult journeys have given many who have traveled the same roads a place to reflect and to feel less isolated."[127] Major themes across his works, in addition to race, gender, and sexuality, include his experiences with extreme poverty, eating disorders, and mental health, including contemplating suicide. Crediting books for saving his life, he shared in an interview that his turn toward writing also gave him a sense of purpose, community and joy: "Being a writer helps me feel I'm doing something useful and necessary."[128] He added, "writing helps me imagine a world outside of the tiny one I felt trapped inside of . . . writing has allowed me to become part of a community that helps others toward thought, creativity and yes, even pleasure."[129] Like each of his publications, *Antonio's Card* reflects a piece of González as both person and author. The potential impact of his words is reason enough to not only keep writing but keep living.

* * *

While children's literature such as *Asha's Mums*, *Tengo una tía que no es monjita*, *A Beach Party with Alexis*, and *Antonio's Card/La tarjeta de Antonio* depict the internal and external factors affecting children of queer parents or relatives, they are equally telling of the internal polemics and rhetorical dilemmas of their creators. This reflects literary theory's long history of debate over the role of the author and authors' intentions when analyzing literature. I part from scholars who argue for the complete irrelevance of authors and their intentions.[130] Nor must the author "die" at the expense of the reader's birth.[131] As Claudia Nelson reminds us, "Among other things, of course, fictional children illustrate adult beliefs about what real children are and need. Thus, *children's literature*, a term tinged with irony by the elided gap between producer and consumer, is both mimetic and prescriptive. It traces a history of childhood that is simultaneously a history of adult *wishes* about childhood."[132] To this, we might add that such wishes about childhood include authors' own desires or fantasies about how they wish their own childhoods might have been different.

At least for the five authors responsible for the four picture books in this chapter, that ideal childhood was rooted in queer women of color and loving households. These picture books exist because authors such as Elwin, Paulse, Cardoza, Johnson, and González took a chance in sharing a glimpse into their world through their own autofantasías. They each mobilized the autobiographical and materialized their autofantasías regardless of place (country) and time (decades apart). Moreover, these picture books materialized and circulated precisely because of feminist and queer of color networks.

In the case of children's picture books, authors as well as illustrators, publishers, readers, and those who listen or look on, regardless of age, can intend or interpret works differently. As a hermeneutic, autofantasía accounts for all of these varying, and sometimes contradictory, interpretations at once. If the overarching goals of this chapter were to present "literary firsts" or the possible beginnings of "by and about" queer of color children's literature across North America, as well as to suggest reading them through their relationship with autobiography, the next chapter shifts to autofantasías as envisioned and executed by publishers.

2

A Tale of Three

Independent LGBTQ+ Picture Book Publishers across North America

I write because it heals me. . . . I publish because it could heal others like me . . . It's about self. And power. And truth.
—Maya Gonzalez

It's a very feelings-y business; that's one of the things about children's publishing generally and about Flamingo Rampant in particular. We make books that often provide the first time a kid has ever seen their family or their experience positively represented.
—S. Bear Bergman

As Maya Gonzalez and S. Bear Bergman emphasized, sharing one's truth by publishing children's literature should be considered not only an act of resistance but also of survival and healing. For Gonzalez, Bergman, and many of the other children's book authors who chose to publish with or create their own small independent presses, their motivation lies in a commitment to personal and social transformation. Fueled by this desire, what specific actions had to occur for queer and trans of color activists across North America to be able to publish picture books or create their own independent presses? How does the decision to become an independent press of LGBTQ+ children's literature help refocus their political goals? When creating an independent press, how does autofantasía manifest or resonate with publishers and the types of picture books or authors they publish?

While queer and feminist independent publishers were already publishing by and about queer of color children's literature during the 1990s and early 2000s, that was not necessarily the publishers' primary objective. Across North America, the 2000s were critical in establishing independent publishers that focused primarily or almost exclusively on publishing children's picture books with a focus on LGBTQ+ of color content. Three publishers stand out in their widespread influence. These include Ediciones Patlatonalli (Mexico, 2004), Reflection Press (US, 2009), and Flamingo Rampant Press (Canada, 2012). Each emerged from their respective country's unique social, political, historical, and cultural context, while also becoming interconnected with their neighboring countries.

When compared with Reflection Press, both Ediciones Patlatonalli and Flamingo Rampant Press share more visible similarities in the tangible picture books they publish. They both, for example, print their picture books exclusively in paperback, and neither press includes authors' or illustrators' photographs within their books. Flamingo Rampant Press does not include biographies either, while Ediciones Patlatonalli provides at least a one- to two-sentence biography for each author and illustrator. For both of these publishers, most of their books are also shorter than the average thirty-two-page picture book—Ediciones Patlatonalli's average page length is twenty-four, while Flamingo Rampant Press' is twenty-eight. All of their books are monolingual, with Ediciones Patlatonalli publishing in Spanish and Flamingo Rampant Press publishing in English, though more recently, some of their titles have also been translated into French and Spanish. However, unlike bilingual or trilingual books that include each language within one book, Flamingo Rampant produces separate versions for each language. In contrast, Reflection Press's books greatly vary in length, with most including additional resources, content, or activities at the end. They also tend to print most of their titles in both hardcover and paperback through print-on-demand (POD), and many of their books are bilingual in both English and Spanish. Each press makes many of these production decisions in an effort to mitigate costs while reaching as many readers as possible.

All publishers have a vision, mission, or set of guiding principles that determine what they publish, and this is also true for children's picture book publishing. While mainstream publishers might be inclined to spend more money on the overall production of a book, they also tend to publish fewer authors from marginalized communities, if they publish them at all. Niche or micro and independent publishers emerge as a response. Ediciones Patlatonalli, Reflection Press, and Flamingo Rampant Press each have a political agenda—or autofantastic publishing practice— reflected in their collective's mission, as well as in the types of books and authors or illustrators they publish. All of Ediciones Patlatonalli's picture books feature adult lesbian relationships; Reflection Press's picture books prioritize nature-based, gender variant or gender expansive communities of color; and Flamingo Rampant Press's collection emphasizes trans and queer characters of all ages, whether white or POC. Each reflects the publisher's own identities, ideologies, political projects, or priorities, which is also evident in their acquisition policies and procedures. These publishers, often privileging a more organic acquisition process or, stated differently, an embodied acquisition practice, prioritize authors, illustrators, and projects that more closely align with their own political projects, often collaborating with first-time authors and longtime activists or community leaders within their sociopolitical networks.

To publish a queer or trans of color picture book is to engage in radical politics. It is an attempt to circumvent or counter white heteronormative patriarchy while facing individual and intergenerational traumas in order to heal oneself and one's communities. Picture books also allow publishers to reimagine a different world for the present, fueled by the past, while looking toward the future. Ediciones Patlatonalli, Reflection Press, and Flamingo Rampant Press have succeeded, partly because of their thematic focus, each intentionality motivated by what they consider political urgencies—aided by a dose of serendipity. Situating these three publishers in relation to one another allows us to consider their unique positions within the larger field of children's literature so that we may excavate the ways in which they are influenced by and, in turn, influence queer and trans of color theory and embodied praxis within autofantastic publishing.

Ediciones Patlatonalli: Lesbian Feminist Children's Literature in Mexico

As in the United States and Canada, Mexican conservative groups like Frente Nacional Por La Familia [National Front for the Family] (FNPLF) have publicly protested children's literature they deem threatening to their expectations for a heterosexual nuclear family—idealized in the religious figures of baby Jesus, Mary, and Joseph. Casting aside his mother's polyamory and that he has two dads—for religiously conservative groups, Jesus has become emblematic of a form of childhood virtue in need of protection.[1] One of FNPLF's primary objectives includes reviewing state-endorsed curricula approved by the Secretaría de Educación Pública [Department of Public Education] (SEP), which is made available to public schools across Mexico.[2] Within FNPLF's vague declaration of "respect toward each individual," one can easily decipher their dismissal of LGBTQ+ individuals.[3]

When analyzing the 2009 preschool educational text *Equidad de género y prevención de la violencia en preescolar* [Gender equity and violence prevention in preschool], FNPLF declared that gender is not socially constructed and queer families should not be normalized by state-sponsored educational materials. However, a 2010 census from Instituto Nacional de Estadística y Geografía [National Institute of Statistics and Geography] (INEGI) found that there were more than 220,000 LGBT households throughout Mexico, of which over 170,000 had children.[4] By 2022, approximately 5 percent of the total Mexican population (or one out of twenty people) identified as LGBTI+.[5] These families often lack access to educational materials that reflect family formations beyond the heterosexual nuclear family. Similarly, LGBTQ+ children, whether raised by straight or LGBTQ+ parents, lack materials that portray their own lived experiences. Reflecting this, of the seventeen children's literature editors in Mexico approached by Adolfo Córdova in 2019, only six had edited a picture book with LGBTQ+ content or content that challenged heteronormativity in any way.[6]

The majority of LGBTQ-themed children's picture books in Mexico are currently imported from the United States and Spain. For example, Lesléa Newman's *Heather Has Two Mommies* was translated by Silvia Donoso into Spanish and published in 2003 by Edicions Bellaterra of Barcelona, Spain. The book eventually made its way into Mexico, where I spotted it at El Armario Abierto, a bookstore specializing in sexuality studies.[7] The translation by Silvia Donoso is unique, however, in that the protagonist's name—and consequently the title—had changed as a result. Replacing Heather with Paula, the Spanish version was titled *Paula tiene dos mamás* and included original illustrations by Mabel Piérola. Newman's story traveled from the US to Spain and then back to North America to be sold in Mexico. Although available in the country, the hardcover sold for the high price of $449 pesos, which was the equivalent of approximately $40 US at the time. In 2023, this 2003 Spanish (rare edition) version was listed on Amazon Mexico for $2,044.99 pesos, which raises the question: Who can afford these translations?[8] Although there are fewer explicitly LGBTQ-themed children's picture books published in Mexico compared to the United States or Spain, those that do exist have been instrumental in shifting the focus of lesbian feminist activism toward children and children's literature.[9]

Ediciones Patlatonalli emerged in Guadalajara, Mexico, as an extension of the lesbian feminist organization Patlatonalli. Its books (including *Tengo una tía que no es monjita* discussed in chapter 1) resulted from the organization's direct involvement within the larger lesbian feminist movement of Latin America and a desire to advocate for LGBTQ+ rights in Mexico.[10] Patlatonalli began publishing under its political campaign and slogan of "Todas las Familias Son Sagradas" [All Families Are Sacred]. Strategically invoking religion, spirituality, and chosen families, this slogan spoke to the manner in which Patlatonalli wove itself into the fabric of Mexican nationalism while also contesting it. This was a political project that arose from the need to situate local politics vis-à-vis national events, and it came at a critical time in Mexico's LGBTQ+ history.

Historian and lesbian activist Norma Mogrovejo credits the political climate of the late 1960s as the impetus for the emergence of Mexico's LGBTQ+ (or LGBTT) movement, which materialized in 1971 as the Frente de Liberación Homosexual de México (FLH), or Homosexual Liberation Front of Mexico.[11] Formed in an attempt to organize a public boycott against a Sears department store in Mexico City after its firing of a gay employee, and following similar incidents across Mexico and the US, Nancy Cárdenas (a Mexican actress, theater director, and the public face of FLH) agreed to an interview on Mexico's popular national television show at the time, *24 horas*.[12] Hosted by Jacobo Zabludowski and airing in 1973, Nancy Cárdenas became the first person in Mexico to publicly come out on national television.[13] Using her local celebrity stardom to catch the nation's attention, Cárdenas discussed discrimination, the lack of laws and rights, and her critiques of the pathologization of non-heteronormative sexualities.[14]

Following the initial work of Nancy Cárdenas and the Frente de Liberación Homosexual de México, other organizations and social movements began to form. Focusing on the lesbian movement, these groups emerged out of political tensions within the wider gay movement on the one hand, and the women's movement on the other. In 1975, a group of lesbians denounced the myth that homosexuality and lesbianism were Western concepts in the Declaración de las Lesbianas de México [Declaration of Lesbians from Mexico] publicly read at the World Conference on the International Year of the Woman.[15] In 1977, women formed the group Lesbos, out of which a splinter organization, Oikabeth, was established in 1978. That year, Lambda formed as a mixed gay and lesbian group, from which Marta Nualart and Guadalupe López co-founded a lesbian group in Guadalajara, Jalisco, in 1986. Initially named Grupo Lésbico de Guadalajara, the group became Grupo Lésbico Patlatonalli de Guadalajara (GLP) by 1989.[16] The organization's name was later shortened to Lesbianas en Patlatonalli and is known today as Patlatonalli, A.C.[17] It remains the longest consecutively running lesbian organization in Mexico, having celebrated its thirtieth anniversary in 2016.

Patlatonalli's decision to publish children's books was initiated by Marta Nualart's personal ties with Melissa Cardoza. Nualart described how she was handed a near-finished version of the book by Cardoza, with whom she was romantically involved at the time.[18] After writing the story, Cardoza asked her friend Margarita Sada to illustrate it, and together they produced the initial prototype of *Tengo una tía que no es monjita*, whose earlier version was titled *Las amigas de mi tía*.[19] Although neither Cardoza nor Sada were members of Patlatonalli, their personal ties with members of the organization, along with Cardoza's gifting of the book to them, resulted in a new direction for the lesbian feminist organization. Upon receiving the story, Patlatonalli was faced with several conundrums, including basic logistical questions like how to reproduce and distribute a children's book and how to become a registered editorial press. In the process of answering these questions, the organization worked with Cardoza on a few changes to the book's prototype, including the new title, the addition of "Ediciones Patlatonalli" to the cover, and the inclusion of a short blurb about the organization on the back, along with the logos of their two funding sources: Astraea Lesbian Foundation for Justice and the Global Fund for Women.[20] In this manner, with the publication of *Tengo una tía que no es monjita* in 2004, the organization Patlatonalli also became Ediciones Patlatonalli, and a new lesbian-focused children's literature press was born in Mexico.

As Nualart noted, Patlatonalli had focused on creating cultural resources from its inception, and at that moment, they noticed a void in lesbian-themed literature, namely that none of it was directed at children. Inspired by *Tengo una tía que no es monjita*, Ediciones Patlatonalli decided to place a call for other lesbian-themed children's stories with the intent of publishing the winner of the competition. *Tengo una tía que no es monjita* would become the first of a series of books focusing on queer families. Maintaining its slogan of "Todas Las Familias Son Sagradas" [All Families Are Sacred], Patlatonalli began to foster a new political line of inquiry, this time directly targeting the notion of families and heteronormativity. Nualart declared:

> Como parte de la sociedad, las familias lésbicas somos una realidad. Nos agrupamos en familias, muy a pesar del esquema heterosexista y monogámico que la propia sociedad conservadora ha intentado perpetuar. Pero insistimos en nuestro derecho a pertenecer en el concepto familiar como insistimos en renombrar y defender nuevas formas de convivencia.[21]

> [As part of society, lesbian families are a reality. We gather as families in spite of the heteronormative and monogamous scheme that mainstream conservative society has tried to perpetuate. But we insist on our right to be a part of the conceptual framework of family just like we insist on renaming and defending new ways of living.]

In accordance with their new political goals, Patlatonalli stressed not only the adults in lesbian families but also the role of children. "Lo que pretendemos no es tanto inventar un mundo diferente" [What we intend is not so much to invent a new world], clarified Nualart; but instead, "hacer que las niñas y niños se sientan cómodos y seguros en ese mundo que ya es diferente para ellas y ellos" [to make sure that girls and boys feel comfortable and secure in a world that is already different for them]. This focus on children as members of a larger lesbian-centered reality within picture book publishing would be a first of its kind in Latin America.

The children's story competition that ensued alongside the publication of *Tengo una tía que no es monjita* resulted in a series of lesbian-themed picture books published by Ediciones Patlatonalli. This competition, or "Convocatoria al Primer Concurso de Cuentos para Niñas y Niños con el Tema Familias Lésbicas" [Contest of Children's Stories about Lesbian Families], was judged by core members of Patlatonalli, along with three honorary judges who included Melissa Cardoza; Silvia Eugenia Castillero, poet and literary magazine editor of *Luvina*; and Baudelio Lara, a psychologist and art critic at the Universidad de Guadalajara.[22] They received a total of fifteen submissions. In an almost unanimous decision, first place was awarded to Juan Rodríguez Matus for his story *Las tres Sofías* [The three Sofías], which was subsequently illustrated by Anna Cooke and published in 2008. In addition to the competition winner, Ediciones Patlatonalli decided to publish other submissions that caught the judges' attention because, as they noted, aside from their own books, "No existen libros infantiles en nuestro país (y son contados en el resto del mundo) que traten el tema de las niñas y niños que nacen y viven en familias lésbicas" [There are no children's books in our country (and few worldwide) that focus on children who are born and live within lesbian families].[23] In 2009, Ediciones Patlatonalli published the late tatiana de la tierra's *Xía y las mil sirenas* [Xía and the thousand mermaids], also illustrated by Anna Cooke, and in 2011, Lorena Mondragón Rocha's *Mi mami ya no tiene frío* [My mommy is no longer cold], illustrated by Dirce Hernández.[24]

Although terms such as "lesbiana" or "gay" are not mentioned within the picture book stories, there are multiple references in the books' paratextual apparatuses. For example, their back covers feature Ediciones Patlatonalli's logo, which depicts two nude women embracing one another. Following a brief summary of the text, along with biographical information about the illustrator and author, we are also given additional information about Patlatonalli:

Las Mujeres en Patlatonalli AC, Lesbianas en una Organización Ciudadana, jugamos diversos juegos, creemos en las Niñas y Niños y nos gusta que conozcan y disfruten sus Derechos; entre ellos, el de Vivir en una Diversidad familiar. Todas las familias son Diferentes. Todas las Familias son Sagradas.[25]

[The women of Patlatonalli, Lesbians in a Civil Organization, play diverse games, believe in girls and boys, and we would like for them to learn and take advantage of their rights; among these, the right to live within a diverse family. All families are different. All families are sacred.]

This summary reconfigures the definition of a diverse family with one that centers queer or lesbian sexuality, all the while prioritizing children.

It is remarkable that Ediciones Patlatonalli was able to publish a series of picture books with lesbian adult characters. It is just as remarkable that each of their books also incorporates Indigenous subjects (e.g., *Las tres Sofías*) or racialized subjects and interracial relationships (e.g., *Xía y las mil sirenas* and *Mi mami ya no tiene frío*) that challenge the racial logics of Mexico. This was intentional, suggesting an autofantastic publishing model that engages multiple political agendas within an intersectional framework. Although all of Ediciones Patlatonalli's picture books include a lesbian adult relationship, they are each told through the perspective of a little girl. Whereas *Las tres Sofías* and *Mi mami ya no tiene frío* are told in first person, *Xía y las mil sirenas* is written in third person. Of all of them, the latter is also the picture book with the most internal conflict, albeit not due to the lesbian relationship.

In *Las tres Sofías*, Sofía, a young girl from an Indigenous community in Istmo de Tehuantepec in Oaxaca, Mexico, reveals the prevalence of her name within her community, including not only her mother, Sofía, but also their neighbor, Sofía Alvarado. "Así le tenemos que decir" [That is how we must refer to her], she explains, "porque somos muchas Sofías viviendo por el miso rumbo" [because there are many Sofías who live around these parts]. We learn that Sofía's mother is situated in a romantic triangle between her deceased husband and her neighbor, Sofía Alvarado. By the end of the book, the triangulation shifts, with Sofía's mother remaining at the center, but with the other Sofías on either side—representing the love between a mother and a child, as well as the love between two women. These three individuals, all named

Sofía, grace the picture book's cover. The two older women embrace in a tight hug while little Sofía plays with her mother's huipil dress, pulling it around her. Like her mom, she wears her hair in braids. The three are centered, looking forward as if posing for a photo, and surrounded by different shades of blue that serve as a frame around them. Despite being united on the cover, their union as a family does not actually occur within the book until much later.

Just before the one-year anniversary of her father's death, Sofía witnesses her mother's audacious transformation as she puts on a brightly colored dress and marches over to the house of the woman she has always loved.[26] She builds up the courage to do so by first confiding in her daughter: "estoy cambiando. Empecé por quitarme el luto; ya cumplí con mi madre y con mi padre, me case para darles gusto. Ahora ella y él ya no están con nosotras." She admits that she is going through a transformation and that she married Sofía's father to please her parents, both of whom are no longer with them. While it is unclear if Sofía's mother loved her husband or was bisexual, it is evident that she has always been in love with Sofía Alvarado. One can only speculate whether she would have eventually left her husband had he not passed away or if her parents were still present. The text also does not clarify or confirm whether the grandparents are in fact dead; "they are no longer with us" could also mean that they left or are not presently there, and this may be why she has chosen this moment.

Regardless of the circumstances that have left her without a husband or parents, Sofía's mother now finds herself free and in a position to seek out happiness:

> Desde hace mucho tiempo me prometí encontrar la felicidad; ahora que me siento libre, he decidido ir a buscarla. Mi vida tiene un nombre: Sofía Alvarado. Ella me ha esperado pacientemente durante todo este tiempo. Nos necesitamos mucho para ser felices juntas.

> [For a long time now, I promised myself I would find happiness; now that I feel free, I have decided to go find it. My life has a name: Sofía Alvarado. She has waited patiently for me during all this time. We need one another immensely to be happy together.]

Although the English translation above reads "I have decided to go find it," the Spanish original allows for a type of gender wordplay for the word "it." When Sofía's mom says she has decided to find happiness, the word "buscarla" may refer to seeking happiness in general, but it can also be translated as "find her"—in this case, referring to the other Sofía. Together, Sofía and her mother assuredly walk over to Sofía Alvarado's house across the street. In the process, Sofía describes herself as her mother's guardian angel, a role that is typically performed by an adult. Sofía momentarily becomes her mother's protector, giving her the courage to move forward and shielding her from any potential disapproval. Consent also plays a role in this story's development. Whereas heteronormative narratives often depict a man kidnapping a woman against her will, this picture book suggests that Sofía Alvarado had already been waiting. Indeed, Sofía's mom knew exactly where to find her; they went directly to the kitchen "donde Sofía la esperaba sonriente tratando de disimular, aunque sabía perfectamente de qué se trataba" [where Sofía was waiting for her while trying to hide her smile, although she knew exactly what this was about]. Smiling discreetly, Sofía Alvarado had been anticipating their arrival, and together they dashed away before anyone could stop them.

Unlike the centrality of the lesbian couple previously mentioned, the lesbian couple in *Xía y las mil sirenas* serves more as a backdrop, rather than driving the plot. *Xía y las mil sirenas* describes Xía's journey, from her city near the sea to her new adoptive family, which includes two mothers, a brother, and a puppy. Employing elements of surrealism and fantasy, Xía meets mermaids, a dragon, and a pony along the way who provide comfort as she adjusts to her new environment. This book is illustrated to capture the likely feelings of uncertainty or fear that one might feel when being taken away from their place of birth, asking us to consider the immediate and initial shift this must present for a child. Rather than being filled with a sense of joy or relief at being adopted, Xía is visibly in a state of despair. Seated next to one of her new mothers, we see her peering out the airplane window, a frown on her face and tears running down both cheeks. We are told that from her window, she sees a lion in a forest, a dragon in the sea, and, across the beach, a thousand mermaids. The illustrations depict the lion, dragon, and a row of mermaids stretched out on the beach. Unlike the other creatures, these magical mermaids will fly to her window to greet and sing to her: "Chica, chica, Xía, Xía, | ven a jugar de noche y de día. | Chica, chica, Xía, Xía, | somos sirenas de alegría" [Girl, girl, Xía, Xía, | come play all night and all day. | Girl, girl, Xía, Xía, | we are joyful mermaids]. This two-page spread illustrates the mermaids in greater detail, swirling around her window. Within this daydream or fantasy world, Xía has another fantasy, imagining herself outside the plane in midair, surrounded by these mermaids. She appears almost like a floating torso as the mermaids contort around her. The one-eyed crowned mermaid in the center holds up Xía, her red tail fin split in two. Then, jolted back onto the plane, Xía asks the mermaids to wait for her as she flies away. Upon arrival to "otro mundo" or another world, Xía meets the rest of her new family. That night, while she sleeps, she dreams she is in space, floating among stars and planets, astronauts, and her silver-plated pony, which becomes her guide and mentor. They eventually arrive on a beach, and Xía desperately calls out for the mermaids to come out and play. To her dismay, there is not a single mermaid in sight. Feeling sad and alone, Xía begins to cry. Only then does she see the mermaids. With each teardrop a new mermaid is formed. With this, the pony imparts wisdom about her new home and assures her the mermaids she saw will always be with her—"estan todas dentro de ti" [they exist within you]—keeping her company as she begins a new life. Ultimately, Xía comes to accept her new life and family.

In contrast, *Mi mami ya no tiene frío* centers a little girl (unnamed narrator) and her single mother who attend a puppet performance. Due to the narrator's desire to see the puppets up close, mother and daughter go backstage after the performance where they meet the puppeteer. The narrator plays with the puppets while the two women chat outside. However, as the days pass, the girl's initial reaction shifts, now feeling upset because her mother is preoccupied with someone else: "Un día mi mamá la invitó a cenar. Ella iba a visitarnos muy seguido y eso me enojaba porque yo tenía que jugar sola" [One day my mother invited her to dinner. She would visit often and that would make me angry because I had to play on my own]. At a distance, we see her mother and another woman toast with a glass of wine, while each sit on either side of a long table. On the adjacent page, a close-up of the protagonist emphasizes her frown. The plot turns when the little girl notes that on one occasion, after going to bed while the women stayed up together, she woke up and caught them kissing. We see a silhouette of the two women embracing under the moonlight coming through an open window. The daughter's frown becomes a look of uncertainty, which is not resolved until the next day when she asks her mother "si eran novias," or if they were girlfriends. Her mother confirms that, yes, they are indeed a couple. The final pages end with her acceptance, reasoning: "Después entendí que se amaban y que mi mami ya nunca tendría frío. Desde entonces somos felices las tres" [Later I understood that they loved each other, and my mom would never again be cold. Since then, the three of us are happy together].

In addition to depicting adult lesbian desire across their picture books, two of Ediciones Patlatonalli's publications (both illustrated by Anna Cooke) further challenge childnormative picture book norms in their provocative incorporation of homosocial nudity. In *Las tres Sofías* this occurs within one very explicit illustration. Before storming over to Sofía Alvarado's house, Sofía's mom shares with her daughter that the two women were childhood friends, having spent all of their time together, and they had always lived across from one another: "Mi mamá dice que desde chiquitas eran inseparables; iban juntas a la escuela, jugaban todo el tiempo" [My mother says that they were inseparable since they were small; they went to school together, playing all the time]. The corresponding illustration depicts them as children, hugging tightly. As they grew older, we are told, their friendship became more intimate. Childhood hugs gave way to feeling comfortable enough to lend one another their clothes and, later, to undressing in front of each other as adolescents or young women: "De jóvenes se prestaban la ropa para lucir bonitas cuando iban a las fiestas" [When they were younger, they borrowed each other's clothes to look pretty when going out]. The author does not say for whom they wished to look pretty. Instead, the accompanying illustration shows the two young women indoors; Sofía Alvarado sits on a wooden bench, completely nude, as she glances toward the reader and away from her best friend, covering her breasts with one arm and gently twisting her body. Sofía's mother has her gaze fixed on her best friend's naked body. Fully clothed, she uses one hand to play with her necklace, as if resting it on her chest over one of her breasts. Her lips are slightly parted. This scene leaves open the possibility of sexual desire among young women, including best friends.

The nudity in *Xía y las mil sirenas* is less sexualized and more prevalent, appearing on the cover and throughout the book as a result of the adult mermaids. Although many of them wear some variation of a bra or nipple covers, others openly expose their breasts. Surprisingly, in one of her last interviews prior to passing, tatiana de la tierra confessed to me her strong disapproval of the illustrations. In particular, she was unhappy with the mermaids' nudity. Known for her explicit lesbian erotic writing in works such as *For the Hard Ones: A Lesbian Phenomenology*, it might seem odd that she would be opposed to nudity. However, her training and knowledge as a librarian meant that she knew her picture book would likely not be acquired by schools as a result—not (only) because of the lesbian couple, but because of the nudity.[27] Here, as in with *Las tres Sofías*, nudity trumps sexuality in challenging potential taboos within children's picture books. Ultimately, Ediciones Patlatonalli made a choice to include these potentially taboo subjects and details throughout each of their books, even if it was, at times, at odds with the authors or risked censorship, in order to maintain their commitments to their own definition of lesbian feminist politics and autofantastic publishing.

Ediciones Patlatonalli's political project is also informed by a desire to represent lesbian families from diverse Indigenous or racial/ethnic backgrounds across Mexico. More precisely, *Las tres Sofías* depicts an Indigenous (Zapotec) same-sex relationship and family. Juan Rodríguez Matus, a gay male Zapotec author who chose to write about a lesbian relationship—an obvious choice given the topic of Ediciones Patlatonalli's competition—set the story near his hometown of Union Hidalgo, Oaxaca. It was inspired by a story his mother shared with him about two women in love.[28] Rodríguez Matus built on this memory to create a story for children that situates lesbian desire, love, and family within Indigenous (Zapotec) communities such as his.

Las tres Sofías should be commended for depicting same-sex desire and relationships in rural Indigenous populations, since urban spaces like Mexico City tend to dominate LGBTQ+ discourse, often overshadowing rural and Indigenous LGBTQ+ communities. The book visually situates the story in Oaxaca among the Zapotec mainly through attire (huipil shirts or dresses and huaraches), though Sofía and her mother also frequently wear their hair braided, and we are also explicitly told the geographic location within the synopsis on the back of the book. Like Rodríguez Matus's book, and the story his own mother told him, LGBTQ+ Indigenous communities exist in Mexico even if they are not always present within mainstream or childnormative literature.

Within the story, we learn that even before living together, Sofía Alvarado had been an integral part of their extended family unit. In their own way, Sofía's mom and Sofía Alvarado raised little Sofía together although they were not yet publicly out. On certain days, while her mom worked and after she had finished her homework, Sofía would spend time with Sofía Alvarado: "Ella es mi amiga como lo fue de mi mamá cuando eran chicas" [She is my friend as she was my mother's when they were little]. The three also spent time working together, going house to house selling *dulces de coco*, or coconut candies. And on other occasions, the three Sofías worked at the local market: "Aquí trabajamos en el campo, aunque mi familia, últimamente, se ha dedicado al comercio de camarones secos, totopos y quesos" [Here we work in the fields, although my family, lately, has focused on selling dried shrimp, *totopos*, and cheeses].[29] The accompanying illustration depicts women and children at the market surrounded by fresh produce, fresh and dried seafood, flowers, baskets, and clay pots (fig. 2.1). Sofía tells us that in her home, her mother is in charge, a nod to Indigenous matriarchal societies. She concludes by reaffirming her new family unit: "Tengo dos mamás tan valientes como yo quiero ser" [I have two moms as brave as I aspire to be].

Following the explicit integration of Indigenous culture throughout *Las tres Sofías*, Ediciones Patlatonalli's other two books depict adult lesbians in racially diverse or interracial relationships (*Xía y las mil sirenas* and *Mi mami ya no tiene frío*). Each takes a slightly different approach in how their characters are racialized, although neither explicitly comments on race or ethnicity within the text. In both stories, a child must deal with internal conflict caused by changes to their environment brought upon them by surrounding adults.

Much remains to be said about each picture book, but what is most intriguing to me (aside from the lesbian content), is how each book integrated racial diversity within the illustrations. For example, in *Xía y las mil sirenas*, racial or ethnic differences appear throughout, beginning with the cover. Mermaids with different skin tones (from very light-skinned to dark brown or black) and different colored hair

Aqui trabajamos en el campo, aunque mi familia, últimamente, se ha dedicado al comercio de camarones secos, totopos y quesos.

En mi casa, la que ha llevado la voz de mando es mi mamá.

Figure 2.1. Sofía and her two mothers walking through a market in Oaxaca; from *Las tres Sofías* [The three Sofías]. Published by Ediciones Patlatonalli. Copyright © 2008 by Juan Rodríguez Matus and Anna Cooke.

(including black, brown, red, blond, and grayish-blue or multicolored) grace the cover. In the bottom-right corner, we also catch a glimpse of a child peering out toward the reader. The child is light-skinned, with dark black eyes, and long, straight, dark-black hair pulled up into two pigtails held together by red hair ties, with short bangs in the front. She can be read as possibly Asian, Asian Mexican, or Asian American.[30] Her racial or ethnic background becomes more noticeable in comparison to her new family since her eyes appear narrower than those of her new moms or sibling. One of her moms is light-skinned with blue eyes (like her new brother) and light-brown or blond hair, while her other mother is dark-skinned with black eyes and dark, curly hair (fig. 2.2). Notably, Xía and her new family appear to speak the same language, or at least we are not told that they do not understand one another. We can interpret this as either an editorial decision made to simplify the complexity of transnational adoptions, or we could conclude that Xía is from one part of Mexico and that her new family lives in another part of the same country. Regardless of the lack of national markers, the book's geographic location is one that includes multiple racial or ethnic backgrounds and phenotypical differences, such as those found in Mexico.

Figure 2.2. Xía with her new multiracial adoptive family surrounded by magical creatures such as mermaids; from *Xía y las mil sirenas* [Xía and the thousand mermaids]. Published by Ediciones Patlatonalli. Copyright © 2009 by tatiana de la tierra and Anna Cooke.

Like Asian Mexicans, Black or Afro Mexicans remain marginalized within Mexico's national discourse, while also rarely being depicted in children's literature.[31] In *Mi mami ya no tiene frío*, the narrator and her mother are both racialized as white or light-skinned, while the puppeteer is racialized as Black or dark-skinned. Like *Xía y las mil sirenas*, this book does not mention or incorporate race or ethnicity within the text, instead relying on the illustrations to visually signal racial differences among characters (fig. 2.3). Both picture books not only incorporate racially diverse characters but also depict interracial relationships between "güeras y morenas," or "light ones and dark ones."[32] In doing so, Ediciones Patlatonalli, in collaboration with illustrators Anna Cooke and Dirce Hernández, suggest their ongoing desire to, at least visually, signal racial differences within Mexico. We might ask ourselves: Is it possible to normalize racial differences by not commenting on them? Or more precisely, is it possible to challenge whiteness when it remains unmarked within the story's text? And what might a lesbian-themed picture book that also dismantles whiteness in Mexico look like?

One of the greatest challenges to publishing these kinds of picture books is the lack of funding. Ediciones Patlatonalli has relied on major funding sources, such as the Funding Exchange, MacArthur Foundation,

Me quedé jugando con los títeres
mientras ellas platicaban.

Figure 2.3. (a) Protagonist surrounded by puppets, and
(b) protagonist's mom with the puppeteer; from *Mi mami ya no
tiene frío* [My mommy is no longer cold]. Published by Ediciones
Patlatonalli. Copyright © 2011 by Lorena Mondragón Rocha and
Dirce Hernández.

Astraea Lesbian Foundation for Justice, COESIDA Jalisco, Semillas, Global Fund for Women, and smaller government grants.[33] They have ranged significantly in both amount and duration. As Patlatonalli members noted, most of the major grants come from international funding sources, which makes the competition pool much larger.[34] Furthermore, the scarcity of local grants speaks to the lack of prioritization of this kind of work by potential Mexican funding sources.

Despite funding troubles, Ediciones Patlatonalli has focused their efforts on strategically distributing the books they can print. From presentations at international book fairs to local artisan markets, members are constantly thinking of creative ways to promote their work, often prioritizing wide distribution over profit. For example, seeking the attention of local governments in both Guadalajara and Mexico City, they distributed copies to elected officials. Although many of their books are now out of print, they often provided free copies during community workshops or to local schools. They also encourage copyleft strategies by providing free PDF versions online.[35]

Perhaps not surprisingly, Ediciones Patlatonalli's children's books have traveled internationally due to the non-profit circuit. Because they were funded by major international foundations, grant organizations have taken a particular interest in the progression of Patlatonalli's initial campaign, "Todas las Familias Son Sagradas." Ana María Enriquez, former director of the Global Fund for Women, mentioned at the Women's Funding Network conference in 2005 that she and her husband read *Tengo una tía que no es monjita* to their child every night.[36] The book also appeared on the cover of the Astraea's 2005 newsletter *Threads*. In a segment on Mexico, Katherine T. Acey, former executive director of the Astraea Lesbian Foundation for Justice, commented, "Patlatonalli's wave of social change has indeed transcended sexual orientation, as well as borders."[37] The series has also made an impact on individuals through the larger international book distribution circuit, with books available for purchase in Spain and for checkout from several public libraries in the US, such as in New York City.[38]

Overall, Ediciones Patlatonalli's picture books reflect Patlatonalli's original lesbian feminist organizational mission statement, aligning politically with wider lesbian feminist activism in Mexico from the 1970s to the present. Patlatonalli (as organization and publisher) prioritizes the lesbian feminist subject, centering a frequently marginalized position within Mexican society and in children's literature. Their picture books also include transborder subjects and incorporate Indigenous and racialized characters that trouble the nationalist ethnic norms of mestizaje. And yet, Ediciones Patlatonalli's ability to publish children's picture books remains confined to NGOs and transnational funding sources. They have also yet to publish a picture book with a queer child at its center; members of Patlatonalli are aware of this limitation and welcome authors willing to take on this task. Still, Ediciones Patlatonalli's series remains Mexico's most radical in its depiction of queer, and specifically lesbian, adult desire in children's picture books.

Reflection Press: Radical Publishing with a Gender Philosophy in the US

Reflection Press began in the United States as a collaborative effort between two partners, Maya C. Gonzalez and Matthew Smith-Gonzalez. Even though it was not officially established until 2009, Maya Gonzalez ventured into children's picture book illustrating much earlier, when she illustrated Gloria Anzaldúa's second children's picture book, *Prietita and the Ghost Woman/Prietita y la Llorona* (1995).[39] Although Gonzalez began illustrating for previously well-established publishers, the limits imposed by the larger children's book industry led her and her partner to create their own press. Both Gonzalez and Smith-Gonzalez utilized their prior artistic and creative experiences to establish Reflection Press. Gonzalez was originally known for her bold queer Chicana artwork, while Smith-Gonzalez, who is trans and white, had a background in architecture to build from.[40] They have also described their collaborative efforts as: "Maya makes the art and words. She sings the song to life. Matthew dreams and tinkers. He makes the work tight."[41] Together, "they make books for the kids they used to be" as well as for "their own two kids so all kids can grow free!"[42]

Located in San Francisco, California, and identifying itself as "a POC queer and trans owned independent publisher of radical and revolutionary children's books and works that expand cultural and spiritual awareness," Reflection Press's mission is "to provide materials that support a strong sense of individuality along with a community model of real inclusion."[43] It envisions "a world rooted in true freedom, respect, and equality, and motivated by the knowledge that everyone is valuable and everyone has special creative gifts to share."[44] Although the press primarily publishes children's picture books, its catalog also includes additional titles such as a YA novella, coloring books and other reference or activity books, and merchandise such as t-shirts and posters. Most of their titles are created by Gonzalez and Smith-Gonzalez, although they have also published several queer bilingual picture books by other authors under their "Queer 2 Queer" mentorship series.[45]

As a political project, Reflection Press prioritizes teaching others how to create their own books, and it also encourages others to consider establishing their own independent presses—all in an effort to counter the profit-driven model of mainstream children's publishing. Their efforts are evident in the programming they do alongside the books they publish. In 2012, Gonzalez and Smith-Gonzalez organized an event titled "Radical and Relevant Children's Books: Fostering a Publishing Revolution from Within" at San Francisco's iconic Women's Building. Concerned with the closing of smaller publishers across the country, this "consciousness cultivating mini-conference" hoped to inspire a "publishing revolution" as a response to "the growing need for children's books beyond the structures of established publishing houses."[46] The event featured three major sessions, one lead by Gonzalez, one by Smith-Gonzalez, and another by Dana Goldberg, whom Gonzalez had previously worked with in her capacity as the executive editor of Children's Book Press. Each session gave participants an insider's view into some aspect of children's publishing. Gonzalez's session, "The Political Act of Children's Book: Sourcing Your Story from Within," aided aspiring authors and illustrators in finding and cultivating a picture book idea through self-reflection, while Goldberg's and Smith-Gonzalez's sessions prioritized the publishing process—Goldberg's "from inside" traditional book publishing, and Smith-Gonzalez's "from outside" traditional publishing or from within alternative and independent publishing, sharing his experiences as co-founder, graphic designer, and publishing manager of Reflection Press.[47]

This mini-conference was followed by the 2013 co-creation of Gonzalez and Smith-Gonzalez's online learning environment for adults, School of the Free Mind, and the 2015 creation of the *Write Now! Make Books* handbook or curriculum for children.[48] Gonzalez also works directly with children, visiting classrooms and encouraging them to tell their own stories. Reflecting on these experiences, she shares, "It is not about art, although art is made. It is about process. It is about self"; for Gonzalez, that means fostering creativity as a conduit for "empowering those who hold the least amount of power and influence in our society."[49]

All of Reflection Press's projects, workshops, and tools fuel Gonzalez and Smith-Gonzalez's joint objective of aiding others in sharing their own truths. This is especially important for individuals and communities who have been silenced or marginalized within children's cultural productions. For the co-founders of Reflection Press, that means addressing and modeling inclusion "by allowing all genders, races, classes, orientations, abilities . . . to stand side by side." Given Gonzalez and Smith-Gonzalez's combined identities and politics, their autofantastic publishing model especially privileges queer and trans of color communities rooted in a holistic and nature-focused approach to gender and sexuality.

What would a gender philosophy or gender theory directed at children look like? Reflection Press's commitment to disrupting the gender binary through gender play launched a series of books that evidence their "Playing with Pronouns" gender philosophy organized around their Gender Wheel. The first iteration of Reflection Press's gender philosophy emerged in Gonzalez's *Gender Now Coloring Book: A Learning Adventure for Children and Adults* (2010). This amalgamation of coloring book, reference guide, and activity book features the Gender Team, a group of children "ready to play and show you the way."[50] Lined up at the bottom of the cover, Gonzalez depicts the six children of the Gender Team whose t-shirts spell out *G-E-N-D-E-R* (fig. 2.4). On closer examination, it becomes apparent that one of them resembles Gonzalez. Depicting herself in child form as the letter "R," this character is brown-skinned, femme, and cisgender. She wears her hair parted in half, with one bun on each side and earrings dangling from her ears. The character reappears throughout the book, including on the very first page where Gonzalez (as author) directly welcomes adult readers: "To parents, caregivers, therapists, social workers, teachers and all the fabulous grown-ups sharing a gender exploration/adventure with children."[51] The character holds a visual representation of the gender wheel in her hands,

Figure 2.4. Cover of *Gender Now Coloring Book: A Learning Adventure for Children and Adults*. Published by Reflection Press. Copyright © 2010 by Maya Christina Gonzalez.

which Gonzalez presents to us on subsequent pages. Switching back and forth, but also coexisting side-by-side, Gonzalez is thus present in the book as both author/parent/adult and child character. Despite the age difference, both versions of Gonzalez are educators and knowledge producers within this autofantastic LGBTQ-inclusive world.

Gonzalez replicated similar versions of herself in prior works as well. For example, she autofantastically inserts herself as the child protagonist in *My Colors, My World/Mis colores, mi mundo* (2007) and *I Know the River Loves Me/Yo sé que el río me ama* (2009)—both published by Children's Book Press.[52] However, even before creating picture books, Gonzalez was painting and drawing herself into her artworks since, as she describes, "everything was self-portraiture in some form or another as I attempted to claim my own face."[53] Childhood drawings were no exception: "As young as 4, I remember drawing my round, Chicana, girl face onto the blank pages in the back of books. On some level I knew I belonged there, despite the fact that I did not see myself in any of the books I came into contact with."[54] Eventually, by drawing and redrawing herself, Gonzalez reclaimed her face and with it, her sense of her whole self.

Like her character, each of the other children who make up the Gender Team are depicted as happy, playful, and confident. Although they each wear a purple shirt and jean shorts on the cover, their individual characteristics make them unique—from long to short hair, dark to light skin, with some accessorizing with jewelry or a hat. Each character further explores their gender and gender expression on subsequent pages.

A key part of disrupting the gender binary is challenging the very categories of "boys" and "girls." Gonzalez explains, "During this time in history, we like to pretend that there are only two types of bodies, male and female, girl and boy. But the truth is that there are lots and lots of different types of bodies. This means there are lots and lots of different ways to feel like a girl or a boy or simply a person on the inside of your body. In fact, there are so many different bodies and ways to feel inside your body, what we really need are more words than just boy and girl."[55] She turns to nature in substantiating her claim, asking readers to "Look at two trees standing next to each other. Even if they're the same kind of tree, like a Pine Tree, they don't grow in the same way. One grows this way, while one grows that way. Each one is free to grow into itself. The same is true for flowers, snowflakes, clouds and even people!"[56]

Gender Now Coloring Book introduces readers to terms like "intersex" and "transgender." While Gonzalez provides short definitions for each, she (as well as Smith-Gonzalez, who designed the layout) notes in smaller text—aesthetically signaling that it is intended for adult readers—other nuances in meaning. For example, in a section titled "Everybody has a body," the font size and placement on the page helps readers to differentiate between simple and more complex definitions. Printed in a larger font, "intersex" is simply defined as having "boy and girl characteristics," while Gonzalez writes in a smaller font positioned parallel to the curves of a tree's roots: "The term intersex is being used here to acknowledge the many perfect bodies that are a mix of what we currently refer to as male and female characteristics, both internal and external. Many historical transgender people may have been intersex."[57] Transgender, meanwhile, is defined as "a boy who changes her body and/or identifies as a girl or a girl who changes his body and/or identifies as a boy." Undoubtedly, not all readers will agree with Gonzalez's definitions. Anticipating this, along with ongoing changes in terminology and definitions, she signals this evolution with a smaller font size that reads: "The term transgender has been evolving over the last 50 years and continues to evolve. For the moment (and for the purposes of this book), transgender is an umbrella term . . . uniting all those whose gender identity does not easily mesh with their gender assigned at birth."[58]

Through the Gender Team, Gonzalez tells us that "some pages are for coloring, some pages are for playing, and some pages are for learning stories about ancestors and nature."[59] Examples of said ancestors or "tr/ancestors" from the United States include We'wha, Cathay Williams, Big Mama Thornton, and Sylvia Rivera.[60] Although Gonzalez only includes very brief descriptions of each, she provides readers with a list of names they can look up themselves to learn more. For example, while historians generally conceive of Cathay Williams as a woman who wore men's clothing, more recent scholarship has reclaimed Williams as trans.[61] Other examples range from individuals like Joan of Arc, to gender categories such as Fa'afafine (Samoan) and Hijra (South Asian), to deities or mythological figures like Guan Yin (Chinese Buddhism) and Ometeotl (Meso-American/Aztec).[62]

Limited views of human gender, sex, and sexuality similarly do not allow us to adequately understand the flora and fauna biodiversity of our own environments. In order to transform these understandings, *Gender Now Coloring Book*'s section "Gender in Nature" incorporates fun facts about gender fluid or transgender animals, which Gonzalez terms "tr/animals." The introduction to this section declares: "Some animals change their bodies to change gender because of things happening in their environment. Some animals spend part of their life as one gender and then when it's time they naturally shift to another gender. . . . Some animals have genders that cannot be thought of as boy or girl, but are a different gender altogether."[63] There may be limitations to assigning or reading gender onto animals, as it risks reducing their complexities to something that will be palatable to humans and aligns with our own gender biases and binary.

As with the historical figures listed above, *Gender Now Coloring Book* offers a list of animals—bears, sea horses, deer, kangaroos, snails, and clownfish—each with brief descriptions of how they challenge our own understandings of gender or sex. This provides details that can serve as a reference point for further research by children and adults. Gonzalez describes: "The girl Clown Fish body is larger than the boy body. And if the girl goes away and leaves the boy Clown Fish with the little fishes, he changes his body into a girl Clown Fish." Further, "All snails are both boy and girl at the same time and they have fabulous swirly shells!"[64] In presentations and interviews, Gonzalez has specifically identified how Disney has promoted gender fallacies, for example, noting that *Finding Nemo* (2003) misgenders Nemo's parent: "If the movie was true to life, Nemo's father would have transitioned to a female fish to act as Nemo's parent."[65] All clownfish are protandry; they are born male, with both male and female reproductive organs, and may transition to female in order to lead. In Disney's *Turbo* (2013), meanwhile, all of the snails are gendered into feminine girl/female snails or masculine boy/male snails without considering that snails are intersex. And yet, Disney continues to dominate children's culture worldwide.

As writer, illustrator, and co-publisher, Gonzalez has the freedom to incorporate as much or as little of herself as she likes. It also means that she need not seek anyone else's approval in what she publishes and can blend literary styles or genres as she sees fit. While much of *Gender Now*

Coloring Book might fall under nonfiction, Gonzalez has also created a world that allows herself, her character, the other Gender Team characters, and readers to merge reality with fantasy, make believe, or otherwise fictional elements. Such is the case on page twenty, where she has drawn herself with giant antlers protruding behind each hair bun. Surrounded by a pair of baby goats (or "kids"), the text reads: "I love taking care of my baby goats so much, I pretend I am [a] goat too." Gonzalez's creative liberties expand to the goats. In contrast to the more realistic goat on page forty-two, these two appear to have wings instead of ears, and their bodies are decorated with flowers. On the following pages, another child shows off a tail fin instead of legs, and a third appears to be a centaur.

One way to interpret these elements of the book is to consider how much of our understandings of gender are socially constructed or fictional. By allowing the Gender Team and child readers to explore and express themselves in multiple ways, this can ultimately create a more loving and supportive environment where children can be their multifaceted selves, regardless of gender identity or expression. For example, one child who might stereotypically be labeled a boy because of their short hair is wearing a dress, whereas other activity pages allow readers to interact with the page by drawing themselves into one of numerous hair styles. Asking readers, "What hairdo do you like?" the page instructs them as follows: "color the hair and draw your own face on the head, or heads, with the hair that feels most like you. Or use the blank one to draw your own hairdo!" With similar activities for choosing an outfit or sharing one's special talents or skills, the book as a whole invites children—and adults—to self-reflect and share a part of themselves while also learning about others. For Reflection Press, "children are communicated to all the time about what is considered right or wrong, good or bad, real or not real, valued or devalued in our culture. . . . Making one's self visible changes the world as we know it and can be seen as a revolutionary or radical act."[66]

As with *Las tres Sofías* and *Xía y las mil sirenas*, *Gender Now Coloring Book* also incorporates nudity. In one version of Gonzalez, her child character is shown nude and is intended to showcase herself as a cisgender girl along with the other Gender Team children in order to discuss anatomy as another component of one's self, gender, or gender identity.

Because people of color and those who are disabled, gender nonconforming, trans, or intersex have historically been put on display or experimented on without their consent, it is important to consider that presenting children this way could potentially be traumatic for some adult readers. The key difference is in the intended audience and gaze. Although adults may read and explain the different nude bodies to children, adults are not the intended audience. The gaze is not intended to be hierarchical, but rather horizontal (i.e., child to child). Children are not likely to be aware of the historical trauma associated with displaying bodies; instead, they can engage with this book as if it were simply a matter of anatomy. Moreover, it is meant to present cisgender, nonbinary, trans, and intersex children with depictions of themselves in order to validate their own bodies. Despite being a pedagogical book, Reflection Press published a modified version under the title of *Gender Now Activity Book: School Edition* (2011), which does not include nude children.

Gonzalez states at the end of *Gender Now Coloring Book*, "everyone is affected by and expresses gender in some way," and she shows this to be true for herself and her family members. She dedicates the book to her child, Zai, whom she describes as "free." Here, one of the ways Zai is free pertains to their gender: "You are beautiful free. May all your days be filled with this knowing," she adds. In Gonzalez's biography at the book's end, she shares how she came out at the age of twenty and was rejected by her family. She emphasizes the importance of finding books to educate and celebrate her child, as well as to acknowledge her queer family and trans partner, Mathew, who has become a co-writer alongside Gonzalez in more recent publications. This "About Maya" page pairs a cropped photograph of Gonzalez with the hair buns of Maya's character at the top, so that both author and character exist visually on that page. Since the publication of *Gender Now Coloring Book*, her family has grown to include another child, Sky (who appears in future projects). In this manner, *Gender Now Coloring Book* is Gonzalez's way of working through her own gender as it fits into a wider gender spectrum that also encompasses her family and greater communities. Since 2010, when the book was published, society's broader engagement with gender and sexuality in children's literature has shifted to include new terminology. Reflecting on the book, she adds, "I choose to use words that are accessible and familiar to the broadest audience possible with the knowledge that language evolves. Our words, even our way of communicating will change as we change. . . . I trust and look forward to the common use of at least 20 amazing new words to describe myself, my community and my thoughts in the future."[67] Her optimism for a broader gender lexicon is encouraging. Indeed, beginning with *Gender Now Coloring Book*, Reflection Press' gender theory has emphasized fluidity, versatility, and gender play, which reverberates across many of their works.

Reflection Press further solidified their gender theory for children in Gonzalez's *The Gender Wheel: A Story about Bodies and Gender for Every Body*, published in 2017. "This is our world," she begins. "Like many things in nature it's round and holds every body at the same time."[68] One need not read this text in one sitting or from cover to cover, since it functions both as a picture book and as an informational or educational guide to bodies, genders, and pronouns. The first part of the book breaks down the boy/girl sex and gender binary, noting, "As a part of nature, human bodies are all different too. Like faces, no two bodies are exactly the same. While people can easily agree that no two bodies are identical, many people believe there are only two kinds of bodies. Girl and boy."[69] In response, she offers a brief history of colonization beginning 500 years ago when "people came to North America from Europe with their beliefs about how they thought the world should be."[70] "Many of their beliefs," she continues, "were linear and rigid. They boxed people in and kept nature out. As the newcomers took the Americas for their own, they forced the people who had lived here for thousands of years to adopt their beliefs about everything, including bodies."[71] Targeting a slightly older audience (ages seven to ten or grades second to fifth), *The Gender Wheel* more explicitly incorporates major themes such as colonization and its ongoing effects on society's limited conceptualizations of gender.

While the beginning of *The Gender Wheel* introduces readers to the stereotypical characteristics of the gender binary (e.g., man/woman; penis/vulva; blue/pink), the primary goal is to share Gonzalez's gender wheel, which includes three concentric circles: (1) the outer Body Circle, (2) the Inside Circle, and (3) the Pronoun Circle at the center.[72] Gonzalez asks, "What can you do to honor nature and the dance we are all part of as things expand and grow?" She suggests, "You can keep your understanding of bodies, gender and pronouns as dancing and alive and current as possible," which she describes as "knowing about lots of different kinds of people and including every body as a normal part of your regular, everyday life."[73] The text continues, "Consider how you think, how you speak, what stories you pass on, what books and movies you look at, even how you learn about nature, or history or cultures. And always remember the wheel and your place in the dance. This keeps Gender NOW!"[74]

Stylistically different, but still recognizable, the six characters that made up the original Gender Team emerge once again. This time, they explicitly share their gender identities as they relate to each circle within the wheel. Gonzalez's character, for example, tells us they describe their body as a "cisgender girl," inside they feel like a "queer femme," and their pronoun is "she."[75] Similar to *Gender Now Coloring Book*, *The Gender Wheel* originally included "each child in their natural or nude state," and was followed by a School Edition published in 2018 with each child clothed (fig. 2.5). Throughout each version of *The Gender Wheel*, and

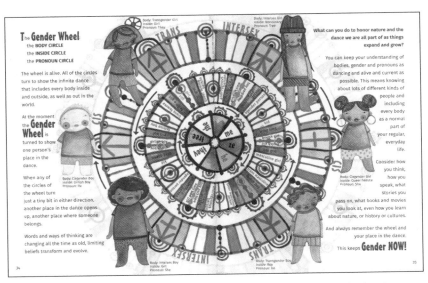

Figure 2.5. Six children around the Gender Wheel; from *The Gender Wheel: A Story about Bodies and Gender for Every Body [School Edition]*. Published by Reflection Press. Copyright © 2018 by Maya Gonzalez.

reflecting Gonzalez's wider gender philosophy, she has continued to emphasize the importance of fluidity, expanding the circle to integrate current understandings of gender, as well as making room for additional future iterations. Visually, this occurs by introducing other characters, such as one resembling her actual child, Sky, as a "freewheeling body." Gonzalez ends with "A note to the reader," which offers instructions on how to make a gender wheel of your own and links to Reflection Press's Gender Wheel resources, which Smith-Gonzalez curates online at www .genderwheel.com.

Gonzalez synthesized her gender philosophy in collaboration with her partner, Matthew Smith-Gonzalez, into two co-authored picture books for slightly younger audiences. *They, She, He, Me: Free to Be!* (2017) and *They, She, He: Easy as ABC* (2019) both emphasize illustrations over the written word.[76] With their focus on "Playing with Pronouns" gender theory, Reflection Press has not stopped at children's literature. Gonzalez's characters have come off the page and been printed onto book bags, posters, stickers, clothing, and, more recently, a Playing with Pronouns card deck. The package includes fifty-two alphabet/pronoun cards with individual characters on each one, along with activity and support cards for a total of eighty-four cards. Their child, Sky, appears in promotional materials online, as well as on their videos that offer game suggestions. For Gonzalez and Smith-Gonzalez, creating their own press was absolutely necessary in order to showcase their gender theory for kids and validate nature-based gender play. Other authors unable to create their own independent press are tasked with seeking out publishers supportive of their and their characters' gender identities and expressions.

Flamingo Rampant Press: Featuring Trans of Color Children's Literature in Canada

Based out of Toronto, Canada, Flamingo Rampant Press began when S. Bear Bergman wrote and self-published two children's picture books, *Backwards Day* (2012) and *The Adventures of Tulip, Birthday Wish Fairy* (2012).[77] Each incorporated gender nonconforming, nonbinary, or transgender themes and characters. Bergman co-founded Flamingo Rampant Press with his partner, j. wallace skelton, both of whom are white transgender activists.[78] Like Gonzalez and Smith-Gonzalez, they also have children (three).[79] Following their first two picture books, Flamingo Rampant Press released six titles each in 2015, 2017, and 2019.[80] Their latest series published in 2022 included both picture books and middle-grade books.[81] Bergman and skelton orchestrated effective crowdsourcing or Kickstarter campaigns to fund all their series. Although Canada provides federal awards and subsidies meant to incentivize underrepresented authors to create more literature, micropublishers such as Flamingo Rampant Press still prefer the independence of crowdsourcing.[82] Bergman explained: "Crowdfunding allowed us to reach out directly to the customers we knew existed even though traditional publishing told us very loudly that they did not exist. We didn't have the resources to start publishing books without pre-sales."[83] As of this writing, Flamingo Rampant Press has published over twenty LGBTQ-themed children's picture books, some of which have also been translated into Spanish and French.

Self-described as a "micropress with a mission," Flamingo Rampant Press's goal is "to produce feminist, racially-diverse, LGBTQ positive children's books, in an effort to bring visibility and positivity to the reading landscape of children everywhere." The mission statement continues: "We make books kids love that love them right back, bedtime stories for beautiful dreams, and books that make kids of all kinds say with pride: that kid's just like me!"[84] In order to cultivate and publish more #ownvoice stories, many of their authors or illustrators are also activists or public figures recognizable among their respective communities. Major themes include trans inclusion, not only within books by S. Bear Bergman such as *Backwards Day* but also others, including Tobi Hill-Meyer's *A Princess of Great Daring!* (2015) and Sophie Labelle's *Rachel's Christmas Boat* (2017). To readers' delight, Flamingo Rampant books even include a "secret message" tucked within the copyright text that reads "you have the right to be safe, strong, free, and utterly fabulous in whatever gender(s) you choose."

Not only prioritizing their own identities but also considering many of the groups historically marginalized, Bergman and skelton choose themes, characters, authors, and illustrators who represent an array of communities and who can speak to pressing sociopolitical issues. For example, Bergman and skelton publish picture books that celebrate their Jewish heritage (e.g., skelton's *The Last Place You Look*, 2017) while simultaneously publishing books from other religions and spiritualities such as queer Muslim identities in El-Farouk Khaki and Troy Jackson's *Moondragon in the Mosque Garden* (2017). Flamingo Rampant Press also encourages us to broaden our definition of what constitutes a Canadian publisher. For example, S. Bear Bergman is originally from Massachusetts (United States) and then moved to Toronto as a result of his relationship with skelton.[85] And like their relationship, which originally started off as transnational, many of their authors and illustrators also span across Canada and the United States. Unlike many of the other publishers discussed herein, Flamingo Rampant Press does not include biographies or photographs of its authors and illustrators at the back of its picture books or on its website. Instead, authors and illustrators often appear in Kickstarter campaign videos and campaign descriptions.

Flamingo Rampant Press emerged at a unique juncture within queer and trans of color children's publishing in that, unlike Ediciones Patlatonalli where all the LGBTQ+ content focuses on adults, their books vary significantly depending on each individual story and the creative autonomy of the authors and illustrators. Despite this, queer desire is limited to adults among their books published within the scope of my research (through 2020). When the focus is on children, they are shown grappling with gender identity instead of sexuality, as I will discuss in the following two chapters. For the sake of this chapter, I want to highlight the ways in which Flamingo Rampant Press also centers nonbinary and trans of color adult characters throughout their books.

Four Flamingo Rampant books exemplify nonbinary or trans of color adulthood. In the first, *Colors of Aloha* (2019), transness is incorporated within the book's illustrations. In the second and third, *The Zero Dads Club* (2015) and *Bridge of Flowers* (2019), gender nonconforming, nonbinary, and trans of color adults are integrated into the story without making their gender identities the central plot line. In the fourth, *M is for Mustache: A Pride ABC Book* (2015), trans of color adults are very much present and celebrated throughout. Each strategy is necessary, allowing the authors, illustrators, and publisher an opportunity to incorporate nonbinary or trans of color identities in subtle and overt ways that validate, normalize, and saturate in order to challenge cisgender privilege and assumptions. Although I will primarily discuss these four books as they relate to nonbinary or trans of color visibility, each title warrants a more in-depth close reading to fully capture their significance and complexities. In what follows, I want to consider how Flamingo Rampant Press, as a publisher working alongside authors and illustrators, employs autofantasía in order to curate collections that mirror their own identities as well as their politics. In this case, that means decentering their own whiteness in order to center nonbinary or trans of color politics and communities.

Colors of Aloha (2019) stands out for its visual incorporation of a trans of color adult character through the figure of Kalani. Narrated by his younger sibling, *Colors of Aloha* follows Kalani as he teaches his sibling and two cousins—Pau and Hinalei—various words in Hawaiian, including colors such as "'ula 'ula (red)," "'alani (orange)," and "melemele (yellow)," among others. Additional terms and translations such as "hale (house)" or "ono (delicious)" are incorporated throughout. *Colors of Aloha* includes and does not differentiate between native Hawaiian terms and Hawai'i Creole English or "Pidgin" ones such as "Unko" [Uncle]. Throughout the book, Kalani embodies the role of educator, associating many of the colors with native Hawaiian culture and landscape. Kalani teaches the children that "taro leaves are 'oma'oma'o (green)," and the awapuhi flower can be "poni (purple)" and "smells sweet like pineapple and makes a beautiful lei."[86] Lessons on flora are paired with fauna. For example, in addition to learning the term for blue, "polu," Kalani also teaches the children about blue parrotfish: "In our legend," he shares, "the parrotfish is the ancestor of all the fish in Hawai'i." Regarding the concept of "aloha," *Colors of Aloha* translates it directly as "love," although, as Stephanie Nohelani Teves argues, the meaning of "aloha" is contested because it is "a burden and a gift, rife with tension because of the ways in which Kānaka Maoli are called by religion, the settler state, and the tourism industry to *live aloha*."[87] In *Colors of Aloha*, the term is also introduced to capture the practice of sharing among loved ones: "On the way, we see Aunty Iwi walking to her tent. Kalani says aloha (love) means looking out for one another and sharing when we have enough." Aloha is invoked again on the last two-page spread as cousin Hinalei yells, "'Look, a rainbow!' Kalani looks up and says, 'The rainbow is the hale where all the colors live close together, in aloha, just like our family.'"

The narrator's home is also used to convey a liminal space between native Hawaiians and current US statehood. Above a couch, a Hawaiian state flag hangs sideways between fishing nets holding up lights on one end, with a Hawaiian or Ikaika warrior mask on the other side. The text on the opposite page reads: "My big brother, Kalani, walks me and my cousins, Pua and Hinalei, home from school every day. We practice hula, play dress up, and look for lizards in the holes of the cinder block wall in front of our hale (house)." The illustration shows Kalani playing a ukulele while sitting between two posters, one of which reads "Kū Kiaʻi Mauna." Above it, smaller triangles make up a larger triangle, referencing the protests against the construction of a telescope ("Thirty Meter Telescope") atop the sacred mountain of Mauna Kea. The second poster includes the partial face of Princess Bernice Pauahi Bishop (1831–1884) in what appears to be either a portrait or photograph. She is likely included because of her advocacy work in support of education, and particularly for establishing Kamehameha Schools through her will.[88] Kalani is equally invested in the education of his sibling and cousins, prioritizing Hawaiian language and culture.

Intertwined within Kalani's lessons on language and culture are others on sexuality and gender. Neither are central to the plot; their implicitness instead functions to normalize queer and trans identities. For example, when Kalani and the children are learning about colors, they are joined by Peleke, Kalani's boyfriend, who is casually integrated into the story: "A voice says, 'What's the game? Can I play, too?' It's Peleke, Kalani's boyfriend! He's like another cousin to me and Pua and Hinalei. Peleke's going to be a famous actor one day, that's why he always wears sunglasses and fancy shirts." Peleke's description is not restricted to his sexuality. His career goals are also highlighted, albeit in ways that are somewhat stereotypical. Peleke remains with the group through the end, partaking in the collective dinner with other loved ones. Kalani therefore "comes out"—at least to readers—through his boyfriend's physical presence, which is well integrated into the book through both text and illustration.

However, the book's treatment of Kalani's gender identity is more subtle. Instead of being mentioned or incorporated directly into the text, it is the illustrations alone that signal Kalani's trans, gender fluid, or nonbinary possibilities. Kalani uses male pronouns, has long hair tied up in a loose bun, full eyebrows, and a smattering of facial hair on his chin—physical characteristics that can apply to anyone regardless of

Figure 2.6. Kalani and his younger sibling; from *Colors of Aloha*. Published by Flamingo Rampant Press. Copyright © 2019 by Kanoa Kau-Arteaga and J. R. Keaolani Bogac-Moore.

their gender or gender identity. Also noticeable, however, is Kalani's bra/ sports bra or chest binder, which is visible throughout the book, beginning with the second two-page spread (fig. 2.6). Kalani and his sibling each sit on a surfboard under the moon. One of Kalani's arms is lifted toward the stars while his other arm rests on his shorts. Between his exposed arm and white tank top, one can spot the underarm portion of a black piece of cloth in the shape of a bra/sports bra or chest binder. It appears again on the following spread. Even though Kalani and the three children are drawn at a distance, with few details (e.g., they do not have eyes or mouths), this black piece of clothing is still very visible under his arm. The second half of the book highlights the piece of clothing further by adding additional detail in the form of a white edge or outline to the bra or binder. When taken together, the facial hair and bra/sports bra or chest binder might suggest someone who has recently begun taking testosterone or transitioning.[89] Amplifying the power of illustrations, this sublet detail provides anyone "in the know" with concrete evidence that indeed at least one of the characters is also or can also be read as trans or nonbinary. These visual maneuvering decisions were enacted by the illustrator, J. R. Keaolani Bogac-Moore, in collaboration with the author, Kanoa Kau-Arteaga—both of whom are native Hawaiians—and were crucially supported by Flamingo Rampant Press. The illustrator, who describes themself as an "Afro-Islander artist" and is known as Keao Lani, also identifies as gender nonconforming, while the author identifies as trans.

Another strategy employed by Flamingo Rampant Press is to incorporate nonbinary, gender nonconforming, or trans of color characters without making their gender identities the primary focal point of each story. Two examples include *Bridge of Flowers* (2019) and *The Zero Dads Club* (2015). While *The Zero Dads Club* is a playful yet necessary critique of gendered holidays, *Bridge of Flowers* is more somber in tone. Both engage and incorporate multiple gender identities tangentially, allowing each character to exist alongside one another in order to validate and normalize the gender spectrum while also validating and normalizing other often marginalized and intersecting identities such as those tied to race/ethnicity and disabilities.

Much of *Bridge of Flowers* comprises two juxtaposed sides, or seemingly opposite perspectives, such as those of the narrator's parents. Apart from the cover and title page, every other page incorporates a gold picture frame that suggests moments or snapshots captured in time. These moments collectively narrate the union and then separation of a queer of color couple, along with subsequent efforts to co-parent two children at a healthy distance—all told from the perspective of their daughter Mona. She describes her first parent as follows: "My Mom, Soraya, is a witch, which mostly means she listens to people talk about their problems and then she makes them potions out of flowers, dirt, spit, rocks, and good thoughts to help them feel better." In contrast, "My Bapa, Kamau, is a scientist. They spend a lot of time looking at tiny pieces of moss through different microscopes." Mom Soraya is visually depicted as femme and in a wheelchair, while Bapa Kamau is butch or masculine presenting, using "they" pronouns and arm braces. For both parents, their gender identities are only one detail of many that make them whole (fig. 2.7). Each parent is also symbolized by a tree: "When my Mom

The thing was, they loved each other but they really didn't like living together.
Mom would spill lipstick and crystals and bacon grease all over everything, and Bapa wanted things to get wiped down clean all the time because otherwise the bacon grease got into their experiments.

When they fought, Mom said that bacon grease and lipstick are magic and Bapa said yes, but so is a clean counter.

So, they stopped living together. Mom said, "You can love someone and they can also really get on your nerves."

Figure 2.7. Mom and Bapa; from *Bridge of Flowers*. Published by Flamingo Rampant Press. Copyright © 2019 by Leah Lakshmi Piepzna-Samarasinha and Syrus Marcus Ware.

and Bapa fell in love they planted two trees, one for each of them. They planted them close but far, so they could be next to each other but still have room to grow." Over time, however, they realized they were better apart: "The thing was, they loved each other but they really didn't like living together." Despite their eventual physical separation and retreat into their own homes, the two remained connected through their children, as well as by the love they had for one another. Incorporating elements of fantasy fiction, this bond materialized into a physical bridge between their two homes: "They wove this bridge so we could always be close to each other, but go away when we needed to."

The siblings are also different from one another and do not always get along but nevertheless work together to reunite their family through disability protests and activism. Whereas the narrator is pensive and quiet, her sibling (who also uses "they" pronouns) is abrupt, active, and visibly disabled. Despite their differences, Mona and Kumar were both able to notice their parents' conflict during an "extra stressful" time in their lives, manifesting in the bridge falling apart: "Our parents were kind of frozen and then said, 'Arg! We'll deal with it later!' and went back to work because that's what parents do when things are too much." Unsatisfied with their response, the narrator mobilizes into action: "I don't always get along with Kumar but we both agreed this was ridiculous and we had to do something. And, people think that people who are quiet don't have magic like people who are always talking about it, but they are very wrong." Each sibling added something to the dirt, and together they magically rebuilt the bridge while inspiring an entire accessibility movement.

Bridge of Flowers was written and illustrated by two disability activists of color. Author Leah Lakshmi Piepzna-Samarasinha has described herself in interviews and on social media as a "witch and intuitive healer."[90] Also self-identifying as "a queer disabled femme writer, organizer, performance artist and educator of Burgher/Tamil Sri Lankan and Irish/Roma ascent," she has authored or co-authors several books of prose and poetry, including *Care Work: Dreaming Disability Justice* (2018), *Tongue-breaker* (2019), and the memoir *Dirty River: A Queer Femme of Color Dreaming Her Way Home* (2015).[91] Even though she is originally from the US, *Dirty River* takes place primarily in Canada, where she lived for several years. In 2006, she co-founded the Asian Arts Freedom School in Toronto, although she currently resides in the US. Meanwhile, illustrator Syrus Marcus Ware, whom I discuss more closely in chapter 5, is known both for his artwork and writing—often centering Black, trans, and disability politics.

Whereas *Bridge of Flowers* uses gender to juxtapose parents and siblings, *The Zero Dads Club* presents a spectrum of genders and gender identities. The gendering of holidays such as Mother's Day or Father's Day leaves many family formations unaccounted for while perpetuating heteronormative nuclear family assumptions. In Angel Adeyoha's *The Zero Dads Club*, Akilah does not want to "paint a dumb tie" and would rather her school cancel Father's Day altogether.[92] Neither she nor Kai have fathers. With the support of their teacher, Miss May, they form a club for others like them. The Zero Dads Club quickly grows from two students to five: Akilah, Kai, Ellie, Matias, and Melanie. Author Adeyoha, whom I will discuss in greater detail in chapter 3, is an Indigenous (Eastern Band Cherokee), trans, and nonbinary activist.[93] Adeyoha and illustrator Aubrey Williams[94] incorporate textual and visual details to destabilize not only Father's Day and gender but also categories such as race, ethnicity, language, and ability. All of the children appear to be racially ambiguous or racialized as non-white either in terms of their names, the terminology they use for their parents, or phenotypically. Equally notable, Ellie wears glasses, and Melanie is in a wheelchair.

Each child shares their family composition along with cards they have drawn for their parents—all of whom challenge on some level the gender binary or assumptions about gender. They include a single mother who presents as femme and enjoys "traditionally masculine" hobbies such as monster truck rallies, as well as two lesbian couples. One is a femme/butch duo. Ellie refers to them as "my Mama and my Baba . . . [who] is kinda like a girl but kinda like a boy. Baba says she's a butch."[95] In contrast, Akilah's moms (or Mom and Mamma) both present as femme. There is also Matias who is cared for by his Tía [Aunt] and Abuela [Grandmother]—who loves soccer and shouts "GOAL" louder than anyone else. Unlike the other children, Melanie is somewhat hesitant to share, but she gains courage from her peers: "Melanie wasn't sure about talking to all these kids at once. But everyone encouraged her and she bravely told them her story."[96] "I live with my Ma," she began; "we go swimming together and to the zoo."[97] Their trips have inspired her future career goals as well: "One day I want to work at a zoo and my Ma says that's a great idea because animals like quiet and I'm good at being quiet."[98] The page to its right shows a large tiger glancing at the audience. Above it, the text continues: "My Ma is a really good Ma and I don't hardly miss when she was my Papa because she's really the same person even though she's my Ma now"[99] (fig. 2.8). Like each of the other children, Melanie does not have a father. Unlike them, her Ma was assigned male at birth and did not transition until she was an adult, after Melanie was born. Throughout *The Zero Dads Club*, each parent's gender is described very matter-of-factly, without any need to elaborate further and without being questioned or challenged.

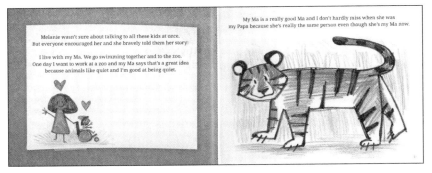

Figure 2.8. Melanie and her Ma; from *The Zero Dads Club*. Published by Flamingo Rampant Press. Copyright © 2015 by Angel Adeyoha and Aubrey Williams.

Certainly, each of the previously mentioned Flamingo Rampant Press books celebrates in its own way adult characters of color who challenge gender roles or assumptions. However, one book stands out in its overwhelming incorporation and celebration of nonbinary and trans of color adult characters, pride, and politics. *M is for Mustache: A Pride ABC Book* (2015) was written by queer Filipina author and activist Catherine Hernandez and illustrated by Marisa Firebaugh.[100] Within the genre of ABC books, *M is for Mustache* follows a typical ABC format and pacing, with each page introducing a new letter of the alphabet using the format, "A is for." The child on the cover proudly displays a drawn-on brown mustache over their smile. A blue headband with bouncing stars pulls back long, dark-brown hair, while an ice-cream-cone-shaped necklace rests atop the ruffles of a rainbow dress. The child holds a rainbow-colored pinwheel and a yellow banner that doubles as the book's title, contrasted against a pale purple backdrop. A partial arm appears to be holding the child's hand, as if linking them to a whole community inside the book.

Hernandez's alphabet within *M is for Mustache* integrates elements of a Pride march in Toronto, Ontario, throughout the text and illustrations. She begins by replacing apple with ally: "A is for Ally, which me and mama try to be every day by speaking up for people who need someone to be on their side."[101] Mother and child stand hand in hand, each holding up a sign: "WE <3 YOU" and "EVERYONE." Hernandez leaves the use of the term "ally" here open to interpretation. For example, if we read the figures as cisgender, they may be transgender allies; if they are heterosexual, they might be understood as queer allies; if they are non-Black, then they might be allies to Black communities; if they are read as able bodied, then they can be seen as allies to disabled communities; and so on. Hernandez does use one identifying marker for the child with the letter "Q," writing "Q is for Queerspawn. Queerspawn is a word for kids as lucky as me to have parents who are lesbian, gay, bi, trans, queer, or two-spirit."[102] From this, we learn that at least one of these identities applies to the mother. And from another illustration, we learn that the narrator's name is Arden—named after Hernandez's own daughter.[103] Narrated through the perspective of this child, or queerspawn, the story interweaves a multicultural celebration of Pride within a Canadian context. Certain letters are marked as Canadian, such as "C is for colours" and "Y is for Yonge Street where all the people cheer us on," which is a reference to Toronto's pride parade route.[104] Geopolitical space and the ongoing effects of colonization are also noted with the letter S, stating that "S is for Smudging. We burn sage to remember that we're marching on Native land."[105]

Alongside child and mom, Aunties or Titas become synonymous with chosen family and trans of color politics. A dynamic group of Titas function as major adult figures or role models, surrounding Arden with love, community, and knowledge as we learn the ABCs. Most if not all of Arden's Titas can be read as nonbinary, gender nonconforming, or trans of color adults. Aesthetically, gender variance and trans of color culture is alluded to with letters such as D for "Doesn't Matter. Like, it doesn't matter where we come from or what body parts we have, we are beautiful."[106] Or W for "Wig," which Tita Fay wears "to go with her beard." And, more directly, the letter N for "Names" acknowledges name changes among trans individuals; we are told: "Some of us choose our own names to match the people we have become."[107] Other letters of the alphabet reference historical figures such as Black nonbinary or trans Stonewall activist, Marsha P. Johnson. Hernandez writes: "F is for the Flowers that Tita Audrey puts in my hair. She tells me stories of a very important person named Marsha P. Johnson, who wore them just like this" (fig. 2.9a).[108] While the text does not delve too deeply into Johnson, it provides curious readers with a name to research. Johnson's inclusion in this book is also a gesture toward transborder coalitions between queer and trans of color communities in Canada and the US.

The book's copious sense of pride is also evident in its presentation of physical contact among characters. Under "K is for Kissing," we are told, "On Pride Day it feels safe for us all to kiss our sweethearts."[109] This page is significant given its focus on kissing as physical contact, especially between same-sex or same-gender and nonbinary or trans individuals, which is rarely represented in children's literature (fig. 2.9b).[110] The illustration depicts diverse families ranging in racial or ethnic backgrounds, genders, sexualities, and ages. Consequently, the use of "sweethearts" here includes not only what we might define as long-term romantic partners but also love among friends and family, including any variation of extended or chosen family.

F is for the Flowers that Tita Audrey puts in my hair. She tells me stories of a very important person named Marsha P. Johnson, who wore them just like this.

K is for Kissing. On Pride Day it feels safe for us all to kiss our sweethearts.

Figure 2.9. Letters of the alphabet including (a) "F is for the Flowers," and (b) "K is for Kissing;" from *M is for Mustache: A Pride ABC Book*. Published by Flamingo Rampant Press. Copyright © 2015 by Catherine Hernandez and Marisa Firebaugh.

Arden's chosen family includes members of the Deaf community. Through the letter H, we learn: "H is for Hands, which we use to sign our happiness in sign language when our Deaf friends march past."[111] Within its accompanying illustration, Tita Fay signs "applause" in ASL (American Sign Language), Arden's mom signs "Pride," and Arden signs "Happy." Certainly, not all prides are accessible and not all prides are safe. Ultimately, *M is for Mustache* features a radically inclusive queer and trans of color reimagining of pride made possible through Flamingo Rampant Press's own autofantastic publishing goals in collaboration with authors and illustrators.

* * *

I chose to focus on Ediciones Patlatonalli, Reflection Press, and Flamingo Rampant Press here because they each exemplify small independent publishers of picture books within their respective countries who have flourished by focusing on a unique community within the larger LGBTQIA+ umbrella.[112] Their success is due in part to each emerging out of a politically conscious community intent on challenging and transforming societal norms, not only through autofantastic children's picture book publishing but more broadly as well. In the following two chapters, I turn from autofantastic publishing and their (mostly) adult characters to children who grapple with their own gender or gender identities (chapter 3) and sexualities (chapter 4).

3

Illustrating Pronouns

Gender Aesthetics and Children's Gender Identities in Picture Books

My work is a dreamspace where I witness, remember, and reflect on my queer and trans herstories. For me, writing is a spaceship into the borderless ancestral past, the puzzle pieces of a manifested queertureverse, and a lifeline back to earth. An earth that is a sacred ground filled with stories—messy, ugly, and wholly beautiful.
—Kit Yan

Our stories are dangerous to the powers that be. When we honor our histories and amplify each other's stories, we hone the sharpest weapon we have, our survival.
—Koja Adeyoha

The powers that be, invoked by Koja Adeyoha above, continue to insist that girls are a certain way and boys are another, that girls like pink and boys like blue. Even though some gender assumptions change over time, like pink being associated with boys through the early twentieth century and with girls today, the perception of a rigid gender divide has remained constant in contemporary society.[1] The widespread conflation of gender with sex or sexuality was further exacerbated by the advent of ultrasound technology, which enabled prenatal screenings of fetal sex and the subsequent sharing of images—both of which became routine practices by the end of the twentieth century.[2] Biotechnologies determining fetal sex have shifted more recently from a private experience (within a doctor's office) to a public spectacle (on social media). As Florence Pasche Guignard noted, the now-infamous gender-reveal party has become "an example of the new forms of ritualization that take place during pregnancy in 21st-century North America."[3] Picture books can be, and indeed have become, a space for another sort of gender reveal: that of gender nonconforming, nonbinary, and trans of color children.

While the prior chapter touched on gender as it pertained to publishers' missions and primarily focused on adult characters, this chapter more closely considers how *children* grappling with their gender and gender identities are centered and depicted in picture books in order to mirror these experiences to younger readers. While all of the picture books in this chapter respond to some variation of the question "are you a boy or a girl?," queer and trans of color authors overwhelmingly continue to incorporate autobiographical details in response—with most authors including child versions of themselves as protagonists exploring gender and gender identities within their autofantasías.

If gender exists on a spectrum, so, too, do picture books seek to articulate this myriad of gender identities. Although I loosely divide these books into those depicting children as (1) gender nonconforming, (2) nonbinary, and (3) transgender, these categories are neither static nor rigid. Instead, and in true queer/trans fashion, many of the books transgress these very categories or ask us to consider other gender identities (such as two-spirit) or incorporate multiple gender identities simultaneously.[4] Additionally, our own language and understandings of gender are constantly changing such that these three categories can be understood as either within or in conversation with other terms such as gender fluid, genderqueer, gender variant, or gender expansive. Although I am emphasizing the three previously mentioned categories (gender nonconforming, nonbinary, and transgender), it is only to provide one possible guide for how to discuss these books and their characters within the larger context of gender and gender identity. Importantly, whether or not we consider them autofantasías depends on how we read the characters in relation to their authors or illustrators.

The first section of this chapter engages the question "are you a boy or a girl?"—often asked of those who color outside the gender lines—by comparing Karleen Pendleton Jiménez's zine and picture books by that very title: *Are You a Boy or a Girl?* (1999/2000/2020) with *The Boy and the Bindi* (2016) and *47,000 Beads* (2017). They each present gender nonconforming (GNC) characters navigating the gender binary. The second category, nonbinary, includes picture books with child characters who challenge the gender binary by identifying with neither, identifying with both, or using pronouns beyond "she" or "he," such as in *Call Me Tree/ Llámame árbol* (2014), *From the Stars in the Sky to the Fish in the Sea* (2017), and *They Call Me Mix/Me llaman Maestre* (2018). Within the third category, children explicitly self-identify or come out as transgender, such as in *Casey's Ball* (2019) and *My Rainbow* (2020).

All the picture books in this chapter portray children's gender transgressions, expressions, or identities across the gender spectrum. These gender-expressive children of color not only navigate a gender-binary society but also present gender-expansive possibilities for all readers, regardless of age. Their journeys are sustained by loving and supportive communities of color—challenging the myth of presumed queerphobia and transphobia often plaguing these communities.[5] Given the genre of contemporary children's picture books, all conclude with "a happy ending," although arriving there looks slightly differently depending on each character and each story's gender motivations.

"Boy or Girl?": Gender Binaries, Gender Transgressions, and Gender Nonconforming Children

Individuals who do not subscribe to society's rigid gender binary are likely to have their gender questioned and challenged, even by children and even as children. Nine years after *Asha's Mums* was published and while the Chamberlain court cases were being tried, queer Chicana author Karleen Pendleton Jiménez compiled and self-published a zine asking exactly this question: *Are You a Boy or a Girl?* (1999, Canada). The following year, Green Dragon Press published a picture book version with the same title (2000, Canada), and in celebration of its twentieth anniversary, Two Ladies Press published a third iteration (2020, Canada), multilingual in English, Spanish, and French, using film stills from the 2008 film adaptation, *Tomboy*. How does the child protagonist navigate their gender expression and gender identity? And how do these books compare to Vivek Shraya's *The Boy and the Bindi* (2016, Canada) and Koja Adeyoha and Angel Adeyoha's *47,000 Beads* (2017, Canada)?

These picture books present child characters who fall under the category of gender nonconforming identities by engaging in practices seen as contrary to their assigned gender. Within the rich history of children's literature, and even if we limit our scope to North America, we will certainly find many picture books that grapple with gender norms imposed on "boys and girls." As I discussed in the introduction, those depicting girls who are tomboys are generally understood as feminist challenges to sexism and patriarchy, whereas effeminate boys are read through a queer lens. Instead, my goal here is to highlight picture books that overtly confront why this question of whether a child is a "boy or girl" is often harmful, unnecessary, or even insufficient. *Are You a Boy or a Girl?*, *The Boy and the Bindi*, and *47,000 Beads* epitomize three autofantasías incorporating cultural or ancestral knowledge to validate the protagonists' gender exploration. While all three may portray cisgender characters (e.g., "girls" who like to do "boy" things or "boys" who like to do "girl" things) and may therefore be understood as "cisgender literature," their authors leave open the possibility of further gender transgressions or nonbinary/transgender identities in their characters' futures, as well as providing categories beyond Western notions of gender such as two-spirit.

All three iterations of Karleen Pendleton Jiménez's *Are You a Boy or a Girl?* narrate a child's struggle with perceived gender and culminate in a mother's reassurance that her child is not alone. In the original 1999 version, Pendleton Jiménez relied mostly on black-and-white photographs to accompany her text, along with a few self-made sketches that she compiled, copied, and stapled into a "zine for progressive children" (fig. 3.1).[6] For its cover, she chose a photograph of herself as a child with short hair, gazing at the camera while wearing a gentle smile. Light enters through a window on the right, making half of the photo appear overexposed while the other (darker) half effectively casts a shadow over part of Pendleton Jiménez's face. Both shadow and light coalesce, yet another metaphor for the child's gender ambiguity. The title, printed in red, looms above this photograph, posing the question: *Are You a Girl or a Boy?* By using a photograph of herself, Pendleton Jiménez presents an autobiographical narrative based on her own childhood experiences. Although she never names herself and writes in the third person, she incorporates photographs of herself at various stages of her early childhood, along with one of her as an adult. The second version of the work,

Are You a Boy or a Girl?

by Karleen Pendleton Jiménez

a zine for progressive children $3

Are You a Boy or a Girl?

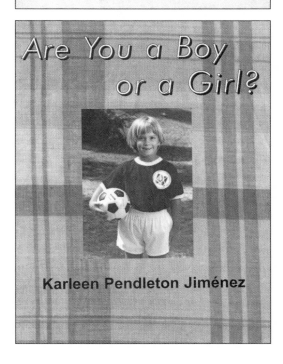

Karleen Pendleton Jiménez

Figure 3.1. Covers of each version of *Are You a Boy or a Girl?*, including the (a) zine-like original (1999, self-published), (b) picture book (2000, Green Dragon Press), and (c) twentieth-anniversary "Tomboy" edition (2020, Two Ladies Press). Copyright © 1999/2000/2020 by Karleen Pendleton Jiménez.

published in 2000, maintains the zine-like aesthetic and includes most of the original photographs and drawings.[7] However, its cover photo was replaced by one of Pendleton Jiménez in a soccer uniform with a ball under one arm and a wider smile. In contrast, the twentieth-anniversary edition illustrated with film stills from *Tomboy*'s short film provides a cartoon version of the protagonist, Alex, on the cover. She is shown at the front of a classroom, holding a bouncy ball.[8] All three versions depict the protagonist with short hair.

Despite different covers and publishers, the premise remains mostly the same. Within each, the child must confront classmates who question her gender expression. The zine's first page is both the title page and the start of the narrative, which begins: "There once was a girl who didn't like girl things | no make up or dresses or dolls | And the people who didn't know | that people are different | couldn't and wouldn't understand." This text is centered and reads like a poem with strategic line breaks and without standard punctuation. It is paired with a photograph of a Cabbage Patch doll in a stroller with a large "X" over it, representing the child's rejection of dolls and "girl things," or childnormative constructions of femininity. Throughout the zine, other children ask if she is a boy or a girl. To drive the narrative arc, Pendleton Jiménez employs repetition emphasized by tone in how the child answers this question. The first time she is asked, she "whispered" back, "I'm a girl."[9] The second time, she "answered" back, "I'm a girl," and the third time, she "yelled" back, "I'm a girl!"[10] Despite her efforts, we are told that "nobody would believe her," causing her to feel "very sad."[11] This sadness boils over onto the next few pages: "they never asked nice. | And sometimes they would laugh. | And the girl was so tired that she wanted to cry. | She grabbed her ball and ran."[12] Instead of a photograph, a hand-drawn sketch of a ball and a string of tears falling in midair cover most of the page. The overwhelming sense of sadness and isolation manifests in the girl's erasure from the page. All that remains are tears—a visceral response to a traumatic moment of invalidation or misidentification regarding the child's gender.

Amidst the trauma, one person is supportive. The mother comes home to find her child crying: "'Honey, what's wrong?' she asked | in long soft words that felt like pillows."[13] Pendleton Jiménez's use of simile here conveys the comfort of her mother's support and is paired with a sketch of differently sized and shaped pillows. Seeking solace in her mother's arms, she shares: "Mama, every day they want to know | if I'm a boy or a girl | and they look at me like I'm a rat | or some hairy animal | and they point and make jokes."[14] Below, a sketch of a rat holding a piece of cheese stares connivingly out from the page. The child's rendering of her experiences at school highlights the recurring and traumatic effects of bullying, which are too often dismissed as classroom teasing.

Her mother takes a deep breath and reassures her, "you'll never be a girl like other girls | and you'll never want to."[15] She continues:

> "Right now it's hard
> because too many people don't know about
> girls like you.
> But ever since there were girls and boys,
> there have been girls who like to do boy things
> and boys who like to do girl things.
> And when you know that
> and you're all grown up,
> you'll know that you can do anything you want to.
> And that's the best way to live."[16]

The author, through the character of the mother, affirms the child's gender transgressions from a historical perspective while also encouraging self-confidence and agency. Within both the 1999 and 2000 versions, it is left up to the readers to imagine possible examples of historical figures who have transgressed gender norms. Notably, the *Tomboy* version incorporates two figures into the illustrations, a dark-skinned person with hair past their shoulders weaving a basket and a light-skinned person with short hair in armor. Though we are not told who these figures are, they loosely resemble or suggest historical figures such as We'wha (nineteenth century, Zuni, Ihamana) and Joan of Arc (fifteenth century, French).

The final spread in the zine version consists of a pair of eyes drawn on the left and no characters on the right. The accompanying text reads: "She looked at her daughter's wet brown eyes | and asked, | 'Do you believe me?'"[17] Instead of immediately answering, the story ends with a final description of the mother, followed by the child's response: "And she felt soft and safe curled into her | mama's big body | that smelled like yellow flowers and chocolates | and she believed her."[18] A floral black-and-white backdrop covers most of the page on the right, surrounding the text, as if enveloping it like a mother hugging their child.

A mother also figured prominently in Vivek Shraya's *The Boy and the Bindi* published by Arsenal Pulp Press. Rather than appearing at the end, the mother, or Ammi, bookends this story, even if she is not shown on the cover. Instead, a child—a boy, according to the book's title—faces forward against the backdrop of a deep purple and blue starry night. Short black hair is visible under a crown of flowers, while dark-brown skin contrasts with a white tank top and a yellow bindi on his forehead, which we will soon discover was placed there by his mother. *The Boy and the Bindi* begins with a close-up of the face of a woman, who, like her son on the cover, glances directly at the reader. Her dark-brown skin contrasts with the gold jewelry decorating her face, while bright red lipstick matches the bindi between her eyebrows.[19] Her eyes are black like her hair, which blows loosely across her face, wrapping around a question posed by the narrator on the second page: "Have you seen my Ammi's dot?" The narrator describes the dot as "a bright and pretty spot" that "comes in every hue." The adjacent page depicts a hand choosing one of several bindis while the subsequent spreads focus on the narrator, standing next to Ammi, inquiring further, "Ammi, why do you wear that dot? | What's so special about that spot?" Ammi clarifies, "It's not a dot . . . | It's not a spot, it's a bindi!" To the right, a child stands in a bedroom, pointing at Ammi's forehead. She squats in front of her son, bringing herself and her bindi within the child's reach. This illustration is the first of three bedroom scenes that incorporate fantastical details. Child and parent stand on a yellow rug in front of a bed. If we look closely, we will notice that the green leaves are not a pattern on the rug, but are instead sprouting outward, around the two figures, as if conjured up through the child's curiosity about his mother's bindi. Ammi further explains the bindi's importance and, completely enamored, the boy asks: "Ammi, can I have a bindi to wear? | Do you have one more to spare?" Indeed, "she smiles and reaches in her drawer. | Ta-da! . . . This one is yours!" she says as she carefully places a yellow bindi on her child (fig. 3.2). By now, the green leaves have grown along with other plants and flowers, transforming the bedroom into a lush garden.

Ammi, not solely wearing her bindi for aesthetic appeal, teaches her son about its cultural and spiritual significance: "My bindi keeps me safe and true." Ammi continues, "My bindi tells me where I'm from. | My bindi reminds me of my mom | And when she gave me my first one." In describing the bindi as such, Ammi makes a direct connection between the bindi and her family, ancestors, cultural background, and

She sticks it on my bare forehead

Figure 3.2. Ammi placing a bindi on her son for the first time; from *The Boy and the Bindi*. Published by Arsenal Pulp Press. Copyright © 2016 by Vivek Shraya and Rajni Perera.

spirituality. The protagonist also feels that connection, noting: "As soon as it's on, I feel so calm— | Like all the noise around is gone." The child sits, legs crossed, almost elevated, surrounded by stars and the greater galaxy or universe. Their eyes are closed as if meditating, and their yellow bindi shines brightly like a distant star.

Within *The Boy and the Bindi*, the question of the protagonist's gender identity is laden with assumptions about who should wear bindis. Traditionally, bindis have been associated with Hinduism, as well as Buddhism and Jainism, though they have not always been associated with women—even if that is currently the dominant narrative.[20] As in Pendleton Jiménez's books above, the school setting (specifically the playground) becomes a place of confrontation: "But when I'm outside, people stare. | Maybe they want a bindi to wear? | My friends at school all want to know: | What is that dot above your nose?" Removed from home life, this scene depicts the protagonist in stark contrast to the other children, even if they are friends. We only see the backs of these three prying children whose light hair and skin provide another visual marker of difference. The protagonist's face is almost expressionless or uncertain. Their body is awkwardly positioned, with one hand in their pocket and the other twisting by their side, the word "Papadam" visible across their tank top.[21] Although this is a moment of external conflict for the protagonist, Shraya does not focus on the boy's response to his peers or whether or not they will accept the bindi. Instead, the following spread depicts only the protagonist (as well as his inner self) surrounded by the cosmos. Perhaps the child responds to their peers, or perhaps they only respond to themselves, but their reflection, nonetheless, is:

> I do not have the words to say
> But if I close my eyes and wait
> My bindi turns into a star, and then
> My forehead turns into the sky, that's when
> All my fears fade out of sight
> And my body feels so light—
> Ammi was so very right!

Since none of the other children knew what a bindi was to begin with, their questions were more likely rooted in cultural or racial and ethnic unawareness rather than gender assumptions. Instead of focusing on the child's peers, the rest of the picture book turns these questions toward readers: "Have you seen my yellow dot? | It's a bindi, not a spot. | Why do you wear a bindi? you say." As readers discover, the bindi becomes a symbol of not only gender nonconformity but also cultural pride and spirituality: "Well, my bindi is like a third eye | watching over me all the time | Making sure I don't hide | Everything I am inside | And everything that I can be." Whomever the boy may become, they will remain culturally connected and protected through their bindi.

Unlike most of the picture books in *Coloring into Existence*, Koja Adeyoha and Angel Adeyoha's *47,000 Beads* does not depict a protagonist on its cover, illustrated by Holly McGillis. One way to interpret this is that its story is greater than any single individual.[22] Indeed, *47,000 Beads* is unique in its incorporation of two-spirit identities and spiritualities that challenge Western ideas of gender and sexuality. Framed in blue borders, yellow-orange flowers, and green vines, circular items dominate the cover, including the centerpiece of a beaded regalia head-band within the top half and a large drum partially visible directly below it. Three drumsticks suspended in midair surround the drum on either side. Together, these four groupings (drumsticks to the right, drum at the bottom, drumsticks to the left, and headband on top) could also connote the four directions (east, south, west, and north).

47,000 Beads' plot hinges on a sense of uncertainty for Peyton, a Lakota youth conflicted about dancing in her community's pow wow.[23] While the cover shows no characters, the first two-page spread includes no text. Instead, readers are initially confronted with two powerful images of sadness and isolation. On the left, a frowning Peyton in an orange t-shirt and jeans is juxtaposed against three other individuals in Indigenous regalia. An elder wrapped in a blanket serves as a visual bridge between Peyton and the others. On the right, we see a close-up of a frowning face as Peyton sits in the corner of a vehicle, looking out the window. Throughout *47,000 Beads*, the illustrations present two depictions of Peyton: as either visibly sad or happily energized, with the former dominating the overall tone. For example, Peyton appears to be in despair as she confesses to her Auntie Eyota that she does not want to jingle dance or wear a dress—both associated with femininity.[24] These melancholic illustrations force readers to contend with Peyton's emotional distress. In rare moments of the book, however, Peyton appears excited and animated, dancing with her eyes, facial expressions, and hands. Peyton wants to dance, but not within the constraints of presumed gender norms.

Peyton has not yet learned about other gender nonconforming, two-spirit, or third-gender people. Even though Auntie Eyota may not have all the answers, she nonetheless realizes Peyton is different and seeks out the help of a two-spirit elder named L. As the two discuss Peyton, L. comments: "I've noticed that I always see her keeping time with her feet, but she doesn't dance. She looks at the dancers like she wants badly to dance. Like in her heart, she is dancing."[25] Auntie Eyota agrees, adding: "Peyton is special, Grandparent. Different. I think her path is two-spirit. I think she wants regalia like her brother and uncle. She feels alone but I know she isn't. I want to show her that she's not."[26] In response, Auntie Eyota and L. sketch out a new regalia design for Peyton and then visit with local community members, asking each to contribute an item. Peyton's mom contributes a ribbon shirt and pants, an auntie contributes a matching beaded belt and headband, a grandmother beads a harness and aprons, a cousin sends armbands and cuffs, and L. makes Peyton's moccasins. The latter include turtles just above the toes, "to give endurance for the dance and to make Peyton's feet feel grounded to the earth."[27]

The final pages depict a public showcase of love and affection for Peyton, with Auntie Eyota announcing: "Peyton, I have a special giveaway for you this time."[28] She shares her own experience as a young girl wanting to drum. "All the drummers were men," she explains, but now "I'm head singer on our drum here. My family believed in me and honored me, and today I am grateful to do the same for you."[29] Peyton unwraps each package while learning who made them. L. adds, "I have such stories to tell you. About people from all the nations who carry two spirits inside of them. I can't wait to tell them to you."[30] Here, the phrase "all the nations" carries two meanings. One references Indigenous or tribal nations, and the other, nation-states such as Canada and the United States (whose flags appear on the adjacent page).[31] The final page reads: "The next day, at the pow wow, in the arena with her auntie drumming an honor song, Peyton was finally dancing. . . . Dancing as herself, not as a boy or as a girl, but as Peyton in her 47,000 beads."[32] Surrounded by loved ones including L., Auntie Eyota, her mother, and other community members, Peyton dances gleefully, her frown replaced by a huge smile (fig. 3.3).

All three autofantasías within this gender nonconforming category provide parallels between their child protagonists, authors, and formative figures in the authors' lives within a culturally specific context. For Pendleton Jiménez and Shraya, that role model was their mother. For K. Adeyoha and A. Adeyoha, it was their two-spirit elder. Beginning with Karleen Pendleton Jiménez, her three versions of *Are You a Boy or a Girl?* provide us with varying degrees of autobiography and autofantasía. For example, the mother's loving and compassionate presence was inspired by Pendleton Jiménez's own Mexican American and mixed-race mother, Elaine Dee Jiménez McCann, who passed away in 1996.[33] Photographs of Jiménez McCann appear toward the end of both the 1999 zine and 2000 picture book. By narrating in the third person, Pendleton Jiménez provides herself with some distance from the story, even if it is her own.

Figure 3.3. Peyton dancing during a pow wow with her new regalia; from *47,000 Beads*. Published by Flamingo Rampant Press. Copyright © 2017 by Koja Adeyoha, Angel Adeyoha, and Holly McGillis.

Of the three versions of her book, the 2020 picture book provides the most flexibility or creative license given its animated short film illustrations. Self-identifying as Chicana and "butch dyke/trans," Pendleton Jiménez often challenges the false dichotomy between a butch lesbian or a transgender person.[34] Reflecting on her character's insistence that she is a girl, she wonders, "If I was telling my story now . . . maybe my character wouldn't be saying 'I'm a girl, I'm a girl, I'm a girl,' but certainly when I was a kid" that was the case.[35]

Vivek Shraya also welcomes exploring gender as something that is constantly shifting. A bisexual, transgender, South Asian artist, Shraya used "boy" in *The Boy and the Bindi* because that was her childhood reality as well.[36] However, this does not mean the child will always identify as such; they very well may come to identify as nonbinary, or trans, or any one of the multiple terms in India for gender-variant individuals such as *hijra*. Or they may dismiss all of these terms and come up with something entirely new. Drawing on her own experiences as a child of Indian immigrant and Hindu parents, Shraya created a character and mother figure modeled after her own, brought to life through the intricate illustrations of Sri Lankan Canadian artist Rajni Perera.[37] Shraya's deeply felt sense of admiration for her mother is evident in the book's acknowledgments, "Special thank you to my dear Ammi for being the eternal source of my gender inspiration," as well as in many of her other artistic endeavors featuring her mother, including a 2016 photo series titled *Trisha* and a 2014 short film titled *Holy Mother My Mother*.[38]

Shifting away from mothers and toward community elders, the inspiration behind *47,000 Beads* draws from the co-authors' experiences as two-spirit and as members of the Eastern band of Cherokee (Angel Adeyoha) and Oglala Lakota (Koja Adeyoha). K. Adeyoha also self-identifies as a lesbian or "butch dyke," while A. Adeyoha's identities include queer, nonbinary, and trans; both are activists in California's Bay Area.[39] The two were partners at the time of the picture book's publication.[40] K. Adeyoha shared that Peyton was modeled after her, suggesting we also consider Peyton's gender as butch.[41] The authors purposely chose to integrate into their book a well-known two-spirit elder, L. Frank Manriquez of the Tongva Acjachemem Indigenous community, who is also K. Adeyoha's Tunwin (Auntie). Manriquez even participated in *47,000 Beads* events, including Two-Spirit Storytime, featuring drag queen Landa Lakes (two-spirit/Chickasaw).[42] Manriquez opened the event with a blessing, reflecting, "In the Native world we are supposed to think of the seventh generation from us and take care of them. Any one of these kids could be two-spirit or be allied with the two-spirit community."[43] The glossary at the end of *47,000 Beads* includes terms like "Pow wow," "Jingle Dress," "Two-Spirit," "Giveaway," and "Honor Song." For its definition of two-spirit, the co-authors emphasize its temporal etymology as "a newer, English word used as a rough translation for older words in the languages of many Tribes and Nations" that can apply to gender as well as sexuality.[44] Importantly, it should only describe Native, Indigenous, or First Nations people.[45]

Taken together, *Are You a Boy or a Girl?*, *The Boy and the Bindi*, and *47,000 Beads* showcase three unique literary and visual strategies for incorporating and depicting gender nonconforming children of color in children's literature. In my specific discussions of each character within this GNC section, I prioritized the pronouns used in the book ("she" in *Are You a Boy or a Girl?*, "he" in *The Boy and the Bindi*, and "she" in *47,000 Beads*) although "they" pronouns can also be used as a way to normalize gender-neutral language while also signaling the possibility of other future identities. This is important given that, as I mentioned above, three of the four authors presently identify as either nonbinary or trans—categories I explore below.

Both, Neither, or Other: Nonbinary Children in Picture Books

Nonbinary children of color characters include those who do not use a pronoun, use multiple pronouns, or use new pronouns beyond "he" or "she" (e.g., neopronouns). Three exemplary picture books depicting nonbinary children include Maya C. Gonzalez's *Call Me Tree/Llámame árbol* (2014, United States), Kai Cheng Thom's *From the Stars in the Sky to the Fish in the Sea* (2017, Canada), and Lourdes Rivas's *They Call Me Mix/Me llaman Maestre* (2018, United States). In the first, a brown child and their peers either do not use pronouns or create their own (e.g., "tree"). In the second, a magical child named Miu Lan is neither boy nor girl, constantly changing their body depending on their needs and desires. In the third, a child realizes they are not alone and eventually finds an embracing community of other nonbinary and trans adults of color who serve as role models. Each picture book is unique in how many children it depicts and whether or not adults are included. Whereas *Call Me Tree* only includes children, *From the Stars in the Sky to the Fish in the Sea* is similar with the exception of the child's mother. Meanwhile, *They Call Me Mix* only includes one child (the protagonist) during depictions of their own childhood, but then other children once the protagonist is an adult. They also vary in their publishers, with the first being published by Lee and Low's imprint, Children's Book Press, known for its multicultural children's literature in the United States; the second, by Arsenal Pulp Press, a small Vancouver-based press in Canada that publishes across literary genres and topics, including many LGBTQ2S+ and BIPOC authors; and the third, self-published in the United States and funded through a Kickstarter crowdfunding campaign. Each one models a literary and visual strategy that prioritizes nonbinary children of color. Together, these three picture books not only provide alternative ways of being beyond "boy" or "girl" but introduce readers to new pronouns including "tree," "they," and "Mix/Mx./Maestre/Maestrx."

Call Me Tree is author/illustrator Maya C. Gonzalez's attempt to challenge the gender binary for a wider audience through subtle or indirect maneuvering of text and illustrations. Written in the form of a poem, or poetic prose, a child urges us to call them Tree. Drawn primarily in colored pencils, introduced on the book's cover and serving as the only human character for the first half of the book, a child can be seen curled up, initially sleeping underground without the sensation of feeling trapped, but rather protected by the earth as if a seed before sprouting: "I begin | Within | The deep | dark | earth." The illustrations also give the sense of being enveloped within a womb or cocoon. This child seedling is fully clothed except for their bare feet. Because clothes along with hairstyles and hair growth are tied to stereotypical depictions of gender, Gonzalez made a choice about how this character might be read. Generally, or at least presently, "gender-neutral" clothes tend to more closely resemble stereotypically "male/boy" clothes. Here, the protagonist wears a t-shirt, suspenders, jeans, and has short dark hair. The child proceeds to burrow their way out, first by dreaming it: "I dream | I am reaching | Dreaming and reaching | Reaching and dreaming." Their body shifts, now lying on their side with one hand up toward the sky, reaching through the earth: "I wake UP | I see sky." This awakening transforms them from a child seedling to a child tree.

The child is first enveloped by golden-brown earth tones, which Gonzalez explained were inspired by the seed pods of an elm tree reminiscent of her own childhood. The rich browns complement the child's own brown skin. Gonzalez alternates between a blue sky (on the first page spread) and a pink sky (on the second spread), which blend into one another on the third spread, culminating in hints of purple. All subsequent pages combine the two seemingly gender-opposing colors, depicting a blue sky with pink clouds. Colored pencils are used over watercolors and ink for added texture. Yellows and greens also dominate the color scheme, both because of their relationship to nature (e.g., sun/sunlight and leaves/plants/grass) and because of what we currently understand to be gender-neutral colors. Green is also the color of the child's shirt, while a yellow bird flies about, reappearing throughout the illustrations.

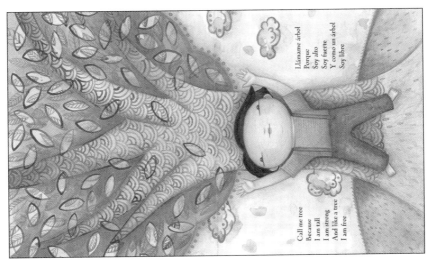

Figure 3.4. Final two-page spread intentionally printed sideways; from *Call Me Tree/ Llámame árbol*. Published by Children's Book Press. Copyright © 2014 Maya Christina Gonzalez.

Never does the child announce a gender pronoun, nor do others gender any of the children in the English version of *Call Me Tree*. In this manner, Gonzalez creates a protagonist whose gender is unclear or unknown to readers, perhaps gender fluid or nonbinary. The book ends with a proclamation: "Call me tree | Because | I am tall | I am strong | And like a tree | I am free." Unlike any of the preceding pages, this one beckons readers to physically turn the book sideways (fig. 3.4). To meet the child face to face, one must readjust their point of view—or turn, topple, shift their perspective—of this child.

Unlike *Call Me Tree*'s more subtle approach to gender, Kai Cheng Thom's *From the Stars in the Sky to the Fish in the Sea* directly challenges rigid gender roles available within childnormative spaces by incorporating fantastical features such as shapeshifting. We are told of a baby born "when both the moon and the sun were in the sky, so the baby couldn't decide what to be." This initial two-page spread juxtaposes the sun on the left page with the moon on the right and two magical creatures on either side: a blue bird with antlers flies across the sun while a fox-like or dog-like pink creature with a pointed nose, long ears, and a long, purple tail fin runs under the moon, up a hill, and toward a blue house. The text continues, "boy or girl? bird or fish? | cat or rabbit? tree or star? | so the baby looked a little like | everything. they looked VERY | strange!" The following spread introduces us to this magically strange baby who uses "they" pronouns. Long pointed ears protrude from the infant's head, while an even longer blue-gray tail fin hangs below its round body; "all the same," we are told, "the baby's mother gave her child a bath | and rocked them in her arms. | 'your name,' she said, 'is Miu Lan.'" They are joined by the two magical creatures, now inside the home. The mom proceeds to sing her baby "a song that her | own mother had sung to | her, long ago":

> whatever you dream of,
> i believe you can be,
> from the stars in the sky
> to the fish in the sea.

The lullaby incorporates references to the child's unique abilities, such as crawling like a crab or flying, concluding with the mother's unwavering support:

> and i'll always be here,
> i'll be near, standing by,
> and you know that [i]'ll love you
> till the day that i die.

Like the adults within the prior GNC section, this mother's love for her child is also unconditional such that even if the child "still couldn't decide" what or whom to be, they "felt loved."

Miu Lan grows into a "strange, magical child who was always chang-ing." We are told that the child could incorporate multiple characteristics of several creatures at once. For example, the child is pictured in one scene with ram's horns, dinosaur or lizard back, fur body, and plant-like tail. On any given day, "they grew feathers and wings to fly | with blue-birds in the mornings, | scales and a tail to swim with | fish in the after-noons, | and fur and paws to play with | puppies in the evenings." And "no matter how many things Miu Lan became, their | mother always

one day, it was time for the child to
go to school they were so excited!
they grew a tail of peacock feathers
and a coat of tiger stripes.

"have fun," said Miu Lan's mother.
but when they got to the school . . .

Figure 3.5. Miu Lan running while waving to their mother; from *From the Stars in the Sky to the Fish in the Sea*. Published by Arsenal Pulp Press. Copyright © 2017 by Kai Cheng Thom, Wai-Yant Li, and Kai Yun Ching.

brought them back into the little blue | house, gave them a bath, and tucked them into bed at | the day's end. as the stars rose, she sang." Notably, although the child can grow other limbs or reshape their body in countless ways, what does not change throughout the watercolor and ink illustrations is the child's short, straight, black hair nor their light-brown or tan skin (fig. 3.5). They share the same skin tone as their mother, who appears with long, wavy black hair and a long red dress. Other details at home provide further visual depictions of magical or fantastical features, including the giant, colorful flora outside the home and faces on objects such as the bathtub or tea kettle, as well as the two previously mentioned creatures (although fantastical, they do not change their shape like Miu Lan). As readers, we might wonder if it was the child's birth that served as a catalyst for all of these magical features or creatures.

Of the three picture books under the category of nonbinary children, Lourdes Rivas's *They Call Me Mix* is unique in portraying the protagonist as both a child and then an adult, as well as being the most "realist" and autobiographical of the three. Like *Call Me Tree*, it references "calling" or naming within its title and is bilingual in English and Spanish. Narrated in the first person, the first two-thirds of the book is told from Rivas's perspective as a child confronting gender stereotypes and in search of language to articulate their nonbinary gender identity. When asked if they are a boy or a girl, or how they can be both, the child responds: "Some days I am both. Some days I am neither. Most days, I am everything in between."[46] The accompanying illustrations incorporate minimal shading against white backdrops. Although most of the pages appear in black and white, pale blue and pink watercolor washes are occasionally used throughout to visually signal the gender binary (e.g., "boy" appears in blue and "girl" in pink). The child's name is also chosen based on assigned gender at birth. "Before I was born," they share, "my mom had two different names ready for me: Daniel and Lourdes. I would be Daniel, like my tío, if they decided I was a boy and Lourdes, like my tía, if they decided I was a girl."[47] The uncle and aunt appear at the top of the page, just above an outline of Mexico, since "both names come from [their] mom's siblings in México."[48] Although these names were meant to honor family members, they remained confined within a gender binary. Of the two options, when the protagonist was born, "everyone decided and agreed that [they were] a girl, so they named [them] Lourdes."[49]

In response to the gender binary, Rivas (as child protagonist) reflects, "I knew in my heart that I could never choose one or the other. I knew in my heart that I wanted to be free every day to just be me, without thinking about choosing only girl or only boy."[50] Even though the child feels this way, they remain bombarded with gender stereotypes and expectations, which results in a painful childhood experience: "Agreeing with others was like ignoring my heart. Ignoring your heart makes everything *very* difficult. You should never ignore your heart."[51] The child remains adrift among a gender binary. That is, until they ask themself: "Where can I fit in?" They are answered by a loving transgender and nonbinary community of color that exclaims: "HERE! We are transgender. We are not one or the other. We flow free like water in a river. We are non-binary. We're not *just* girls. We're not *just* boys. We're both and everything in between" (fig. 3.6).[52] As readers, we are not told how the protagonist found this community. Instead, they appear almost magically, as if summoned by a wish. Only, instead of one fairy godmother, the protagonist now has an entire community behind them. They appear racially diverse and carry signs that read "This is your community" (in English and Spanish). Their initial response to Lourdes is also significant, since they present both "transgender" and "non-binary" as options; whether these two terms overlap, or each serve as umbrella terms, or have one subsumed under the other, is not as important as simply

Figure 3.6. Lourdes as a child when they first discover a nonbinary/transgender community; from *They Call Me Mix/Me llaman Maestre*. Self-published. Copyright © 2018 by Lourdes Rivas and Breena Nuñez.

stating that these communities exist and that the protagonist can find refuge in them. Surrounded and supported, Rivas learns, "it's okay to disagree with everyone who looks at me and says I am a girl. It's okay to say, '. . . Instead of she, you can just say my name or use they.' Go ahead, try it!"[53] This moment also presents a potential pause in the story where readers might take a moment to model this.

All three picture books use distinct literary strategies for moving the plot forward—each motivated by the authors' and illustrators' goals for their nonbinary characters. *Call Me Tree* is not driven by conflict, whereas *From the Stars in the Sky to the Fish in the Sea* presents and resolves conflict during the second half of the book, while *They Call Me Mix* incorporates challenges and resolutions throughout most of the book. Instead of introducing conflict within *Call Me Tree*, Maya Gonzalez employs the use of a character's sense of wonder and discovery to drive the story. First the protagonist becomes aware of themself, and then their environment, including all the surrounding trees introduced halfway through the picture book: "Trees! | More and more trees | Trees and trees | Just like me! . . . All trees have roots | All trees belong."[54] Upon initially surveying these additional tree kids, one is likely to notice that they appear to be from different racial or ethnic backgrounds, although these categories are never confirmed nor denied. Instead, readers may impose these identities onto the children depending on how they might read skin tones or hair color, texture, style, and length. All of the children are dressed in shorts or pants and tops or sweaters, all in an assortment of colors.[55] For example, one of the darker-skinned kids wears a purple hoodie, conjuring up images of Black youth such as Trayvon Martin, who was murdered two years prior to the book's publication.[56] Within *Call Me Tree*, this child tree can exist as they are, without fear of violence, alongside the other tree children.

The intentional omission of pronouns also allows readers more options when considering each tree kid's gender identity. Although each tree is different, they each have roots. In an interview, Gonzalez shared, "I only create to heal. For myself and then, by being witness, others."[57] Within the book, the protagonist is firmly planted in place and yet, from that position, can not only see or witness the other trees but be intertwined with them in a complex network of dark-brown roots that form spirals and hearts—symbolizing community, interconnectedness, continuity, and love. When asked to identify the overarching concept within *Call Me Tree*, Gonzalez responded: "I would say that it's the culmination of what can happen when we connect with nature personally, relationally, and universally. Nature is a perfect resource to help us see through societal projections and feel powerful within ourselves and with each other even when times are rough."[58] Nature also gives Gonzalez the space to explore genders beyond the binary. Within *Call Me Tree*, Gonzalez "opens up the possibility that it's ok not to know the gender of a child. No matter what their gender identity may be, what is valuable is that they feel free, strong, a sense of belonging and appreciative of difference and sameness in themselves and others."[59] Yet, readers and reviewers continue to gender the child, shares Gonzalez: "Despite the fact that there are no gender specific pronouns, reviewers have assumed the main character is a cisgender boy. The main character is actually based on someone assigned girl. The specificity doesn't matter as much as the opportunity to notice the assumption."[60] When considering these gender assumptions, there is also the question of diction and translation that can influence a book's reading.

In choosing to publish *Call Me Tree* with Lee & Low's Children's Book Press rather than self-publish (see Reflection Press, chapter 2), Gonzalez had to give up some autonomy over her creative choices. For example, she does not explicitly state the picture book's focus on gender-neutral language within the text, nor on the book's dust jacket, summary, or any other features of the peritext. Instead, this topic becomes evident as the focal point of the book's epitext within its paratextual features such as Lee & Low Books' webpage where viewers can "read why Maya Christina Gonzalez decided to make her new picture book *Call Me Tree* completely gender free." It includes links to a letter from Gonzalez to readers, urging: "When sharing this book, you may want to include that it's gender free as part of the conversation in your classroom, library or home."[61] Without Gonzalez's letter, readers may have completely missed the book's gender play/subversion. However, by only including this information online rather than within the book itself, the onus falls on the gender-conscious adult to acknowledge the messaging vis-à-vis gender. Unlike Gonzalez's other works that include these discussions or resources within the text, making this book's gender discussion only available online within the publisher's website drastically limits which adults—and, by extension, which children—have access to this wider gender free framework.

The publisher was also responsible for *Call Me Tree*'s translation from English to Spanish.[62] Despite Gonzalez's effort to not use pronouns for any of the children in the English text within the book, the limitations of Spanish and what might be considered "formal Spanish" in the context of children's publishing include an erroneous gendernormative slippage on the very last page:

Call me tree	Llámame árbol
Because	Porque
I am tall	Soy *alto* [emphasis added]
I am strong	Soy fuerte
And like a tree	Y como un árbol
I am free	Soy libre

Although one can argue that "árbol" [tree] is already gendered in Spanish as masculine, the Spanish translation avoided a direct reference to masculinity in reference to the child's gender up until the line "Soy alto" [I am tall], since "alto" refers to a tall boy, man, or male. It is not surprising, then, that Spanish readers are likely to conclude that the child is male or uses he/him/his pronouns. Gender limitations are notorious in Spanish and in Spanish translations, although recent efforts are attempting to change that. Gender-neutral alternatives to the masculine ending "o" and the feminine ending "a" include the subversive use of "x" or "e"; for example, Latinx or Latine and pronouns like ellx or elle. Lee & Low could have chosen to use "altx" or "alte," even if these are not considered "grammatically correct" in formal Spanish. At the very least, they might have used another word, phrase, or expression to reference the child's height if they wanted to adhere to Gonzalez's desire not to assign a particular pronoun to the child. This slippage speaks to the ongoing tensions between the gendered constraints of romance languages such as Spanish and efforts to change this.

One of *Call Me Tree*'s major contributions to a gender-neutral or nonbinary lexicon is its introduction of "tree" as another pronoun option for characters and readers. Although Gonzalez only hints at this new pronoun option here, her other self-published books make that claim more explicitly. In *Call Me Tree*, the request to be referred to as "tree" has multiple meanings. First, the children in the book may be *like* trees, using it as a metaphor for being grounded, among other qualities. Secondly, the child protagonist may be referring to their own name. Thirdly, the child protagonist may be sharing their pronoun, in this case, "tree." In a message to readers at the end of the book, Gonzalez exclaims, "I'll call you tree if you call me tree!" In subsequent publications, including *They, She, He, Me: Free to Be!* (2017) and *They, She, He: Easy as ABC* (2019)—both co-written with her partner Matthew Smith-Gonzalez— the pronoun "tree" appears alongside others like "they," "ze," "she," and "he" (fig. 3.7). These two picture books accomplish an enormous feat using only a handful of words and repetition. Like other books by Reflection Press, they also contain multiple narratives, which serve different pedagogical purposes and have distinct literary implications. A reader may choose to read only the first section, the "story," or they might read any of the subsequent sections, such as the section titled

Figure 3.7. Children with "tree" and "ze" pronouns; from *They, She, He, Me: Free to Be!* Published by Reflection Press. Copyright © 2017 by Maya Gonzalez and Matthew Smith-Gonzalez.

"Pronouns" or another section titled "For the Grown-Ups" where the authors list resources like links to Merriam Webster's singular "they," noting, "Yes, it's grammatically correct."[63] The books also offer ideas for creating additional pronouns: "You can change pronouns from *he* to *she* or from *she* to *he*, you can use new ones like *ze* or create your own like *tree!*"[64] It even caught on with celebrities like Keiynan Lonsdale, who declared "tree" as their pronoun in a 2018 Instagram post.

Meanwhile, Kai Cheng Thom's *From the Stars in the Sky to the Fish in the Sea* incorporates the previously visited trope of unwelcoming peers at school as a major driving force within the narrative. Unlike *Asha's Mums* (chapter 1) or *Are You a Boy or a Girl?* and *The Boy and the Bindi* above, the resolution to Thom's picture book provides a transformative space where the protagonist is no longer the only "odd" or, in this case, nonbinary child. The love and affirmation Miu Lan receives at home during the first half of the book is strongly contrasted with their experiences away from home. Miu Lan's initial excitement at going to school is squashed when they discover that "the other students were either boys or girls: they had no feathers, no scales, no leaves, no fur, no fins—not even any sparkles! no one invited Miu Lan to play." In a traumatic scene, a boy yanks on one of Miu Lan's peacock feathers as other children stare and join in humiliating them. Even when Miu Lan attempts to appear as a childnormative "boy" for a day, their play options become scrutinized over gender, since "'boys don't play hopscotch!' said a little girl," while a little boy asks, "are you a boy or a girl, anyway?" In response to several children who at once ask, "what are YOU supposed to BE?" Miu Lan shouts, "I DON'T KNOW!" and then gallops "out of the playground on horse's hooves," swims "through the stream with a fish's tail," and soars "up the hill on eagle's wings."

Giant tears run down the child's face, forming a giant puddle as the child approaches home and jumps into their mother's arms. Miu Lan's mother asks, "how was school?" as she had each day. This time, Miu Lan responds with a question: "i can't decide what to be! why do i have to be just one thing?" Miu Lan's mom admits: (1) it isn't always easy being different, (2) one can only be who one is, and (3) she does not know what Miu Lan might do to make friends aside from encouraging them to always be who they truly are. Overall, she listens to, affirms, and loves her child. This exchange also reveals that parents do not always have all the answers and fosters a renewed sense of self-worth and confidence in Miu Lan, who decides to be whomever they choose at school once again. This time, the children admire Miu Lan and learn to get out of their own comfort zones by also galloping like horses, climbing like monkeys, and swimming like fish. Collectively, they had learned that it was "fun to be many different things." And Miu Lan, who was "always changing, felt happy."

Although one may initially read Miu Lan as another nonbinary or trans character who must be exceptional—in this case, magical—to fit in, I want to offer a different reading based on the picture book's final scene at school.[65] Not only do the other children change by accepting Miu Lan as they are, but they themselves are physically transformed as well. Returning to the book's beginning, we should recall that Miu Lan was born while the sun and the moon were both in the sky at the same time. If this is the cosmic influence or rationale for this child's magical abilities—and, therefore, their nonbinary identity—then the conditions of their magic are not exceptional or uncommon since the moon can often be seen during the daytime. Building on this logic, even though the child is initially understood as magical or exceptional, their creation is not, and that also means that there are likely many more children who were also born during this timeframe (of both sun and moon) and are, therefore, just as magical—or just as nonbinary. And while one reading of the illustrations might suggest that the other children are only using their imaginations to make-believe they can fly or swing from a branch, another interpretation would suggest that Miu Lan shows the other kids their own inner selves, which may also be just as magical or nonbinary. This is especially visible with the character ("boy") who had previously pulled Miu Lan's feathers. Not only do they confess they had been jealous of Miu Lan, but they are now also depicted with wings flying alongside Miu Lan. Their clothes have also transformed; they now wear a pinkish-red skirt over their pants. Similarly, all the other children have grown additional limbs or fantastical features such as fins, tails, and elongated ears. Thus, by the end of the book, Miu Lan is no longer the only magical child, but just one of many others, who, when loved and validated, can also show off their inner and outer nonbinary selves.

Kai Cheng Thom's work spans multiple genres. Identifying as trans and of Chinese descent, her formal biography on the publisher's website reads: "Kai Cheng Thom is a writer, performance artist, and psychotherapist in Toronto." Thom first published the lines of the mother's lullaby included in the picture book within her novel *Fierce Femmes and Notorious Liars: A Dangerous Trans Girl's Confabulous Memoir* (2016, Metonymy Press, Canada). Though this novel is listed as a "work of fiction" on its copyright page, it is described online (on both the publisher's and Thom's websites) as "the highly sensational, ultra-exciting, sort-of true coming-of-age story of a young Asian trans girl." In an interview, Thom shared, "I wanted to prove to myself that I could write a longform fictional narrative that was inspired by my life. . . . To write my life, but to do so in a way that put relationships between trans people, rather than the expectations of cis people, front and centre."[66] According to her first "Dear Charity" letter within the novel, the protagonist's mom used to sing this lullaby to them and then they sang it to their baby sister, Charity. The lullaby is almost identical in both picture book and novel—with only minor changes to some of the words and punctuation, though the general sentiment and imagery remains the same.[67] Although we may not know whether Thom's own mother actually sang her this lullaby, its inclusion in her novel and then within her picture book signals its significance for the author.

"Stars" and "fish" also become important motifs for Thom across her creative works. For example, in *I Hope We Choose Love: A Trans Girl's Notes for the End of the World* (2019), Thom mentions "star" or "stars" multiple times, including in references to Sylvia Rivera's and Marsha P. Johnson's STAR organization.[68] In another example, she equates all "brilliant trans women" to stars.[69] Meanwhile, Thom incorporates "fish" as a reference to trans women who "pass" as described in *Fierce Femmes and Notorious Liars*. In an interview, she explained its limitations: "the experience of passing is violent because it is something done to you. . . . You are put in the position of either not being authentic about who you are in order to hold onto privilege and safety, or of being really honest and putting yourself in danger."[70] We see Miu Lan's attempt at passing as a "normal" child when they hide their magical features and shapeshifting abilities. The despair that follows is not because Miu Lan is magical or nonbinary, but because of society's limiting beliefs. Instead of focusing on gender dysphoria, Thom proposes an emphasis on gender euphoria, "the state of joy or delight in one's being, one's gender presentation," since "for trans people, gender euphoria isn't a feeling that one can just force oneself to have. It must be fought for. . . . It is something that is passed on, from one trans sister to another."[71] Certainly, with the help of Miu Lan, a whole community of nonbinary or trans children can begin to explore their own gender euphoria.

From the Stars in the Sky to the Fish in the Sea is unique in being the only co-illustrated picture book within *Coloring into Existence*. Co-illustrators Wai-Yant Li and Kai Yun Ching knew "it was definitely a risk!" They shared, "While we both had pursued our own artistic endeavours, neither of us had ever fully illustrated a children's book from start to finish, nor had we collaborated this extensively together."[72] Wai-Yant Li primarily works in watercolor and inks, whereas Kai Yun Ching is better known for ceramics.[73] "From the font to the pencil sketches, to the final watercolour paintings," they reflected, "every aspect of the images were reviewed together, reworked and finalized as a team. When we look at the pages, we see both our perspectives represented so strongly. Most importantly, we had a continual feedback process with family and loved ones."[74] With input from their respective communities, Kai Yun Ching, Wai-Yant Li, and Kai Cheng Thom created an affirming picture book that centered an Asian Canadian and nonbinary child.

Conversely, Lourdes Rivas does not depict schools nor peers as the culprits of bullying against the protagonist in *They Call Me Mix*. Rivas, an educator, may have wanted to portray schools as a place of learning rather than bullying or exclusion. A temporal shift occurs two-thirds into *They Call Me Mix* in which Lourdes (the character) transforms from a child to an adult and teacher. Only then is a school setting introduced into the picture book. "I grew up and became a teacher," Lourdes tells us as they explain their gender identity.[75] "I am a non-binary teacher. I teach my students about respecting all genders. We practice with each other."[76] Under these words, an adult version of Lourdes is depicted with short hair and a button-down shirt. They hold up either a chalkboard or tablet that reads "Maestrx Lourdes" while encircled by five of their students. Although "Maestrx" and "Maestre," Lourdes's gender-neutral versions of "teacher," are not included within the English text, they stand out in both the illustration and Spanish translation, challenging Spanish gender norms that dictate "Maestro" for "male" teachers and "Maestra" for "female" teachers. The next spread expands the setting to a wider view of the classroom with the Spanish alphabet above a large chalkboard.[77] Hanging on it are six headshots depicting other nonbinary individuals, including Lourdes's friends previously shown on prior spreads. Lourdes explains to readers, "I teach my students that non-binary people look, dress and sound all kinds of different ways. I teach my students that it's okay to change and play with words to make them fit us."[78] Referring to themself, they continue, "My students learn to call me Mx. Lourdes because I am a mix!"[79] While the prior page focused on Lourdes's gender-neutral terms in Spanish for teacher, this page introduces readers to "Mx." as a gender-neutral alternative to either Ms., Miss, Mrs., or Mr. in English. For both "Maestrx" and "Mx.," incorporating an "x" transforms it into gender-neutral spelling, while also providing the "e" in "Maestre" as another option.

Rivas elaborated on the inspiration and process behind creating *They Call Me Mix* in an interview for *Se Ve Se Escucha: A Language Justice Podcast*. They explained, "This book came about because I just needed something to use in my classroom . . . to introduce myself to kids."[80] In 2014, Rivas enrolled in Maya Gonzalez's online learning community, School of the Free Mind, in order to learn how to create a children's book but was unable to complete the program since that was also their first year of teaching. However, during the next two years, Rivas gained "a lot of practice" telling their story in a "kid friendly way," noting, "I found myself re-telling this story to my students, introducing myself, and talking about being transgender and non-binary to kindergarteners."[81] By 2016, Rivas began drafting the text for their picture book toward the end of their second year teaching and reenrolled in Gonzalez's online school in 2017 after completing a full first draft of the text.[82] When asked if they feel their picture book has "helped [them] reclaim any part of language," they shared, "Definitely, I feel so much more empowered to, to kind of mess up the way that Spanish is structured, like the binary. . . . I do feel more comfortable now un-gendering a lot of the words as I'm speaking, even to my classroom or my colleagues—it's been a journey."[83]

Because *They Call Me Mix* was self-published, Rivas was also responsible for finding an illustrator. Breena Nuñez's website describes her as a cartoonist who "creates diary comics that often explore themes surrounding the awkwardness of racism, being a queer Afrodescendiente from the Bay Area, and understanding what it means to be Central American from the U.S." in order to "help BIPOC folks give themselves permission to express their personal stories through the language of comics."[84] Nuñez shared her illustration process for *They Call Me Mix* on social media. After the book was published, she reflected, "Thank you a million times over for asking me to illustrate this valuable story. . . . Whenever life would get me down I always remembered how happy I felt [when] I was ink washing these pages; and knowing that Lourdes is spreading so much light to young trans and non binary Latinx kids in today's world."[85]

The pedagogical component of *They Call Me Mix* manifests in the relationship between teacher and students (within the book), as well as between Rivas and readers (beyond the book). The final spread, speaking directly to the reader, states on the left page: "And you too, can decide for yourself. If you ever feel in your heart that you don't agree with what people say you are, remember that there are many of us out there cheering you on. Speak your truth! Live your truth!"[86] To the right, another affirmation serves as the final page of the story: "Being transgender is being free. Being transgender is fearless. Being transgender is beautiful."[87] Rivas dedicates *They Call Me Mix* to "every student I've ever worked with, from Lynwood to San Francisco to Boyle Heights to Oakland to Berkeley." They end with a "Note to the Reader," which states: "For the past five years, I've been teaching Kindergarten. . . . I witness the strong (and very binary) ideas kids have around gender every day. They almost always ask 'are you a boy or a girl?'"[88] Rivas continues, "In no way is this a story about all transgender people. In no way is this a story about all non-binary people. This is simply my story. I wrote it out and pursued its publication so I can use it in my classroom to bring back imagination and possibility to the way kids approach and think about gender."[89] Like several of the previously mentioned books, *They Call Me Mix* warns against assuming pronouns: "Pronouns can be as personal to someone as their name. One should never assume to know a person's pronoun, just like we don't go around assuming we know people's names. It's okay to ask. And if someone shares their pronouns with you, don't question them. Thank them for sharing and use those pronouns in the same way you would use their name after meeting."[90] Rivas concludes their note to readers by reminding them, "It's also okay to reimagine a whole new pronoun for yourself. Play with it and live your truth!"[91]

Like Rivas's character in *They Call Me Mix*, both Miu Lan in *From the Stars in the Sky to the Fish in the Sea* and the protagonist in *Call Me Tree* are each living their own truth within their respective literary worlds. Although I have discussed each character as an example of a nonbinary child, one can also consider how each may fit under the larger transgender umbrella. Of the three picture books, only *They Call Me Mix* includes the term "transgender" in relation to nonbinary identities. The next section will more closely examine trans of color children in picture books.

Transgender Kids in Picture Books

How do kid characters come out as trans in children's literature? While, as previously mentioned, all of the picture books within this chapter could potentially depict transgender children, two stand out in their conspicuous portrayal of trans kids of color: Trinity and DeShanna Neal's *My Rainbow* (2020, United States) and Kit Yan's *Casey's Ball* (2019, Canada). Within both, trans of color identities become intertwined with navigating societal gender expectations. In their book published by Kokila, an imprint of Penguin Random House, the daughter/mother co-authoring duo narrate just a tiny fragment of Trinity's transition as a child who is also Black and autistic, or, as described on the dust jacket, "*My Rainbow* is a celebration of showing up as our full selves with the people who see us fully." The second picture book, *Casey's Ball*, was published by Flamingo Rampant Press and depicts an Asian Canadian (or Asian American) child who recently came out as a transgender boy. In both cases, the child protagonist identifies as transgender from the very beginning of the book. Rather than questioning whether or not the kids are trans, each plot is driven by how the child must navigate some aspect of their trans identity within a predominately cisgender world—all while supported by their loving families of color.

My Rainbow and *Casey's Ball* differ in their approaches to gender expectations. For Trinity, gender expectations manifest around the length of her hair, highlighted on the cover and throughout the picture book. Trinity's own short, black, tightly coiled or kinky hair is slightly visible on the cover with a rainbow-colored array of flowers in bright shades of red, orange, yellow, blue, and purple emerging from it. Sparkles emanate from her hair and dark black eyes. One hand is placed on her chest, as if holding onto her heart, and the other lifts up the flowers in her hair. These colorful flowers will be transformed within the book into a bright pink, teal, and purple wig—with the pink and teal dominating, slightly resembling the paler or more muted colors of the pink-and-blue transgender pride flag.

In comparison, Casey's experience with gender expectations mostly pertains to which soccer team he may join as a transgender boy. Only his legs are visible on the cover, but as we will soon discover, the color of his socks reveals his participation as a new member of the boys' team. The dark-green socks match the green uniform worn by the boys' team, which contrasts to his blue uniform on the first two-page spread where a smiling kid runs across the field kicking a soccer ball. Above, the text reads: "I'm Casey and I'm joining a soccer team today!" On the sidelines, a water bottle with Casey's name on it sits among another soccer ball, a bag of snacks, a light-blue towel, and a pink-and-purple sports bag. He discusses his gender identity on the second spread, as he reveals why he is joining a new soccer team: "I used to be on the girls' team and my uniform was blue, but now that everyone knows I'm a boy, I'm switching to the boys' team and getting this new green one instead."

Within both picture books, the protagonists' family and community members are integral to validating their trans of color identities and gender expressions. In *My Rainbow*, Trinity's mom constantly affirms all her children, encouraging them to explore who they are and who they can become. When Trinity and her siblings play with dolls, they make-believe that sometimes their dolls are video gamers and other times they are astronauts, since "their dolls could be anything, just like Mom said they could!" The dolls are also racially diverse, from the lighter-skinned doll with rainbow hair and a yellow dress on the title page to several brown- and black-skinned dolls with braided or curly hair. Collectively, they serve both to validate the range of girlhood and femininity that can exist for Trinity and her siblings, as well as to bring attention to how Trinity's own gender identity is intertwined with how she views her hair. Contemplating her doll's "long, curly hair and beautiful dark skin," Trinity worries she cannot be a girl because her own hair is short.

Her mother reminds her that, like herself, girls can also have short hair. Within the illustration, the mom touches her own short hair as she gazes toward a thought bubble with five floating heads—presumably all girls or women, each with different hair styles from completely shaved off or buzzed to shorter, natural curls and dreadlocks. Visually parallel to her mother on the opposite page, Trinity frowns, pushing back: "I don't think you understand, Mom. I'm a transgender girl." She holds one hand over her heart while the other presses up into her mother's thought bubble, as if pushing it away. This is an important gesture, because Trinity is articulating, both with her words and body language, that her gender identity, at least in that moment, requires longer hair. The text continues: "Trinity let out a *big* breath, as if she'd been holding it forever. 'People don't care if cisgender girls like you have short hair. But it's different for transgender girls. I *need* long hair!'" Although trans girls and women can and do have short hair, we should consider Trinity's own sense of self and agency here as she vocalizes her needs. Acknowledging her cisgender privilege, her mom eventually agrees, "You're right. It is different for me." This exchange between mother and daughter takes place among Trinity's other family members and their pet pig, Peter Porker.

After struggling with what to do next, Trinity's brother Lucien comes up with a solution. Leading his mother across the street, with Peter Porker close behind, the three enter a beauty shop full of wigs. Despite all the choices, none are quite right. To this, Lucien responds: "Trinity needs her very own rainbow!" Unlike the other text within the story, this one appears in a much larger, crayon-like, colorful font, as if handwritten on the store's wall, and is surrounded by hair extensions ranging in color, resembling a rainbow. Behind the counter, a smiling employee wears one name tag with their name "MAYA" and another with their pronouns "THEY/THEM." The beauty supply shop also provides Peter Porker an opportunity to explore their own gender—first by wearing a wig and then by painting their hooves with nail polish. That night, Trinity's mom "sat down with her laptop, a hair needle, thread, and a wig cap." Even though "she had never made a wig before," she "threaded the hair into the cap like the online videos showed. She sewed late into the night, weaving love into every row." She eventually dozes off only to be awaken by Trinity sobbing in the bathroom the next morning: "Trinity's eyes sparkled. She was crying tears of joy! She ran her fingers through the curls. 'It's me, Mom. My hair has finally come! It's my rainbow!'" Trinity appears four times on this two-page spread, each time from a slightly different angle as she gleefully poses with her new wig. She thanks her mom, hugging her as she proudly declares, "I love my rainbow," as the rest of her family joins them in the bathroom (fig. 3.8). Here, the bathroom, a space usually associated with privacy, becomes a space of recognition and validation. First, self-validation, when Trinity initially glances back at herself in the bathroom mirror while wearing her new wig, and then familial, when her entire family enters the space to show their support. The final page depicts the whole family once again—mom, dad, siblings, and pet pig—encircling Trinity with the words "And we love you, my heart" above them.

Like *My Rainbow*, Casey's family and community are equally supportive. This includes assisting Casey in practicing for his soccer games and cheering him on during his games. Casey, who hopes to score a goal one day, practices constantly after school. "Sometimes," shares Casey, "my brother and sister help me kick the ball back and forth. I can't kick the ball very far yet, but I'm getting better." Each sibling is slightly different in skin tone. The brother wears blue and yellow and has shorter

Figure 3.8. Trinity thanking her mom for her new wig; from *My Rainbow*. Published by Kokila, an imprint of Penguin Random House LLC. Copyright © 2020 by Trinity Neal, DeShanna Neal, and Art Twink.

hair, whereas the sister wears a pink crop top and has longer hair pulled up into a messy bun. A dotted triangle on the field connects the three as they kick the ball back and forth. This occurs while Casey wears his green uniform, implying the siblings' support of his transition from the girls' team to the boys' team. Despite the gendered teams, *Casey's Ball* challenges gender-associated colors by making the girls' team's uniforms blue, a color stereotypically associated with boys. The visual juxtaposition of Casey in both uniforms at the beginning of the text is also powerful because, aside from changing colors (blue to green) and team mascot (dolphin to lizard), nothing else has changed about his body. In other words, Casey did not need to present himself any differently or change any aspect of himself in order to identify as trans and switch teams. Specifically, Casey's pink-and-purple sports bag remains the same, as does his hair in terms of style and length.

Casey's physical appearance—and hair in particular—does carry significance within the story, although not for the reasons one may initially suspect. Hair, as previously noted since chapter 1, is often racialized and gendered. In *Casey's Ball*, it is not whether Casey's hair is too long to be considered "boy's hair," but rather a matter of how longer hair may affect one's performance in soccer—regardless of gender. Casey explains what occurs when he attempts to kick the ball: "Sometimes my hair gets in my eyes. When it does, I miss the ball and someone else kicks it." A frustrated Casey is depicted three times on this spread. First, standing as the ball comes his way, his arms are up as if attempting to reach his hair to move it out of his face. It falls around his head, straight and dark brown, nearly shoulder's length. Next, we see him after having just attempted to kick the ball while falling backward, arms and legs flailing. Lastly, he lies on the ground, one arm covering his face in a gesture of embarrassment or defeat. By this point, a member of the opposing team has run off with the ball. Just like Lucien in *My Rainbow*, one of Casey's siblings knows how to help. His sister gives Casey one of her hair ties, and his expression immediately changes to one of excitement as arrows around his head point toward his own messy bun—just like his sister's (fig. 3.9). Now he will be able to see clearly while he runs and kicks the ball. Here, too, Casey's mother provides further validation by telling him that "ponytails are for any kid, boys or girls or neither or both." While this should be true regardless of time period, ponytails or buns on boys or men, now commonly referred to as "man buns," became a contemporary cultural phenomenon, further contributing to an acceptance of Casey's hairstyle. But although "man buns" may be credited for popularizing the idea of a "masculine" hair bun, men from across

Figure 3.9. Casey dealing with his hair while playing soccer; from *Casey's Ball*. Published by Flamingo Rampant Press. Copyright © 2019 by Kit Yan and Holly McGillis.

different cultures or religious beliefs have had long hair or have worn it in some type of ponytail or bun for various reasons throughout history. What *Casey's Ball* reminds us of is that, indeed, anyone can wear a hair bun regardless of one's gender. And, more importantly, hair need not be gendered at all.

Like his family, Casey's coach and teammates also embrace him as he joins the boys' team. His coach encourages him to "keep practicing, dude!" He kneels next to him with one hand on Casey's shoulder and the other with his fist up and the words "fight on!" embedded within the illustration. Casey grins proudly, holding a ball under one arm and emulating his coach with his other hand, also up in a fist. Whether or not the coach or teammates know Casey is transgender is not important to the book's plot—allowing readers to decide for themselves. Instead, what we do witness is a team that embraces Casey, even when he accidentally scores a point for the opposing team. Disappointed in himself, he asks his coach if he "can still be on the boys' team," and his coach assures him he can: "Keep trying and keep learning! You're doing great, Casey. We're glad to have you on our team." As Casey learns, no one is perfect, and that is okay. In the end, team spirit prevails, and everyone cheers when they go out for pizza: "We're the Great Green Lizards, and we love to play! We're the Great Green Lizards, and today is our day!" Casey's nonchalant acceptance as a member on the boys' team is noteworthy given the historical and more recent media controversies over transgender athletes.[92] And in a nod to queer athletes, illustrator Holly McGillis (who also illustrated *47,000 Beads*) sneaks in a queer couple by depicting two of Casey's soccer team opponents holding hands off to the side.

While I consider both *My Rainbow* and *Casey's Ball* autofantasías, *My Rainbow* is also clearly autobiographical, whereas *Casey's Ball* is primarily fiction. Their three authors (like most in this chapter), share a celebrity status among their respective communities and are primarily known for their other accomplishments outside of children's literature. Co-authors Trinity and DeShanna Neal gained national attention after winning an appeal against Medicaid in the state of Delaware. Trinity Neal even visited with former president Barack Obama and former first lady Michelle Obama in 2016. Meanwhile, Kit Yan is a queer, transgender, Asian American poet, playwright, and performer. Their numerous accolades include the Jonathan Larson Grant (2021) and the Kleban

Prize for Libretto (2021). All three authors rely on their own nuanced and intersecting identities to inform how they choose to depict trans of color children within their respective picture books.

During her actual childhood, Trinity Neal began verbalizing she was a girl since she was a toddler, at age three. At the time, she was attending a specialized preschool for children with disabilities. DeShanna recalls that, during speech language therapy, children were asked their name, age, and "if they were a boy or a girl. And each time she would say she was a girl."[93] As a result, DeShanna Neal "would get something sent home in her folder from her speech therapist, her teacher, or the school phycologist about how [she] would need to work with [her] child."[94] This included worksheets meant to assist T. Neal in "understand[ing] the differences between boys and girls."[95] Rather than consider she could be transgender, the preschool assumed she was having difficulties distinguishing between binary gender roles because of her autism. This not only demonstrates the challenges faced by transgender children but compounds the added challenges resulting from also being an autistic child.[96] On a separate occasion, D. Neal was told, "You need to fix your child. . . . Your child is going to be gay."[97] Another time, a child therapist instructed the parents to each be more "feminine [mom] and masculine [dad]" and to "smack their child" when she behaved like a girl.[98] All of this contributed to depression and anxiety. By age four, T. Neal had been diagnosed with clinical depression. She recalls, "I didn't like what the teachers kept saying to me. . . . Always calling me a boy . . . And then sometimes I'd get nightmares about them."[99] Her mother adds, "she stopped speaking. She became withdrawn and she just stopped interacting with anyone at school and at home."[100]

With her parents' support, Trinity Neal began socially transitioning by age four. "I told my parents I was a girl. Then, they actually listened!" she recalls, sharing how initially she wore her mother's dresses and wigs.[101] That was until, T. Neal says, "Mom gave me a dress and I was so happy."[102] DeShanna Neal adds, "and she was smiling. . . . If we hadn't listened to her and addressed her the way she knew she was, I would not have this child. I think she would have taken her life."[103] Unable to find a supportive elementary school, D. Neal quit her job and began homeschooling her daughter and her older brother Lucien (who was expelled "after he bit a classmate who called Trinity a 'sissy'").[104] D. Neal explains,

"We had to homeschool because we wanted our child to continue to live. And that was really hard." Despite the financial hardships (dropping below the poverty line), she knew this was the best option for her family. She elaborates: "Here I am fighting the civil rights for my daughter as a trans person. But then there is also that added fact that she is a Black person too."[105] By this point, T. Neal's parents were also educating themselves about transgender identities as well as learning about the staggering statistics of violence against Black trans women. But even though she had socially transitioned, it was not until T. Neal was seven, after having joined a soccer team (like Casey), that she "wanted the correct terminology for what society would call her."[106] Only then did she learn of the term "transgender." At age twelve, her request for puberty blockers was approved by her doctor but denied by her insurance. In a handwritten note submitted during the appeals process, T. Neal expressed: "I don't want to be a boy, or I'll be sad for the rest of my life. Please give me my blockers. It'll be a dream come true." By age thirteen, on April 6, 2016, she "became the first transgender minor in Delaware to receive puberty blockers by Medicaid."[107] Although this was a victory, she would need to request reauthorization every three months, which prompted her to eventually opt for a two-year implant instead. Since then, T. Neal has shared that she legally changed her name and gender, found a supportive high school (graduating in 2022), and had Genital Confirmation Surgery (GCS).[108] Her mother, now divorced, founded the Intersections of Pride nonprofit organization and continues to advocate for all her children as well as for herself as a queer, disabled single parent.[109]

My Rainbow debuted on October 20, 2020, just before T. Neal's seventeenth birthday. The picture book was illustrated by Art Twink, a trans of color artist who believes "art is for creating community and safety in a world that offers very little of either."[110] Together, along with Trinity and DeShanna Neal, the three created a book that captured a lived childhood experience of a Black autistic transgender girl who wanted long hair but had difficulties growing her own because "she hated how it made her itchy" on the back of her neck.[111] After a virtual book reading, Cree Myles from All Ways Black asked both authors why hair was important to who they were as a person. T. Neal answered first, sharing, "It is the way you express yourself. And honestly, for me, it makes me feel happier. It makes me feel like me. . . . It's best to choose your own hair that suits you. That's my reason."[112] D. Neal also reflected on the societal pressures placed on Black women because of their hair, as well as her position as a cisgender Black woman.[113] "My natural hair is curly and kinky and is beautiful," she shared. "And I made sure my children grew up knowing hair is beautiful, Black hair is beautiful. All Black hair is good."[114] Simultaneously, D. Neal wanted to validate her daughter's "intersections and the fact that her hair is curly, but she is autistic and certain textures and sensations bother her," while also acknowledging her own cisgender privilege since "[i]t doesn't work the same way for [her] as it works for [her daughter]."[115] Choosing to focus *My Rainbow* on hair allowed T. Neal's autofantasía to also be an autobiography because, in this case, the ideal experience or "fantasy" occurred for her in that moment of putting on her rainbow wig. *My Rainbow*, then, becomes a way to honor, hold space for, or visually and textually capture that specific experience and to share it with others. Even the inclusion of Lucien's cello and Peter Porker are based on reality. T. Neal's actual pet pig, Peter Porker, a miniature potbellied pig, is featured on almost every spread of the picture book.[116] Instead, it is within *My Rainbow*'s illustrations that non-fiction and fiction are blurred. For example, illustrator Art Twink embellished certain details within the artwork—namely, anthropomorphizing Peter Porker as they try on wigs or paint their own hooves.

In contrast, Kit Yan's autofantasía is less autobiographical and more fictionalized. Although Yan does not share the same name as their protagonist, both are racialized as Asian or of Asian descent. We might assume Casey is Asian Canadian since the book was published by Flamingo Rampant Press (Toronto, Ontario, Canada). Or, if considering Yan's own identity, Casey could also be read as Asian American. Yan's one sentence website bio is a bold statement about race, migration, and place: "Kit Yan is a Yellow American New York based artist, born in China, and raised in the Kingdom of Hawaii."[117] Yan first began performing as a slam poet while in college and then as one of the leads in the traveling poetry musical group Good Asian Drivers from 2008 to 2010.[118] Since then, Yan and their co-performer Melissa Li's many projects include releasing an album (*Drive Away Home*) and co-creating musicals (*Interstate* and *MISS STEP*). Yan has also collaborated with other writers such as Simone Wolff (*Mr. Transman* and *(T)estosterone*) and Jess X Snow (*Safe among Stars* and *Invasion*). In 2016, Yan's solo performance, *Queer Heartache*, was published as a poetry collection. Most recently, they wrote *Cancelled* (2020), a one-act musical centering transphobia within a Gay–Straight Alliance. Since the epigraph at the beginning of this chapter, Kit Yan has revised their artist statement, adding:

> I am who I am because I am Asian, I am transgender, and I was raised poor in Hawaii. I love all of these things about me and my stories reflect the experiences I've had—the time I got a blood transfusion because I stopped taking T without consulting my doctor, the time I went on tour with my best friend who I was in love with, but who was in love with our drummer, the time in my life when I took step aerobics classes with older women who kicked my ass and made me feel free in my body. Without all these memories, I wouldn't have stories. And without these stories I wouldn't remember.[119]

Storytelling, Yan reminds us, is not only about sharing one's stories with others but about sharing them so we do not forget them ourselves. These stories, or memories, not only inform Yan's writing but also provide a platform for them to publicly process experiences, emotions, identities, and politics.

Unlike Trinity Neal, Kit Yan's gender identity and journey has been more fluid. For example, while T. Neal has used "she/her/hers" pronouns since she was a child, Yan's pronouns vary. At times, they have used "they/he/she" pronouns simultaneously—other times, only one or two of these. As of the time of this writing, Yan primarily uses the pronoun "they" and self-identifies as both queer and trans. When asked about their trans identity for the "I AM: Trans People Speak" video campaign, Yan shared: "I love being trans. I think it's a beautiful thing. . . . It took me a while to get here honestly, to be able to say that I love who I am and I love being trans. I love having experienced life in different genders, in fluid gender, as a queer person and finding community in that. I really love being able to be a part of a community that is experiencing the world in that way as well."[120] Gender is also a major theme across all of Yan's work. For example, the album *Drive Away Home* includes a track titled "Third Gender," written and performed by Yan. In it, they explore their gender identity, while also challenging cisgender assumptions:

> Cuz sometimes my gender is boy,
> who looks like a girl,
> who likes boys.
> And sometimes my gender is trans.
> And sometimes my gender is chillin' out in between.
> But most of the time my gender is "Fuck you! Mind your own
> business!"[121]

The end of the track includes a nod to gender fluidity as a resistance to the gender binary: "There may be as many as a million genders, identities, and sexualities just floating around, waiting for the right person to snatch them up, put them on, and proudly parade around in their new skin."[122]

In a 2021 Playwrights Horizon Master Class, Kit Yan also acknowledged that identity formation is a process (internally and externally) that can benefit from an audience who can relate to being trans, noting, "engagement is very important to me. . . . It has always been helpful for me to know that other trans folks are telling their stories or receiving mine."[123] And just like Yan, Casey explores his own gender identity and expression. However, instead of a stage, Casey's arena becomes the soccer field within the pages of a picture book. As an autofantasía, *Casey's Ball* provides Yan an opportunity to reimagine one more version of the trans of color child they might have been.

For both Yan and Casey, family is a vital component of their lives. Reflecting on coming out to one's family, Yan shared how, when they first began "talking to [their] parents about being trans, it wasn't easy," in part because of language barriers and limited translations or definitions for terms such as "transgender." Instead, a family spiritual advisor was able to assuage the parents' concerns by incorporating culturally specific religious or spiritual concepts such as reincarnation: "our spiritual advisor said to my parents—and particularly [to] my mother who was having a hard time at that moment—that who I am today is a result of previous lives. . . . It's like an extension or a manifestation of who I was previously. And I think after hearing that in terms of talking about lives and reincarnation, my parents sort of came to a different place and said, 'oh, well that makes a lot of sense.'"[124] As Yan describes, it became important for their parents to contextualize their trans identity within their own cultural and spiritual backgrounds. Although Casey's mom is only visually depicted twice within the picture book, her presence and validation are assumed throughout. And like Yan, Casey also has two siblings. In interviews and performances, Yan has implied that their younger sibling, Edwin, may also be queer or trans, or is at least a strong ally.[125] This suggests another reading of *Casey's Ball* in which we might consider Yan in the role of one of the older siblings and Edwin as Casey.

The characters Casey and Trinity each depict just one way to exist as a trans of color kid. As DeShanna Neal reminds us, "We represented something you didn't see often. Which was that a family of color accepted a trans child."[126] Even though she was referring to her actual family unit, the same can be said for the picture books *My Rainbow* and *Casey's Ball*. Picture books with trans of color characters have the potential to validate trans of color readers. They may also provide their family members, and all other readers, with an opportunity to evaluate their own cisgender or white privilege—but only if they are, at least to some degree, open to hearing these stories. This is why Kit Yan often says, "My work has universal themes, but it is not actually for everyone."[127] Like other titles mentioned throughout *Coloring into Existence*, *My Rainbow* was also included within Republicans' "Krause's Book List" of titles to be banned in schools.[128] "What's so scary about us?" asked Trinity Neal while being interviewed by Vice Magazine regarding transgender bathroom rights.[129] One can only hope that books like *My Rainbow* and *Casey's Ball* may eventually contribute to countering anti-trans discourse and actions such as ongoing battles over bathroom rights or book bans. In the meantime, T. Neal has a message for other trans kids: "Never give up. Keep fighting."[130]

* * *

All picture books in this chapter should remind us that children can make important decisions about their own genders and gender identities. In dividing the books into three categories (GNC, nonbinary, and transgender), it was not my intention to suggest linear or evolutionary progress; each category is equally valuable, just like all genders are important. Moreover, the characters themselves should not be seen as static within their genders, instead, allowing them to exist or be read through ongoing discussions of gender fluidity and gender expansive embodiment. For the sake of this chapter's length, I had to limit the titles discussed even though there are many others worthy of inclusion.[131] Although now, more than ever, there exists a plethora of picture books on gender nonconforming, nonbinary, and transgender children, more are still needed. And although each one focuses specifically on gender, we must also consider how they overlap—albeit some more than others—with questions of children's sexuality, which I discuss in the following chapter.

4

Showing and Telling

Children's Sexuality in Queer of Color Children's Literature

What society feeds you as flaws are your superpowers.
—Myles E. Johnson

We should be more open to accounting for feelings, intu-
itions, and behaviors as manifestations of knowledge.
—Ernesto Javier Martínez

Imagine if we had been children who could love freely,
knowing that our love is just as valid as any non-queer love
that exists.
—Adelina Anthony

One of the greatest taboos in children's literature is child sexuality.
Despite adult fears, most children are not asexual. Parenting resources
like Bonnie J. Rough's *Beyond Birds and Bees: Bringing Home a New Message to Our Kids about Sex, Love, and Equality* (2018) and NPR segments
like "The Birds and the Bees: How to Talk to Children about Sex" attempt
to broach the subject.[1] Directed at older children and youth, Cory Silverberg and Fiona Smyth's *You Know, Sex: Bodies, Gender, Puberty, and
Other Things* (2022) is another useful resource, while picture books
for younger children lag behind.[2] Even LGBTQ+ picture books rarely
acknowledge children's sexuality. As with adults' sexuality, discourse
surrounding children's sexuality has been amplified since the eighteenth
century alongside society's efforts to regulate such sexuality, which Foucault outlined in *The History of Sexuality*, noting that "it would be less
than exact to say that the pedagogical institution has imposed a pon-
derous silence on the sex of children and adolescents."[3] Instead, within
Western society, "the sex of children and adolescents has become, since

the eighteenth century, an important area of contention around which innumerable institutional devices and discursive strategies have been deployed."[4] Leading this charge, Foucault explained, would be "educators, physicians, administrators, and parents."[5]

Children's sexuality remains widely debated. It is not surprising that, even in fields like sexology or child development, studies of children's explicit sexual desire are limited.[6] Apart from parents' understandable trepidation in volunteering their children for studies of sexuality, there is also children's own inability to provide consent to the ethical standards of human-subject review boards. As child psychologists and experts in children's sexual development are aware, children do explore their bodies, masturbate, develop crushes on one another, and experiment among themselves. After delivering a talk on children's sexuality, Italian-Australian scholar Maria Pallotta-Chiarolli was asked a question that has been frequently demanded of her: "why did you teach your daughter about masturbation at such a young age?" Her response to this question is often: "I did not teach my daughter to masturbate, but I did not discourage it when I was aware that she was doing it."[7] Elaborating, she explained, "Children grow up with a sexuality, sexual desires and curiosity about their bodies and soon discover for themselves what makes them feel good. They need to be protected and cared for, and certainly not made vulnerable to sexual abuse. But this means actually teaching children to be comfortable, confident and articulate about their bodies so that they will not passively allow anyone to exploit them."[8] Pallotta-Chiarolli's research further details her own parenting choices, which include "queerly raising" her daughter, teaching her about the clitoris, and not shaming her for masturbating.[9] However, children simply knowing about sexuality can be cause for alarm. As childhood studies scholar Kerry H. Robinson put it, "children who have an understanding of sex and sexuality are often 'othered' as unnatural children,' with 'unnatural knowledge.'"[10]

Another problem lies not only in admitting that children have sexualities but in attempting to label them. When children are not deemed asexual, heterosexual desire is often presumed and encouraged. Hetero- and cisnormative parenting effectively raises "boys" within hypermasculinity and "girls" within hyperfemininity without allowing or even admitting to categories beyond these binaries. Often under the cloak of playful childhood innocence, these little boys are then encouraged to kiss little girls or to role-play as "princes" charged with saving little girls or "princesses." These types of narratives are perpetuated in fairytales and Disney films, with any deviation from the heteronormative script causing potential alarm. As far as queer children are concerned, Eve Kosofsky Sedgwick reminds us that, at least within revisionist psychoanalysis, "the healthy [male] homosexual is one who (a) is already grown up, and (b) acts masculine."[11] This limiting definition leaves little room for queer children. Although, as I mentioned in the introduction, Sedgwick and others in queer theory have offered poignant rebuttals.[12]

Certainly, not all children are judged equally. Even though children of various races/ethnicities, religions, abilities, genders, and sexualities might be considered sexual beings, children of color in North American societies are more often hypersexualized or judged as adults when compared to their white, heteronormative, cisgender counterparts.[13] Among queer children, queer children of color are often racialized and sexualized differently by society in ways that do not afford them the same presumed innocence.[14] With this focus on queer of color children, my intent is not to argue that they are the only children who experience sexuality. Instead, beginning with the assumption that most children experience some form of sexuality or desire, I am particularly interested in how queer of color adult authors integrate these experiences into their writing.

While previous chapters offered examples of queer and trans of color authors creating LGBTQ+ children's literature—and while we might be able to do a queer or autofantastic reading of specific (or all) children's literature—this chapter focuses on queer of color authors who more explicitly explore queer children's sexuality in their works. Within YA or adult literature (not intended for children), queer of color authors might explore children's sexuality by recalling their own childhood experiences. However, titles that explicitly represent or depict queer of color children exploring their sexuality are rare within children's picture books. Notable exceptions include queer of color authors who use gender as a metaphor for sexuality while also announcing to readers beyond the scope of their books that their characters are queer, as in Myles E. Johnson's *Large Fears* (2015), or they may explicitly articulate and depict queer desire among children of color, as in Ernesto Javier Martínez's

When We Love Someone We Sing to Them/Cuando amamos cantamos
(2018). These picture books challenge readers to grapple with children's
sexuality, not only as a theoretically abstract concept but as autofantastic
manifestations of their author's own queer childhoods, to be shared with
other (potentially) queer kids.

Not for Children: Queer of Color Authors Reflecting on Childhood Sexual Experiences

In response to children's presumed asexuality or heteronormativity, it
has become commonplace for LGBTQ+ adults to reminisce about their
childhood love interests and sexual awakenings.[15] In part, these desires
fuel the "born this way" discourse around sexuality, emphasizing nature
over nurture. Within queer literature, these narratives about one's childhood mostly appear in adult and YA novels, as well as in non-fiction and
autobiographical or life writings. Such stories abound, including common scenarios like Katherine James's: "I've always been attracted to girls,
even when I was a little girl."[16]

Recounting memories of her childhood, Audre Lorde explained one
of her earliest encounters of curiosity about her own body and that of
another child's. In *Zami: A New Spelling of My Name*, she recalled, "I
found my first playmate when I was around four years old. It lasted for
about ten minutes. . . . Suddenly I realized that there was a little creature
standing on a step in the entryway of the main doors, looking at me with
bright eyes and a big smile. It was a little girl. She was right away the
most beautiful little girl I had ever seen alive in my life."[17] Lorde recalls
wanting to keep her—as in pretending to be her mother and also as in
desiring her. Lorde vividly remembered her amusement over the child's
name, Toni: "The name called up a picture book I was just finished reading, and the image came out *boy*. But this delectable creature in front of
me was most certainly a girl, and I wanted her for my very own—my
very own what, I did not know—but for my very own self."[18] Toni says to
her, "Play with me, please?"[19] Lorde cannot believe she is real and even
contemplates the possibility of her being a doll: "Was her bottom going
to be real and warm or turn out to be hard rubber, molded into a little
crease like the ultimately disappointing Coca-Cola doll?"[20] Just as she is
about to check, her mom interrupts, leaving her with a longing to find

the girl another day and recreate the encounter: "I don't know how long I looked for Toni every day at noontime, sitting on the stoop. Eventually, her image receded into that place from which all my dreams are made."[21] What is most unique about Lorde's experience is that it occurred while she was only four years old, but became formative in her own sense of self-awareness and awareness of others.

Childhood sexual experiences at only a few years older than Lorde in her experience described above include trans Latinx icon Sylvia Rivera who, in "Queens in Exile, the Forgotten Ones," describes being sexually aroused at age seven and sexually experimenting with an older cousin.[22] Similarly, in "The Boy in Fear Who Became a Latino/a LGBT Advocate in Philadelphia," David Acosta narrates how he first became aware of his "interest and attraction both romantic and sexual to boys" while at a boarding school between the ages of seven and eleven.[23] Numerous authors in Lisa C. Moore's edited volume, *Does Your Mama Know? An Anthology of Black Lesbian Coming Out Stories* (1997), recount similar childhood experiences. Stephanie Byrd recalls being around six or seven when she was first called a lesbian. After learning the definition of the word, she proclaimed that she was, indeed, a lesbian because she was in love with her next-door neighbor. Then, at age twelve, she submitted a school assignment listing her three aspirations in life: being a "brain surgeon, a lawyer, and a lesbian."[24] Meanwhile, Donna Allegra described "discovering [herself] as a lesbian after reading *The Well of Loneliness* when [she] was 9 years old," whereas Tonda Clarke revealed that she masturbated and had her first girlfriend by age ten.[25] The anthology also includes a contribution from Jewelle Gomez, who was delighted to learn the term "bulldagger": "I was so happy at thirteen to have a word for what I knew myself to be."[26]

Numerous other examples of LGBTQ+ children's sexuality can also be found in works of fiction, such as the eleven-year-old in Carla Trujillo's *What Night Brings*, the sisters in Terri de la Peña's *Faults*, the protagonist in Charles Rice-González's *Chulito* who recalls a memory of himself as a boy kissing his best friend Carlos,[27] and the young boys who explore their sexuality during sleepovers in Craig S. Womack's *Drowning in Fire*.[28] Even if not always explicitly autobiographical, authors tend to draw on what they know, what they have experienced, or what they imagine to be plausible among children. By accepting or sharing that these feelings of same-sex desire and sexuality or sexual exploration occurred during childhood, authors effectively validate their own queer adult existence. But why are most of these narratives confined within YA or adult literature? What would it look like to share them in picture books for children who might also be curious about or already exploring their sexuality?

The Pink Planet: Gender and Homosocial Metaphors for Black Queerness

Unable to find a children's book that spoke to his personal experience as a gay Black boy, Myles E. Johnson self-published *Large Fears* in 2015. A writer and popular cultural critic, Johnson is best known for his contributions to the *New York Times*, *Essence*, and *Buzzfeed*. In a 2018 interview with *Lumina Journal*, when Johnson was asked how he started writing and when people started to pay attention, he explained, "I've been writing my whole life. Folks started caring around four years ago because of my personal essays, then I self-published a children's book and my readership has been evolving ever since."[29] On the impetus for writing *Large Fears*, Johnson reflected, "I had this prayer on my heart that I wanted to work out some childhood trauma through my art."[30] He realized this while visiting his family: "I was one day in my room at my mama's house dancing to George Michael and the name Jeremiah Nebula popped into my head. I stopped dancing and got a notebook and asked myself who this person was. And it became clear he was a child and that the language needed to be a bit more simple and friendly."[31] Unlike his other writing, which includes essays on popular culture, he described that "writing a children's book was freeing and helped [him] fall back in love with creation."[32] Johnson did not attempt to publish the book with a mainstream press, as he "was so convinced it would get rejected that [he] didn't bother," opting instead to crowdfund and self-publish.[33]

Large Fears was illustrated by artist and designer Kendrick Daye, who describes himself as "a southern boy, a neer-do-well, a halogenic hipster setting up art-camp" in Harlem.[34] His illustrations include collages of boldly painted multicolor backdrops with black-and-white cutout characters drawn primarily in pencil. Johnson's text and Daye's illustrations combine to form an introspective picture book that confronts childhood traumas. Gender provides a metaphor for the child's queer sexuality, which Johnson does not identify within the story itself, but rather in epitext features within its paratextual scope, like the crowdfunding campaign prior to the book's publication and interviews in which he describes the book. In this case, the child is queer because the author is telling us he is, even if that disclosure occurs outside of the picture book (fig. 4.1).

Figure 4.1. Cover of *Large Fears*. Self-published. Copyright © 2015 by Myles E. Johnson and Kendrick Daye.

Large Fears focuses on the inner struggles of Jeremiah Nebula, who loves pink and daydreams of traveling to Mars. "Little Jeremiah was not a bullfrog," begins the story, "He was a boy with skin like hazelnut." In this comparison, bullfrog is made synonymous with tough, rough, and un-pretty, whereas hazelnut refers to the rich color of his skin: dark and beautiful. Johnson describes the child feeling "like an alien on the playground." Although we are not told why, we can surmise that it has to do with gender stereotypes about what it means to be a "boy" or a "girl." In this context, his love of pink things like flamingos and pink tulips could isolate him from other children. At the same time, he might also be understood as gender fluid or gender variant. With an array of interests, Jeremiah's sense of isolation or alienation is further evident in the accompanying illustration, which depicts him in a side profile, standing alone, facing away, with his back to the text and a somber expression on his face. The black-and-white pencil sketch of him contrasts starkly with the bright-yellow splatter across most of the two-page spread, along with a pale-pink layer beneath it.

Jeremiah's inability to fit in results in his desire to find a more welcoming environment. "Each night, little Jeremiah dreamed of going to Mars," we are told. "But he feared what he would see on each star on his way. For some kids, stars are bright lanterns in the sky. For Jeremiah, stars were scary worlds standing between him and his dreams of Mars." Whereas fairy tales might have us believe that we can "wish upon a star" like Pinocchio and be granted our deepest desires, or that stars are like diamonds in the sky such as in the lullaby *Twinkle, Twinkle, Little Star*, Jeremiah is highly skeptical and even suspicious of them. Instead, the words "WiSh UpOn A MaRs" are printed at the top of the page, appearing like a heading or title similar to the chapter titles of a chapter book or novel. These mixed upper- and lower-case headings indicate the major themes of each particular spread. In this case, reaching Mars is Jeremiah's greatest desire, describing his utopia as follows: "on Mars everything would be pink, and he'd find a world full of little black boys who loved pink things, too." Although Jeremiah may have learned other facts about Mars at home, in school, or elsewhere, his autofantasía of the red planet reimagines the rocky, extremely cold, and hostile Martian atmosphere as a pink planet inhabited by other Black boys like himself.

How explicit would a little boy have to be for us to acknowledge that this is a declaration of same-sex desire? Although gay desire or queerness is never explicitly conveyed in the text, it is nonetheless implied by Jeremiah's continued longing for the color pink and little Black boys like himself. This ideal homosocial representation of the planet Mars in *Large Fears* provides Jeremiah with an imaginary space in which he can meet and befriend others like him. Of course, not all boys who like pink are queer, nor should we conflate gender with sexuality. The point, however, is that Jeremiah wants to be surrounded by other little Black boys like himself who, at least on Earth, might also be considered odd, different, or queer like him. He may not yet know that he is or will grow into a queer boy and, eventually, a queer adult. And although the author and illustrator present us with a gay Black boy, we could also read Jeremiah as genderqueer, nonbinary, or trans—even if the child does not yet have the language to articulate such identities. Jeremiah's desire for a whole planet of boys like himself could also invite discussions about non-monogamous or poly networks and chosen family. At least within the text, Jeremiah does eventually imagine himself meeting others in space, explaining, "He would play silly games with outer space pals." Although these "pals" are not depicted in the book's final page spread, readers can easily decipher that he means others like himself.

Should readers miss Jeremiah's queerness within the text, they may find themselves instead encountering *Large Fears'* metadata that reveals him as such. In the book, the boy is queer because the author and illustrator say so in the picture book's epitextual elements. Before the book existed in physical or tangible form, the #LARGEFEARS hashtag and Kickstarter campaign presented Jeremiah as a young gay and Black boy. Potential sponsors were offered a direct petition from Jeremiah Nebula in the form of an introductory letter, which described his mother as wise, recounting her saying: "everything we see, hear, touch, and smell is a story ready to be told," and "everyone deserves to be able to tell their story. She says that it's PARAMOUNT."[35] In introducing himself, he shared, "Who am I? I'm a boy that likes pink with black skin and I never quite fit in and during recess I don't have many friends. But then, I went to Mars and I met Mr. Kendrick and Mr. Myles, and they said we could be friends and they even helped me tell my story about Mars and all the stars I landed on and called it "LARGE FEARS." And they even said I reminded them of them when they wore smaller sneakers and ate PB&J. They have very nice beautiful mommies too."[36] Jeremiah can grow up to be just like Johnson and Daye. Although Jeremiah's queerness can only be inferred from his own letter to potential campaign donors, the author and illustrator undeniably confirm it: "We wanted to see a queer black boy represented in children's books and instead of waiting for it to come to be, we created it. . . . We spent over a year designing the story and world that our young queer black boy, Jeremiah Nebula would thrive in. We fought, cried, thought, and edited to make sure this world was honest, artful, and inspiring. Today, I am happy to say that our large dream came true due to our diligence."[37] Like author and illustrator, Jeremiah also had hurdles to overcome. In order to reach Mars, Jeremiah would first have to confront his greatest fears, beginning with those that were internal or internalized.

The planet Mars, at least as understood within Western astronomy, is named after the Roman god of war, who is modeled after the Greek god of war, Ares.[38] The planet has two moons, Phobos and Deimos, named after Ares's sons, whose names mean "fear" and "dread," respectively.[39] It is fitting, then, that Jeremiah must confront his own fears manifested in the form of stars. Unlike the big balls of fire or hot helium gas that our own star (our sun) is made of, which might warrant their own set of concerns, Jeremiah's stars more closely resemble planets or moons. His imagination leads him up into space, "but instead of landing on Mars, he landed on a star" with giant butterflies the size of skyscrapers. He wonders whether these orange-and-black winged creatures (resembling monarch butterflies on Earth, only these are made of gold) would like him or if, instead, they would want him dead. Two very different scenarios; after all, Jeremiah did tell us on the first spread that he had large fears for every large dream. On this star, he also imagines "fireflies as big as his head with gold vines on their bodies, that treated him like a wild coyote." He worries they might not understand him. These giant butterflies and fireflies, despite their size, do not give any indication that they might try to hurt him, much less want him dead; yet they represent tiny insecurities that, at least internally, seem like gigantic obstacles.

Interestingly, the illustrations also depict Jeremiah as a giant towering over skyscrapers, but with no other person in sight. Alone apart from the giant insects, Jeremiah becomes further engulfed by anxiety and fear.

However, his facial expression seems more inquisitive than sad. Little Jeremiah jumps from star to star, facing quicksand on one star and tiny robots on another. On this latter star, the tiny robots provide his first interaction with a humanoid object, in the sense that they each have a head, two eyes, and a mouth, along with arms and legs. Touching one and saying hello to another, "They buzzed around and treated little Jeremiah like he wasn't even there. Jeremiah was a ghost that was given no attention or care. Those little robots didn't budge or judge. The little robots made Jeremiah feel like an invisible monster, and little ghoulish Jeremiah cried big tears that turned into a waterslide that he slid down onto another star." Usually a fan of monsters, he does not enjoy feeling like an invisible monster himself. Despite the tiny robots' presence across this star, Jeremiah finds himself completely ignored, made to feel invisible to the point of tears, calling his whole existence into question. It is not until he reaches "A LaZy StAr," where "all the houses leaned on each other," that he discovers a TV depicting "big Jeremiah living a great life."

Little Jeremiah's journey from star to star eventually leads him back home to his mother. Titled "HoMe On EaRtH," the two-page spread indicates his joy in returning back to reality: "This place looked like his home, but little Jeremiah wasn't sure. . . . He had to find the one thing that would let him be sure he wasn't still lost in a daydream—his mom!" No longer fixated on catastrophizing his fears within his head (or "daydreams"), Jeremiah, for a brief moment, is unsure of where he is. We are told, "Little Jeremiah burst through the door. He found his mom in the kitchen making dinner. It was home after all!" Now feeling safe, "Little Jeremiah sat on the kitchen floor and watched his mom make space sandwiches made with slices of cheese that came from the moon. She also made asteroid juice that little Jeremiah drank with stardust straws." These references to the moon, asteroids, and stardust are not meant to be taken literally. Likely, either these details remain Jeremiah's private thoughts, or perhaps he and his mother make-believe together, each contributing an off-planet detail. But what if, within the picture book's world, Jeremiah's mom was not confined to earth? What if she could also travel to the moon for slices of cheese? Whether figuratively or not, Jeremiah's mom is his superhero. Within the illustration, she stands as if posing for a photo, legs body-width apart and hands on her hips (fig. 4.2).

Figure 4.2. Jeremiah and his mother; from *Large Fears*. Self-published. Copyright ©
2015 by Myles E. Johnson and Kendrick Daye.

There are evident parallels between Jeremiah in *Large Fears* and
Max in Maurice Sendak's classic *Where the Wild Things Are* (1963) in
terms of their investment in boyhood through fantasy and travel. Both
of their authors are also queer, although Sendak was closeted when he
published his book and throughout most of his life.[40] Both are also marginalized because of race or ethnoreligion: Johnson as Black and Sendak
as Jewish. Both Max and Jeremiah fantasize about leaving their homes,
and indeed they do (within their imaginations), only to return by the
end of the book. Notably, Max is attempting to escape his mother who
is never visually depicted within the illustrations. In contrast, Jeremiah's
mother represents a Black mother providing for, nourishing, consoling,
and supporting her child. Despite his vivid imagination and daydreams
of far-off planets, Jeremiah's mother remains central to his conception
of home. In a subsequent illustration, Jeremiah kisses his mother on
the cheek, after which "he looked up and told Mama Nebula about his
mind's adventures while she prepared cosmic snacks. . . . Little Jeremiah
told Mama Nebula about how he wanted to go to Mars, but those stars
with the fears that were large kept him from the trip to Mars."

We might ask, why would Jeremiah daydream of stars that made him fearful instead of automatically landing on Mars? Why would he impose these unnecessary obstacles upon himself? What does it mean to fail, even within one's own imagination? The answers lie in his mother's poignant response: "Little Jeremiah, those stars are all fears that you made up because you are smart and have a wonderful imagination. If you want to go to Mars, you can go to Mars. If you want to be a star, you can be the biggest star. Everything you need is right inside of you." Unsure, he asks, "What if I want to be the biggest star in the world and play laser tag or dolls on the Milky Way?" Mama Nebula responds, "You should prepare to play away. Anything you want will happen as long as you know you are your imagination's captain. It controls where your rocket ship lands." His mother's encouragement leads to a newfound confidence as he smiles widely while the two embrace.

Large Fears can also be understood as speculative fiction and Afrofuturism. An entire galaxy becomes Jeremiah's playground, with him easily navigating from one star or planet to another with neither a spacesuit nor spacecraft. He is also able to see into the future, presenting himself and readers with a future populated by a thriving queer Black community. Unsurprisingly, Myles Johnson's love of writing is intertwined with his passion for speculative fiction: "That's my core. That's how I feel in love with writing. . . . I was, and still am in many ways, the little boy obsessed with sci-fi, monsters, and *The Twilight Zone*. Even now, I always have just this constant ongoing projector in my head of worlds, monsters, and situations that are otherworldly but serve as a critique of the world."[41] Johnson enthusiastically adds, "I love, love, love the work of Samuel R. Delany, Octavia E. Butler, Toni Morrison, Ray Bradbury, and Chuck Palahniuk."[42] Among this list of notable science fiction authors, the first two brought about the advent of Afrofuturism, which, as I mentioned in my book's introduction, was a term coined by Mark Dery and popularized by Alondra Nelson.[43] As Ytasha L. Womack described it, "Afrofuturism is an intersection of imagination, technology, the future, and liberation."[44] Within *Large Fears*, this future must include the liberation of gay Black children such as Jeremiah.

Mars also offers a symbolic alternative or parallel universe created by Jeremiah. To return to *Where the Wild Things Are*, while Max conquers land and rules as king over the "otherly" wild monsters, Jeremiah would rather make friends than wage war or rule over others. And unlike Max, who wears a gold crown atop his head as a symbol of dominance or entitlement, Jeremiah's crown becomes a symbol of Black pride that evokes discourses countering the misconception that only European cultures come from royalty. The outlined three-pronged crown is reminiscent of work by AfroLatinx artist Jean-Michel Basquiat.[45] In describing Basquiat's crown motif to children, Jauaka Steptoe explained how "crowns represented many things, such as power or strength, and [Basquiat] often 'gave' crowns to others in his artwork as a sign of respect."[46] In a similar manner, Kendrick Daye includes a crown on Jeremiah's t-shirt as a way to signal that he is special—not only is it a crown, but it is a crown with wings. Basquiat's crowns are now iconic, adorning artworks and even book covers such as on *Life Doesn't Frighten Me*, a collection of poetry by Maya Angelou paired with artwork by Basquiat. It is fitting, then, to imagine that Daye might grant Jeremiah a crown as a sign of protection against his own fears. Basquiat's possible influence on Daye can also be inferred from the colorful abstract backgrounds that appear throughout *Large Fears*, as well as some of the shapes superimposed on these backgrounds, such as lightning bolts (another Basquiat motif). Under the title "ThE WhOlE WiDe GaLaXy iS YoUr PlAyGrOuNd," Johnson ends with four blocks of text, which I would like to quote here at length:

Little Jeremiah would blink those bright stars he called eyes and imagine he was on Mars. He would imagine it so well that it became true. He would look at himself in the mirror and realize that he was a superstar, with all of his pink toys and his favorite pretty flowers that ate fireflies.

Little Jeremiah would live and run in a dream come true. He would play on those stars. He would make fun of those large fears, or explore them when he was feeling especially brave.

He would play tag with those mean butterflies with the mean eyes. He would play silly games with outer space pals. Little Jeremiah is not a bullfrog, but a dream come true.

Little Jeremiah is not his large fears. Jeremiah Nebula is a superstar, just like you.

Satisfied and with a renewed sense of confidence, Jeremiah relaxes, propping up his chin on his arms while lying outstretched on his stomach. Almost identical to the cover art, these illustrations differ in that the final image depicts Jeremiah out in the galaxy, surrounded by countless stars. Pink and yellow zigzags or lightning rods surround his head, as if to symbolize his thoughts or imaginative power. Circling back to Johnson's epigraph at the beginning of this chapter, Jeremiah's "flaws"—in this case his fears about who he is or might become, about others judging him, and about being lonely or invisible—have been transformed through his mother's words of encouragement and his own imagination into his superpowers radiating outward across the galaxy.

Johnson's picture book made headlines when it was released, both because it was labeled the first children's book about a gay Black boy and because, as a result, its purpose as a political project sparked public controversy among renowned authors, editors, educators, and literary critics. Meg Rosoff's now infamous comments included: "You don't have to read about a queer black boy to read a book about a marginalised child. The children's book world is getting far too literal about what 'needs' to be represented. You don't read . . . Alice in Wonderland to know about rabbits. Good literature expands your mind. It doesn't have the 'job' of being a mirror."[47] Although Lewis Carroll's *Alice's Adventures in Wonderland* may be read as potentially subversive, Rosoff's comment frames it as a touchstone of childnormative children's literature. Her other comments included: "I really hate this idea that we need agendas in books. A great book has a philosophical, spiritual, intellectual agenda that speaks to many more people—not just gay black boys. I'm sorry, but write a pamphlet about it. That's not what books are for."[48] The debate that ensued speaks to the ongoing effects of childnormativity within children's literature, whereby only white heterosexual characters and experiences are normalized as universal, becoming yet another moment for reinforcing the Western, modernist assumptions about art and politics. In response, Debbie Reese, literary critic and founder of American Indians in Children's Literature (AICL), pushed back: "all books have agendas."[49] Edith Campbell agreed, adding, "I *do* need to read about a queer black boy. I *do* need the children's book world to be much more literal about what, about who needs to be represented and I need that more than I need to read about self absorbed middle class white kids in apocalyptic

England. I need mirrors like Jeremiah Nebula to remind me that I can face my fears. I need him to remind me how fearfully white the world is."[50] The white world Campbell references exists not only in what we might call "classic" children's literature but in children's material culture more broadly, including contemporary children's media and picture books. Titles like *Large Fears* not only serve as mirrors for historically marginalized communities but also challenge dominant culture's limiting beliefs regarding what constitutes universal appeal.

Serenatas as Affirmations of Queer Love between Boys of Color

As with Jeremiah above, I suggested we might understand certain characters as queer because their author tell us so—even if outside the scope of the story—expanding queer worlds beyond the boundaries of the page. While commendable, such picture books *imply* queerness without explicitly depicting queer desire among children within the text or illustrations. As previously discussed, LGBTQ+ children's literature often prioritizes gender over sexuality among children, while reserving queer desire for adults. It should not surprise us, then, that the next step for authors of queer children's literature is to depict queer desire among children in picture books.

Until recently, this has primarily taken place in picture books published outside of North America. For example, the bilingual book from Spain *El viejo coche/The Old Car* (2008) narrates the life of two boys (Andrés and Pablo) who are best friends as children and who, as they get older, fall in love. In *La fiesta de Blas* [Blas's party] (2008), also from Spain, the boy protagonist (Blas) considers his sexual identity as he experiments with another boy who likes him, but he ultimately decides he likes a girl instead. Unlike the other picture book titles, this one explicitly describes children's sexuality, including the two boys' erections. Meanwhile, the French title *Jérôme par coeur* (2009), which was translated into English and published in the US as *Jerome by Heart* in 2018, depicts the mundane joy experienced by two boys (Raphael and Jerome) who like each other. This picture book is unique in that the cover illustrates queer desire among children by depicting the two boys holding hands while bicycling. In contrast, *Prva ljubezen* (2014), which was translated from

Slovene into Spanish and published as *Mi primer amor* [My first love] in 2016, is a disheartening story of two boys who like each other but are separated by teachers and then parents. With these books in mind, *When We Love Someone We Sing to Them/Cuando amamos cantamos* (2018) may be recognized as one of the first children's picture books by a queer author to explicitly depict queer desire between children within North America—certainly the first in North America by a queer of color author who centers queer of color children (fig. 4.3).[51] Written by Ernesto Javier Martínez and illustrated by Maya Gonzalez, it not only implies queer sexuality among children but narrates a story of reciprocated desire between two boys of color, who are surrounded by supportive parents.

In *When We Love Someone We Sing to Them*, Martínez does not shy away from narrating queer desire among boys. Employing anaphora embellished with similes and spanning across three spreads, the unnamed narrator describes his attraction for another boy: "My heart? My heart zoomed like a bird the day we met. My heart fluttered like the wind in the grass when you held my hand. My heart beat as loud as the rain the afternoon we spent together."[52] Each statement emphasizes some aspect of nature: a blue bird in the first, green grass in the second, and blue and green that combine to form blue raindrops between green willow branches and leaves that encapsulate the two boys in the third. An element of fantasy underlines Gonzalez's accompanying illustrations. The analogy between rapid heartbeats and a bird's speed could have depicted a bird flying beside or above the two boys. Instead, Gonzalez's hyperbolic proportions depict a bird that not only is giant in size but can carry the two boys on its back, nestled between its swift wings. As if looking downward, the bright-green backdrop suggests grass below. It is imprinted with foliage and flowers at various stages of bloom, alluding to the budding feelings between the two boys. The imagery also suggests the seemingly magical sensations of having feelings for someone else, as if being confined to the ground is no longer possible and one must instead glide up above the Earth. The boys' desire is so strong, in other words, that it shakes up their whole world and sense of reality. Atop this giant singing blue bird and looking at one another, the boys exist in their own world or fantasy.

In comparing this spread to *Large Fears*, here too, we have a giant winged creature. Only instead of multiple giant butterflies made of gold

Figure 4.3. Cover of *When We Love Someone We Sing to Them/Cuando amamos cantamos*. Published by Reflection Press. Copyright © 2018 by Ernesto Javier Martínez and Maya Gonzalez.

that might want to harm a gay Black boy, this winged creature cradles and supports these two queer boys of color. Like Jeremiah, the narrator's love interest has curly hair and slightly darker skin compared to the protagonist. He also shares Jeremiah's wider nose. In my comparative, autofantastic reading, perhaps Jeremiah can one day become like this other boy—free to proclaim and enact queer love.

By the third spread in this six-page sequence within Martínez's picture book, the narrator's feelings materialize into an adorable date under a willow tree—a queer take on a "play date." Remnants of a picnic are scattered under the willow tree, except instead of sharing lunch, they had pressed their own lemonade infused with sweet honey and red strawberries sliced into hearts. Despite the willow holding them—creating a sense of security—the boys' feelings are too strong to remain hidden.

The next spread, in contrast, does not include any text. Instead, Gonzalez depicts the narrator releasing all of his feelings for the other boy in the form of sonorous markings that reverberate through the boy's body and outward into the world. They are carried along on the wings of butterflies and decorated with flowers and spirals in various tints of pink or purple, adding further movement to the image. The boy holds a willow branch in one hand and a love letter in the other. This page stands out from the others because of the lack of text apart from within the artwork, in which the name of the boy's love interest is revealed: Andrés.

The book concludes with the protagonist serenading Andrés, each boy surrounded by a loving parent. Whereas Martínez's story shows being in love through song, Gonzalez's illustrations communicate this through markings on the body. From the very first page, the love between father and mother is depicted visually through symbols imprinted on their skin, as if their love was burrowed into or tattooed on their flesh for everyone to see in the form of a flower, or xochitl. These symbols also become activated by song. When serenading his wife, for example, they appear along the father's face, neck, and hands. One can also spot a flower imprint on the narrator's mom as she is awakened by the serenade. Similar symbols then surround the protagonist and Andrés, culminating in a flower design that bonds the two boys together as their hands converge on the final page (fig. 4.4).

The back of the picture book includes definitions for concepts such as "serenatas," or serenades, which Martínez describes as "a Mexican

Figure 4.4. Protagonist and Andrés joined at the hands; from *When We Love Someone We Sing to Them/Cuando amamos cantamos*. Published by Reflection Press. Copyright © 2018 by Ernesto Javier Martínez and Maya Gonzalez.

tradition of *singing to someone who you love*."[53] They are best performed "early in the morning or late at night because the goal of singing a serenata is to surprise the person you love. Imagine them sleeping peacefully in their bed and then, like a dream, they hear beautiful music as they slowly open their eyes."[54] The protagonist's father explains: "it's our way to hug with sounds."[55] Martínez first introduces serenatas in the form of love and affection among family members—between the protagonist, his father, and his mother. Recalling a Mother's Day memory, the boy and his father serenade his mother while she is still in bed. In another scene, the father promises, "when you start to feel the Xochipilli way, I will sing with you, it will be my honor, we will share what's in your heart someday."[56] Despite his personal upbringing with serenatas, Martínez has described how his queer sensibilities and consciousness eventually made him question their presumed heteronormativity: "Very quickly I started to feel a little bit alienated from it because there weren't songs for boys who loved boys."[57] He continued, "As a young gay boy, this brought me sadness and left me concerned that my feelings were not important to those around me. I grew up loving music, loving my community and family, but I was so sad about not being included that at one point, I stopped singing. Inside, I wanted a song—a healing, loving song all my own—and a community that I could trust would listen."[58] Creating a picture book on serenatas allowed Martínez to revisit and respond to these childhood traumas and feelings of alienation (similar to Jeremiah and, by extension, Johnson).

Martínez deliberately intertwines Mexican American/Chicanx, Mexican, and Mexican Indigenous traditions. "In my imagination," he explains, "Xochipilli, the Mesoamerican god of creativity and song, is flowing through you when you feel love and sing like this. Like a thousand flowers blooming, he is bringing joy to the one you love."[59] The extended definition on the last page adds: "Xochipilli is the Mesoamerican Nahua god of creativity, art, song, writing, and dance. His name is made up of two nahuatl words: xochitl ("flower") and pilli ("prince"/"child"). He was often depicted in a cross-legged and/or seated position with sacred, magical flowers covering his body. Flowers," explained Martinez, "carried very important ritual meanings for the Nahuas of Mesoamerica. Among other things, flowers represented love, fertility, growth, and enchantment and were sometimes associated with queer/two-sprit people in Nahua culture. The Nahua people still continue to inhabit Central Mexico to this day."[60] Xochipilli has also been linked to feasting, pleasure, beauty, and love.[61] Martínez's references to Xochipilli throughout the picture book suggest this figure's approval of love between boys, further queering Xochipillli in the reader's imagination.

The father's support within the book is central to his son's sense of self. Despite Martínez's own struggle with feeling that he was not fully seen at home, or more accurately *because* of this sense of isolation, he created an autofantastic world where fathers are supportive of their queer children. Father and son appear together on the cover and throughout much of the book. Readers will discover that the cover illustration is also included within the story, representing the day the boy tells his father he likes another boy. The two are joined by a butterfly perched atop a guitar. A symbol of migration and transformation, the butterfly's presence throughout also alludes to Latinx immigrant and queer identities. The back of the book explains: "Butterflies are called 'papalotl' by the Nahuatl-speaking people of Central Mexico (Nahuas).

Some contemporary queer Latino/a/xs call themselves the Spanish form, 'mariposa' as a powerful affirmation of femininity and as a way to pay respect to their own process of self-acceptance and transformation."[62] Having been transformed by his affection for another boy, the son summons his father for help:

> And so, one day, I asked Papi
> to help me sing my butterfly song,
>
>   my serenade—
> for a boy in town, for a boy bright brown,
> who smelled like fresh rain, wet earth, and lemonade.[63]

This stanza is visually spaced to emphasize—through line breaks and blank or white space—the boy's strong desire for his own song or serenade that he could dedicate to his sweetheart. He reiterates:

> This boy is special,
> I told Papi.
> He makes my heart hum, sing!
> At school
> I never eat lunch without him.
> At recess, we squeeze
> together on the swing.[64]

Martínez could have created a story where the father did not support his son's affection for another boy. Instead, the father's initial silence marks his contemplation, as he sighs and looks out the window. Redirecting readers from the father's initial uncertainty or hesitation, Martínez emphasizes the boy's cheerful response as he notices his father looking in the direction of the other boy's home, "near the tienda, by the willow!"[65]

The father's acceptance reverberates throughout the remainder of the book. He asks his son, "What song should we sing for your friend?"[66] Here, "your friend" stands in for "the boy you like." While the father may not yet have the words, he demonstrates unquestionable support through the language of song—his love language. This is visually depicted as the dad and son's bodies contort in midair to form the shape of a heart. Importantly, this is also the first time the flower imprint appears on the protagonist, on his right cheek. Now, like his father, the son also has markings on his skin symbolizing that he, too, is in love. The boy asks his father, "teach me a song for a boy who loves boys."[67] Not knowing any, his father responds lovingly, "Let's make a new song, a great song, for your butterfly-garden-love-joy."[68] Together, they create new language, or love terms, for boys who love boys.

Both boys have supportive parents. The protagonist's father, for example, sings by his side, whether that means practicing his son's new love song or singing next to his son when serenading Andrés. This physical gesture further amplifies the song through the father's own voice, while his physical body visually becomes a symbolic hug or shield around his son. Although this picture book is significant for its depiction of gay love between boys of color, the relationship between father and son is just as important. In fact, not only are these the only characters depicted on the cover, they are the only two characters who speak, resulting in a book that serves as an extended conversation between the two. The illustrations also depict Andrés's accompanying parent or caregiver appearing to be supportive of the exchange between the boys. They smile and wave alongside Andrés as he is serenaded.[69] Flowers, a butterfly, and the same love symbols that appeared on the narrator's parents emanate from the boy toward Andrés's window, joining the two boys together. Coming full circle, the final spread not only physically bonds the two boys but also depicts the father flying above them, his body contorted in the exact same manner as it was in the book's opening spread. While in the first spread he sang to his beloved wife, in this last one he sings for his son and his son's blossoming love for another boy.[70]

As Martínez's autofantasía, it should not surprise readers that, like the protagonist in his picture book, Martínez also sang alongside his father as a child. Martínez, a "queer Chicano-Rican educator and writer," grew up singing in a trio with his brother and father.[71] "Early on," he shared, "I learned that music held powerful magic for Latino immigrant families like mine," and through this he discovered "how music could communicate love, history and *sabiduria* [wisdom], while also providing comfort and reinforcing community in a foreign land."[72] Though the boy protagonist is not given a name, it would not be too farfetched to refer to him as Ernesto, even if Ernesto the protagonist and

Ernesto the author did not share the same queer childhood. Or rather, through autofantasía, Martínez is able to imagine a different coming-out narrative for his former child self, which includes a different response from loved ones. Within the picture book, the boy can serenade another boy without fear and amidst an abundance of joy. Martínez reflected, "What's significant about serenades for me is that someone is risking. . . . It's sometimes like humiliation because *te vas a aventar* [you're going to go for it], you know, you're going to sing to the person you love. And what I realized as a queer person, as a young person, is that what was missing for me was people witnessing . . . and appreciating and approving of my expression of love."[73] In contrast, the boy protagonist does not demonstrate this sense of alienation; his queer desire is witnessed and validated. Martínez continued, "We used to be hired to sing serenatas for other people. I just remember the shift in people's bodies, how they appreciated being serenaded. And then I just knew that profoundly was missing for me as a queer person. And so part of this is that kind of healing energy around something that's so culturally significant in Mexican culture."[74]

Since one of the major goals of the picture book is to speak directly to Latinx communities, *When We Love Someone We Sing to Them* was published as a bilingual book in English and Spanish. Martínez reiterated the importance of language, noting,

En dos idiomas. Es importantísimo porque en parte, fíjate que la historia cuando me nació, me nació así en el corazón, me nació en español. . . . Y en parte me nació porque yo tenía que sanar mi relación con mi papa que falleció en el 2013 de cáncer de páncreas.[75]

[In two languages. It is incredibly important because in part when I created this story, when I felt it in my heart, it first emerged in Spanish. . . . And it did so in part because I had to heal my relationship with my father who passed away in 2013 from pancreatic cancer.]

Thus, language, community, family, and healing intertwine throughout Martínez's autofantasía—especially as it pertains to his relationship with his father. Although the two were close, and Martínez felt loved, he needed to write the book to "sanar" [heal] part of his relationship with his dad. Writing this story became, for Martínez, "a new avenue to really kind of honor how [his] dad expressed love and to tell a new story for young people that wasn't that story, but that was a healing story."[76] In choosing to depict a serenade, Martínez pushed back against heteronormative assumptions about who can serenade whom. Contemplating the possibility of being the one who is serenaded, Martínez shared, "And part of it is the surprise. . . . Someone is sitting in their home or sleeping in their bed. And then they're hearing music and they're like: Is that? Is someone . . . OMG is that for me? And then you peek, you kind of comb your hair, then you peek outside . . . and you're like: 'They're singing to me.' . . . So that's a beautiful moment."[77] Indeed, Martínez captures this moment within the text, while Gonzalez beautifully illustrates Andrés's initial surprise.

This picture book also represents a deeper relationship between authors and illustrators, for the relationship between Martínez and Gonzalez goes beyond a traditional author/illustrator collaboration. Mainstream children's publishers generally accept a story first and then outsource the illustrations to an artist, rarely allowing for any communication between author and illustrator. Instead, *When We Love Someone We Sing to Them* grew out of a mentor–mentee relationship between the two, with Maya Gonzalez fulfilling not only the role of illustrator but also mentor, editor, collaborator, and friend. In 2016, Martínez secured funding for a "Queer Latinx Youth Storytelling Project," which included a six-week workshop with Gonzalez for members of AJAAS (Association for Jotería Arts, Activism, and Scholarship) interested in writing children's literature, noting that "the experience was nothing short of transformative."[78] Out of this queer Latinx space, Martínez created the Jotería Storytelling Project (JSP), which includes himself as well as Maya Gonzalez, Rigoberto González (author of *Antonio's Card*), and queer Chicana filmmaker Adelina Anthony. From these networks and collaborations, Martínez formed the Femeniños Project in 2018 to highlight his joint projects—picture book and short film (*La Serenata*). In Gonzalez's own words, "This book represents our mentorship journey. It is a strong-hearted book that passes on our queer beauty and fabulousness from the inside OUT while creating a new vision of the world. Our LGBTQI+ kids deserve to know our power and the world we want to create with them. We are the revolution."[79]

Martínez agreed, commenting, "working with Maya and writing this book, I learned that creating children's books can be a form of cultural medicine, both for the queer person of color revisiting their past and for the larger community eager to see themselves represented. The story I wrote for this book heals me and the boy that I was. And it is with gratitude that I offer it to my community."[80]

Wrapped in Martínez's gift to his community are the lyrics of "a song for a boy who loves a boy," reprinted at the end of the book. Titled "Jardín de Mariposas" [Butterfly Garden], the song was written by Héctor H. Pérez, a Grammy-nominated artist from the Bay Area and a family friend of Martínez.[81] Inspired by the musical genre's bold declarations of love, it has been said that "this is the first Mexican bolero to honor a queer boy's courage to express his love through song."[82] As Lawrence La Fountain-Stokes reminds us, "bolero is a music of seduction."[83] Even if the general public might assume heteronormative love or affection, the wider musical genre allows for greater queer possibilities or sensibilities. As bolero scholars have noted, the gender ambiguity of many songs can afford queer readings of them, depending on who is doing the singing and to whom they are singing.[84] The lyrics of "Jardín de Mariposas" detail the excitement and anticipation of becoming enamored with someone:

Buscando tu canción	[Searching for your song][85]
Encontré esta melodía	[I found this melody]
Pintada de arco íris	[Painted in rainbow]
Y llena de alegría	[And full of joy]
En tono enamorado	[In tones of love]
Con guitarra a mi lado	[With guitar by my side]
Yo te escribo miles versos	[I write you thousands of verses]
Eres el quien mas quiero	[You are the one I love most]
Mi lindo compañero[86]	[My sweet companion]

The song goes on to describe the visceral responses to liking someone, such as "Mis ojos se me llenan | Cuando tu me miras" [My eyes fill up | When you gaze at me] and "Mi piel se pinta rosa | Cada ve[z] que tu respires" [My skin turns pink | With each breath you take]. It also suggests writing verses and singing as an appropriate response to say "Te quiero" or "I love you." "Jardín de Mariposas" concludes by repeating once again:

> Eres el quien mas quiero   [You are the one I love most]
> Mi lindo compañero[87]   [My sweet companion]

In Spanish, the word for "companion," *compañero*, is gendered masculine, presenting the love interest as a boy. And although the narrator's gender is not revealed within the song itself, it is sung by a male vocalist and intended to be a song by and for boys. Moreover, Martínez affirmed that "all proceeds from the sale of the song will be donated to Somos Familia, a non-profit [organization] dedicated to queer Latinx youth and their families."[88]

Pérez created the song specifically for *La Serenata*, a 2018 short film adaptation of Martínez's picture book directed by Adelina Anthony, which is also listed alongside the song at the end of the picture book. Some of the biggest differences between the book and the film pertain to the father and the love interest. Whereas the mother plays more of a leading role in the short film compared to the book, the father's hesitation when he first registers that his son (Luis) likes another boy (whose name is changed from Andrés to Pichi) is more drawn out, creating moments of tension between the characters. Additionally, *La Serenata* ends just as the boy is about to begin his serenade, leaving the ending open to interpretation as to whether or not his feelings are reciprocated. *La Serenata* has received numerous accolades, including being featured on HBO as a winner of the Latinx Short Film Competition. Since the film's release, Martínez has gone on to develop a script for a feature-length film and has also participated in the 2020 Sesame Street Writers' Room Program.[89]

The impetus for writing *When We Love Someone We Sing to Them* is also apparent from the larger proposal that Martínez calls the Femeniños Project, which includes collaborators Martínez, Maya Gonzalez, Adelina Anthony, Hector Pérez, Jorge G. Martínez Feliciano, Omar Naim, and Pamela Chávez. Building on Gonzalez's articulation that writing books is a radical act, the Femeniños Project website offers the following statement: "Queer adults communicating with queer children is a radical act of intergenerational healing and transformation."[90] Martínez has also articulated the Femeniños Project's philosophy when responding to the question of what impact he hoped the book would have:

> We understand that children's books have a very interesting structural dimension to them. Children's books can offer adults the opportunity to reflect on their youth. And queer adults often, our youth, haven't always been the best. And so it gives us the opportunity to reflect on our own lives and then to write children's books that don't dumb down the world for children and don't re-harm them with our injures, our old injures, but that then pass on information and knowledge. . . . We really see this not just as entertainment, but as a political project to accompany our familias [families] as they grow in all these beautiful directions.[91]

Alongside *La Serenata*, Martínez's picture book has also received numerous accolades. It was featured on the American Library Association's 2019 "Rainbow list" of notable LGBTQ+ children's literature and has earned two International Latino Book Awards: Best Children's Picture Book (2019) and Best First Book for Children (2019).[92]

* * *

Both Martínez and Johnson provide queer boys of color who encounter their picture books with a glimpse into what their own childhoods might hold. The picture books also offer imaginative alternatives to the authors' actual childhoods. Whereas *Large Fears* hints at Black queerness through Jeremiah's longings for his own pink planet full of other Black boys like himself and through the encouraging words of his mother, the protagonist in *When We Love Someone We Sing to Them* exists in a world where boys can like boys and boys can proclaim their love for one another without ridicule and alongside loving and supportive parents. Might we imagine a world that begins with a text's seedling (initial idea) and creation (picture book), that then expands to include its distribution, engagement from readers, and relationship to similar books? Through their characters, both authors (and their respective illustrators) engage in queer of color worldmaking—not in the more traditional, literary sense (e.g., the world confined within the pages of a single book or series of books), but in the more expansive sense that also accounts for the ways said characters and books impact authors/ illustrators and readers.

Large Fears and *When We Love Someone We Sing to Them*, alongside the other picture books included throughout *Coloring into Existence*, collectively engage in a kind of worldmaking or worldbuilding that has the potential to modify our actual lived experience within our current, literal world. More precisely, these books aim to shatter our existing assumptions about the current world by presenting two "possible worlds" where boys of color can love and be loved by other boys of color.[93] In providing alternative worlds or realities, this emerging queer of color literary field also provides a blueprint for enacting social change and transformation. As I will show in the following chapter, reading practices can be just as transformative and necessary in the act of worldmaking.

5

Autofantastic (Mis)Readings

Rendering Colors beyond the Rainbow

Collecting texts makes selves and worlds.
—Natasha Hurley

When queers read . . . they do so as a form of survival just as
much as a way to gain pleasure, develop knowledge and skill,
and make a mark on the world.
—Ramzi Fawaz and Shanté Paradigm Smalls

In an interview with Marcela Arévalo Contreras, I confessed my initial misreading of the protagonist featured in her 2013 children's picture
book *De los gustos y otras cosas* [Of one's likes and whatnot].[1] To my surprise, this was a story narrated by a little boy, and not a little girl as I had
presumed. How had I misgendered the protagonist? More importantly,
how does the child's gender—as intended by the author or as read by the
audience—situate the book as either heteronormative or queer (in terms
of the child's sexuality) or as gendernormative or gender nonconforming
(with respect to the child's gender)? In prior chapters, I outlined autofantasía as a literary, artistic, and publishing technique incorporated by
authors, illustrators, and publishers. This chapter shifts the perspective
from those creating children's picture books to those reading or being
read to. In this regard, autofantasía can function as a reading practice,
occurring either by (1) projecting oneself onto the story, or (2) projecting the creators (e.g., author, illustrator, or publisher) onto the story.

This chapter invites us to reconsider *how* we read. Paula M. L. Moya
tells us that, "insofar as literature is a system of formalized mechanisms
enabling social communication via culturally-specific forms of aesthetic
expression, the meaning of any given work of literature is only fully realized in the particular interaction(s) between a text and its readers."[2]

Meanwhile, José Esteban Muñoz suggests that "to access queer visuality we may need to squint, to strain our vision and force it to see otherwise, beyond the limited vista of the here and now."[3] To be clear, an autofantastic reading practice is an inherently political reading practice—one which, in the words of Cathy J. Cohen, is "guided by [a] type of radical intersectional Left analysis."[4] Autofantastic reading requires active reading strategies meant to topple power dynamics. Beginning with Marcela Arévalo Contreras's *De los gustos y otras cosas* (Mexico), followed by picture books from Gloria Anzaldúa (United States), Jacqueline Woodson (United States), and Syrus Marcus Ware (Canada), I use this chapter to map and model an autofantastic reading practice for each. Whereas one might read queerness and queer of color politics or aesthetics across all four, Ware also beckons us to autofantasize through trans and disability justice. Whether accidental or intentional, "misreadings" or autofantastic readings provide provocative engagement with children's literature that might otherwise fall outside of a queer and trans of color archive, survey, or canon.

Anomalous Queerness: Normativity or Oxymoron in *De los gustos y otras cosas*

Ambiguous titles and abstract covers can lead readers to be pleasantly surprised by a story's unfolding. I stumbled upon *De los gustos y otras cosas* while perusing the children's literature section of an LGBTQ+ bookstore, Voces en Tinta, in Mexico City.[5] Its cover featured crisp title lettering and water-colored fish against a white backdrop. Most of the fish are colored in shades of greens, blues, and browns, swimming toward the bottom-left corner. In contrast, a lonesome bright-red fish swims in the opposite direction, away from the school, toward the top-right corner, persuading readers to turn the page. Both its color and the direction in which it swims visually mark it as "different," "unique," or "queer," going against the norm, even if that means doing so alone. Communicating a similar theme, the title and dedication pages also each depict lonesome creatures. The title page includes the silhouette of a small animal, perhaps a squirrel, atop an abstract figure resembling a playground climbing dome, looking in the direction of what appear to be three tiny blue clouds. On the dedication page, a tall bird resembling a heron or wild turkey stands at the center, surrounded by abstract rocks and grass.

Without any additional cues about the book's content, readers are met with a full-page prologue written by Ana Francis Mor on the adjacent page. "Esta es la historia de un gato con los ojos al revés" [This is the story of a cat with backward eyes], begins Francis Mor, promising a picture book of "un mundo al revés," or an upside-down world. Francis Mor proceeds to critique what she calls dominant narrative "absurdities," stating, "the story you and I have been told is poorly constructed: I was told that boys were a certain way and girls were another; that white people were a certain way and Indigenous peoples were another; and in this manner, a whole bunch of absurdities."[6] Perpetuated by heteropatriarchy and colonialism, such absurdities continue to ostracize marginalized voices within children's literature. Speaking in the second person, Francis Mor asks readers, "And you, what have you been told?"[7] Coaxed to suggest additional dominant narratives, the reader or listener might identify those perpetuating heteronormativity, queerphobia, transphobia, ableism, classism, and so on. As Francis Mor notes, combating such literary absurdities requires counternarratives: "Being able to write better stories now is very important and I like that this book is an example of how to tell them. . . . A world without these stories is an incomplete world. . . . *Here begins the story of an editorial press that talks about an upside-down world*" (emphasis added).[8] Francis Mor is referring to the book's publisher, Ediciones Chulas, established in 2013 by the Mexican feminist collective Las Reinas Chulas.

Known primarily for their cabaret and theater, Las Reinas Chulas was founded in 1998 by Ana Francis Mor and three others (Cecilia Sotres, Marisol Gasé, and Nora Huerta).[9] They embarked on a new trajectory into publishing based on a desire to "offer texts that function as tools to raise awareness, bring joy, and lead to reflections on humor and pleasure, with critical attention toward reality and dominant discourses, but above all, fully committed to human rights."[10] In 2013, they published their first two books, Arévalo Contreras's *De los gustos y otras cosas* and Francis Mor's *Manual de la buena lesbiana, 2* [The good lesbian's manual, part 2]. The first debuted at a *presentación de libro*, or official book release event, on November 19, 2013, at Teatro Bar El Vicio in Mexico City, and it featured both authors (Arévalo Contreras and Francis Mor).[11] Emphasizing radical feminist politics, Ediciones Chulas positions itself as "Las 'A' que le faltan a la literatura. Por otrAs narrativAs contemporAneas" [The "A" missing from literature. For or in favor of other contemporary narratives].[12] In the Spanish original, the capital "A" is used to counter the gender-normative and masculine use of "o" by emphasizing a feminine/feminist "A" instead. Self-proclaimed radical feminists, their call for transgressive narratives positioned the press as a type of literary corrective that would promote counternarratives.

With such a politically profound stance on behalf of the editorial press—echoed within the Prologue—I was not at all surprised that, like me, Francis Mor was also convinced that the protagonist in *De los gustos y otras cosas* was a little girl rather than a little boy. Her rave review would not have positioned it as "un mundo al revéz" [an upside-down world] had she thought otherwise. As with all my interviews associated with this picture book, I confessed my initial misgendering to Francis Mor only to have her affirm that up until that very moment, she had herself assumed similarly: "Pues, yo siempre entendí que era una niña platicando con su mamá" [Well, I always understood it as a little girl speaking with her mother].[13] When I asked how she might respond to the author's proclamation that the protagonist is a boy instead of a girl, she shared:

A veces cuando escribimos queremos decir unas cosas y decimos otras. Yo me quedo con lo que yo leí, ¿me explico? Porque a partir de que abro el libro, el libro es mío, y la historia es mía, y me parece también que no necesariamente es importante. A la mejor yo me cedo con que el personaje es niña porque yo deseo que sea niña, porque yo deseó que sea una niña diciendo que le gusta [otra] niña.[14]

[Sometimes when we write we want to say one thing but say another. I will stick with what I read, does that make sense? Because from the moment I open the book, the book is mine, and the story is mine, and I think that it is not necessarily important. Perhaps I believe the character is a girl because I wish she was a girl, because I wish she was a girl stating that she likes another girl.]

Paging through the book, I pointed out whom I thought was the pro-tagonist and whom I thought was the mother. Francis Mor concurred, adding, "Para mí siempre fue una niña. . . . Que cada quien se acomode el saco. Eso me parece bueno" [She was always a girl to me. . . . To each their own. That seems good to me].[15] As with my own, Francis Mor's autofantastic reading generated a queer character proudly transgressing gender norms and proclaiming her desire for another girl. This mis-reading is more than simply a queer reading; this literary "slippage" or autofantastic reading was made possible thanks to the picture book's uniquely abstract illustrations.

De los gustos y otras cosas marks the second collaboration between author and illustrator. Ilyana Martínez Crowther also illustrated Arévalo Contreras's first book, *Los abuelos son de Marte* [The grandparents are from Mars] (2008). The two were childhood friends who have known one another for over thirty years.[16] Martínez Crowther, who now lives in Canada, spends her time between the two countries and is primar-ily known as a graphic designer and visual artist. Within *De los gus-tos y otras cosas*, her characters appear to be rough cutouts from black construction paper, giving the illusion of black silhouettes with jagged edges. White colored pencil or chalk is used sporadically to highlight certain features such as a character's eyes, nose, mouth, or hair, creating the overall effect of childnormative doodles on a classroom chalkboard. These characters are surrounded by abstract figures or shapes that only loosely correspond with the text and appear to be watercolors or pen sketches, although some objects also appear as black cutouts. Like the cover, each page defaults to a white backdrop. Although minimalist at times, each figure—no matter how small—stands out against the white-ness of the page.

De los gustos y otras cosas is written in verse, monolingually in Span-ish, as a dialogue between a child and their mother. The book opens with the text: "It turns out that the other day I was talking to mom about that girl who is always on my mind."[17] These lines span three pages and introduce the two characters that reappear throughout the remainder of the book (fig. 5.1a). The conundrum, however, is deciding who these characters are in relation to the dialogue and written text. One figure is a floating oval head with short curly hair, while the other is slightly smaller in scale, wearing a dress, with longer hair parted across the

Lo importante es respetar el querer de los demás"

y hasta ponerte corbata"

Figure 5.1. (a) Characters as floating heads, and (b) tie hanging on a clothesline; from *De los gustos y otras cosas* [Of one's likes and whatnot]. Published by Ediciones Chulas. Copyright © 2013 by Marcela Arévalo Contreras and Ilyana Martínez Crowther.

middle into two pigtails. At times, abstract shapes and colors surround the characters, approximating what could be interpreted as thought bubbles hovering over both figures.[18] The following four pages expand on the crush: "it's just that, seriously, she has eyelashes that reach the moon and when she looks at me I feel a taste like that of prickly pear fruit."[19] This imagery emphasizes the crush's physical appearance (long eyelashes) and the observer's visceral response. Whereas others might say someone is causing them to feel butterflies in their stomach, here we are told that the protagonist feels *like* sweetness. On its own, the text presents poetic details about a child's crush on a little girl.

Despite the lack of pronouns attributed to the protagonist, *De los gustos y otras cosas* includes a lot of gender-relevant content. For example, when the child and mother discuss other things that each of them likes and dislikes, the child's list includes "dragons and monsters, which by the way, do not scare [them]."[20] The mother validates the child's interests, which she summarizes as including the little girl from school, cars, pirates, bugs, and wearing ties. Although the mother affirms that "cada quién tiene sus gustos" [everyone has their own likes or preferences], the child's likes might be gendered as stereotypically masculine. If the protagonist is read as a girl, liking another girl indicates queer desire among children, whereas liking cars, pirates, bugs, and ties might suggest a tomboy or butch masculinity. If the protagonist is read as a boy, however, their likes are instead stereotypically hetero- and gender-normative. And, of course, these need not be the only options.

Part of the visual ambiguity results from the fact that most of the pages illustrate objects or items, rather than the characters themselves. For example, instead of depicting a child wearing a tie, there is an illustration of a tie hanging on a clothesline, leaving the reader to decipher who is speaking (fig. 5.1b). Given that the book is a dialogue between a child and a mother, one could reasonably assume that one of the two figures is the child (girl with pigtails), and the other is the mother (larger talking head with shorter hair). Alternatively, if we accept the author's original intention, the male protagonist is on the right in fig. 5.1a and the girl he likes is on the left, even though she never speaks within the text. This, however, would also mean that the mother is never depicted. Thus, we would have an invisible mother and a love interest who is visible but unable to voice her thoughts or desires. Both mother and girl are only evident through the boy, who speaks and is visible. Indeed, like his heteronormative desire for a girl, his likes and dislikes, and his position as the protagonist who is both seen and heard also replicate gender stereotypes—not at all in line with a feminist upside-down world.

Only on the last two pages is *De los gustos y otras cosas* overtly queer. The protagonist candidly notes that while they like girls and their mother likes coffee, their aunt likes another woman named Maité. The two women lean into one another, smiling, as they emanate colorful multi-sized hearts. Like the other characters, they are drawn in white chalk over black paper that appears to be cut out and placed over a white background. Aesthetically, the two women are gendered as stereotypically femme by their shoulder-length hair, even though the aunt was inspired by the author's own lesbian sister (Cristina), whose own hair is much shorter. While this last spread might be enough to label this picture book as queer in content, it would not be enough to consider it the "upside-down world" Francis Mor so highly affirmed in the book's prologue.

Francis Mor and I were not alone in "misgendering" the protagonist through our autofantastic reading. On November 14, 2018, Arévalo Contreras shared an anecdote on social media based on a book talk. Although her picture book is geared toward younger children, this presentation was given to middle school youth. Afterward, a young girl approached her: "Thank you for writing this book. I do not like girl's shoes nor dresses, but my grandmother says that if I do not wear them, she is going to take me out of school because she doesn't want a lesbian granddaughter."[21] The young girl proceeded to hug the author and then bursts into tears. Arévalo Contreras reassured her, "No one has a right to tell you how you should be. Don't ever forget this."[22] She gifted her a copy of the picture book in hopes that the grandmother might read it and have a change of heart. It may have been that the young girl was responding to the lesbian couple on the last page; however, based on what she shared, she may have also identified with the protagonist—whom she may have read as a girl who does not like what are stereotypically gendered as girl shoes or dresses.

Other readers also assumed the protagonist was queer or emphasized that their gender could be open to interpretation. For example, a social media post recommending *De los gustos y otras cosas* read: "A little girl speaks with her mother about another little girl who is always on her mind. Beautiful for little ones."[23] Similarly, in an opinion article published in the mainstream newspaper *La Jornada Aguascalientes*, Raquel Castro described how the picture book "nos cuenta de una niña enamorada de otra niña" [tells the story of a little girl in love with another little girl].[24] Meanwhile, Adolfo Cordova's review described the picture book as

> Un poema que habla de un personaje (quizá un niño según la ilustradora) al que le gusta una niña . . . [También] es posible interpretar que el protagonista sea niña y le guste otra niña, igual que su tía.[25]

> [A poem that speaks of a character (perhaps a little boy according to the illustrator) who likes a little girl . . . It is [also] possible to interpret the protagonist as a girl who likes another girl, just like her aunt.]

Although it is unclear how Cordova obtained the illustrator's perspective, if he is correct, she may have not intended to be ambiguous about the protagonist's gender. Regardless of her intentions, however, her abstract illustrations did just that. Author Arévalo Contreras, meanwhile, revealed that she modeled the protagonist after her own son, just like the aunt is modeled after her own sister.

I also want to highlight that while the author and her family are light-skinned, the figures in the book are solid black silhouettes. Just as the protagonist has been commonly misgendered, these characters could also be read as racially Black, regardless of the author's or illustrator's intentions. What is fascinating, if also not surprising, is the absence of race or ethnicity from reviews of *De los gustos y otras cosas*. Compounded with Mexico's history of Black erasure, this suggests that most readers likely see these as silhouettes of light-skinned characters. As with gender and sexuality, an autofantastic reading could also mean approaching these characters as Black or Afro-Mexican.

Ultimately, these issues of race, gender, and sexuality raise a question: if the author says it is so, is it? What if the author envisions their story one way and the illustrator interprets it another? Or, regardless of what either one says or intended, what if the reader understands something else entirely? This picture book demonstrates that an author's intentions can drastically contradict a reader's interpretation. Like myself, readers "misgendered" or chose to read the protagonist's gender as that of a little girl and, in doing so, privileged their own autofantastic reading of this picture book. Similar to interpreting creative expressions such as works of art, children's picture books are also worthy of such complexity, yielding an array of nuanced and often contradictory interpretations. *De los gustos y otras cosas*' more abstract illustrations, along with the text's own omission of the protagonist's gender, lend themselves to complex autofantastic interpretations and associations by readers. Like Francis Mor and so many others, I too wished for or fantasized about a particular narrative and therefore saw and read a queer story between two little girls of color.[26]

Let the Child Alter Ego Speak: Gloria Anzaldúa's Prietita

Gloria Anzaldúa, whose concept of autohistoria I mentioned in the introductory chapter to *Coloring into Existence*, wrote extensively throughout and about her life. Best known for her essays and poetry, she also published two children's picture books sharing the same protagonist named Prietita, a Mexican American girl, or Chicanita. In her first, *Friends from the Other Side/Amigos del otro lado* (1993), Prietita befriends Joaquín, an undocumented boy from Mexico. Throughout the book, Prietita comes to his aid by defending him against bullies, hiding him from border patrol agents, and helping to heal the boils on his arms. Prietita reappears in Anzaldúa's second picture book, *Prietita and the Ghost Woman/Prietita y la Llorona* (1995). This time, her mother is ill and in need of an herb (rue) located beyond a fence she is forbidden to cross. Guided by la Llorona, she eventually finds the rue. In both picture books, Anzaldúa inserts her child alter ego, manifested in the form of Prietita, as a witness to injustices and an active participant in challenging the status quo.[27] Both picture books were published by Children's Book Press and share not only characters (Prietita, Doña Lola, Teté) but major themes. Although border crossing and feminist inferences figure prominently in both, an autofantastic reading also allows us to consider Prietita's embodiment of queerness.

Anzaldúa's association with the nicknames Prietita or Prieta first appeared in writings published prior to her picture books. In September

1979, Anzaldúa began drafting an essay or *autohistoria*, "La Prieta," which she published in 1981 as part of *This Bridge Called My Back*.²⁸ Deemed la Prieta, the dark one, or la Prietita, the little dark one, Anzaldúa struggled throughout her life with multiple complex identities and politics. However, once a contested label, la Prieta metamorphosed into Anzaldúa's own alter ego and reemerged throughout her works, including in an unpublished novel or collection of stories also titled "La Prieta," and as the protagonist in her published stories for children.²⁹ She spoke openly about her desire to write children's books to present alternative narratives from those of white authors or characters. Recalling her youth, she explained, "When I went to school all we had were white books about white characters like Tom, Dick, and Jane, never a dark kid, una Prieta. That's why I write for children, so they can have models. They see themselves in these books and it makes them feel good!"³⁰ In addition to questions of representation, Anzaldúa's picture books deal with serious topics, challenging readers to reexamine preconceived notions of childhood and childnormative experiences.

Both *Friends from the Other Side* and *Prietita and the Ghost Woman* emphasize border crossings, with the first highlighting the US–Mexico border, whereas the second asks us to consider the lines between private property and public property, or the privatization of natural resources. Within *Friends from the Other Side*, Anzaldúa creates a literary world where child's play is routinely interrupted by a culture of fear and intimidation because of citizenship status. As a result of one border, in this case the US–Mexico border, more borders are made between, for example, citizens and non-citizens. Anzaldúa begins *Friends from the Other Side* with a note from the author, describing how she grew up in South Texas near the Rio Grande, where, she says, "many women and children . . . had crossed to this side." The initial pages of *Friends from the Other Side* create a stark contrast between Prietita and Joaquín, and between child's play or leisure and child's work. While Prietita enjoys the summer playing outdoors, perched on a mesquite tree and freely observing everything around her from the comfort of her own backyard, Joaquín works outdoors, walking from house to house selling bundles of firewood he carries on his back. This initial page correlates Joaquín's need to work with his position as a border-crosser. Prietita inquires, "Did you come from the other side? You know, from Mexico?" Joaquín is also linguistically marked as an outsider because, as Prietita keenly observes, "his Spanish was different from hers." As their friendship develops, Prietita is privy to Joaquín's reality as an undocumented boy. On a visit to his home, Anzaldúa tells us that Joaquín and his mother lived in a "tumbledown shack with one wall missing. In place of the wall was a water-streaked tarp." The front door appears to be made of similar material. These tarps hang loosely, secured only at the top, leaving the space fully exposed to hazardous weather or potential intruders—also evoking the vulnerable status mother and son share because they are undocumented.

Most of the action in *Friends from the Other Side* centers on two distinct incidents in which Prietita intervenes on Joaquín's behalf. Both are tied to his status as undocumented. The first example is a jarring depiction of bullying rooted in xenophobia. A group of boys confront Joaquín as he leaves Prietita's home: "Look at the *mojadito*, look at the wetback!" calls out Prietita's cousin, Teté. A second boy remarks, "Hey, man, why don't you go back where you belong? We don't want any more *mojados* here." Even the diminutive form of *mojado* used by the first boy does little to mask this direct form of harassment and hostility from similarly racialized subjects. They, like Joaquín, have similar hair and skin tones, resembling one another to such an extent that Joaquín could easily be their cousin or sibling. Instead, Joaquín is targeted because of his citizenship status. The text is paired with equally jarring illustrations. Three boys stand with their backs to the reader. One of the boys (possibly Prietita's cousin) points a finger at Joaquín, who looks almost minuscule in comparison to the boys. This confrontation seems to draw the attention of the surrounding dogs and cats, which can be seen on the edges of the page, observing. Meanwhile, Prietita refuses to remain a casual observer, choosing to confront her cousin and his friends on the following spread: "What's the matter with you guys? How brave you are, a bunch of *machos* against one small boy. You should be ashamed of yourselves!" Her cousin responds, "What's it to you? Who asked you to butt in, Prietita?" Eventually the boys decide Joaquín is not worth the trouble and leave. The illustrations depict Teté (or one of his friends) twice on this spread: on the left page, facing Prietita and Joaquin with a rock in one of his hands, and on the right page, with the word "Bully" written across the front of his green shirt and fists closed as he walks away (fig. 5.2).

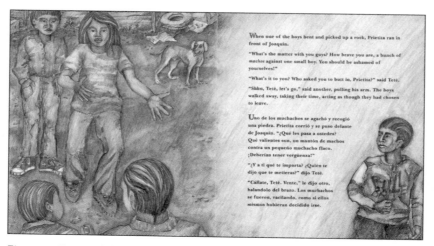

When one of the boys bent and picked up a rock, Prietita ran in front of Joaquín.

"What's the matter with you guys? How brave you are, a bunch of *machos* against one small boy. You should be ashamed of yourselves!"

"What's it to you? Who asked you to butt in, Prietita?" said Teté.

"Shhh, Teté, let's go," said another, pulling his arm. The boys walked away, taking their time, acting as though they had chosen to leave.

Uno de los muchachos se agachó y recogió una piedra. Prietita corrió y se puso delante de Joaquín. "¿Qué les pasa a ustedes? Qué valientes son, un montón de machos contra un pequeño muchacho flaco. ¡Deberían tener vergüenza!"

"¿Y a tí qué te importa? ¿Quién te dijo que te metieras?" dijo Teté.

"Cállate, Teté. Vente," le dijo otro, halandolo del brazo. Los muchachos se fueron, vacilando, como si ellos mismos hubieran decidido irse.

Figure 5.2. Prietita defending Joaquín; from *Friends from the Other Side/Amigos del otro lado*. Published by Children's Book Press. Copyright © 1993 by Gloria Anzaldúa and Consuelo Méndez.

This bullying scene foreshadows an immigration raid by border patrol agents that is depicted toward the end of the book. Once again, child's play is interrupted—this time by the state. While playing lotería, Joaquín and Prietita suddenly hear a neighbor's cries, "[¡]La migra!" [The Border Patrol!]. The sense of urgency in the woman's voice is echoed by Joaquín's reaction to the news as he "jumped out of his seat," concerned for his mother. Once mother and son are reunited, Prietita guides them to la curandera's house. As they hide, Prietita and la curandera ("the herb woman" or healer) watch "from behind the curtains" while "the Border Patrol van cruise[d] slowly up the street. It stopped in front of every house."

Here, too, Anzaldúa takes this opportunity to further complicate the us-versus-them paradigm. "While the white patrolman stayed in the van," we learn that "the Chicano *migra* got out and asked, 'Does anyone know of any illegals living in this area?'" Like the bullying incident, this event emphasizes tensions within Chicanx or Latinx communities, while also challenging how Border Patrol agents are imagined by interrogating the role that communities of color play in relation to state institutions like Immigration and Customs Enforcement (ICE) under the US Department of Homeland Security.[31] The tension caused by the presence of these agents is mitigated by the witty response from another neighbor: "They heard a woman say, 'Yes, I saw some over there,' pointing to the *gringo* side of town—the white side. Everyone laughed, even the Chicano *migra*." Although this is meant to provide comic relief, the woman's response is not entirely unfounded, given that undocumented immigrants are often employed as domestic workers or day laborers. Once the Border Patrol agents drive off, Joaquín and his mother resurface. Edith M. Vásquez reads this incident as exemplary of childhood *travesuras*, or antics, observing: "Prietita and Joaquín perform heroically, humanely. Yet they disobey legal, political, and social strictures. En este sentido, son niños traviesos" [In this regard, they are naughty children].[32] These acts of illegality might also be considered in relation to ongoing immigration debates. Revealing her deep convictions, Anzaldúa observed in an interview with Linda Smuckler that "children are these little people with no rights."[33] Moreso, undocumented children pose a unique and considerable challenge to children's rights discourses in the United States because they have even fewer protections.[34]

Border crossing in *Prietita and the Ghost Women* does not directly involve the US–Mexico border or questions of citizenship status like it does in Anzaldúa's first children's picture book. Instead, Prietita becomes a border crosser when she crosses a property line without being authorized to do so. The book begins at the site where *Friends from the Other Side* ends—the curandera's garden. Prietita tends the garden while the older woman hangs laundry to dry. They are interrupted by Prietita's younger sister Miranda, who runs toward them, frightened. Their mother has become ill with "the old sickness again" and needs the curandera's healing powers.

The character known as la curandera, or the healer, appears in both picture books, although she is referred to differently. In *Friends from the Other Side*, readers know her as "the herb woman" with "healing powers" in English and as "la curandera" in the Spanish text. In contrast, she is referred to as "la curandera" in both the English and Spanish text within *Prietita and the Ghost Woman*; she is also given a name, Doña Lola. For la curandera to heal Prietita's mother, she needs ruda, or "leaves from the rue plant," to complete the proper remedy. Prietita "watched closely as *la curandera* sketched the rue" plant for her. There is only one problem: where to find it. Doña Lola cautions Prietita, "Well, I know there is some in the woods of the King Ranch. . . . But it is dangerous to go in there. I've heard that they shoot trespassers. . . . It is not safe for a little girl." Even though Doña Lola verbalizes this, she cannot possibly believe it is an altogether impossible task for Prietita, since she is the one who drew the rue plant for her and directed her to King Ranch, although she does not outright tell her to go, instead leaving that up to Prietita. Initially, Prietita walks alongside the barbwire fence surrounding King Ranch. Having no luck in spotting rue, and "making sure that nobody was watching, she squeezed under the barbwire and entered the King Ranch." On one level, Prietita's border-crossing experience serves as an allegory for those who cross national borders in search of a better life, but we might also consider her border crossing to be an act of reappropriation or reclaiming; she is taking back what the King Ranch owner deemed their own: the land and everything on it, including the flora and fauna.

Most of the picture book consists of Prietita wandering through the woods within King Ranch on her quest to find the rue plant. In the process, she gets lost, asking various creatures for help along the way. First, she spots a white-tailed deer drinking water by a lagoon. In response to Prietita's plea for help in locating the rue plant, she thinks "she heard her say, 'Follow me,' so she started after her" until the deer "was out of sight." In a similar fashion, Prietita meets and then follows several other animals, including a red salamander, a white-wing dove, lightning bugs, and, most surprisingly, a jaguarundi, "like the pictures she had seen of the jaguars in ancient Mexico." Intermixed among her encounters with these creatures, she hears a faint crying or wailing, which she eventually discovers belongs to la Llorona. Overcoming her fear, Prietita asks her for help. Obliging Prietita's request, "the ghost woman floated along the edge of the lagoon and Prietita followed her. Soon the woman stopped and pointed to a spot on the ground." A rue plant glistened under the moonlight. After picking some of its branches, Prietita follows la Llorona once again, this time as she guides her out of the woods and toward the barbwire fence before disappearing.

The book concludes with Prietita spotting a search party comprised of concerned neighbors who had gone searching for her. Doña Lola is among them and is not at all surprised when Prietita tells them of la Llorona. Insinuating she may know more, she shares, "Perhaps she is not what others think she is." As other scholars have mentioned, Anzaldúa provides readers with a Chicana feminist revisionist narrative of la Llorona.[35] In *Light in the Dark/Luz en lo oscuro* (2015), Anzaldúa reflects: "Fantasy is not just a coping with reality, a correction of reality, or a supplement to reality. A dream/fantasy frees you from the confines of daily time and space, from your habitual identity."[36] Here, la Llorona, too, can escape her patriarchal origin story. In this reimagining, she is no longer a myth, nor an "evil" woman who murdered her children; instead, la Llorona serves as Prietita's guide and companion—an almost angelic or spiritual protector. "My symbol for la herida de [the wound of] colonialism and the trauma of the conquest is la Llorona," Anzaldúa shared in interviews, in part because she is constantly wailing, a symbol of historical trauma.[37] In *Prietita and the Ghost Woman*, her wailing becomes a beacon of hope, reuniting Prietita and la curandera with medicinal plants and ancestral healing practices.

An autofantastic reading allows us to also read Prietita (and other characters) as queer. Drawing from Anzaldúa's own life, Prietita represents more than a rebellious girl engaging in "childish travesuras or antics"; she is a queer child coming to terms with her queerness.[38] In *Borderlands/La Frontera*, Anzaldúa writes, "Being lesbian and raised Catholic, indoctrinated as straight, *I made the choice to be queer*."[39] Here, queer functions as a political marker, something one chooses. And yet, like *Borderlands*, the original essay "La Prieta" has been ignored or overlooked as queer scholarship, despite Anzaldúa's explicit engagement with queer thematics. Anzaldúa concludes "La Prieta" with the following: "We are the queer groups, the people that don't belong anywhere, not in the dominant world nor completely within our own respective cultures. Combined we cover so many oppressions. But the overwhelming oppression is the collective fact that we do not fit, and because we do not fit *we are a threat*."[40] Similarly, picture books that "cover so many oppressions" are seen as a threat.

Friends from the Other Side and *Prietita and the Ghost Woman* are not usually included in LGBTQ-themed children's literature bibliographies. Indeed, one could easily dismiss each for their lack of overt queer content. However, in other writings and interviews, Anzaldúa herself tells readers to read critically and between the lines. For example, in her essay "To(o) Queer the Writer," she reminds us that, "I don't always spell things out. I want the reader to deduce my conclusions or at least come up with her own."[41] While we can certainly read Prietita as a tomboy, we can also autofantasize Anzaldúa's queerness onto Prietita. If, as readers, we challenge assumed heteronormativity as a child's default sexuality, Joaquín, too, may register as queer, as can any of the other characters within either picture book. For example, Joaquín is targeted because of both his immigration status and his presumably effeminate demeanor.[42]

Potential censorship limitations likely prevented Anzaldúa from publishing her picture books as explicitly queer texts. Anzaldúa was mindful of the publishing industry for children's literature, explaining: "I have to struggle against the standards and marketing strategies in children's book publishing."[43] She elaborated on this in a 1996 interview with Andrea Lunsford. Commenting on bilingual children's books, Anzaldúa described her dilemma: "How much can I get through the censors in the state of Texas in any particular children's book? Texas has more stringent censorship rules than the other states, and most publishers can only do one book for all the states. So the publishers tend to be conservative because they want to get these books into the schools. How much can I get away with pushing at the norms, at the conventions?"[44] This palpable threat of potential censorship is also likely why there is no reference to Anzaldúa's sexuality in her biography at the end of either picture book. Unless one is already familiar with her, it would be easy to miss her contributions to queer theory and queer Chicana scholarship by solely reading her picture books. However, research into Anzaldúa's life and additional publications can reveal her counternormativity.

Anzaldúa's picture books are political commentaries. As she tells us in *Light in the Dark*, published posthumously, "The artist uses the imagination to impose order on chaos; she gives psychic confession form and direction, provides language to distressed and confused people."[45] As autofantasías, *Friends from the Other Side* and *Prietita and the Ghost Woman* present us with a younger version of Anzaldúa the author, who was constantly rewriting and reimaging herself in her writings. "The paradox in reading, making art, and making self is that the artist must simultaneously remember and forget self and world," Anzaldua theorized; "Creation is really a rereading and rewriting of reality—a rearrangement or reordering of preexisting elements."[46]

Anzaldúa, like other foundational feminist and queer of color authors (e.g., Cathy Cohen, Audre Lorde, Merlo Woo, Beth Brant, and Barbara Smith, among others), knew what was at stake if their political framework did not also include an intersectional analysis of power.[47] Since her early publications, Anzaldúa engaged in queer of color critique even if her works are not always accepted as foundational to the modern queer canon. It is not surprising, then, that her children's picture books have also been dismissed by queer audiences or those seeking queer children's literature. That, coupled with the limitations imposed on her by children's publishing during the 1990s, require us to, instead, use an autofantastic reading strategy to illuminate the queerness in Anzaldúa's picture books. This allows those of us most familiar with her writings to reach for *Friends from the Other Side* and *Prietita and the Ghost Woman* precisely because we can recognize her and her political discourse within Prietita.[48] While Anzaldúa intentionally and overtly inserts herself within her children's literature, others such as Jacqueline Woodson leave snippets or breadcrumbs of themselves for us to follow and rearrange.

Piecing Together Queer of Color Critique in Jacqueline Woodson's Picture Books

At only three years old, Woodson learned to write her full name: Jacqueline Amanda Woodson. Her imaginative storytelling as a child was often met with opposition from adults who could only understand her stories as lies. Despite her writing and storytelling abilities, however, reading did not come so easily. She often read slowly and reread the picture books that she already knew instead of choosing new ones. Now an adult, Woodson takes great pride in reading slowly, which she shared in a 2019 TED talk titled "What Reading Slowly Taught Me about Writing."[49] There are several narratives a writer tells and retells about themselves, whether in biographies, memoirs, interviews, or on a website's Frequently Asked Questions page. Writing at age three and reading slowly are two of Woodson's, but others include literary influences like Virginia Hamilton, Toni Morrison, and James Baldwin. Hamilton's *Zeely* was especially impactful, having been "one of the first books [she] read that was by an African American about African American people."[50]

Woodson's vivid imagination and ability to dream up fantasies proved ideal for her career as a writer. Once her storytelling became recognizable as fiction, others realized her craft. Such was the case with Woodson's sister Odella, who overheard her singing a song she had made up. She refused to believe Woodson created the piece since it was "too good."[51] Pleased with her sister's unintended compliment, Woodson simply looked away smiling. Eventually, her teachers and family came to regard Woodson as a writer. When inquiring about her writing, her mother would say, "Just so long as you're not writing about our family." In response, Woodson thought, "And I'm not. Well, not really. . . ."[52] Actually, she is. In many ways, Woodson has followed in Hamilton's footsteps, winning many of the same accolades, including the Hans Christian Anderson Award and the MacArthur Genius Award. Both are internationally recognized Black women authors of children's and young adult literature. Yet each rose to literary fame during different historical eras, and Hamilton was heterosexual while Woodson is queer.

Woodson currently lives in Brooklyn, New York, with her partner Juliet Widoff. They have two children, Toshi Georgiana and Jackson-Leroi. Author of over thirty books, Woodson is best known for her YA novels and middle-grade chapter books like *Brown Girl Dreaming* (2014), a memoir in verse that received the Coretta Scott King Award, the National Book Award, a Newbery Honor, and an NAACP Image Award, among others.[53] Approximately a third of her publications are picture books. Overall, Woodson's corpus reveals a kind of fragmented autofantasía, or pieces of herself that are scattered throughout all her writings, including her picture books. Fragments of Woodson's person, family, and history are embedded in almost everything she writes, regardless of whether they are published as autobiography or fiction.

Using autofantastic reading practices, I will reassemble these fragments into a collage of Woodson's queer of color worldmaking that includes intergenerational perseverance, healing, and transformation. Beginning with *Show Way* (2005), an autobiographical family history from slavery to the present, overlapping narratives can be traced throughout her picture books, including *The Other Side* (2001) and *The Day You Begin* (2018). Together, these books reveal how Woodson has negotiated her desire to write with the limitations imposed by either herself or mainstream publishing with regard to sexuality. Although none of her picture books to date are explicitly queer, I engage them using an autofantastic queer of color lens that considers Woodson's position as a Black lesbian author of children's literature.

Illustrated by Hudson Talbott and adorned with the Newbery Honor Book seal, *Show Way* (2005) is a historically rich picture book that interweaves intergenerational trauma with Black resilience. Although we do not yet know young Soonie, the book begins with her great-grandmother, who at age seven "was sold from the Virginia land to a plantation in South Carolina without her ma or pa but with some muslin her ma had given her. And two needles she got from the big house—and thread dyed bright red with berries from the chokecherry tree." Forced away from her child, Soonie's great-grandmother's mother grips similar items, creating a symbolic link between mother and daughter. Her parents and younger sibling watch hopelessly while she is pulled away—the last in a line of children tied together by a rope.

Show Way unapologetically and in great detail documents slavery's inhumane treatment of Black communities and their mundane acts of resistance. Examples of the former include the sale and separation of families, manual labor, physical exploitation, and incidents of whipping. Woodson also notes the historical erasure of Black names from the archives and collective memory, describing in the case of Soonie's mother that "history went and lost her name." While Woodson may not know her name, she refuses to forget these ancestors. As she put it, "I thought as I was writing *Show Way* that I'd make up a name for her, and then I thought no, I think this needs to be written down that we did lose some of our history on this journey."[54] These women remain part of her lineage, and she honors them by including them in this picture book, even if she can only list them as "Soonie's Mama" and "Soonie's Great-grandma." *Show Way* also showcases couples who "jumped broom," marrying symbolically because they could not do so legally. In the first example, she writes, "Soonie's great-grandma grew up, jumped broom with a young man named Ensler." They had a child, Mathis May, who was also sold away. When she grew up, she too "jumped broom with another slave." While this practice did not prevent couples from being separated, its inclusion here demonstrates how some Black couples pushed back against white supremacy by redefining or reconfiguring marriage as a form of resistance.

Evidenced by countless ads for "runaway slaves" across the United States' historical record, enslaved persons actively sought freedom. Unlike the printed ads of slave owners that have been preserved on paper, however, the ways in which enslaved persons escaped have been passed down through oral histories. In the case of Woodson's maternal lineage, she documents the oral history of "show ways" or "freedom quilts" that her ancestors used during the Underground Railroad.[55] Historians continue to debate the extent to which quilts were used by individuals attempting to escape slavery; however, as Woodson herself has affirmed, oral histories are not likely to leave a paper trail. As she tells it, "Nobody was going to go up in the big house and say, master, can you write down this story about how we're escaping using these quilts [during] the Underground Railroad?"[56]

In Woodson's family's version, the story begins with Soonie's great-grandmother, who was raised in South Carolina by Big Mama. This figure, an adoptive mother to enslaved children in that region, told them stories "in a whisper about | children growing up and getting themselves free." The illustrations on the following spread contrast day and night, geometrically divided to give the impression of fabric pieces quilted together. In a large triangle at the top of the spread, Big Mama not only teaches Soonie's great-grandmother how to sew but passes along secrets embedded within the quilt's design. She points to a large star at the quilt's center with one hand, and gestures to indicate discretion with the other. In another triangle, a group studies a quilt by candlelight as they make their way through the night, under the protection of darkness. After Big Mama passes, Soonie's great-grandmother continues the tradition with her own daughter, Mathis May, who learned before she was taken away. Those around her "whispered what no one was allowed to say: That Mathis know how to make . . . a Show Way." Pieces of cloth come together in quilted patches that resemble a map: "Go to log cabin. Stay on Drunkard's path. (Walk in a Zigzag line) to Crossroads. Look for Wild Geese Flying to find North Star."

Woodson reminds us that even the abolishment of slavery did not translate into freedom and equal rights. The Reconstruction era, Jim Crow laws, and the Civil Rights era all saw Black communities remain targets of white supremacy. Woodson documents this history through quilting, continuing from Soonie's mother to Soonie, and from Soonie's daughter (Georgiana) to Georgiana's daughters (Caroline and Ann).[57] Even if they "didn't much need that secret trail to the North anymore," they continued to sew quilts "to remember." For example, Caroline and Ann are depicted participating in a political action, "walking in a line to change the laws that kept black people and white people living separate." The girls march hand-in-hand for the possibility of change. As they march, they are held up by quotes from Frederick Douglass, Harriet Tubman, Ella Baker, Langston Hughes, Sojourner Truth, and others, stitched together onto a black quilt that provides the solid ground or foundation from which to journey forward.

The next spread grapples with the possible implications of protesting while remaining hopeful. Caroline and Ann "were a little bit scared sometimes, but pinned inside their dresses were Show Way patches Grandma Soonie had given them." The sisters are surrounded by a collage of newspaper clippings, photographs, and sketches depicting historical moments of racial tensions and racism in the US, such as a *New York Times* headline announcing the 1954 Supreme Court decision *Brown v. Board of Education*. Another headline reads, "3,000 Troops Put Down Mississippi Rioting and Seize 200 as Negro Attends Classes: Ex-Gen. Walker is Held for Insurrection." Written on various signs are "Gate X. Colored Entrance," "Imperial Laundry Co. We Wash for White People Only," and "Death to All Race Mixers! Keep White Public Schools White by Massive Armed Force!" Hateful photographs, such as a group of white boys holding up a confederate flag, are juxtaposed against more hopeful ones, like a young Black girl encouraging her community to vote and an image of Martin Luther King Jr.

Show Way's final pages shift in perspective from third person to first, as Woodson narrates her birth and then the birth of her first child, Toshi. We see Woodson at seven, her mother telling her, "All the stuff that happened before you were born is your own kind of Show Way. There's a road, girl. . . . There's a road." Woodson sits on her bed with scissors in one hand and cloth in the other, surrounded by yarn, needles, and colorful scraps of fabric that connect her back to the quilts or *show ways* of her ancestors. Her bed floats among the stars, held up by the figure of a large Black woman smiling down on her. "And I grew up, tall and straight-boned," Woodson narrates, "writing every day. And the words became books that told the stories of many people's Show Ways." Now an adult, Woodson is pictured sitting at her desk, her hair short and wearing a white t-shirt and jeans, subtly marking her as a tomboy, butch, or gender nonconforming. The book ends with her own child: "Had a baby and named that child Toshi Georgiana. Loved that Toshi up so. Yes, I loved that Toshi up. So some mornings, I start all over. Holding tight to little Toshi, I whisper a story that came before her." Thus, the story, or Woodson's retelling of her family's history, begins all over again, this time continuing with her daughter.

Woodson wrote *Show Way* in honor of her matriarchal lineage, having dedicated the book "For my family and in loving memory of the women who came before us." This is echoed in the summary provided on Woodson's website, which reads: "This is the story of seven generations of girls and women who were quilters and artists and freedom fighters."[58] Under her website's section "Why I wrote it," Woodson explains, "After my grandmother died and my daughter was born, I wanted to figure out a way to hold on to all the amazing history in our family. I wanted a Show Way for my own daughter."[59] Woodson and her wife contemplated different options for getting pregnant. "Having grown up for most of her life without her own father's presence," Woodson and Juliet "decided they did not want their child to face that particular kind of struggle," instead asking "a white male friend to be Toshi's biological father."[60]

Although Woodson wanted to honor the women in her family who came before her, it is curious that she does not mention her older sister Odella or her wife, Juliet. In terms of partners, *Show Way* does explicitly name husbands or other male partners like Ensler and Walter Scott. As a whole, this book accomplishes a great deal and could have also very easily depicted Woodson's queer family at the end. This raises the question of whether an earlier version of *Show Way* might have included Juliet and if it was the publisher's or Woodson's decision not to include her. As I have shown throughout *Coloring into Existence*, queer of color picture books have been published in North America since 1990. In fact, *Asha's Mums* was published the same year that Woodson published her first picture book on Martin Luther King Jr. and her first chapter book, *Last Summer with Maizon* (1990).[61] However, unlike Rosamund Elwin and Michele Paulse, Woodson did not publish *Show Way* with a small independent feminist press, but rather with G.P. Putnam's Sons, a division of Penguin Young Readers Group.

Show Way is similar to Woodson's *This Is the Rope: A Story from the Great Migration* (2013) in that both depict intergenerational storytelling through material goods: quilts in *Show Way* and rope that gets passed down from one generation to another until it reaches the present in *This Is the Rope*. Woodson referred to the latter picture book as a "fictive memoir," having been inspired by her family history. In particular, it recounts her mother's move from Greenville, South Carolina, to Brooklyn, New York, in 1968 as part of the Great Migration: the movement of African Americans from the rural south to northern cities between the early 1900s and mid-1970s. Woodson shared, "When I began writing it, my mom was still living. She didn't live to see the final book but I think it would make her very proud."[62] Although Woodson has called the book "a work of fiction," her family was part of the Great Migration, having traveled from South Carolina to New York. By inserting her family's story, and by choosing a young Black girl as the narrator, she inadvertently invites an autofantastic projection of herself onto the character, even if that child has not yet come out as queer.

This is also the case in two additional picture books inspired by Woodson's childhood experiences: *Sweet, Sweet Memory* (2000) and *Visiting Day* (2002). The first is dedicated to both of Woodson's grandfathers, although the specific events were shaped by the death of her grandfather Gunnar Irby in 1970. Like protagonist Sarah's grandfather in the story, Woodson's grandfather was also known for his gardening and passed away when she was a child. Sarah also wears a white dress for the funeral, just like Woodson did.[63] On the other hand, *Visiting Day* depicts a little girl's visit to her father in prison and was inspired by Woodson's uncle. Woodson elaborates in an "Author's Note" at the end of the book: "When I was growing up, I had a favorite uncle," Robert, who "went to prison when I was very young. . . . I knew that some of my happiest moments in childhood were spent getting on that bus to go visit him."

In this manner, both *Sweet, Sweet Memory* and *Visiting Day* each provide glimpses into Woodson's childhood, her many experiences, and her identities. Referring to her sexuality in a 2014 NPR interview with Terry Gross, Woodson grappled with "not quite knowing as a child or still figuring things out," stating, "the closest I came to it as a kid was being called a tomboy because I was kind of rough and tumble, but I also still wore ribbons."[64] She also recounted how her mother would "get upset with [her] 'cause she said [she] walked like [her] dad." Woodson described initially coming out in her late teens to a housemate who was also queer: "Like suddenly a light went on, and I thought, this is what it is." Although this did not happen until college, Woodson also admits her love for her child-hood best friend, Maria.[65] Close friendships such as these can be read as queer possibilities among friends who may grow to love one another, whether that love is strictly platonic or more intimate and romantic.

Meanwhile, *Pecan Pie Baby* (2010) asks us to consider both Wood-son's childhood and adulthood. Like *Show Way*'s depiction of Woodson as a mother alongside her daughter Toshi, *Pecan Pie Baby* also depicts motherhood—this time, with baby number two. Also a work of fiction, one can easily read this book as a depiction of a single Black mother with one child and another on the way. And while Woodson has shared that she does not like pecan pie, what if we autofantasized Woodson onto her picture book? One could either liken Woodson to the little girl who is upset at no longer being the youngest—a fact she shared in *Brown Girl Dreaming*—or to the mother who resembles Woodson as an adult and her experience with her own children.[66] As written on her website: "Jackson-Leroi—our son—was on the way and Toshi—our daughter—had decided, once she knew it was a boy, that she didn't want a baby in the house after all. By then, of course, it was way, way, way too late."[67] Jokingly, she adds, "She's since come to like him but she does complain about him breaking her toys! And yes, both of them love pecan pie. But I actually don't like it very much."[68] As with *Show Way*, this could have easily been an explicitly queer picture book, had both mothers been de-picted. Even without changing the text, an illustration showing a queer household in a family portrait would have accomplished this. Yet, as with *Show Way*, we are only given glimpses into, or breadcrumbs about, Woodson's family—as neither book explicitly depicts the children's sec-ond mother or indicates that they are a queer and interracial family. This is a recurring tension or point of queer erasure in her picture books, further exemplified in her biography statement at the end of *Pecan Pie Baby*: "She lives with her family in Brooklyn, New York." As with Gloria Anzaldúa, what is peculiar is that her queerness is omitted in her picture books, even if she is out in real life.

In addition to history and family, a central theme underlining many of Woodson's publications is that of interracial friendships and relationships, which she attributes to growing up in New York City. Her younger brother, Roman, is mixed race (Black and white), as are her children. In her middle-grade and YA novels, she often includes mixed-race characters and interracial friendships, such as in her first chapter book, *Last Summer with Maizon*, and *I Hadn't Meant to Tell You This*, among others. In *From the Notebooks of Melanin Sun* (1995), for example, a Black teenage boy's mother comes out as a lesbian, and he grapples not only with her sexuality but with her having a relationship with a white woman. Woodson has also had partners from different racial or ethnic backgrounds. She met her wife, who is white and Jewish, in the 1990s when Juliet was a medical student.[69] But what if they had met as children?

What if we autofantasized Woodson and her partner onto picture books such as *The Other Side* (2001)?[70] For example, the two girls in this picture book may be drawn to one another not only because they are of different races—one Black and one white—but also because, perhaps, they like one another. Like a line between Black and white, the fence featured in E. B. Lewis's vivid illustrations becomes symbolic of racial segregation. "That summer," narrates Clover, "the fence that stretched through our town seemed bigger. We lived in a yellow house on one side of it. White people lived on the other. And Mama said 'Don't climb over that fence when you play.' She said it wasn't safe." Clover also describes how that summer, "there was a girl who wore a pink sweater." She noticed, "Each morning she climbed up on that fence and stared over at our side. Sometimes I stared back. She never sat on that fence with anybody, that girl didn't." Curious, the narrator eventually makes her way over to the fence and introduces herself. She learns the other girl's name, Annie Paul: "'I live over yonder,' she said, 'by where you see the laundry. That's my blouse hanging on the line.'" Clover notices Annie's smile, sharing, "She had a pretty smile. | And then I smiled. And we stood there looking at each other, smiling."

One may interpret this as queerly seeing one another, or as some kind of queer recognition toward each other. Throughout these two spreads, they inch closer and closer to one another until, at last, they briefly touch on the next spread (fig. 5.3). The two girls hold each other's hand as Annie helps Clover onto the fence. However brief, this moment is visually captured or frozen in time within the illustration. And even

Figure 5.3. Interracial interactions among girls in *The Other Side*. Published by G. P. Putnam's Sons, a division of Penguin Putnam Books for Young Readers. Copyright © 2001 by Jacqueline Woodson and E. B. Lewis.

though the fence is a border or marker of racial division, it momentarily serves as a queer space, a borderland or third space, a physical place on which the girls may sit and be queer: "That summer me and Annie sat on the fence and watched the whole world around us." Clover's other friends, also drawn to this third space, eventually join them. The book ends with Annie longing for a future without the fence: "Someday somebody's going to come along and knock this old fence down," and Clover replying, "Yeah . . . Someday."

One of Woodson's more traditional, conventional, or childnormative children's picture book, however, is *The Day You Begin* (2018). Yet, when read through the lens of autofantasía, its queerness can be seen within all of the shy or socially awkward children who do not quite fit in at school.

Here, autofantasía functions as a way to reconcile personal and public histories of marginalization. Instead of queer outcasts, the children will eventually make space for one another, forming their own queer world. Coupled with Woodson's poetic voice, Rafael López's colorful illustrations encapsulate a general message of acceptance despite differences. Woodson opens and closes *The Day You Begin* with: "There will be times when you walk into a room and no one there is quite like you." Both lyrical and cyclical, for each verse of "There will be times when," there is a child who queerly stands out from their classmates—whether because of their skin, hair, accent, food, socioeconomic status, or a more intangible sense of difference. Although the ending repeats this, the line continues: "There will be times when you walk into a room and no one there is quite like you until the day you begin to share your stories." In doing so, the protagonist Angelina discovers that,

> . . . all at once, in the room where no one else is quite like you,
> the world opens itself up a little wider
> to make some space for you.

As the book's title emphasizes, Angelina's initial hesitation and sense of isolation upon entering her classroom is replaced with wonder. The day one begins, she learns, occurs when:

> . . . every new friend has something
> a little like you—and something else
> so fabulously not quite like you
> at all.

In this manner, the book equally emphasizes similarities and differences, or possibly even coalitional praxis, a cornerstone of queer women of color theory since *This Bridge Called My Back*. Woodson's use of "fabulous" also gestures toward a queer vernacular of *fabulousness*.[71]

The Day You Begin was inspired by the poem "It'll Be Scary Sometimes," published in Woodson's *Brown Girl Dreaming*.[72] The poem honors her great-grandfather (William Woodson) and her great-great-grandfather (William J. Woodson), who "was born free in Ohio, 1832."[73] The verse mentions W. J. Woodson's occupations and participation in the US Civil War, which led to his name being included on the Civil War Memorial: "William J. Woodson, United States Colored Troops, Union, Company B 5th Regt."[74] His son, W. Woodson, was "the only brown boy in an all-white school." Woodson recalls her mother telling her, "*You'll face this in your life someday.*" And although "*It'll be scary sometimes,*" she need only "*think of William Woodson | and you'll be all right.*"[75]

How readers see either Woodson or themselves reflected in *The Day You Begin* depends on how the book is autofantasized. One potential reading strategy involves projecting Woodson onto the protagonist as a queer Black girl who feels different from those around her; another is to project oneself onto the protagonist or any other characters. This is not original or unique, as it is common for heteronormative audiences to assume heteronormativity, cisgender audiences to assume cisnormativity, and able-bodied audiences to assume ability. White audiences, meanwhile, tend to assume whiteness unless told otherwise. However, even then they are likely to project whiteness or refuse to accept a character's race or ethnicity, such as with Rue in the Hunger Games.[76] If not explicitly told a character's race, ethnicity, gender, or sexuality, one may consciously or unconsciously assume the content of an author's identities or project one's own identities as readers onto characters.

However, it can also be radical to project one's own identity in cases where that identity is traditionally marginalized. For example, many of us (in this case, folks who are queer) assume people are queer unless told otherwise. Many of us also do this while reading or watching films, an act of resistance against assumed heteronormativity. In the case of Woodson's work, her characters might be read as queer in this way. Although she does not explicitly mark them as such, she does attempt to write against normative narratives: "I feel compelled to write against stereotypes, hoping people will see that some issues know no color, class, sexuality. . . . I write from the very depth of who I am, and in this place there are all my identities."[77] What is interesting about her reflection here is that her books are in fact very much about race, class, and sexuality. The issues that "know no color, class, sexuality" are those generally understood to be "universal," such as love, triumph, loss, death, or acceptance. Yet, these too are saturated with identity politics. According to one of Woodson's biographers, "Jacqueline is also one of the few children's authors who is out as a lesbian. She has been a vocal activist for the LGBT community, and several of her books feature gay characters. Still, it makes her uncomfortable to be defined by any one thing. As she says, 'It makes me nervous when an identity tries to push the others away as opposed to letting me be a writer first.'"[78] Like Woodson herself, along with her characters and readers, we too might continue to grapple with these intersecting axes of identities and power.

The sites where Jacqueline Woodson's explicitly queer content is evident are in her chapter books or novels, such as *The Dear One* (1991) and *The House You Pass on the Way* (1997). The first introduces a teen struggling with her tomboy or butch identity, while the latter depicts an older lesbian relationship. More recently, her novel *After Tupac and D Foster* (2008) was challenged in schools because of its queer content. Despite the name, *Autobiography of a Family Photo* (1995) is not actually an autobiography, although in interviews she does say that "emotionally, it was completely autobiographical, . . . like that's who I was at that age, the sense of being on the outside, the sense of watching the world, of bearing witness from a powerless position"; but also, "From an event standpoint, a lot of it I made up."[79] Considered an adult novel or, as a biographer wrote, "not a book teachers would be able to use in a classroom," it is written from a child's and youth's perspective. The reason for not including it in the classroom likely has to do with the overwhelming traumas experienced by key characters, including incidents of sexual assault, molestation, and incest, as well as detailed descriptions of sexual experimentation and sex at a young age, including between girls. Although Woodson stated that most of the novel's details were made up, one cannot help but notice how its major events parallel those included in her memoir *Brown Girl Dreaming*.

Woodson's writing also appeared in the edited collection *The Letter Q: Queer Writers' Notes to Their Younger Selves* (2012), in which she shared a childhood story of desire for her best friend Maria while grappling with her emerging butch identity.[80] Evidently, as biographer Laura L. Sullivan tells us, "Though all of her stories are vastly different, dealing with everything from teenage pregnancy to homophobia, she says they are all ways in which she is trying to work through the same story."[81] Like Anzaldúa's autohistorias and autofantasías, Woodson, too, is attempting to retell her story on her own terms. And in her own words, Woodson confessed, "I think I'm telling that story again and again in different ways and constantly figuring it out maybe just a little more deeply than the last time."[82] While she may have felt like an outsider, much like the protagonist in *The Day You Begin*, as she has gotten older, she has expressed moving from "a place of isolation to one of belonging."[83] She offers hope to her readers: "I don't think I have a message aside from what I believe myself, which is that we all have a right to be here."[84] For Woodson, writing is "what I know how to do in order to feel powerful and to make others feel powerful."[85]

By reassembling Woodson's picture books and then intertwining her novels, essays, and interviews, we are able to capture more of who she is as a whole person. If we only focused on her picture books, we would have a more limited and skewed perspective. That is, of course, unless we read her picture books through autofantasía. For example, other signs of her queer of color community in picture books might include an autofantastic reading of *We Had a Picnic This Sunday Past* (1997), where the narrator's favorite aunt is described as "the smart one" and "doesn't want to marry." The narrator casually adds, "and maybe me and Paulettte [her best friend] won't, either." We can also queer other characters such as the unmarried aunt in *Our Gracie Aunt* (2002), who agrees to care for a niece and nephew after their mother (her sister) dies, despite her not knowing the children very well. One could surmise, for example, that the aunt and her sister were estranged due to the aunt's queer sexuality.

Though overt queer content is not always evident in her picture books, Woodson wholeheartedly advocates for intersectional curriculum, even if she doubts an instructor's ability to teach it. In a 2016 interview with the *New York Times*, Woodson expressed skepticism over teachers introducing queer of color literature: "A teacher who is uncomfortable with queer issues isn't going to teach a book with gay characters."[86] She adds, "Someone who has never dealt with people of color and is teaching in an all-white classroom is probably not going to be able to really unpack a book that deals with race from the perspective of someone of color."[87] This reminds us that an author's target audience is not limited to young readers; adults such as educators or parents, who either purchase books directly or otherwise encourage their circulation among youth and children, must be considered. Authors must also navigate the editors and book publishers who decide what is published, critically contributing to the lack of overt queer content in children's picture books. In response, reading Woodson's work through an autofantastic lens allows readers to superimpose queerness and queer of color visuality onto all of her picture books.

Love and Embodiment in the Art, Activism, and Writing of Syrus Marcus Ware

An autofantastic reading can beckon not only queerness or racialness but also transness and disabledness, such as in the picture books of Syrus Marcus Ware. His political identities span many movements as a Black/ mixed race, transgender, disabled activist, artist, and scholar based in Toronto, Ontario.[88] He is also a core member of Black Lives Matter Toronto and is active in abolitionist and climate change movements.[89] Born in Montreal, Quebec, Ware is an identical twin to his sister, Jessica Lee Ware, who resides in the US. Prior to arriving at picture books, Ware was already a well-established artist. His "Love Letters" art series asked strangers to write letters to activists, which he then mailed to them. This project identifies many of the tenets important to Ware and led to his next series, which included drawing large-scale portraits of activists, most of whom were also Black, queer, trans, or disabled. Within both projects, Ware emphasized love while celebrating individuals often relegated to the margins by mainstream society. "My work shifted so radically when I started anchoring it around the survival of all of my people," he reflects, noting: "my work became about resiliency, it became about support, it became about love. . . . All of my artistic projects, all of my activist projects have been trying to get closer to this understanding of how we all get to make it."[90] Political notions of Blackness, queerness, transness, and disabledness are all present throughout Ware's work. When they are not always obvious, we can employ an autofantastic reading practice to seek them out, to allow them to radiate through and beyond the pages of the book, such as in his picture books *Love is in the Hair* (2015), *Bridge of Flowers* (2019), and *I Promise* (2019). The first was both written and illustrated by Ware, whereas the last two were written by others but illustrated by Ware.

In Ware's charming picture book, storytelling and hair are integral to showing love within a queer Black family. Written in the third person, *Love is in the Hair* introduces readers to Carter, a curious child who cannot sleep in anticipation of tomorrow, or the "Very Big Day" when her parents and new baby sibling are due to arrive home from the hospital. Until then, Carter is being cared for by Uncle Marcus and Uncle Jeff. *Love is in the Hair* was inspired by Ware's experiences as an uncle (to Aeshna and Zora) and father (to Amélie Carter Ware-Redman). As an autofantasía, his picture book parallels Aeshna's experience awaiting her baby sister, but names the protagonist after his daughter's middle name, Carter. In this manner, he is able to infuse a little bit of each one into his protagonist. Ware's focus on love, both within the book's title and throughout the narrative, reflects his own belief that "love is a fundamental part of human existence. It's the thing that makes us get up in the morning. Love of ourselves. Love of coffee. Love of our children. . . . Love guides a lot of my decision making. It's an action. A feeling. A memory. A hope for the future. An adjective."[91] Dedicated to his beloved family, *Love is in the Hair* is a meditation on honoring oral traditions and intergenerational knowledge.

Ware incorporates the act of storytelling between characters in *Love is in the Hair* as a nod to the oral traditions of communities of color in order to validate their own familial histories. He implores us to "consider what we want to remember and how we want to remember it, building an archive of our movements going forward to ensure that intergenerational memory can inform our activism, community building, and organizing."[92] In *Love is in the Hair*, Carter's uncles enact this remembrance. Having been awoken, "Uncle Marcus settled onto the edge of the bed, carefully moving his hair out from under him as he sat down."[93] Carter glances "at her uncle's hair with wonder. It was full of beads, fabric, shells and jewels, memories and stories and magic."[94] She climbs onto her uncle's lap as he shares two stories with her. The first story and bead mark Carter's own birth: "This bead is from a very special day 4 years ago, when you were born."[95] Noticeably, the illustration takes us away from Canada to New York City, setting this memory within the picture book in the United States for those who might be able to recognize the hospital.[96] The choice of New York reflects Ware's ties to the city through various family members currently residing there, including his twin sister (who resembles Carter's mother).

The second bead and its accompanying pink thread represent the time when both of Carter's uncles met at a music festival where Uncle

Jeff was selling jewelry. Uncle Marcus shares, "I've worn [the metal bead] in my hair ever since."[97] Uncle Jeff adds: "I liked you from the first moment!"[98] As a result, "That thread is from the day we decided to be each other's family."[99] Their recollections of that day vary, as the two engage in a lighthearted disagreement wherein Uncle Marcus recalls purchasing jewelry from Uncle Jeff, while Uncle Jeff recalls gifting him the jewelry. Even though "they always remembered parts of the story differently," what mattered most was that it was captured among the stories in Uncle Marcus's dreadlocks (fig. 5.4a).[100] Here, the uncles' playful disagreement is not a critique of oral history, but an endorsement of shared authority in telling one's history.

This initial interaction between the two men also reflects Ware's ideological critique of modern-day capitalism. "As much [as] possible," Ware described during an interview, he tries "to do bartering and trading."[101] He would like to believe Rinaldo Walcott's claim that our society is nearing the end of capitalism, exclaiming, "I absolutely hope that's true!"[102] Until then, Ware worries more now as a parent, noting: "An anxiety gets fostered in us that we have to have enough to keep this little one alive and growing. . . . That anxiety doesn't make me want to make more money—it makes me want to . . . grow my own food."[103] Like the author, Ware's characters also embody this sense of social responsibility.

While this is not the first time Black hair has been central to a children's picture book (e.g., bell hooks's *Happy to Be Nappy*, 1999), we can also situate *Love is in the Hair* within contemporary Black is Beautiful campaigns (e.g., Kobena Mercer's work on hair as a symbolic material) and Black Lives Matter politics.[104] In line with Marlon Riggs's call for the transformative power of Black-on-Black gay love, this picture book disrupts notions of heteronormativity by presenting readers with a loving gay Black couple who relish in self-affirmation and provide powerful role models for Carter and other children.[105]

For Ware, Blackness serves as an adjective and an aesthetic, proclaiming, "I would absolutely put that as an adjective on everything." "Thankful and hopeful because of blackness," Ware's embrace of Blackness is also informed by his experiences as Black Canadian, as well as his active role in political spaces such as Blockorama (the name of the Black queer and trans stage at Toronto Pride) and Black Lives Matter (BLM) Toronto. As a core member of BLM Toronto, for example, Ware called for Pride

Figure 5.4. (a) Carter surrounded by two uncles in *Love is in the Hair* (2015, Flamingo Rampant Press), and (b) Miracle with her two dads in *I Promise* (2019, Arsenal Pulp Press). Copyright © 2015 by Syrus Marcus Ware; 2019 by Catherine Hernandez and Syrus Marcus Ware.

to disassociate with local police, among other demands.[106] He is also the Founding member of the Prison Justice Action Committee of Toronto. As an aesthetic, the color black is just as powerful in influencing Ware's artistic sensibilities, describing the color as "the essence of all colours. All light of the universe is absorbed from the colour black."[107] Ware's fascination with how the color black is coveted within color theory leads him to broader inquiries over black/white dichotomies and the power of Blackness.[108] Ware fuses Blackness with a black aesthetic in most (if not all) of his creative endeavors, including the previously mentioned large-scale portraits of activists and community figures, many of whom are also Black.

In *Love is in the Hair*, Ware's use of the color black throughout the picture book quite effectively conveys the color's strength. From the characters' black hair to silhouettes of trees or buildings to solid black walls or shadows, the color black is essential to the book's illustrations. Numerous illustration details warrant praise; however, one that might have been different pertains to the visual depiction of queer coupling. Early in the story, when Carter cannot sleep, she seeks out her uncles asleep in the living room. Interestingly, only Uncle Marcus is visibly sleeping on the sofa bed, even though, given the language in the text ("found them on the sofa bed, fast asleep"), one can presume that Uncle Jeff is lying next to him. This visual omission cannot be a matter of space, as there is ample negative space within the spread—raising the question of whether Uncle Jeff was omitted to nullify any possible censorship debates over two queer Black men in bed together (even if they were only sleeping).

Given Ware's own position on Black trans visibility and parenting, can we also read Carter's uncles (as well as Carter) as transgender, nonbinary, or gender nonconforming? In 2017, Ware's publication in *TSQ: Transgender Studies Quarterly* contested "the erasure of racialized and Indigenous histories from white trans archives, time lines, and cartographies of resistance."[109] Furthermore, he argued, "Black trans archives live in the moments of shared story, of names called, of gatherings and celebrations in public space. Our archives live in our bodies and minds, and they span time and space."[110] For Ware, he is his own archive, just like his archive is also made up of his artistic expressions such as his picture books.

A few years before *Love is in the Hair*'s publication, Ware became pregnant with his daughter, Amélie Carter. Ware and his partner at the time, Nik Redman, who is also Black and trans, feared the degree to which they would face transphobia or cisgender assumptions about birthing. Deciding who should carry the baby was not difficult for Ware; explaining, "Nik is older than I am. . . . I had a lot of time in terms of fertility; I planned to carry the child."[111] However, "There were a lot of questions. Can you have top surgery and still breastfeed? How long do you have to be off hormones?"[112] Ware also wondered if he "would be able to handle being 'she'd,'" or if he would be able to have a "frank discussion about [his] 'ovaries' or menstrual cycles with a doctor."[113] They sought out answers and, when these were not readily available, plunged forward anyway. In describing the process, Ware shared: "I am ready to be pregnant and it is challenging and terrifying. . . . I have been off hormones for about two years and then you go through the process to make sure your ovaries are still functioning."[114] The next phase (looking for sperm donors) led to new challenges, such as when their application was flagged since, "How could two men be in need of insemination?" they were asked.[115] This could have easily deterred him and Redman. Instead, Ware reflected, "I felt confident that despite wanting to be pregnant, I was still a man. . . . I believe that, as a man about to carry our child, I have a lot to offer our child in terms of questioning gender rigidity in our society, and teaching the world about alternative ways of parenting. Perhaps it was this hope that got me through that time in the waiting room, unsure of what to expect."[116] Since medical professionals did not always have the answers or could not always understand their concerns, Ware and Redman had to seek out answers and, in the process, become mentors—even designing a course ("Trans Fathers 2B") for other trans men hoping to parent. Ware also shared details from his pregnancy in "Boldly Going Where Few Men Have Gone Before: One Trans Man's Experience," published in *Who's Your Daddy? And Other Writings on Queer Parenting*.

Ware has continued to document his experiences parenting as a Black trans father. However, he was not fully prepared for the racial discourse that would follow giving birth to a light-skinned child who passes as white. In "Confessions of a Black Pregnant Dad," Ware shares, "We anticipated that being trans dads would be a huge hurdle on our road to parenthood and therefore prepared by planning how we would deal with transphobia and gender expectations."[117] Instead, they were most surprised by the racial politics: "In the end, our experience of racialization as black men raising a baby who reads as white to many has been by far one of our biggest sources of external curiosity and often frustration."[118] Though not referenced directly within *Love is in the Hair*, its illustrations can also yield a discussion of mixed raced or interracial families. On the one hand, the characters across the book present different ways of embodying Blackness. Like Ware's own daughter, the final spread includes an image of a light-skinned baby in a thought bubble. The baby is being held by Carter, who faces forward toward readers.[119] In Carter's hair, one can also spot two pieces of fabric intertwined—symbolizing the newly formed bond between siblings, as well as the intergenerational sharing of knowledge and customs across multiple shades of Blackness.

Just like at first glance, none of the characters in *Love is in the Hair* "appear" to be trans, neither do they "appear" to be disabled. And yet, intertwined in everything Ware does is also his strong sense of disability justice. Accordingly, we could use an autofantastic reading to also decide that any or all of the characters in *Love is in the Hair* are also disabled or neurodivergent. Outside of the picture book, Ware has worked to challenge limiting definitions of disability, instead asking us to consider disability as a spectrum that includes not only physical disabilities (which may or may not be visible) but also neurological differences, among others. For example, Ware's contribution (co-authored with Zack Marshall) for the edited volume *Trans Bodies, Trans Selves: A Resource for the Transgender Community* considered the broadness of the term "disability," such that, "for many people, disability is about a sense of difference. But it is also about the diversity of human experience" such that in an ideal world, "all human bodies, minds, and ways of thinking [would be] celebrated."[120]

Ware unabashedly discusses his own disabilities in interviews, lectures, and his writing as integral to who he is. For example, he has shared that he was disabled since he was a child because he was born with two and a half kidneys and a double ureter, which required multiple surgeries.[121] He developed lupus and other autoimmune diseases as well as a neurological condition that affects his memory.[122] Ware was also institutionalized in psychiatric detention. All of these factors contribute to his sense of self as "disabled and mad," terms he proudly reclaimed.[123] "My practice is very much connected to my experience of disability," Ware emphasized, proclaiming, "And I guess what I would mean by that is that I desire disability. . . . Figuring out how to center and celebrate disability as a big part of who I'm creating work about, who I'm doing portraits of, who I'm talking about in my work."[124] Disability informs Ware's artistic practice not only in terms of content or themes but also the manner in which or "how" he works. Ware described the physical effects of creating art that would result in periods of rest and recovery, as well as the challenges of his body needing certain things while his mind needed others.[125] He remains committed to his craft, noting that individuals who are disabled are not simply "a potential audience to develop. We are artists, we are professionals, we are all sorts of things. So you don't just make space in the audience for us, you make an accessible stage that we can climb up onto and be part of delivering a spectacular presentation."[126] For Ware, his spectacular creative endeavors include his picture books.

In addition to writing and illustrating *Love is in the Hair*, Ware also illustrated two subsequent picture books: *Bridge of Flowers*, written by Leah Lakshmi Piepzna-Samarasinha and published by Flamingo Rampant Press (chapter 2); and *I Promise*, written by Catherine Hernandez and published by Arsenal Pulp Press. Both were published in 2019. When comparing the two, a notable similarity is their inclusion of Black and gender nonconforming, nonbinary, or trans characters, although disabled characters and politics are, at least initially, more apparent in the first than the latter. Aesthetic markers of Blackness include, for example, dark or Black skin, whereas pronouns such as "they" are used in each book's text to signal gender nonconforming or nonbinary characters.

Although I discussed *Bridge of Flowers* in chapter 2 from a publisher's perspective, here I will highlight Ware's artistic contributions in centering disability justice. Throughout the illustrations, obvious or overt visual markers of disability included incorporating items used by characters who are disabled, such as a wheelchair (Mom Soraya), arm braces (Bapa Kamau), and a metal prosthetic leg (protagonist's sibling, Kamur). Depicted on the cover as well, Kamur wears shorts throughout the book, exposing their prosthetic leg. Additionally, one two-page spread stands out in providing possible solutions for making our world more accessible. The spread features nine circles of various sizes, each one depicting a separate space or scene. They are all held together by a black backdrop framed in gold. In one of the circles, an activist meeting flyer announces it is wheelchair accessible, provides ASL, is scent free, and offers childcare and gender-free bathrooms. In another circle, a speaking mouth says, "Sure, I'll use the mic!" Other circles include "Stop Gap" ramps, automatic doors, and pedestrian crossing stoplights that beep, as well as a "Memo" with work conditions including a "4 hr work day" and "1 week vacation every 2 months." Another circle emphasizes sleep by depicting a bed with Zs across it. Of all the circles, the largest one includes a banner at the top announcing "MAD PRIDE," which can be interpreted as a march or celebration of MAD individuals, or, more specifically, MAD LGBTQ+ individuals.

When disabled characters and disability justice are not as overt, an autofantastic reading of *I Promise* can help us identify disability within this book as well. Ware's *I Promise* cover art resembles his prior portraiture series in the sense that it boldly depicts large-scale Black figures. Unlike his twelve-by-six-foot drawings, however, he was limited by the book's ten-by-eight-inch dimensions. Instead, to create the effect of a large-scale drawing, Ware drew extreme close-ups of the two characters' smiling faces—one adult and one child. Even these faces do not fit on the page, spilling off the cover for readers to imagine or piece together. For example, the child may or may not be bringing their hand or a finger toward their mouth. A skeptical reading might suggest that these characters are not "whole." Instead, if we build on Ware's politics around disability justice, what if we also consider this as an example of reclaiming bodies not deemed "whole"? We might also ask ourselves, what does it take to read disability onto a page or character? Throughout the book, these two figures, identified as the Mama and "kiddo," go about their evening routine (having a snack in the kitchen, doing their hair, brushing their teeth, putting on their pjs, and getting into bed) while the child asks their mother questions about other children and their families.[127] In the process, and intermixed within the illustrations, readers are introduced to these other families. Most of the characters appear as grayscale sketches, while sporadic colors highlight certain details within the illustrations (e.g., purple socks, green polka dots, or a yellow wall). Although any of the characters can be read as disabled (as well as trans), one family stands out in their autofantastic possibilities.

I Promise opens with a child asking their Mama a question while in a kitchen. "You know Miracle from swim class," the child begins. "If she has two dads, where did she come from?" This is juxtaposed with a second spread depicting three new individuals (and one stuffed animal) on a bed. While the protagonist does not use pronouns, Miracle uses "she." Ware draws Miracle lying in bed with her eyes closed as her two dads read her a bedtime story (fig. 5.4b). This page plays with gender primarily through hair, as well as attire. For example, Miracle appears to have either partially shaved or shorter hair like one of her dads while the other father has longer, fuller hair. This father also wears a thin bow tie that resembles more of a necklace than a tie since he wears it with a tank top. Both parents wear shorts. While we can assume both parents are fathers because the text tells us so, we can also read them as a gender nonconforming, nonbinary, or trans family.

As for disability, at first glance Miracle and her two fathers do not "appear" to have physical disabilities. All invisible or partially visible disabilities notwithstanding, however, we might autofantastically interpret the two parents as each having legs of different lengths. Without this autofantastic reading, some might assume that one parent sits with one leg under their knee while the other parent sits with one leg under the blanket. Given what we know of Ware, however, many of his artistic projects incorporate multiple forms of disabilities, including individuals who use leg prosthetics. Such was the case not only with Kamur in *Bridge of Flowers* but also with one of the activists Ware drew a large-scale portrait of, Yousef Kadoura, a disability activist who co-hosts the podcast *Crip Times* and describes himself as a "Lebanese Canadian actor, writer and producer, as well as a right leg below knee amputee."[128] Miracle, too, could be read as disabled. Only her head and a hand are visible, whereas the rest of her body is covered under a blanket. Here, I want to return to Ware's incorporation of beds throughout his picture books. In *Love is in the Hair*, I considered the meaning behind not showing the two uncles in bed. In *Bridge of Flowers*, a bed was depicted as a space of rest and disability justice. Here, too, I want to consider beds and bedrooms as political spaces where individuals navigate a slew of power dynamics. In the case of *I Promise*, the children are usually in bed surrounded by loving parents. Within a disability framework, as Ware describes, beds can have added significance since "in a non-disabled household" the bed might be "only a space that is occupied 8 hours of the night. But for the rest of us, it can become this space where it's a community center, it's a school, it's a workplace, it's everything, it's our art studios, it's our protest rallies."[129] This shift in perspective redefines "time and space. And that's what crip time means to [Ware]—this absolute necessity to embrace the expansion of time and this need to root it in the idea that we go at the slowest pace of the slowest person."[130] Beds, or the spaces individuals occupy as they manage, heal, or deal with their disabilities, can look very different. Even though Miracle and her two fathers may not appear to have a visible physical disability from an ableist perspective, we might apply an autofantastic reading to discover that they do. The synopsis on the back cover of *I Promise* describes it as capturing "the honest and intimate moments of queer parenting in all their messy glory." Ware's illustrations remind us that Blackness, transness, and disabledness are also part of that messy glory in need of celebration.[131]

All three of Ware's picture books are powerful examples of queer of color children's literature. Although different in many ways, when read through autofantasía, one can also identify Ware's emphasis on Black trans disability justice in each. Infused with love, *I Promise*, *Bridge of Flowers*, and *Love is in the Hair* provide us with hopeful responses to an unjust world.

* * *

In some ways, any analysis one conducts is informed by who we are. As readers, we bring our own assumptions, biases, histories, lived experiences, and expectations to our active engagement with texts. Though not a new practice, I hope my engagement with "misreadings," which I call autofantastic reading, can provide an umbrella term for practices so many of us already do consciously or unconsciously. As an overarching reading practice, it incorporates strategies such as queer reading, trans reading, BIPOC reading, and disability reading to create a subversive reading practice that serves the underrepresented or historically marginalized "self" and our politics.[132] An autofantastic reading centers not only what is being read but *who* created the object of analysis and *who* is doing the reading. Throughout this chapter, I have modeled my own autofantastic reading of picture books by Marcela Arévalo Contreras, Gloria Anzaldúa, Jacqueline Woodson, and Syrus Marcus Ware. I hope I have also shown that autofantastic reading, as I define it, is very clearly a political practice, operating from the bottom up, as a way to see ourselves, to bring ourselves into focus, to color ourselves into existence.[133]

Coda

When Chupacabras Protest, Chabelita's Heart Emerges

I always felt that when I was talking publicly, I was talking mainly to the children, to the young, which is to say to the future.
—James Baldwin

It is a beautiful and mysterious journey to come into deeper relationship with your creative power. . . . I encourage you to allow the page to rise up and meet your hand. Allow the page to open up and express your heart of hearts through your strong hand. Allow your mind to let go and watch as you let yourself play freely. . . . This is the revolution of self claiming self. This is the revolution of coloring ourselves and our communities into reality.
—Maya Gonzalez

My book's title is, in part, inspired by Maya Gonzalez's words above. *Coloring into Existence: Queer of Color Worldmaking through Children's Literature* began with a promise and an invitation to excavate the ways one can engage queer and trans of color authors, illustrators, publishers, and readers through the hermeneutic of autofantasía. In closing, I want to return to queer of color theory and queer feminists of color specifically, who inspired my research. First, I return to Gloria Anzaldúa, who passed away in 2004, the same year that Melissa Cardoza and Margarita Sada published *Tengo una tía que no es monjita*. Although Anzaldúa is best known for *Borderlands* and co-editing *This Bridge Called My Back*, her posthumous publication *Light in the Dark* (2015) encapsulates her philosophical corpus. As she reminds us, "identity, as consciously and unconsciously created, is always in process—self interacting with different communities and worlds. . . . Identity is multilayered, stretching in all directions, from past to present, vertically and horizontally, chronologically and spatially."[1] These words remind me that we all exist in a much larger, interconnected world. Even when centering the self (auto), we exist beyond ourselves. As Indigenous (Bay of Quinte Mohawk) lesbian Beth Brant shared, "somewhere inside I knew that *alone* did not mean *lonely*. I knew there was a community out there and that we were looking for each other."[2] Enacting autofantasía need not be an individualistic or solitary project, but one of political urgency and community building.

Coloring into Existence is both a case study for employing the various interpretative and methodological elements of the hermeneutic of autofantasía (e.g., literary strategies used by authors, artistic techniques used by illustrators, publishing guidelines used by publishers, and reading practices used by readers), as well as my persistence in documenting the emergence of a new literary archive, one that traces the possibilities of queer and trans of color children's picture books as an evolving worldmaking practice across North America. Some of the picture books within *Coloring into Existence* are very well known, while others rarely if ever appear on LGBTQ+ reading lists. I hope my research can lead more audiences to discover or rediscover the titles within. Below I will explore how we might expand the genre of "picture book" to include other texts that are otherwise excluded, while also suggesting other applications for autofantasía beyond picture books. Finally, I conclude with a personal reflection on my own journey from writing about queer of color children's picture books to creating my own.

Picture Books and Beyond

A major goal of *Coloring into Existence* has been to identify the parameters of an emerging literary field and its archive of queer and trans of color picture books, which I am proposing began in North America with the publication of *Asha's Mums* in 1990 and continued through 2020—a year plagued with the COVID-19 pandemic and tumultuous US elections. No doubt, the years between concluding research for and publishing this book will have seen new titles that should also be included within this North American literary archive. And, despite my best efforts to identify all of the books that merit inclusion, I acknowledge that this task is never fully complete. Not only are newer titles created, but our definitions for key terms such as "queer," "trans," "people of color/BIPOC," "North America," "children's literature," and even "picture books" continue to change over time.

When examining picture books, certain texts (such as those created by James Baldwin and Maya Gonzalez) do not quite fit neatly into the category of children's picture books, or they might purposely resist categorization altogether. For example, at nearly one-hundred pages in length, where should we put James Baldwin's *Little Man, Little Man: A Story of Childhood*? In the introduction to the 2018 edition of Baldwin's book, Nicholas Boggs and Jennifer DeVere Brody refer to it as an "experimental, illustrated literary work."[3] Illustrated by Yoran Cazac and originally published in 1976 by Michael Joseph, Ltd., in London and Dial Press in New York, Baldwin dedicated the text to his friend and mentor, Black artist Beauford Delaney.[4] Its four-year-old protagonist, TJ, was inspired by or modeled after Baldwin's own nephew, Tejan Karefa-Smart, who had demanded, "When you gonna write a book about MeeeeeEEE!?"[5] Boggs and Brody surmise that *Little Man, Little Man* was "ostensibly written as a children's book" even if it was billed as a "child's story for adults."[6] Baldwin thought highly of children, noting: "Children, not yet aware that it is dangerous to look too deeply at anything, look at everything, look at each other, and draw their own conclusions."[7]

Aside from its page count, however, the book also includes seemingly taboo subjects for children's literature—during the 1970s and today—like police violence, drug and alcohol addiction, dysfunctional relationships, and poverty. One of its greatest strengths is that it proudly depicts the joy of Black quotidian life in Harlem through the actions of three kids: the protagonist TJ and two older neighbors, seven-year-old WT and eight-year-old Blinky. Blinky, we are told, displays a certain tomboy aesthetic: "She don't hardly never wear a dress herself. She always in blue jeans. Look like she do everything she can to be a boy. But she ain't no boy. Blinky is a girl. But she don't like girls."[8] From an autofantastic perspective, this description of Blinky provides many gender and sexuality possibilities, even if these are not directly explored in the book. She is instead relatively marginalized for being "a girl."[9] In the story, Blinky primarily shadows WT and, by extension, TJ.

The strongest bonds occur between male characters. TJ and his father share quality time together by seeing a movie or going to the beach. His father also reaffirms a sense of pride in Black culture: "he took him to the Apollo Theater, so he could see blind Stevie Wonder. 'I want you to be proud of your people,' TJ's Daddy always say. TJ proud of his people, just like he proud of his Daddy. His Daddy one of them people; they boss people."[10] Baldwin's references to the Apollo Theater situate TJ's father within a longer history of Black culture and pride at the heart of Harlem (fig. C.1).[11]

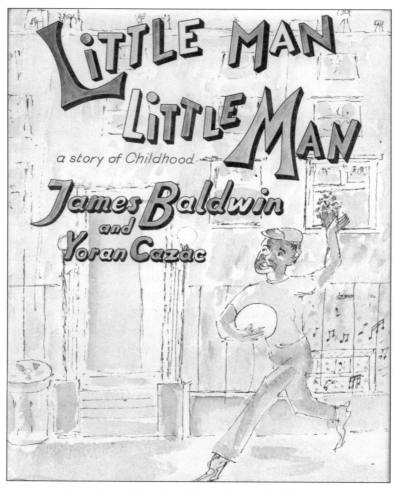

Figure C.1. Cover of *Little Man, Little Man: A Story of Childhood*. Published by Michael Joseph Ltd. Copyright © 1976 by James Baldwin and Yoran Cazac.

Like most of the authors in *Coloring into Existence*, Baldwin was primarily known for his other talents. A public figure, social critic, and author, he also *happened* to write a children's book. Although this was the only book he wrote that was directed at both children and adults alike, the quote from Baldwin in the epigraph above emphasizes how children were a target audience and focal point for his other works as well. For example, in "The Negro Child—His Self-Image," a 1963 speech delivered to educators, he rightly called out US hypocrisy: "What passes for identity in America is a series of myths about one's heroic ancestors."[12] Baldwin also cautioned that the US must change or else it will self-destruct: "America is not the world and if America is going to become a nation, she must find a way—and this child must help her to find a way to use the tremendous potential and tremendous energy which this child represents. If this country does not find a way to use that energy, it will be destroyed by that energy."[13] Using this figurative child as a stand in for Black children and their wider Black community, Baldwin declares the limitations, inherent racism, and structural oppression of education in the US. Children were also central to Baldwin's *The Evidence of Things Not Seen*, which featured the Atlanta child murders between 1979 and 1981 that primarily targeted Black boys: "It is very clear that whoever is murdering the children wants them to be found as they are found: this brutally indifferent treatment of the child's corpse is like spitting in the faces of the people who produced the child."[14] Much like his critiques of US society and public education, Baldwin here condemns the continual failing of the US toward Black children and their communities.

If Baldwin's *Little Man, Little Man* defied categorization because it may be too long for a children's picture book, other works might be considered too short. I return to Maya Gonzalez, this time as she advocates on behalf of chupacabras marching for equal rights. Though chupacabras may hold little credibility except within folklore or fantasy fiction, they materialized on paper from Gonzalez's imagination as a short, illustrated story for children in response to our world's calamities. *The Interrupting Chupacabra* (2015) defies categorization as an unconventional illustrated story for children and adults. Created as a black-and-white six-page PDF handout rather than a traditional book, *The Interrupting Chupacabra* was meant to be printed, colored, cut, and compiled into a short booklet or "sample book for practice."[15] The booklet offers an example for anyone who wants to make their own book under Gonzalez's "Write Now! Make Books" curriculum. This sample or practice book was intended to inspire other novice authors along with Gonzalez's three rules, which are also listed on the back: (1) "Everyone is an Artist," (2) "There is never a right or wrong way to make art," and (3) "Art is always an act of courage."

Like the children's picture books already mentioned throughout *Coloring into Existence*, I want us to also seriously consider this "story of silly suspense and intriguing interruption."[16] Immediately noticeable are the cutout and gutter lines, suggesting that this is a work in progress rather than a polished product. Gutter lines are typically only visible to editors, writers, and illustrators during pre-production. Leaving them visible here is a way of visually marking the book as one that is still being created or is at least not yet published. This "incomplete" version, however, is the finished product from Gonzalez, who leaves it up to readers, or "colorers," to color, cut, and fold the PDF into a finished product for them. On the sample book's cover, a profile view of a creature's head with razor-sharp teeth and a comically long tongue extends upward toward the title. Gonzalez's name appears to the right of the tongue, and to the left of it are the words "color by" along with a blank space to be filled in by whomever is coloring this sample book project.

The "About the Author & Illustrator" section of *The Interrupting Chupacabra* includes a brief biography of Gonzalez that concludes: "What she loves just as much as making books is teaching other people (and especially kids!) how to make their own! She also fancies herself a pretty stylish chupacabra!"[17] Instead of a photograph, Gonzalez includes an illustration of herself as a "stylish chupacabra" with eccentric jewelry, bulging eyes, fang-like teeth, and tattoos across her arms. Below Gonzalez is a section titled "About the Colorer" with the words: "Tell us a little about yourself here." Whereas children's picture books are usually collaborations between an author and illustrator, this illustrated story more closely resembles the collaborative efforts of comic books that tend to include and credit the penciller, inker, colorist, and letterer among others. A large blank circle provides a space for the "Colorer" to illustrate themself. The second half of the PDF page serves as the title page for the completed book, with the word "Interrupting" divided into two separate lines, creating the visual effect of an actual interruption. The letters do not align and instead almost merge or interrupt one another, whereas the word "chupacabra" is printed in a different font, further creating the illusion of chaos. Two "monsters"—not as scary as the one on the cover—adorn separate corners of the page, with one hanging upside-down as they gaze toward one another. Like its adjacent biography page, this title page also provides the person doing the coloring a blank line for writing in their name (fig. C.2).

In the tradition of knock-knock jokes, this one begins with the words "Knock! Knock! Who's There?" However, neither of the two characters—a cow and a goat grazing on a hilltop within a fenced outdoor area—knocks nor responds.[18] Instead, both glance off toward the edge of the page as the words, and those who are responsible for uttering them, approach. The next spread answers the call: "Interrupting chupacabra." At this point, readers, like the animals, have yet to see who is answering and approaching. With only sounds to guide their thoughts,

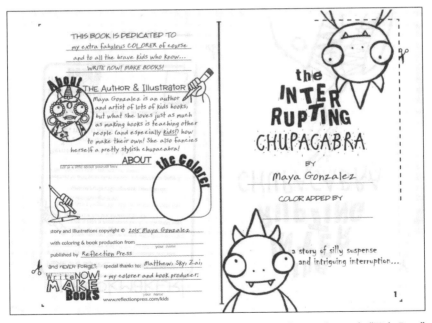

Figure C.2. Sample "Copyright, Biography, and Dedication" page alongside "Title Page" of *The Interrupting Chupacabra*. Published by Reflection Press. Copyright © 2015 by Maya Gonzalez.

the startled goat imagines a terrifying chupacabra similar to the one on the booklet's cover, with piranha-like teeth and an extremely long, drooling tongue reaching out toward its potential prey. In anguish, the goat is seen on the next page frantically running past a row of houses. From within their homes, cows yell out statements such as "Chupacabras on the rise!" "They're monsters!" and "Chupacabras to blame for everything!"[19] What readers may not initially notice are the tips of two horns of "actual"—according to the author's imagination—chupacabras slightly visible at the bottom left-hand corner.

The final two-page spread is the most detailed and revealing. Readers finally see the approaching group of chupacabras as they march toward the homes of the cows and goats. They continue to chant in a call-and-response manner while holding protest signs that read "I'm a mother not a monster" and "Interrupt unfair treatment." The mother holds the sign in one hand and a baby chupacabra with the other. Two other chupacabras hold up a banner that reads: "Chupacabras unite!" Another holds a sign crossing out the stereotypical image of the terrifying chupacabra while hugging a goat holding its own sign with the words "Goats for truth," illustrating the importance of allies or accomplices within political movements and protests. The goat could also very well be the chupacabra's partner, implying inter-species relationships. In contrast, the cows' prejudice is evident from a sign on one of their homes that reads: "Chupacabras go home!" If we consider chupacabras to be a marginalized population here and the discrimination they face (e.g., chupacabraphobia) to be a metaphor for xenophobia, queerphobia, or other forms of hate or discrimination, this sample story turns out not to be so lighthearted. Instead, what may be initially labeled a simple or silly story can also be simultaneously understood as a complex textual and visual narrative about preconceived prejudices, discrimination, hateful speech, political protest, community, and love.

Maya Gonzalez's work extends well beyond the confines of childnormative children's picture books. Instead, she pairs her artistic skills with community needs and healing practices to produce cultural materials that challenge common assumptions about children and their communities. While I have primarily examined picture books in *Coloring into Existence*, I want to pause in order to reemphasize that the very format and target audience of contemporary children's picture books reinforce childnormativity. As I stated in the introductory chapter, industry standards for children's picture books tend to dictate that they be thirty-two pages, printed in color, emphasize illustrations over text, have larger font sizes in comparison to novels or other literature, and contain a varied typography. How did we as a society come to understand or accept this as childnormative? Why have we normalized the picture book format as the most acceptable, appropriate, and expected genre for children's print media? Considering Baldwin's *Little Man, Little Man*, and Gonzalez's *The Interrupting Chupacabra* provide additional options.

This brings me to other genres or cultural materials beyond children's picture books where one might also identify and apply autofantasía. For example, with the exception of a few works that were mentioned in passing, I deliberately excluded chapter books or novels from consideration here in order to narrow down my research focus. However, these too can be experienced through autofantasía. When considering queer and trans middle-grade, YA, or adult novels, one might begin with any of the numerous titles by Jacqueline Woodson, or perhaps with Malinda Lo's *Huntress* (2011) or *A Line in the Dark* (2017), Benjamin Alire Saenz's *Aristotle and Dante Discover the Secrets of the Universe* (2012), Gabby Rivera's *Juliet Takes a Breath* (2016), Adam Garnet Jones' *Fire Song* (2018), or Karleen Pendleton Jiménez's *The Street Belongs to Us* (2021), among countless others.

Even ephemera such as stickers, buttons, and posters may compel an autofantastic analysis.[20] For example, one might contemplate the manner in which lesbian feminist collectives such as Grupo Producciones y Milagros by Rotmi Enciso and Ina Riaskov utilize the concept or figure of a child, specifically a little girl, in their calcomanías, or decals and stickers, which they also replicate on infant onesies, toddler tank tops, and protest posters. Likewise, paper dolls of queer of color artists like Janelle Monáe or the Family Pride memory matching game set that depicts an array of families could serve as other examples.

Still, I want to reiterate that autofantasía is not limited to, and should not only be applied to, children's picture books or even children's material culture. Rather, I am suggesting that the hermeneutic of autofantasía can be useful when analyzing not only literary genres like novels, plays, and poetry but also film, art, photography, and other media. The underlying current in all of these is the question of how individuals (creators as well as the audience) interlace the autobiographical and political with the fictionalized.

Praxis behind *Chabelita's Heart/El corazón de Chabelita*

In 2016, I was invited to share my initial thoughts on autofantasías at the Gloria Anzaldúa "El Mundo Zurdo" conference. In my talk, I reflected on my own childhood, identifying critical moments when I was socialized into heteronormativity, as well as moments I can now claim as my queer Chicana beginnings.[21] Once when I was on the playground during recess, a boy insisted that I not wear purple because it meant I was "gay." Although this happened in the 1980s, his linking the color purple to queer identities was not entirely wrong. The colors purple, violet, and lavender are in fact associated with early gay and lesbian movements and organizations, as well as with the persecution of queer individuals during the "lavender scare" of McCarthyism under former president Dwight D. Eisenhower.[22] While I may have not known the definition of gay then, much less its historical association with lavender, the tone in my classmate's voice made it clear to me that he saw it as something repulsive I should shun. Unbeknownst to either of us at the time, I was already queer—even if I was only a child, and even if I could not yet articulate it.

Part of the problem with the idea of publicly coming out is how that act tends to negate all of the queer moments that took place before the public confession of our desires. For example, I vividly remember being in first grade and getting ready for picture day. I had short hair tucked to the side by a hairpiece and wore a white-and-pale-pink cotton dress. My ensemble included a pair of Minnie Mouse earrings, which my mother purchased specifically for this occasion. The set also included a matching Minnie Mouse necklace. My mother looked forward to receiving my photographs, which were accompanied by headshots of the rest of my class, along with headshots of the school's principal, vice principal, and my first-grade teacher. In the class photograph, I was featured in the second row, fifth person from the left. To my mother's surprise, I was not wearing the necklace. I could have told her I lost it, but unfortunately for me, she quickly spotted the necklace on another one of my classmates: bottom row, third girl from the left. My mom was livid, repeatedly asking why one of my classmates was wearing my necklace. What I could not quite articulate at that moment was that, at least within my world, she was not a random girl; I liked her more than just as a friend. I was taken by her smile and could not deny her request to borrow my necklace. A few years later, I would develop a crush on another girl, this time the neighbor beside my childhood home. She was a couple of years older than me, and I did everything possible to spend time with her. I also remember playing with dolls and creating queer couplings among them, dressing myself like what might be considered a tomboy, and being curious about one of my middle-school teachers who was rumored to be gay.

I share these moments, or queer beginnings, because they have shaped me into the queer Chicana I am today. And while I did eventually come out as a teenager, I wonder how my childhood might have been different if I had known or learned about others like me. What is the purpose of telling our stories, or of sharing our stories with children or with our childhood selves? My childhood consisted of silence—literal silence imposed by my father. I was often not allowed to speak. Meanwhile, I witnessed my father struggle with English and my mother battle with depression. In my extended family, we dealt with traumas ranging from mental health crises and cancer to sexual violence and suicides—all topics we were not allowed to discuss. How might my childhood have been different if I had felt whole? Heard? To answer these questions, I imagine my current self having a conversation with my younger child self through autobiographically inspired autofantasías.

Anzaldúa and Gonzalez, like many of the children's book authors and illustrators in *Coloring into Existence*, inspired those around them to create—to share themselves with the world, to tell their stories. They accomplished this by deliberately inserting themselves within the text and illustrations of their works. Utilizing autofantasía as a literary and aesthetic technique, they recreated their childhoods or adulthoods in order to comment on themes and sociopolitical issues outside of what is usually considered to be appropriate content for children.

Inspired by Anzaldúa and Gonzalez, I too have autofantasías I want to share. Growing up, my family and friends called me María, Mari, and Marilou, or Chabelita and Isabela for Isabel. Just as I had many nicknames, I now reimagine myself into multiple forms as I draft and sketch my own autofantasías. Sometimes my illustrations look like variations of me, while other times there is no apparent resemblance. As I wrote and sketched the initial draft for my first children's picture book (well over ten years ago), I was reminded of everyone who had touched my life and the future generations of queer children of color who will continue to struggle for visibility, representation, autonomy, and a more just world.

By not restricting autofantasías to a specific time or place, authors, illustrators, and publishers may move freely through space—intentionally recreating themselves within their works in order to bring attention to sociopolitical problems. Such is the case with my own picture book, *Chabelita's Heart/El corazón de Chabelita*, published in 2022 by Reflection Press, in which I reimagine myself in first grade. *Chabelita's Heart* can be summarized as follows: "With the support of her loving Chicanx family, a girl named Chabelita discovers it's okay to like other girls." On the cover, I depict two kids, Chabelita and her new friend and crush, Jimena (fig. C.3). Within my "Note from the Author," I share a shortened version of what I shared above:

> When I was in first grade, my mom gave me an earring and necklace set for picture day.
> To my mom's surprise, I was not wearing the necklace in my class photo because I had lent it to a little girl I liked. . . .
> This book is for everyone, but especially for anyone who can relate to Chabelita and Jimena. Shine brightly like Jimena and love boldly like Chabelita.
> *With love,*
> *Isabel*

At the center of *Chabelita's Heart* is certainly all the joy and awe of a childhood crush between Chabelita and Jimena, from that first moment they meet and throughout the development of their relationship.

Another element joining these two characters is that sense of identification and relatability around being Latinx and sharing migration histories. For Chabelita, that is represented by her father, who migrated from Mexico. For Jimena, it is her mom who has been deported to Honduras. But even though they are both Latinas, they are different; Chabelita is Chicana, or Mexican American, and Jimena is Honduran American and Garifuna (or Black and Indigenous)—at least from her mother's side.

Figure C.3. Cover of *Chabelita's Heart/El corazón de Chabelita*. Published by Reflection Press. Copyright © 2022 by Isabel Millán.

Together, I hope their racial and ethnic backgrounds challenge how we conceptualize who belongs under categories such as "Latinx." Another goal of mine was to depict that it is possible to discuss both sexuality and migration simultaneously, since queer-themed picture books do not have to exist in a vacuum, away from other intersecting oppressions or lived experiences.[23]

I also wanted to subvert stereotypical gender roles by, for example, depicting Chabelita's father in the kitchen making her breakfast, and her mother driving the family car. Moreover, both parents are very present and supportive of Chabelita's queerness. Within my life, even though my mom and sisters, and most of my extended family and communities are supportive, I no longer have a relationship with my father because of his own queerphobia. *Chabelita's Heart* was my opportunity to create a father figure who was also supportive of his queer daughter.

It was equally important for me to not limit queerness to only Chabelita and Jimena. Understandably, many queer picture books present a queer character (or two) surrounded predominately by heterosexual or heteronormative characters. After all, that can be the reality for many queer folks, especially children, who have not yet come out or found others like them. This is why I also wanted, at least within the subtext of *Chabelita's Heart*, to provide the possibility of other queer characters. We see this with Jimena's aunt, tía Aurora, whose gender might fall under the label of butch or gender nonconforming (fig. C.4). She is also an artist and Jimena's primary guardian until she can be reunited with her mom. As I like to mention in public readings or talks where I have presented *Chabelita's Heart*, I also wanted to present Jimena's mom as queer or pansexual and in a possible relationship with tía Aurora. Perhaps Jimena and her mom were just about to move into tía Aurora's home before her mother was detained and deported. In this example, "tía" or aunt functions as a title of endearment for chosen family rather than biology. This is just one version of the story I like to tell myself when it comes to Jimena's mom and tía Aurora. And if you look closely, their relationship is on display in an art piece hanging in tía Aurora's art room. An art piece of a younger Jimena on a swing hangs close by, suggesting her importance as well within this queer family. Stylistically, I drew tía Aurora's artwork in a manner that resembled the characters of *Tengo una tía que no es monjita*, yet another way I hope to honor that book's impact on me.

One activity that occurs within the book's storyline—and can also serve as an example of an accompanying activity for readers of *Chabelita's Heart*—is the choosing and drawing of role models. Chabelita chooses Nancy Cardenas, a historical lesbian figure from Mexico (see chapter 2), and Jimena chooses Berta Caceres, an Indigenous environmental activist

Figure C.4. Tía Aurora's home; from *Chabelita's Heart/El corazón de Chabelita*.
Published by Reflection Press. Copyright © 2022 by Isabel Millán.

from Honduras. My focus on Mexico and Honduras was inspired, once
again, by *Tengo una tía que no es monjita*. You may recall that author
Melissa Cardoza is from Honduras and illustrator Margarita Sada is
from Mexico. Cardoza had also migrated to Mexico and published the
book while living there. In considering the characters for *Chabelita's
Heart*, I asked myself what would have happened if Cardoza had instead

migrated to the US. I was so taken by Cardoza and Sada's picture book that I completely shifted my research focus toward queer of color children's literature and therefore dedicate my own picture book and this larger research project to them. In many ways, they are my role models.

The illustrations were by far the most challenging aspect of creating *Chabelita's Heart*. Although Gonzalez reminded me, "Everyone is an artist," I was not "formally" trained as an artist and had no prior experience illustrating picture books. I ultimately decided on a mixed-media collage style for the illustrations. This allowed me to create one item, detail, or character at a time, making modifications along the way to items rather than whole spreads.[24] Inspired by Margarita Sada's larger brush strokes, I wanted to emulate that in my abstract backgrounds. I then used acrylics, markers, and other materials to draw, color, and cut out each character and tape them onto each spread.

There was a moment while creating some of the earlier sketches and thumbnails that I was pleasantly surprised with the revelation that I would need to change the story in order to accomplish the illustrations. While my personal experience and original version of the text included a necklace and earring set, this was simply more jewelry than I wanted to draw on each kid.[25] Fortunately, that lead me to bow ties! Including them on both Chabelita and Jimena was also a way to highlight gender variance, not only for them but for readers, since the last page of the picture book includes an interactive bow tie activity along with its own hashtag #chabelitasbowtiefriends. In an accompanying bow tie demo video, I share, "The nice thing about cutouts is that you do not have to stay in the lines."[26]

Creating this picture book allowed me to reimagine my own childhood—as I wish it could have been, while being held by an entire community of loved ones. That community includes Maya Gonzalez and Matthew Smith-Gonzalez from Reflection Press. I am delighted to be the third author published by Reflection Press under Gonzalez's mentorship. Throughout this process, Gonzalez taught me that creating *Chabelita's Heart*—both the text and illustrations—was necessary for my own sense of self. Although I knew this on a theoretical level, the act of finishing this book and holding it in my hands was indeed transformative. As other authors conveyed in prior chapters, sharing my picture book with loved ones and reading it aloud in public has also transformed me.

I simply cannot explain the joy I feel when someone—child or adult—tells me they see themself in one of my characters. Even though creating my picture book was a deeply personal and transformative journey, I am grateful for anyone who can read it and gain something from it. Syrus Marcus Ware titled his 2017 essay in *Canadian Art*, "All That We Touch, We Change," referring to Octavia Butler's quote from *Parable of the Sower*, "All that you touch | You Change. | All that you Change | Changes you."[27] This is a fitting reminder of the cyclical process of creating, sharing, receiving, and being transformed by children's picture books.

ACKNOWLEDGMENTS

This book has truly been an act of love, sacrifice, and resilience. Above all, it is an act of love for queer and trans of color communities, authors, illustrators, publishers, readers, and all the picture books that serve as the primary sources for this research. I want to first begin by thanking all of those responsible for creating the picture books in *Coloring into Existence*. This project began with one picture book and then a paper for a course while I was a graduate student at the University of Michigan. I want to thank all of the faculty I had the pleasure of working with, especially Nadine Naber, Maria Cotera, Lawrence La Fountain-Stokes, and Yeidy Rivero. I also benefited from writing workshops with both Nadine Naber and Sarita See, as well as enlightening conversations with fellow peers including, but not limited to, Lani Teves, Kiri Sailiata, Lee Ann Wang, Chris Finley, Matt Blanton, Cristina Solis, Anthony Kim, and Mindy Mizobe. I am equally grateful to friends and colleagues in Mexico who provided feedback, aided me in locating sources or archives, and who I turned to when I needed help on translations including, but not limited to, Cristina Serna, Coco Gutiérrez-Magallanes, Norma Mogrovejo, Circe Sandoval Diaz, Bea G. Alonso, and Miriam Ruiz Hernández. I also greatly benefited from a postdoctoral fellowship at the University of Texas at Austin. A special thank you to Ana Raquel Minian and Monica M. Martinez. While there, I had the enormous privilege of spending time in Anzaldúa's archive at the Benson Latin America Collection. While at Kansas State University, I could not have asked for a better group of colleagues and friends than Shireen Roshanravan, Norma A. Valenzuela, Melisa Posey, and April Petillo. At my institutional home, the University of Oregon, I would like to thank all of my colleagues within the Department of Women's, Gender, and Sexuality Studies including Kemi Balogun, Jamie Bufalino, Ana-Maurine Lara, Gabriela Martínez, Judith Raiskin, Yvette J. Saavedra, Yvonne Braun, and Priscilla Yamin. Within my affiliated department of Indigenous,

Race, and Ethnic Studies, I am grateful for all of you, although I want to especially thank Ernesto Javier Martínez, Lynn Fujiwara, and Laura Pulido. I am equally grateful for Sangita Gopal and Michelle McKinley for their support within the Center for the Study of Women in Society and the Women of Color Group, whose writing workshop impacted the early stages of this book. I would also like to thank those of you whom I have had the privilege of getting to know through CLLAS, Latinx Studies, and English (especially Lynn Stephen, Cecilia Enjuto-Rangel, Audrey Lucero, and Betsy Wheeler). Throughout the years, my research benefited from conference presentations across my various disciplinary fields including ASA, NWSA, ChLA, MALCS, NACCS, and MLA. I wish I could list all of the individuals within and across each one who has directly impacted me, either through our conversations or through their research. These are just a few: Norma Cantú, Karleen Pendleton Jiménez, Rita Urquijo-Ruiz, Marivel Danielson, Mary Pat Brady, Richard T. Rodríguez, Frederick Luis Aldama, David Vásquez, Anita Revilla Tijerina, L. Heidenreich, Jennifer Miller, and countless others. I also want to thank everyone who has read either individual chapters or some version of this manuscript, especially Maria Cotera, Juana María Rodríguez, Nat Hurley, Julia L. Mickenberg, Karen Mary Davalos, Mike Murashige, and Yvette J. Saavedra, as well as the wonderful team at New York University Press, including Eric Zinner, Furqan Sayeed, and Ainee Jeong. This book was also possible thanks to the various funding sources and research support I have received throughout the years from each of the previously mentioned universities, as well as the Arne Nixon Center for the Study of Children's Literature, and visits to numerous archives across the US, Canada, and Mexico. The staff at the San Francisco Public Library Special Collections were especially helpful during the pandemic. I also had the privilege of being a recipient of the Institute for Citizens and Scholars (formerly Woodrow Wilson) Career Enhancement Fellowship (2021–22), which allowed me to complete this book. Once again, to Melissa Cardoza and Margarita Sada for putting me on this path of children's literature, and then later to Gloria Anzaldúa and Maya Gonzalez for sustaining me through this journey with your theories and practices. Thank you for allowing me to reach out, beyond the page, and to consider my role within the larger world and universe. I am always grateful for all my loved ones and family—given and chosen—who remain ever-supportive and who have held me or sustained me during my work. My beloved nina Angie passed as I was completing this book. Even though she was unable to see it in print, I know she would have been proud. My family and chosen family is also expansive, and I could not have done this without you. Many of you are already mentioned above, but to the list I will also add Cetine Dale, Dean Gao, and the Martinez family (Anayvette, Lupita, and Diego Luna), as well as newer family members from the Saavedra side, including Leonor, Jorge, Crystal, Andrew, Bianca, and Diego. I want to especially thank my mom, Aurora, sisters, Revecca and Christina, and nieces, Emma and Penelope, whose love I constantly feel even though we are many, many miles apart. All of you have always been my cheerleaders, and you have also always served as my inspiration. I hope to continue to make you proud. My partner, Yvette J. Saavedra, holds a very special and central place in my heart and this work. Not only is she my love and my home, but I have also had the privilege of calling her by many titles including co-chair, colleague, family, wife, and so many more. She has been beyond supportive of me. I am forever grateful to all the ways she was there, cheering me on, and never doubting me or this book.

NOTES

INTRODUCTION

Epigraph: Neal and Neal, back cover of *My Rainbow* (2020); Nodelman, introduction to *More Words about Pictures*, 10.

1 The first DQSH took place in December 2015. See "Drag Queen Story Hour," RADAR Productions, quoted 2018, www.radarproductions.org; "About," Drag Queen Story Hour, quoted 2018, www.dragqueenstoryhour.org; Una Lamarche, "Drag Queen Story Hour Puts the Rainbow in Reading," *New York Times*, March 19, 2017, www.nytimes.com. In 2022, the organization changed its name to Drag Story Hour (DSH).

2 Charlotte Allen, "Opinion: What I Saw at Drag Queen Story Hour," *Wall Street Journal*, October 9, 2019, www.wsj.com.

3 This specific incident occurred on January 26, 2019; "Armed Man Disrupts Houston Library during Drag Queen Storytime," *OutSmart*, January 29, 2019, www.outsmartmagazine.com. In response, librarians created a DQSH resource guide, which begins with the following statement: "Many libraries across the country have been hosting or participating in Drag Queen Story Hours. A few have experienced pushback from some members of their community. To support libraries facing challenges we have established this collection of resources. We will continue to add to it and welcome your contributions." See "Libraries Respond: Drag Queen Story Hour," American Library Association, September 19, 2018, www.ala.org.

4 Hate crimes against LGBTQ+ communities and spaces are all too common. These include individual attacks as well as mass shootings such as Pulse (Florida) in 2016 and Club Q (Colorado) in 2022.

5 See "Florida Man Convicted of Murdering 3-Year-Old 'Gay' Son," *The Advocate*, July 19, 2005, www.advocate.com.

6 See Rowe Michael, "What Is Says about Us When a 17-Month-Old Boy Is Beaten to Death for 'Acting like a Girl,'" *Huffington Post*, August 5, 2010, www.huffpost.com.

7 Further details of this case were captured in the Netflix documentary series *The Trials of Gabriel Fernandez* (2020).

8 Anthony's mother stood by while her boyfriend tortured the boy for at least five consecutive days. See Kit Ramgopal and Karin Roberts, "Man Charged with Killing Boy, 10, Who Reportedly Came Out as Gay," *NBC News*, June 27, 2018, www.nbcnews.com.

9   See Julie Turkewitz, "9-Year-Old Boy Killed Himself after Being Bullied, His Mom Says," *New York Times*, August 28, 2018, www.nytimes.com.

10   There are many others over ten years old such as Carl Joseph Walker-Hoover (11 years old; died by suicide); if we also count teens, examples include Gwen Araujo (15), Sakia Gunn (15), Lawrence King (15), and Angie Zapata (18). Even though I am only focusing on children of color, I do so because it is within the scope of this project and not because I am arguing that homophobia or transphobia are more prevalent in communities of color, nor am I saying that white children have not also been victims of similar hate crimes.

11   Muñoz, *Cruising Utopia*, 95.

12   I do not mean in terms of Existential Philosophy or of equating Being with Reason, Rational Thought, or Rationality. Instead, I am thinking about it in terms of the state of being alive and thriving. For a philosophical discussion, see Jaspers, *Philosophy of Existence*; Gordon, *Existence in Black*; Tillich, "Existential Philosophy."

13   The organization GLAAD compiled a list of actions taken by the Trump adminis-tration related to LGBTQ+ laws and policies; see "GLAAD Accountability Project: Donald Trump," www.glaad.org. According to data collected by the Southern Poverty Law Center, there were over seven hundred "incidents of hateful harass-ment" in the first week following the election; see "Update: Incidents of Hateful Harassment since Election Day Now Number 701," Southern Poverty Law Center, November 18, 2016, www.splcenter.org. Other striking statistics included: "Over 2,500 educators described specific incidents of bigotry and harassment that can be directly traced to election rhetoric. These incidents include graffiti (including swastikas), assaults on students and teachers, property damage, fights and threats of violence"; see "The Trump Effect: The Impact of the 2016 Presidential Election on Our Nation's Schools," Southern Poverty Law Center, November 28, 2016, www.splcenter.org.

14   "Florida's Governor Signs Controversial Law Opponents Dubbed 'Don't Say Gay,'" *NPR*, March 28, 2022, www.npr.org.

15   For example, Texas State Representative Matt Krause circulated a list of over 800 books he wanted banned, which includes some of the titles I discuss in *Coloring into Existence*; see Bill Chappell, "A Texas Lawmaker Is Targeting 850 Books That He Says Could Make Students Feel Uneasy," NPR, October 28, 2021, www.npr.org.

16   Douglass, "The Color Line."

17   This address was delivered by Du Bois in 1900 at the Pan-African Conference or-ganized by H. Sylvester Williams in London from July 23rd to 25th, a year before Du Bois published "The Freedmen's Bureau" (1901) and years before he published *The Souls of Black Folk* (1903). According to archival records, the end of the speech lists the following four individuals and their titles in this order: Alexander Walters (Bishop), President Pan-African Association; Henry B. Brown, Vice-President; H. Sylvester Williams, General Secretary; and W. E. Burghardt Du Bois, Chairman Committee on Address. See Pan-African Association, "To the nations

of the world, ca. 1900," W. E. B. Du Bois Papers, Special Collections and University Archives, University of Massachusetts Amherst Libraries, https://credo.library .umass.edu. According to Alexander Walters's *My Life and Work*, "Prof. DuBois, chairman of the Committee on Address to the Nations of the World, submitted the following, which was adopted and sent to the sovereigns in whose realms are subjects of African descent" (257). Contemporary scholars generally credit Du Bois as either the sole author or primary author of this address. For example, Rothberg lists DuBois as sole author; see Rothberg, "W. E. B. Du Bois in Warsaw," 187n1.

18 Perry, *Vexy Thing*, 244–45.

19 Perry, 245.

20 Some scholars suggest its origins lie in the colonial era, while others trace the song to the Cursillo movement within the Catholic Church in Spain during the 1940s; see Gómez-Quiñones and Vásquez, *Making Aztlán*; Azcona, "Chicano Movement Music."

21 The popular Spanish version of this song goes as follows: "De colores, | De colores se visten los campos de la primavera | De colores, | De colores son los pajaritos que vienen de afuera | De colores, | De colores es el arco iris que vemos lucir | Y por eso los grandes amores de muchos colores | Me gustan a mi." E. Martínez translated these lyrics "with much poetic license," as follows: "Many colors, | In spring the fields don many colors | Many colors, | The birds that come from afar have many colors | Many colors, | The lustrous rainbow that we see has many colors | And that is why the great loves of many colors | Are so pleasing to me"; see "About 'De Colores,'" in E. Martínez, *De Colores Means All of Us*. Her book was meant as a "transformative, feminist worldview that can help move us toward a rainbow century," and her engagement of rainbows is rooted in the Indigenous epistemology of Turtle Island's "Warriors of the Rainbow"; see Vinson Brown, *Voices of Earth and Sky*, quoted in E. Martínez, *De Colores Means All of Us*, xviii.

22 M. Gonzalez, *Claiming Face*, especially chapter 6, "The 3 Rules," 73–80.

23 Rankin and Neighbors, "Introduction: Horizons of Possibility," 1.

24 This question, along with the goal of publishing the "books that are missing," was at the forefront of Janine Macbeth's Indiegogo campaign, "#ReadInColor: Diverse Books for Every Kid," to fund Blood Oregon Press in 2016, www.indiegogo.com.

25 Larrick, "The All-White World of Children's Books," 63–85.

26 Although I focus on queer and trans of color children's picture books, LGBTQ+ YA novels have also been overwhelmingly white. See Jenkins, "Young Adult Novels with Gay/Lesbian Characters and Themes, 1969–92."

27 These statistics are based on an infographic created by David Huyck and Sarah Park Dahlen with data compiled from the Cooperative Children's Book Center (CCBC), a research library of the School of Education at the University of Wisconsin–Madison; see Huyck and Dahlen, "Diversity in Children's Books 2018," *Sarah Park Dahlen* (blog), June 19, 2019, https://readingspark.wordpress.com.

CCBC has been generating statistics on multicultural children's picture books since 1985. It is unclear if the Latinx category also includes Latin American characters and/or authors. As of 2018, CCBC began documenting disability, religion, LGBTQ+, and gender.

28 Huyck and Dahlen, "Diversity in Children's Books."

29 Anzaldúa, "La Prieta," 199.

30 Anzaldúa, 208.

31 Sedgwick, "How to Bring Your Kids Up Gay," 20. The decision to shift from sexuality to gender was made in 1973 and appeared in the 1974 seventh printing of the DSM-II, the 1980 DSM-III, and subsequent versions under modified names (e.g., Gender Dysphoria within DSM-V in 2013); see Beek, Cohen-Kettenis, and Kreukels, "Gender Incongruence/Gender Dysphoria and Its Classification History"; Tosh, *Psychology and Gender Dysphoria*.

32 Edelman, *No Future*, 19, 31.

33 Edelman, 31. Edelman's *No Future* was also the cause of much debate at the 2005 MLA annual convention. See José Esteban Muñoz's response, "Thinking beyond Antirelationality and Antiutopianism in Queer Critique," in "Forum: Conference Debates," published as Caserio et al., "The Antisocial Thesis in Queer Theory."

34 Bruhm and Hurley, *Curiouser*, xxxiii–xxxiv. Emphasis in original.

35 Bruhm and Hurley, xxxiv.

36 Direct quote is from the special issue's abstract online; see also Gill-Peterson, Sheldon, and Stockton, "Introduction."

37 The collection resulted from a conference or an "Interdisciplinary Workshop at Williams College, May 3–5, 2013," titled "Worlds of Wonder: The Queerness of Childhood" (https://sites.williams.edu/worlds-of-wonder/); Fishzon and Lieber, *The Queerness of Childhood*. Also see Bohlmann and Moreland, *Monstrous Children and Childish Monsters*.

38 Kid, "Queer Theory's Child and Children's Literature Studies," 185.

39 The IRSCL traces its origins to the Frankfurt Colloquium of 1969 organized by members of the Institute for Children's Literature Research; a year later, the IRSCL was founded on May 30, 1970, while its first conference was held in October 1971 in Frankfurt, Germany (see "About IRSCL," IRSCL, www.irscl.com). The ChLA began as a joint project between Anne Jordan and Francelia Butler, who met along with other scholars on August 20, 1973, and the first conference took place March 15–17, 1974, at the University of Connecticut (see Gay, "ChLA: 1973–1983").

40 Anyone interested in beginning research in children's literature should also consult its "General Bibliography" (2429–2432); see Zipes et al., *The Norton Anthology of Children's Literature*. For a discussion of the relationship between comics and children's literature, see Hunt, *Children's Literature*, especially chapters 8 through 10; Hatfield, "Comic Art, Children's Literature, and the New Comic Studies"; Hatfield and Svonkin, "Why Comics Are and Are Not Picture Books"; Nodelman, "Picture Book Guy Looks at Comics"; Aldama, *Comics Studies Here and Now*. For

a discussion of the role of illustrations within comics, see Harvey, *The Art of the Comic Book*.

41 For fifteenth-century rhymes, see Opie, "Playground Rhymes and the Oral Tradition." For an early eighteenth-century example, see W[hite], *A Little Book for Little Children*; although it was considered an educational book at the time, it includes topics such as intoxication, fighting, and shooting a frog, which could be considered taboo subjects today. An impressive feat at over 2,000 pages, *The Norton Anthology of Children's Literature* collects over 200 original works for children from the 1600s to the present, "tracing the historical development of genres and traditions through 350 years of children's literature in English" (Zipes et al., xxxii). For histories of children's literature written or translated into English, see Nikolajeva, *Aspects and Issues in the History of Children's Literature*; Hunt, *Children's Literature*; Hunt, *International Companion Encyclopedia of Children's Literature*; Lerer, *Children's Literature*; Grenby and Immel, *The Cambridge Companion to Children's Literature*; Reynolds, *Children's Literature*. For Latinx and Latin American examples from the 1800s and 1900s, see Brady, "Children's Literature."

42 Such as manga or European classics like *Alice's Adventures in Wonderland*. See Coats, *Looking Glasses and Neverlands*; Clark, *Kiddie Lit*. For a brief history of manga, see Ito, "A History of Manga in the Context of Japanese Culture and Society."

43 For a broader discussion of gender and school stories, see Clark, *Regendering the School Story*.

44 See Taylor, "U.S. Children's Picture Books and the Homonormative Subject"; Millán, "Contested Children's Literature"; J. Miller, "A Little Queer"; J. Miller, "For the Little Queers"; DePalma, "Gay Penguins, Sissy Ducklings . . . and Beyond?"; Capuzza, "'T' Is for 'Transgender'"; Epstein, "We're Here, We're (Not?) Queer"; Lester, "Homonormativity in Children's Literature."

45 In 2012, Jamie Campbell Naidoo published a notable reference book on LGBTQ+ children's picture books and chapter books; see Naidoo, *Rainbow Family Collections*.

46 For an overview of the history of children's book illustrations, see Feaver, *When We Were Young*; M. Miller, "Illustrations of the 'Canterbury Tales' for Children"; Lewis, *Reading Contemporary Picturebooks*.

47 See Lewis, *Reading Contemporary Picturebooks*, xvi, as well as chapter 1, "Modern Picturebooks: The State of the Art."

48 Thirty-two pages is currently the industry standard; however, others generally range from twenty-four to forty or forty-eight pages. They are usually multiples of eight due to double-sided printing and printer signature groupings of sixteen pages each. Many contemporary picture books do not include page numbers.

49 See Nodelman, *Words about Pictures*; Hunt, *Children's Literature*; Nel and Paul, *Keywords for Children's Literature*.

50 Paratextual features include "title pages, covers, endpapers, dedications, author notes, book jackets, advertisements, promotional materials, associated websites

and such"; these are divided into peritext, or "those contained within the covers of the book," and epitext, or "those that are outside the book itself," such as advertisements, promotional materials, and websites (Serafini, "Design Elements of Picturebooks," 6). Also see Genette, *Paratexts*.

51 Zipes, "The Twists and Turns of Radical Children's Literature," vii. For additional discussions of political context as it relates to children's literature, see Mickenberg, *Learning from the Left*; Mickenberg and Nel, *Tales for Little Rebels*.

52 Dupriez, *A Dictionary of Literary Devices*; Jones, "Getting Rid of Children's Literature," 290.

53 Abrams, *The Mirror and the Lamp*, 6.

54 Exceptions include picture books such as Charlotte Steiner's *Tomboy's Doll* (1969). For a literary history of tomboys, see Abate, *Tomboys*.

55 Bruce Mack's *Jesse's Dream Skirt* originally appeared under the pseudonym "Morning Star" as an illustrated story in *Magnus: A Socialist Journal of Gay Liberation* (1977). Larry Hermsen completed the accompanying illustrations. The story was later revised (including new illustrations by Marian Buchanan) and published as a picture book by Lollipop Power, Inc., an independent feminist press, in 1979. See Marian Buchanan, "A Better Version of Jesse's Dream Skirt," Marian Buchanan's personal website, July 9, 2015, www.marianbuchanan.com. For varying interpretations, see Swartz, "Bridging Multicultural Education"; Dykstra, "Trans-Friendly Preschool"; Tunks and McGee, "Embracing William, Oliver Button, and Tough Boris"; Herzog, "Sissies, Dolls, and Dancing"; Flores, "Teachers Working Cooperatively with Parents and Caregivers When Implementing LGBT Themes in the Elementary Classroom."

56 Cases of gender-neutral parenting inspired by this book include Storm Stocker, the child of Kathy Witterick and David Stocker. The parents stated in an email delivered in 2011 to those around them: "We decided not to share Storm's sex for now—a tribute to freedom and choice in place of limitation, a standup to what the world could become in Storm's lifetime." The *Toronto Star*, along with ABC's *The View* (among others), reported on this case. See Linsey Davis and Susan Donaldson James, "Canadian Mother Raising 'Genderless' Baby, Storm, Defends Her Family's Decision," *ABC News*, May 20, 2011, https://abcnews.go.com.

57 It sparked conflict within the lesbian community because of its focus on breakups as opposed to depicting positive lesbian relationships. See Crisp, "Setting the Record 'Straight.'"

58 E. Ford, "H/Z."

59 From birth, and even prior to birth, society genders and divides children into socially acceptable categories such as "girls" and "boys." Additionally, as Steven Bruhm and Natasha Hurley illustrate in their introduction to *Curiouser: On the Queerness of Children*, "There is currently a dominant narrative about children: children are (and should stay) innocent of sexual desires and intentions. At the same time, however, children are also officially, tacitly, assumed to be heterosexual," creating the "statistically 'normal' child" (ix–x).

60 These age parameters are not finite categories; they blur and blend into one another, varying across specific sociopolitical and historical contexts. See Ariès, *Centuries of Childhood*.

61 The consequences of not providing adequate adult supervision could potentially lead to inquiries from Child Protective Services and be framed as neglect or child abuse. For example, it may not be childnormative within our contemporary Western society for a five-year-old to walk to and from kindergarten. Or it may not be childnormative for a six-year-old to stay home alone. Simultaneously, as Juana María Rodríguez has observed, the policing of children's space has led to "No Adults Allowed Unless Accompanied by Children" signs, including within spaces such as Queer Pride; see J. M. Rodríguez's chapter "Who's Your Daddy? Queer Kinship and Perverse Domesticity," in *Sexual Futures, Queer Gestures, and Other Latina Longings*, 31.

62 Sánchez-Eppler, "Childhood."

63 Sara Ahmed details the tension between parents and children in her discussion of willful girls and willful children. See chapter 3 in *Living a Feminist Life*, as well as *Willful Subjects*. Also see Halberstam, *Wild Things*; Brady, *Scales of Captivity*.

64 North America is not synonymous with the United States and must be understood as also encompassing Canada and Mexico. Given my research focus, this grouping notably excludes Greenland, the Caribbean, and the subcontinent of Central America (i.e., Guatemala, Belize, El Salvador, Honduras, Nicaragua, Costa Rica, and Panama). When I use the term "Americas," I mean the continents of North and South America, as well as the Caribbean. See Shukla and Tinsman, *Imagining Our Americas*; Levander and Levine, *Hemispheric American Studies*; Siemerling and Casteel, *Canada and Its Americas*.

65 See Adams, *Continental Divides*.

66 See Saldívar, *Border Matters*.

67 The field of border studies emerges from the rich collisions between Chicana/o/x and Latina/o/x studies, Latin American studies, and transnational feminisms. See Anzaldúa, *Borderlands/La Frontera*; Mignolo, *Local Histories/Global Designs*; Saldívar-Hull, *Feminism on the Border*; Brady, *Extinct Lands, Temporal Geographies*; Fregoso, *MeXicana Encounters*; Belausteguigoitia and Melgar, *Fronteras, violencia, justicia*.

68 Anzaldúa, *Borderlands/La Frontera*; specifically, see the first half of this book, titled "*Atravesando Fronteras*/Crossing Borders," including the following definition: "*Los atravesados* live here . . . in short, those who cross over, pass over, or go through the confines of the 'normal'" (3). All direct quotes from *Borderlands* pertain to the first edition.

69 See Echeverría, "*Queer*, manierista, *bizarre*, barroco."

70 This includes canonical texts by queer women of color such as the Combahee River Collective, "The Combahee River Collective: A Black Feminist Statement" (1977/78); Moraga and Anzaldúa, *This Bridge Called My Back: Writings by Radical Women of Color* (1981); B. Smith, *Home Girls: A Black Feminist Anthology* (1983);

Lorde, *Sister Outsider: Essays and Speeches* (1984); and Anzaldúa, *Borderlands/La Frontera: The New Mestiza* (1987). See Ferguson, *Aberrations in Black*; Ferguson, "Queer of Color Critique"; Chambers-Letson, *After the Party*.

71 For an example of scholarship that engages more directly with how children read or respond to picture books, see Deliman, "Picturebooks and Critical Inquiry."

72 For a thorough engagement with identity politics, see Alcoff, *Visible Identities*; J. M. Rodríguez, *Queer Latinidad*.

73 I began to theorize autofantasía as a literary technique in "Contested Children's Literature: Que(e)ries into Chicana and Central American Autofantasías."

74 Halsall, "Translator's Preface," in Dupriez, *A Dictionary of Literary Devices*, x. Emphasis in the original.

75 See Berta-Ávila, Revilla, and Figueroa, *Marching Students*; Escudero, "Organizing While Undocumented"; Seif, "'Coming Out of the Shadows' and 'Undocuqueer.'" I also discuss disability and trans identities in chapter 5.

76 For Shirley Chisholm, see Russell-Brown, *She Was the First!*; for Emma Tenayuca, see Tafolla and Teneyuca, *That's Not Fair!*; for Mary Golda Ross, see Sorell, *Classified*; for Kamala Harris, see Grimes, *Kamala Harris*.

77 Bridges, *Through My Eyes*.

78 Archival examples include the Historic Iowa Children's Diaries collection (e.g., Belle Robinson's 1877 diary, which she began writing at the age of thirteen). Visit the Historical Iowa Children's Diaries digital collection at https://digital.lib.uiowa.edu.

79 Soto, *Reading Chican@ Like a Queer*.

80 E. Hernández, *Postnationalism in Chicana/o Literature and Culture*.

81 Spear, "Introduction," 1.

82 Keating, "Appendix 1: Glossary," in *The Gloria Anzaldúa Reader*, 319.

83 Anzaldúa, "The New Mestiza Nation," 216.

84 Anzaldúa, "now let us shift . . . the path of conocimiento . . . inner work, public acts," 578.

85 Anzaldúa, *Interviews*, 243. Also quoted in Keating, *EntreMundos/Among-Worlds*, 35.

86 Anzaldúa, "now let us shift . . . the path of conocimiento . . . inner work, public acts," 540.

87 Anzaldúa passed away before she could complete her Prieta series of short stories. However, she discussed the series and Prieta/Prietita character in numerous interviews before her death. Although autohistoria is primarily understood as a retelling of one's past and as temporally situated in one's past, she hinted that this may not always be the case, not only with autohistoria but with any autobiography: "what it becomes is an experiment in autobiography, and the point I'm trying to make is that autobiography is not just lived experience but also experiences that are imagined or fantasized. So I have Prieta from the 1980's looking back. . . . I also have her going into the future and doing the same thing" (Anzaldúa and de la Peña, "Interview," 2).

88 Aldama, "Magical Realism," 334–35.

89 See Linda Hutcheon's discussion of women's autobiography in *The Politics of Postmodernism*; see also Smith and Watson, *Reading Autobiography*; Vázquez, *Triangulations*; Bost, *Shared Selves*.

90 Dery, "Black to the Future," 736; as Alondra Nelson and others have argued, although Dery coined the term, "the currents that comprise it existed long before." See A. Nelson, "Introduction: Future Texts," especially 14n23 (which references Kodwo Eshun). See also Eshun, *More Brilliant than the Sun*.

91 Thomas, *The Dark Fantastic*, 18. Thomas distinguishes between her concept of "the Dark Fantastic" and Afrofuturism or the Black Fantastic; her concept considers the work of mainstream and predominantly white creators, while the other two privilege Black creators.

92 Ramírez, "Cyborg Feminism"; Ramírez, "Deus Ex Machina." Also see her discussion of Chicanafuturism as it relates to Afrofuturism in "Afrofuturism/Chicanafuturism: Fictive Kin."

93 Prior iterations appear, for example, in Benvenuto Cellini's original memoir written in Italian circa the mid-1500s (published posthumously in 1728); reflecting on a conversation with an inmate, he wrote: "Mi cominciò a domandare, se io avevo mai auto fantasia di volare" [He began to ask me, if I ever had an auto fantasy of flying]. Here, "auto fantasia" loosely translates to "self-fantasy," "personal fantasy," or, more simply, a fantasy or desire. Thomas Roscoe first translated Cellini into English in 1822 (Cellini, *Memoirs of Benvenuto Cellini*). Twentieth-century examples, meanwhile, include translations of the German philosopher credited for phenomenology Edmund Husserl's *Ideen zu einer reinen Phänomenologie und phenomenologische Philosophie II* (1952); Alexander Wolf and Emanuel K Schwartz's research on psychotherapy (1958); and Leon Livingstone's analysis of Spanish autobiographies, in which he writes, "no como historia, sino como poesía. Autofantasía" [not like history, but like poetry. Autofantasy] (1982); see Spanish translations by Ideen, II Buch (97), quoted in Notas Bioliograficas (378), and English translation by Richard Rojcewicz and Andree Schuwer. Wolf and Schwartz, "Irrational Psychotherapy: An Appeal to Unreason (III)"; Livingstone, "Autobiografia y autofantasia en la Generacion del 98: Teoria y practica del querer ser," quote from page 300.

94 I translate "monjita" as "little nun" to emphasize the diminutive form of "nun"; this title can also be translated as "I have an aunt who is not a nun" or as "I have an aunt who is not a dear nun."

95 As I will discuss in chapter 1, Johnson also self-published another coloring book (*A Day with Alexis*) prior to *A Beach Party with Alexis*, which may or may not be read as a picture book; see S. Johnson, *A Day with Alexis*.

1. LITERARY FIRSTS

Epigraph: Quoted in Lauro Vazquez, "An Interview with Rigoberto González," *Letras Latinas Blog*, January 22, 2012, http://letraslatinasblog.blogspot.com.

1 The original lawsuit was filed in 1998 under the title *"Chamberlain et al v. The Board of Trustees of School District No. 36 (Surrey) and Others."* See *Chamberlain et al. v. The Board of Trustees of School District No. 36 (Surrey) and Others*, 1998 CanLII 6723 (BC SC), Canada.

2 The policy was referred to as "District Policy B64–95/96" in *Chamberlain v. Surrey School District No. 36*, 2002 SCC 86 [2002] 4 SCR 738–39, Canada, https://scc-csc .lexum.com.

3 The "GALE Resolution" was dated April 10, 1997; the "Three Books Resolution," which specifically targeted *Belinda's Bouquet*, *Asha's Mums*, and *One Dad, Two Dads, Brown Dads, Blue Dads*, was dated April 24, 1997. For a summary of each resolution, see *Chamberlain v. Surrey School District No. 36*, 2000 BCCA 519, 4, Canada.

4 *Chamberlain v. Surrey School District No. 36* (2000). GALE-BC continued compiling LGBTQ+ educational resources. For example, in 2000, they produced *Challenging Homophobia in Schools*, a handbook "with comprehensive sections on rationale, background information, classroom strategies, lesson plans (kindergarten to grade 12), and resources" (Carter, "Vancouver, Canada," 103).

5 *Chamberlain v. Surrey School District No. 36* (2002).

6 *Chamberlain v. Surrey School District No. 36* (2002).

7 *Chamberlain v. Surrey School District No. 36* (2002).

8 *Chamberlain v. Surrey School District No. 36* (2002).

9 "School Board Rejects Books with Gay Parents for Bad Grammar," *CBC News*, June 13, 2003, www.cbc.ca.

10 For a discursive discussion of this policy and how it compares to other countries, see Ferfolja, "LGBT Equity and School Policy."

11 Tim McCaskell, then a board member of the Equity Department, was one of the individuals who sought out LGBTQ+ materials; see McCaskell, *Race to Equity*; McCaskell, *Queer Progress*.

12 For a brief history, see McCaskell, "Fighting Homophobia in Toronto Schools"; Russell, "Equity Undone." The Triangle Program was also challenged by queer and queer of color communities for is initial inability to integrate an intersectional or race-based analysis; see Snider, "Race and Sexual Orientation."

13 The author/illustrator published the coloring book *A Beach Party with Alexis* under the name "Sarita Johnson-Calvo," although she also went by "Sarita Johnson-Hunt" or just "Sarita Johnson," which is the name she presently uses. I will mostly use "Johnson-Calvo" when crediting her as author for copyright purposes; otherwise, I will refer to her as Sarita Johnson. The copyright page for *A Beach Party with Alexis* lists 1991 as the original copyright date, although it was later published by Alyson Wonderland, an imprint of Alyson Publications, Inc., in 1993. 1991 marks the year the coloring book was completed (in accordance with US copyright law). Sarita Johnson, email correspondence to author, February 22, 2022. Johnson also indicated to me that prior to *A Beach Party with Alexis*, she created another coloring book titled *A Day with Alexis*, which may or may not

count as a picture book; as of this writing, its publication date is unknown (see my discussion of Johnson within the US section of this chapter). Sarita Johnson, email correspondence to author, February 22–23, 2022.

14 *Antonio's Card* was published by Children's Book Press. Although not an explicitly feminist press, it was created by Harriet Rohmer in an effort to publish authors of color and stories for communities of color. Within gay of color scholarship, see Michael Hames-García and Ernesto Javier Martínez, *Gay Latino Studies: A Critical Reader.*

15 See Hunter and Polikoff, "Custody Rights of Lesbian Mothers"; Robson, "Making Mothers"; Rivers, *Radical Relations*; Gutterman, *Her Neighbor's Wife.* Despite both groups being framed as "predatory," gay men have been positioned as a greater risk to children. For example, Rivers notes that "gay fathers usually fought for visitation rights while lesbians fought for either visitation or outright custody," at least between 1967 and 1985 in the United States ("In the Best Interest of the Child," 918). Also see Becker, "Child Sexual Abuse Allegations against a Lesbian or Gay Parent in a Custody or Visitation Dispute"; George, "The Custody Crucible."

16 Within the US, data on children raised by queer parents maintains that there were no negative consequences to their well-being.

17 Ferguson, "Queer of Color Critique," 2.

18 Canada's version of English closely aligns with Great Britain given its continued relationship to the Crown under its constitutional monarchy. I maintain original spelling of titles and direct quotes throughout.

19 Elwin and Paulse, *Asha's Mums*, 4.

20 Elwin and Paulse, 7.

21 Her brother, Mark, is not depicted elsewhere in the text. It may be that he no longer lives with the family or only temporarily lives with them.

22 Jackson, "Performing Show and Tell," 164.

23 *Chamberlain v. Surrey School District No. 36* (2002).

24 *Chamberlain v. Surrey School District No. 36* (2002).

25 *Chamberlain v. Surrey School District No. 36* (2002).

26 C. Mitchell, "What's Out There?," 115.

27 See Collins, *Black Sexual Politics.* In addition to gender and sexuality, butch-femme dynamics have historically been both raced and classed. See Somerville, *Queering the Color Line*; Keeling, "Ghetto Heaven."

28 Karen Coats engages in color symbolism within children's literature in "Visual Conceptual Metaphors in Picturebooks: Implications for Social Justice."

29 One detail in the backdrop of the last spread depicts one of the staircases and circular outline of the architecture in Ontario's Science Centre located in Toronto, Ontario. The first level includes a Van de Graaff electrostatic generator, or silver sphere, which visitors can touch for a "Hair-raising Experience": www.ontariosciencecentre.ca.

30 Elwin and Paulse, *Asha's Mums*, 14.

31 Elwin and Paulse, 14.

32 Elwin and Paulse, 14.

33 "About," Canadian Scholars, www.canadianscholars.ca. For a detailed discussion of Canada's Women's Liberation Era from 1960 to 1988, see P. Mitchell, *About Canada*. Also, Women's Press should not be confused with the Canadian Women's Press Club (CWPC) founded in 1904.

34 Interview with members of Women's Press; see Acton, Bobier, and Martin, "Women's Press," 20.

35 See the copyright page for each picture book.

36 Neither anthology lists Elwin, Paulse, or any other name as editor; instead, each title page states, "Edited by The Lesbian Writing and Publishing Collective," and attributes copyright to Women's Press. *Dykeversions* includes, "The Book was produced by the collective effort of the members of the Women's Press," while *Dykewords* adds, "This book was produced by the collective effort of Women's Press and is a project of the Lesbian Manuscript Group."

37 Other titles Elwin either edited or co-edited include *Getting Wet: Tales of Lesbian Seduction* (1992, with Allain), *Out Rage: Dykes and Bis Resist Homophobia* (1993, with Oikawa, Falconer, and Decter), *Tangled Sheets: Stories and Poems of Lesbian Lust* (1995, with Tulchinsky), and *Countering the Myths: Lesbians Write about the Men in Their Lives* (1996).

38 See Honychurch, "Crossroads in the Caribbean."

39 Rosamund Elwin's daughter, Aziza, recounts her mother's migration story as part of her effort to honor her mother during Mother's Day. See Aziza Elwin, "My Mom Rosamund—A Woman of Distinction," in "Our Moms . . . the Original Women of Distinction," YWCA Toronto, May 13, 2012, http://blog.ywcatoronto.org.

40 "Naomi James Obituary," Dolan Funeral Services, 2018, www.dolanfuneral.com.

41 "Naomi James Obituary."

42 Elwin, "Introduction," 10.

43 Lorde's mother was born in Carriacou and met and married Lorde's father in Grenada before migrating to the US from Grenada. Lorde's father was from Barbados.

44 Lorde, *Zami*, 255.

45 M. Smith, *Kinship and Community in Carriacou*, 199.

46 M. Smith, 200. For another reading of M. G. Smith's engagement with Carriacou lesbianism or zami, see Apter, "M. G. Smith on the Isle of Lesbos: Kinship and Sexuality in Carriacou."

47 Paulse, quoted in "Contributors' Notes" at the end of *Dykeversions*, 184.

48 Paulse, quoted in "Contributors" at the end of *Lost Communities, Living Memories*, 6. In her book chapter, Paulse also explains her involvement with this collection, including her doctoral thesis and interviews on Tramway Road in Cape Town, South Africa. See Paulse, "'Everyone Had Their Differences but there Was Always Comradeship.'"

49 Paulse, quoted in "Contributors' Notes" at the end of *Dykeversions*, 184.

50 She explains further: "This meant I was born on the Cape Province and belonged to the 'Coloured,' meaning 'mixed' race." Paulse, "Commingled," 43–45.

51 See "Contributors' Notes," in Elwin, *Dykewords*, 266.

52 Elwin and Paulse co-authored a second children's picture book, *The Moonlight Hide and Seek Club in the Pollution Solution* (Women's Press, 1992), illustrated by Cheryl Henhawke. Within the story, the moon is unwell due to pollution by humans and has fallen on Earth. A group of children work together and, with the support of their parents, clean the moon and nurse her back to health. Savvy readers may pick up on the plural use of "Mei's dads," even if the accompanying illustration only depicts one dad.

53 "About the Front Cover," 6–7.

54 "About the Front Cover," 6–7.

55 Elwin, "My Mom Rosamund."

56 Elwin.

57 Elwin.

58 Last names were surmised based on the "Contributors' Notes" at the end of the anthology, since the two statements only listed first names ("Michele and Nila" and "Ellen and Maureen"); see Paulse et al., "Notes about Racism in the Process," 11–15.

59 Paulse et al., 11.

60 Paulse et al., 12.

61 Paulse et al., 12–13.

62 Paulse et al., 13.

63 As quoted in Niedzwiecki, *Print Politics*, 4.

64 Lisa Rochon, "Race Issue Splits Women's Press," *Globe and Mail*, August 9, 1988, C58.

65 For additional commentary, see Philip, "Journal Entries against Reaction," 97.

66 Michele Paulse also co-authored a letter published in *Kinesis* in which she and three others outlined why they were withdrawing from the 2nd Pan-Canadian Conference of Women and Words organizing committee. They concluded that "it is not the task of black women and women of colour to educate white women about racism"; see Silvera et al., "Racism Stops Women and Words," 27. For additional critiques of multiculturalism, see Morton, "Racism in the Arts"; Wong and Guo, *Revisiting Multiculturalism in Canada*; Chan, "Inner Hybridity in the City."

67 Mayo, *Disputing the Subject of Sex*, 102.

68 Mayo, 102.

69 Melissa Cardoza, personal communication to author, 2012.

70 In Spanish, the original quotation reads, "Creo que para ella no había más opciones y le causaba sorpresa que fuera una monja que no usara hábitos ni rezara." Quoted in "Polémico libro sobre familias lésbicas dirigido a niños," *Infobae*, February 26, 2005, www.infobae.com.

71 "Le dije que además de no ser monjita, era lesbiana y le expliqué que yo tenía novia y que las mujeres podíamos hacer eso." Quoted in "Polémico libro sobre familias lésbicas dirigido a niños."

72 Melissa Cardoza, personal communication to author, 2012.

73 I initially began to consider this picture book as an autofantasía in Millán, "Contested Children's Literature."

74 Same sex marriage laws in Canada, the US, and Mexico.

75 See Curb and Manaham, *Lesbian Nuns*; Franco, *Plotting Women*; Evans and Healey, *Queer and Catholic.*

76 On globalization and Latin America, see Canclini, *Consumers and Citizens.*

77 See Bell, Haas, and Sells, *From Mouse to Mermaid*; Faherty, "Is the Mouse Sensitive?"; Towbin et al., "Images of Gender, Race, Age, and Sexual Orientation in Disney Feature-Length Animated Films"; D. Hurley, "Seeing White."

78 Marta Neri, personal interview, 2010; *Tengo una tía que no es monjita*, directed by Julia Robles. See also "Anuario 2007," Teatro en los Estados, 2007, 77, www .teatromexicano.com.mx.

79 MacCann, *White Supremacy in Children's Literature*. Other examples include Klein, *Reading into Racism*; Nel, *Was the Cat in the Hat Black?*; as well as public scholarship and blogs such as Debbie Reese's popular online platform *American Indians in Children's Literature* (AICL), https://americanindiansinchildrensliteratu re.blogspot.com.

80 Unlike British colonization, Spanish colonization relied on a Casta system, with numerous racial/ethnic hierarchical classifications. See Saavedra, *Pasadena before the Roses*, especially chapter 1.

81 See Bennett, *Colonial Blackness*; Vinson III and Restall, *Black Mexico.*

82 See Candelario, *Black behind the Ears*; Rivero, *Turning Out Blackness.*

83 See Hall, *Naming a Transnational Black Feminist Framework*; López Oro, "A Love Letter to Indigenous Blackness"; Lambert, "We Are Black Too"; Anderson, *Black and Indigenous.*

84 Vinicio Chacón, "Feminista: 'Honduras es laboratorio de las más crudas políticas neoliberales,'" *Semanario Universidad*, June 19, 2013, https://historico .semanariouniversidad.com.

85 See Cardoza, *13 colores de la resistencia hondureña.*

86 Rosa María Laguna Gómez, personal interview, 2010. Also see "Las Manchas de la Luna," CENART, 2021, www.cenart.gob.mx; email correspondence "El Mejor Corto, Prepas de la UDG," Musas de Metal listserv, March 18, 2008.

87 This short film is available online: www.youtube.com/watch?v=HSh1eJ-nY_o.

88 As previously mentioned, *A Beach Party with Alexis*'s original copyright lists 1991 and was then published by Alyson Wonderland in 1993. Johnson also created another coloring book titled *A Day with Alexis*. During our initial conversation, Johnson was unsure about the copyright year but mentioned that she may still have a copy of it among her things and would look for it. If published prior to 1990, and if we decide it is also a picture book, it will force us to reconsider *Asha's Mums'* current designation as "literary first" across North America. Sarita Johnson, email correspondence to author, February 22–23, 2022.

89 Mickenberg and Nel, *Tales for Little Rebels*, 1.

90 Rather than address the trauma or contextualizing the geopolitical climate sur-
    rounding 9/11, these books opt for "simplistic narratives of character empower-
    ment adapted from self-help literature." Kid, *Freud in Oz*, 185. Also see Lampert,
    Children's Fiction about 9/11.
91 See C. Nelson, "Writing the Reader"; Sipe and McGuire, "Picturebook Endpapers."
92 Kirby, "Reading with Uncle Sam."
93 Alyson Wonderland began in 1990 and published LGBT-themed children's litera-
    ture; it was an imprint of Alyson Publications, Inc., which was founded in 1980 by
    Sasha Alyson and specialized in LGBT literature. Children's Book Press began as
    an independent press; in 2012 it became an imprint of Lee & Low Books.
94 Fernandez, "Children of the Rainbow," 378–82.
95 Alyson Wonderland Book Listings describe the coloring book as follows: "A
    Beach Party with Alexis, by Sarita Johnson-Calvo, $3.00. Alexis is giving a beach
    party, with a little help from her mothers. A beautifully drawn coloring book
    that will help children learn about diversity. The illustrations follow Alexis as she
    plans and then hosts her beach party, from making the invitations to watching the
    sunset. Alexis' guests include people of many races, body types, and in many dif-
    ferent family configurations. Ages 2 to 6." See "Alyson Wonderland Book Listing,"
    Queer Resources Directory, 1994, www.qrd.org. Also see Sarita Johnson, email
    correspondence to author, February 22–23, 2022.
96 Sarita Johnson, email correspondence to author, February 22, 2022.
97 Sarita Johnson, email correspondence to author, February 22, 2022. In May 2020,
    Crayola unveiled its "Colors of the World" skin tone colors.
98 Sarita Johnson, email correspondence to author, February 23, 2022.
99 R. González, *Antonio's Card*, 4.
100 R. González, 6.
101 I used "first mother" instead of "birth mother" in order to not assume or normal-
    ize giving birth as the only way one can become a mother. Although I am aware
    that by labeling one as first and the other as second, I am also creating a hierarchy.
    My goal here is only to distinguish between the two women.
102 Presumably, the plural use of "women" implies one's mother, as well as perhaps
    a grandmother, aunt, or stepmother. Despite this heteronormative logic, it does
    adequately describe Antonio's situation whereby he has, indeed, two mothers.
    R. González, *Antonio's Card*, 12.
103 R. González, 12.
104 R. González, 15.
105 R. González, 17.
106 R. González, 17.
107 R. González, 18.
108 R. González, 18.
109 R. González, 10.
110 R. González, 29.

111 R. González, 29.

112 R. González, 30.

113 Johnson's biography appears under "Contributors," quoted on page 88. She contributed an illustration for issue 13; see Hemphill, "If Freud Had Been a Neurotic Colored Woman."

114 See S. Johnson, "Occupation."

115 Examples include her illustrations in the following: *Sinister Wisdom*, 1989; *Aegis: Magazine on Ending Violence against Women*, no. 41 (1986): 17.

116 Johnson does not recall when she created this coloring book. Sarita Johnson, email correspondence to author, February 22–23, 2022.

117 Sarita Johnson, email correspondence to author, February 22–23, 2022. As I was completing the copy edits for this book, I received an email from Johnson stating that she had found copies of *A Day with Alexis* and would mail them to me; email correspondence to author, March 9, 2023. I received two copies in late March. Visually, one of the greatest differences is that these illustrations appear pixelated. The only text on the cover and title page reads: "A Day with Alexis © Sarita Johnson-Hunt." It does not include a copyright date. Although I was unable to fully analyze it within this book, I look forward to more closely engaging this coloring book in the future.

118 Her newest website can be found at https://saritajohnson.myportfolio.com.

119 R. González, *Soledad Sigh-Sighs*, 32.

120 R. González, 32.

121 R. González, 30.

122 R. González, 30.

123 Lauro Vazquez, "An Interview with Rigoberto González," *Letras Latinas Blog*, January 22, 2012, https://letraslatinasblog.blogspot.com.

124 Vazquez.

125 Jenna Herbert, "An Interview with Rigoberto González," *English at Saint Rose* (blog), October 7, 2013, https://stroseenglish.wordpress.com.

126 Vazquez, "An Interview with Rigoberto González."

127 Herbert, "An Interview with Rigoberto González."

128 Herbert.

129 Herbert.

130 Barthes, "The Death of the Author." I agree with Barthes on a few points, namely that a text is "a multi-dimensional space in which a variety of writings, none of them original, blend and clash" (146). He also argues, "Classic criticism has never paid any attention to the reader; for it, the writer is the only person in literature" (148).

131 I find useful the work of literary scholars such as Paula Moya, in which both author and reader can exist simultaneously, "interacting within a dynamic system of communication through which the manifold ideologies that shape and motivate humans' diverse cultural practices are circulated." Moya, *The Social Imperative*, 8. Although *The Social Imperative* as a whole privileges the reader

(as do I in chapter 5), it is especially useful when considering the sociopolitical implications of close readings.

132 C. Nelson, "Writing the Reader," 223.

2. A TALE OF THREE

Epigraph: Maya Gonzalez, "The Ghosts and the Writing: My First Novella," *Maya Gonzalez Blog: Life, Art, Activism*, July 7, 2017, www.mayagonzalez.com; S. Bear Bergman, quoted in Shea Fitzpatrick, "Yes, There Are Queer-Positive Children's Books That Are Actually Good and Not Horribly Depressing," *Medium's The Queue*, October 25, 2017, https://medium.com.

1 One may argue Mary was polyamorous because she had two simultaneous relationships (one with God and/or the Holy Spirit and one with Joseph). However, one may also argue that she did not consent to an encounter with God and is therefore a survivor of sexual assault.

2 Post-Revolution Mexico prioritized the institutionalization of public education through the conceptualization and development of new departments, positions, and organizations invested in the role of children as future citizens. In 1921, the Secretaría de Educación Pública (SEP), or Department of Public Education, was formed in an effort to centralize and organize the educational system on a national level. This new department was led by José Vasconcelos, who was assisted by Gabriela Mistral of Chile. Both would prove to be controversial figures, even to this day; Vasconcelos, for his construction of Mexican identity under what he referred to as "la Raza Cósmica," which romanticized an Indigenous past and glorified the mixing of peoples through colonization, and Mistral, who advocated morality, civility, and strict gender roles in children's education, and whose influence spread across Latin America. For a history of children's literature in Mexico, see Rey, *Historia y muestra de la literatura infantil Mexicana*; for Latin America, see Peña Muñoz, *Historia de la literature infantil en América Latina*.

3 "Revisar los libros de texto de la SEP que se distribuyen a nivel nacional en primarias y secundarias, para proponer mejores a los contenidos educativos con base en el respeto de la persona." Frente Nacional Por La Familia, "Análisis de los libros de texto de la SEP," PowerPoint presentation slides, n.d.

4 Formerly the National Institute of Statistics, Geography, and Informatics: https://inegi.org.mx.

5 See "Encuesta Nacional Sobre Diversidad Sexual y de Género (ENDISEG), 2021," INEGI, June 28, 2022, https://inegi.org.mx; and "Conociendo a la población LGBTI+ en México," INEGI, June 28, 2022, https://inegi.org.mx.

6 "Pregunté a 17 editoras mexicanas de literatura infantil y juvenil si alguna vez habían editado un libro en el que hubiera personajes cuya preferencia sexual fuera distinta a la norma o alguna trama que naturalizara la diversidad sexual entre ese grupo tan heterogéneo de lectores. Del total, sólo seis respondieron afirmativamente. Seis libros más otros seis (de no ficción), que encontré para este artículo, escritos y publicados originalmente en México en 40 años de historia de la

edición de LIJ moderna." See Adolfo Córdova, "Los días felices: Diversidad sexual y libros para niños, niñas, niñes y jóvenes," *Linternas y bosques: Literatura infantil y juvenil*, June 28, 2019, modified January 28, 2020, https://linternasybosques .wordpress.com.

7   "El Armario Abierto, librería especializada en sexualidad."

8   The quantity and price fluctuate, as does the exchange rate between pesos and dollars. For example, on February 19, 2021, three copies were available on Amazon within the US (listed in US dollars): $64.50, $113.08, and $149.50; on March 21, 2023, one copy was listed for $79.79 and another for $164.79. Within Amazon Mexico (amazon.com.mx), only one copy was available for $2,044.99 pesos (approximately $109.93 US dollars at that time) on March 21, 2023.

9   Within this chapter, I do not include children's picture books that gesture toward queer families such as *Esta familia que ves* (2013), written by Alfonso Ochoa and illustrated by Valeria Gallo, or middle-grade chapter books or YA novels such as *Sombras en el arcoiris* (2017), by M. B. Brozon.

10   See La Fountain-Stokes, "La política queer del espanglish."

11   The student movement was particularly strong, ending in the student massacre of Tletelolco that the Mexican government of the time attempted to hide. Within Mexico, "LGBTT" had historically been used more than "LGBTQ."

12   Mogrovejo refers to her as FLH's "main public face" in *Un amor que se atrevió a decir su nombre*, 313. Also see Mogrovejo, "The Latin American Lesbian Movement"; Ian G. Lumsden, *Homosexuality, Society, and the State in México* (Mexico: Solediciones, 1991) as referenced in Cantú, *The Sexuality of Migration*, 89.

13   Evidently, nonheteronormative sexualities were practiced before then, and many were publicly ostracized, such as in the controversial case of Los 41 in 1901. Cárdenas's case was different because she chose to publicly out herself.

14   See Mogrovejo, *Un amor que se atrevió a decir su nombre*, 64–65.

15   See Mogrovejo, "The Latin American Lesbian Movement," 319.

16   See a timeline of Patlatonalli's history: "LesbiHistoria," Patlatonalli, https: //patlatonalli.org.mx.

17   "Lesbianas en Patlatonalli A.C.," Patlatonalli document, courtesy of Rosa María Laguna Gómez, 2010.

18   Marta Nualart, personal interview, 2010.

19   "My Aunt's Friends." Marta Nualart, personal interview, 2010.

20   According to Rosa María Laguna Gómez, each book goes through an editing process where more prototypes are made and then shown to children and literature/ language specialists who provide additional feedback.

21   Quoted from Nualart's public remarks at a presentation she gave on *Tengo una tía que no es monjita*. Marta Nualart, email correspondence to author, January 2, 2011.

22   The competition accepted submissions during approximately two years, with a final deadline in 2004. Marta Nualart, personal interview, 2010.

23   Official competition results; Patlatonalli document, courtesy of Marta Nualart, 2010.

24 It should be noted that Anna Cooke is also related to one of the founding
    members of Patlatonalli. Additionally, they had intended on publishing a fourth
    lesbian-themed picture book by Rosamaría Roffiel; however, production delays
    resulted in the book being published in 2001 by Prensa Editorial LeSVOZ instead.
    See "'El secreto de las familias,' de Rosamaría Roffiel," LesVoz, October 18, 2021,
    www.lesvoz.org; Roffiel, *El secreto de las familias* [The secret to families]. In 2010,
    Roffiel—author of *Amora* (1989)—read her story aloud alongside Mondragón
    Rocha during a Patlatonalli event in Mexico City's Somos Voces (known at the
    time as Voces en Tinta).

25 This description appeared on the back cover of *Tengo una tía que no es monjita*,
    with slightly different variations for its other books.

26 Death is rarely mentioned in contemporary children's picture books, with the no-
    table exceptions of books that are explicitly about death and mourning or events
    like Día de los Muertos. Within *Las tres Sofías*, Sofía's mother participates in a
    public display of mourning for her deceased husband by wearing black. Whereas
    some widows might remain in mourning for the remainder of their lives, cultural
    norms, religious differences, and personal preferences dictate how and for how
    long one mourns. To perform luto, Sofía's mother had to wear black, and although
    she participated in the public mourning of her husband for almost one year,
    she also made a personal choice to *quitarse el luto*, or end her public display of
    mourning. Sofía observed how her mother stopped the mourning period before
    the one-year anniversary of her father's death and how she seemed distracted or
    pensive. In this context, *quitar* means to remove, and here she is actively remov-
    ing the visual marker—a black shawl—that designates her as being in mourning.
    This is Sofía's mother's first step toward Sofía Alvarado.

27 tatiana de la tierra, personal interview, 2011. De la tierra also experienced coming
    out in the classroom while teaching. See de la tierra, "Coming Out and Creating
    Queer Awareness in the Classroom."

28 Juan Rodríguez Matus, personal interview, 2010.

29 Totopos, a type of tortilla chip that originates in Oaxaca/Zapotec; and the famous
    Oaxacan quesos (cheeses).

30 For discussions of Asian Mexicans, see Delgado, *Making the Chinese Mexican*;
    Chew, "Mexicanidades de la Diáspora Asiática."

31 For a comparative study of Asian Mexicans and Afro Mexicans, see Ng'weno and
    Siu, *Comparative Raciality*.

32 See Belausteguigoitia and Melgar, *Fronteras, violencia, justicia*.

33 "21 Aniversario Patlatonalli AC," Patlatonalli, brochure, 2007.

34 Martha Neri, personal interview, 2010; Rosa María Laguna Gómez, personal
    interview, 2010.

35 Martha Neri, personal interview, 2010; Rosa María Laguna Gómez, personal
    interview, 2010.

36 Acey, "Letter from the Executive Director," 2. Also see within this same newsletter,
    "Patlatonalli, Guadalajara, Mexico: Astraea Grantee Spotlight," 4–5.

37 Acey, 2.

38 Marta Nualart, personal interview, 2010.

39 Gonzalez also illustrated several picture books by poet Francisco X Alarcón for Children's Book Press, including *Laughing Tomatoes and Other Spring Poems/ Jitomates risueños y otros poemas de primavera* (1997).

40 Gonzalez identifies as queer and Chicana, is biracial (white mother and Mexican father), grew up Catholic, was born in California, and then moved to Oregon when she was seven. As an adult, she moved to San Francisco where she currently resides. See Reisberg, "Maya Gonzalez."

41 See the co-authors' biographies at the end of Gonzalez and Smith-Gonzalez, *They, She, He: Easy as ABC*.

42 Gonzalez and Smith-Gonzalez, *They, She, He: Easy as ABC*.

43 "Mission and Values," Reflection Press, https://reflectionpress.com.

44 "Mission and Values."

45 These include Ernesto Javier Martínez's *When We Love Someone We Sing to Them*, Juan A. Ríos Vega's *Carlos, the Fairy Boy*, and my own picture book, *Chabelita's Heart*, which I discuss in the Coda.

46 See the full conference schedule at https://reflectionpress.com/conference/.

47 The major sessions included: (1) "The Political Act of Children's Books: Sourcing Your Story from Within" with Gonzalez, (2) "The View from Inside: The Publishing Process from Query Letter to Finished Books" with Goldberg, and (3) "The View from Outside: Creating Your Own Path to Publishing" with Smith-Gonzalez. See the full conference schedule at https://reflectionpress.com /conference/. Worksheets and handouts from this event are available as a 23-page zip file.

48 See "About Maya" at the end of M. Gonzalez, *Ma Llorona*, 163.

49 M. Gonzalez, *Claiming Face*, 1.

50 M. Gonzalez, *Gender Now Coloring Book*, 8.

51 M. Gonzalez, 1.

52 Within each, she inserts herself as the child protagonist. Her use of autofantasía first takes readers through a world of colors as she describes her childhood home, and then through a love letter or poem describing her affinity for rivers. She writes in the first person and includes a personal statement at the end of *My Colors, My World*: "The little girl in this book is me. I also modeled her after a doll I had as a kid—a big, round-headed doll my aunt made . . . [that] reminded me of me. . . . I faced a number of challenges as a very young person. I turned to my environment to search out my reflection and a sense of belonging." As for *I Know the River Loves Me*, Gonzalez begins, "I am here to visit one of my best friends in the world, the river. She loves me." Although the protagonist's name is never mentioned, those familiar with Gonzalez and her artwork can identify aspects of Gonzalez in both the text and illustrations. Additionally, Gonzalez's biography at the end of the book begins with, "Maya Christina Gonzalez is a river lover." This page includes two photographs of her next to rivers. Her hair is split in two and

tied up like that of her character, which she has also drawn with a pronounced chin, mole, and ear piercings that resemble her own.

53 M. Gonzalez, *Claiming Face*, 8.

54 M. Gonzalez, 7.

55 M. Gonzalez, *Gender Now Coloring Book*, 2.

56 M. Gonzalez, 3.

57 M. Gonzalez, 3.

58 M. Gonzalez, 3.

59 M. Gonzalez, 8–9.

60 M. Gonzalez, 32–33.

61 Arkles, "No One Is Disposable."

62 M. Gonzalez, *Gender Now Coloring Book,* 26–35.

63 M. Gonzalez, 38.

64 M. Gonzalez, 39–41.

65 Gonzalez presented at the 2020 Transform Challenging Behavior Online Conference and shared a handout with participants titled "Keeping the Perspective Alive."

66 M. Gonzalez, *Claiming Face*, 38.

67 M. Gonzalez, *Gender Now Coloring Book*, 49.

68 M Gonzalez, *The Gender Wheel*, 5.

69 M. Gonzalez, 13.

70 M. Gonzalez, 13.

71 M. Gonzalez, 13.

72 In "A Note to the Reader," Gonzalez tells us that the faint circle around the outside of the Gender Wheel represents a fourth circle or "more to come" (*The Gender Wheel*, 41).

73 M. Gonzalez, *The Gender Wheel*, 35.

74 M. Gonzalez, 35.

75 M. Gonzalez, 35.

76 I discuss ABC books, including *M is for Mustache*, at length in my book chapter "Apples Begone," expected 2024.

77 Originally from Massachusetts, he moved to Toronto, Ontario, as an adult.

78 S. Bear Bergman, email correspondence to author, March 27, 2023.

79 See FAQ: www.sbearbergman.com/faq. Bergman also discusses his experiences parenting three children in an interview with Rabbi Moskowitz; see Mike Moskowitz, "Two Dads Talking about Talking about Gender," Congregation Beit Simchat Torah (CBST), YouTube, March 8, 2021, www.youtube.com /watch?v=_lh7d_Oa2ig.

80 Bergman's third picture book, *Is That for a Boy or a Girl?*, debuted as part of the first set of titles in 2015 along with skelton's *The Newspaper Pirates*; skelton's second book, *The Last Place You Look*, was included in the 2017 book set.

81 See the "Flamingo Rampant: Adventure!" Kickstarter campaign for their "2021 season of feminist, culturally-diverse books celebrating LGBT2Q kids, families,

and communities!" www.kickstarter.com/projects/flamingorampant/flamingo
-rampant-adventure.

82   Unlike the United States or Mexico, Canada provides federal funding for cultural
productions, including the publishing of children's literature, through entities like
the Canada Council for the Arts and the Government of Canada's Book Fund.
These federal funds can also be supplemented with local or provincial funds,
such as those awarded by the Ontario Arts Council, the British Columbia Arts
Council, and the Government of British Columbia's Book Publishing Tax Credit
Program. However, federal funding does not, in and of itself, eliminate oppression
or social hierarchies.

83   S. Bear Bergman, email correspondence to author, March 27, 2023.

84   Flamingo Rampant Press website: www.flamingorampant.com.

85   See "Are you married? Do you have children?" and "Where do you live?" under
FAQ, www.sbearbergman.com.

86   Awapuhi refers colloquially to a group of "ginger plants," though they encompass
different species and families (Zingiberaceae and Commeliancaea). Within *Colors
of Aloha*, the text and illustrations reference the species Dichorisandra thyrsi-
flora, commonly known as "blue ginger" even though it looks purple. The plant
is similar to red ginger, although white ginger and yellow ginger flowers are more
commonly used in leis.

87   Teves, *Defiant Indigeneity*, 24.

88   According to the Pauahi Foundation: "When Pauahi was born, the Native Hawaiian population numbered about 124,000. When she wrote her will in 1883, only
44,000 Hawaiians remained. Pauahi witnessed the rapid decline of the Hawaiian population. With that decline came a loss of Hawaiian language, culture and
traditions. She believed education would offer her people hope and a future,
so she left her estate—about nine percent of the total acreage of the Hawaiian
kingdom—to found Kamehameha Schools." See "A Legacy of a Princess," Pauahi
Foundation, quoted 2023, https://pauahi.org.

89   It is also possible that Kalani be read as intersex.

90   The longer quote reads: "My piece, 'Crip Magic Spells,' comes from several places
in my life. It's partially from my own practice and identity as a disabled femme of
color witch and intuitive healer, thinking about how often I have used magic to
keep myself alive, remind myself of my power and inherent goodness, and navigated my PTSD, as well as ableism, racism and oppression, how I feel like my and
our disabled lives are a spell we are writing into existence." See Alex Locust, "An
Interview with Sins Invalid Performer: Leah Lakshmi Piepzna-Samarasinha," Paul
K. Longmore Institute on Disability, San Francisco State University, 2016, https:
//longmoreinsitute.sfsu.edu.

91   See Piepzna-Samarasinha's extended biography in Leah Lakshmi Piepzna-
Samarasinha, "Leah Bios for Press Kit," Brown Star Girl, https://brownstargirl
.org.

92   Adeyoha, *The Zero Dads Club*, 2.

93 See "Who Is Angel?," Angel Adeyoha: Integrative Coach, http://integratetheveil .com; "Performance: Two-Spirit Story Hour," San Francisco Public Library, YouTube, November 20, 2021, www.youtube.com/watch?v=EQe64Vse_ww.

94 Not to be confused with Aubrey Williams (1926–1990), the Guyanese artist known for his oil paintings. I believe Williams (illustrator of *The Zero Dada Club*) is a digital/animation artist of color based in the US; however, as of this writing, I was unable to confirm any biographical information for them.

95 Adeyoha, *The Zero Dads Club*, 20.

96 Adeyoha, 26.

97 Adeyoha, 26.

98 Adeyoha, 26.

99 Adeyoha, 27.

100 On social media, Firebaugh identifies as a "proud mixed race Chinese-American."

101 C. Hernandez, *M is for Mustache*, 2.

102 C. Hernandez, 18.

103 See Catherine Hernandez, "Why Was My Queer Children's Book Too Radical for Kindergarteners?," *Huffington Post*, June 23, 2015, updated June 24, 2016, www .huffingtonpost.ca.

104 C. Hernandez, *M is for Mustache*, 4, 36.

105 C. Hernandez, 20.

106 C. Hernandez, 5.

107 C. Hernandez, 15.

108 C. Hernandez, 7.

109 C. Hernandez, 11–12.

110 See Naidoo and Lynch, "Global Rainbow Families," 34.

111 C. Hernandez, *M is for Mustache*, 9.

112 Among other presses is My Family! (USA), started by Cheril N. Clarke and Monica Bey-Clarke, a Black lesbian couple who has published books such as *Keesha's South African Adventure* (2016); and Arsenal Press (Canada), which is much larger and publishes not only LGBTQ+ picture books but also middle-grade chapter books and YA novels.

3. ILLUSTRATING PRONOUNS

Epigraph: Kit Yan, "Artist Statement," Kit Yan's personal website, quoted 2020, https://kityanpoet.com; Koja Adeyoha, "Keynote Address," presented at the Butch Voices National Conference, 2017, www.butchvoices.com.

1 See Paoletti, "The Gendering of Infants' and Toddlers' Clothing in America"; Paoletti, *Pink and Blue*.

2 Larkin, "Authentic Mothers, Authentic Daughters and Sons." Larkin also links prenatal ultrasounds to consumer culture and middle-class motherhood.

3 See Guignard, "A Gendered Bun in the Oven."

4 As I will discuss below, two-spirit can be understood as both a gender identity and a sexuality.

5 By this, I do not mean that queerphobia or transphobia do not exist in communities of color, but rather that queerphobia and transphobia are also prevalent within dominant white culture.

6 This zine-like picture book version can also be described as an illustrated poem or DIY picture book. Throughout, I refer to it as a zine since it is labeled as such and in order to differentiate this original picture book from the other two versions. Pendleton Jiménez immediately sold out of the original 100 black-and-white copies at a Clit Lit event for lesbian writers. Her second printing consisted of 500 copies with a red-and-black cover. I consider both the black-and-white copies and red-and-black cover copies as 1999 originals. Figure 3.1 depicts the latter. Karleen Pendleton Jiménez, personal interview, 2011.

7 Tim McCaskell requested copies for the Toronto District School Board's "Equity Department" curriculum and connected Pendleton Jiménez with Green Dragon Press, who agreed to publish the children's book version with financial assistance from the TDSB and the Linden School, an all-girls independent school in Toronto. In 2000, it was a Lambda Literary Award Finalist. Karleen Pendleton Jiménez, personal interview, 2011.

8 For a discussion of the short film, see Urquijo-Ruiz, "Tomboy."

9 Pendleton Jiménez, *Are You a Boy or a Girl?*, 3.

10 Pendleton Jiménez, 5–7.

11 Pendleton Jiménez, 8–9. The photograph in the original zine is cropped within the picture book version.

12 Pendleton Jiménez, 11.

13 Pendleton Jiménez, 12.

14 Pendleton Jiménez, 13.

15 Pendleton Jiménez, 14.

16 Pendleton Jiménez, 14–16.

17 Pendleton Jiménez, 17.

18 Pendleton Jiménez, 18.

19 Notably, the mom's association with red is also evident within the text; unlike most of the book's text (printed in black), the mother's dialogue is printed in a dark red or burgundy color.

20 See Kanhai, *Bindi*.

21 "Papadam" refers to a thin, crispy bread popular in India.

22 I believe McGillis identifies as a nonbinary white illustrator based in Canada; however, as of this writing, I am unable to entirely confirm this. K. Adeyoha mentioned she provided regular feedback on the picture book's illustrations; Koja Adeyoha, personal correspondence to author, March 28, 2023.

23 The Lakota nation's lands have been reduced to small reservations located primarily in South Dakota or on the border between North Dakota and South Dakota within the US.

24 Adeyoha and Adeyoha, *47,000 Beads*, 6–7.

25 Adeyoha and Adeyoha, 12.

26 Adeyoha and Adeyoha, 13.

27 Adeyoha and Adeyoha, 21. This could also be interpreted as a reference to Turtle Island.

28 Adeyoha and Adeyoha, 21.

29 Adeyoha and Adeyoha, 24.

30 Adeyoha and Adeyoha, 25.

31 Within the illustrations, L. carries a Canadian flag, while a person next to them holds up a rainbow version of the US flag.

32 Adeyoha and Adeyoha, *47,000 Beads*, 27.

33 Pendleton Jiménez details her mother's racial/ethnic mixed-race ancestry in an essay titled "'Tell Them You're Mexican,' and Other Motherly Advice."

34 Karleen Pendleton Jiménez, personal interview, 2011; also see her website, www.karleenpj.com.

35 Karleen Pendleton Jiménez, personal interview, 2011; also see her website, www.karleenpj.com.

36 Michelle Munroe, "Nurturing Your Children's Gender and Identity with Vivek Shraya," Parent and Community Engagement Office, TDSB, YouTube, July 13, 2022, www.youtube.com/watch?v=9My0B-9A4NU. This also applies to her first book, *God Loves Hair* (2010), a memoir of herself as a "mom-loving, god-loving, queer Indian boy in Edmonton"; see Vivek Shraya, "Slow Bridges," *Gaysi: The Gay Desi*, July 28, 2010, http://gaysifamily.com.

37 Katherine Brooks, "Artist Vivek Shraya Channels Her Mother in Stunning Recreated Photos," *Huffington Post*, May 19, 2016, www.huffpost.com. For more on Perera, see "About," www.rajniperera.com.

38 *Trisha* was the title of a photo series honoring Shraya's mother; however, the name Trisha should not be confused with her mother's name, which she prefers not to share. This photo essay is also available on Shraya's website; see "Trisha," Vivek Shraya, https://vivekshraya.com. For the short film, see "Holy Mother My Mother," Vivek Shraya, 2014, https://vivekshraya.com.

39 For more on K. Adeyoha, see "Keynote Speaker Biography" and "Keynote Address," Butch Voices National Conference, 2017, www.butchvoices.com. For more on A. Adeyoha, see "Who Is Angel?," Angel Adeyoha: Integrative Coach, http://integratetheveil.com.

40 Both have discussed poly or open relationships and non-monogamy on social media. As of this writing, they are no longer together, and K. Adeyoha is in the process of changing her last name; Koja Adeyoha, personal correspondence to author, March 28, 2023.

41 Koja Adeyoha, personal correspondence to author, March 28, 2023.

42 The event was held in 2018 during Pride Month in San Francisco. David Elijah Nahmod, "Two-Sprit Storytime Teaches Kids about Native Americans," *Bay Area Reporter*, June 6, 2018, www.ebar.com.

43 Nahmod, "Two-Sprit Storytime Teaches Kids about Native Americans."

44 Adeyoha and Adeyoha, *47,000 Beads*, 28. For other definitions of two-spirit or scholarship on queer Indigenous theory, see Driskill, et al., *Queer Indigenous Studies*. Two-Spirit organizations include Bay Area American Indian Two-Spirits (BAAITS), which hosts an annual Two-Spirit Pow Wow (www.baaits.org).

45 Adeyoha and Adeyoha, *47,000 Beads*, 28.

46 Rivas, *They Call Me Mix*, 5.

47 Rivas, 6

48 Rivas, 6.

49 Rivas, 7.

50 Rivas, 9.

51 Rivas, 11.

52 Rivas, 16.

53 Rivas, 18.

54 For other readings, see Avilés, "Chillante Pedagogy, 'She' Worlds, and Testimonio as Text/Image"; Avilés, "Reading Latinx and LGBTQ+ Perspectives"; Lopez, *Calling the Soul Back*.

55 One child wears overalls and another a jumpsuit; none wear skirts or dresses.

56 For discussions of hoodies and the criminalization of Black youth, see R. Ford, *Dress Codes*, especially chapter 12; Lane et al., "The Framing of Race."

57 Maya C. Gonzalez, personal interview, 2016.

58 James Michael Nichols, "'Call Me Tree': A Children's Book with No Gender Specific Pronouns," *Huffington Post*, April 4, 2015, updated December 6, 2017, www.huffpost.com. Also see San Francisco Public Library, "Author Maya Gonzalez: A Holistic Approach/Children's Books as Activism," speech delivered at the Association of Children's Librarians (ACL) Institute, YouTube, April 10, 2015, www.youtube.com/watch?v=AVr4PBv45vc.

59 Nichols, "Call Me Tree."

60 Nichols, "Call Me Tree."

61 Maya Gonzalez, "Why Create a Gender Neutral Picture Book?," *The Open Book Blog*, Lee and Low Books, January 29, 2015, https://blog.leeandlow.com.

62 The Spanish translation copyright lists Lee & Low Books Inc., while the copyright page names the translator as Dana Goldberg, former Executive Editor for Children's Book Press.

63 Gonzalez and Smith-Gonzalez, *They, She, He, Me*, 38.

64 Emphasis in original; Gonzalez and Smith-Gonzalez, 29.

65 Although I will argue against this, some may read the protagonist as perpetuating a common trope in transgender children's literature—that of the "extra special," "magical," or "useful" trans or nonbinary child. As others have commented, this double-edged sword can both validate transgender children and cause undue stress or pressure on them to resolve their peers' or society's problems; Maya Gonzalez discussed this at length in her 2015 ACL speech referenced above. Also see skelton, "Not Exceptional or Punished"; Laura Jimenez, "Trans People Aren't Mythical Creatures," *Booktoss* (blog), September 24, 2018, https://booktoss.org;

Wargo and Coleman, "Speculating the Queer (In)Human." Countering critiques of trans exceptionalism, Thom emphasizes that "trans people deserve magic"; see Fariha Róisín, "'Trans People Deserve Magic': An Interview with Kai Cheng Thom," *Hazlitt*, December 8, 2017, https//hazlitt.net.

66 Róisín, "Trans People Deserve Magic."

67 For example, the picture book is written in all lowercase letters. Thom, *Fierce Femmes and Notorious Liars*, 33.

68 Thom, *I Hope We Choose Love*, 106.

69 "There is something that happens to brilliant trans women. . . . We burst into being; we give birth to ourselves. We burn like stars in the fight to survive. Like mayflies, we soar ever so briefly, then fall." Thom, *I Hope We Choose Love*, 139. Thom's second picture book, *For Laika: The Dog Who Learned the Names of the Stars*, tells the story of Laika, the dog who became the first living organism to orbit around the earth only to have her rocket burst into flames on her way back down to earth. Here, too, stars are equated with sacrifice.

70 Róisín, "Trans People Deserve Magic."

71 Kai Cheng Thom, "Pursuing Happiness as a Trans Woman of Color," *BuzzFeed LGBTQ*, October 10, 2015, www.buzzfeed.com.

72 Although all three creators of *From the Stars in the Sky to the Fish in the Sea* are Asian Canadian, two write their first or given name before their family or surname (Kai Cheng Thom and Wai-Yant Li), while the third writes their family name first followed by their given name (Kai Yun Ching). The first or given names are: Kai Cheng, Wai-Yant, and Yun Ching; family names are: Thom, Li, and Kai. See "The Best Canadian Book Covers of 2017," *CBC Books*, December 22, 2017, www.cbc.ca.

73 Wai-Yant Li is especially known for creating ceramic dishes (e.g., mugs, bowls, etc.) with faces on them similar to the tub in *From the Stars in the Sky to the Fish in the Sea*. See their artwork here: https://creationsli.com. Kai Yun Ching can be found here: www.instagram.com/kaiyunching/.

74 Quoted in "The Best Canadian Book Covers of 2017."

75 Rivas, *They Call Me Mix*, 27.

76 Rivas, 27.

77 Spanish because it includes "Ch ch" between the letters "C c" and "D d." Although "Ch" and "ch" are no longer used as single letters, they still visually emphasize Spanish over English.

78 Rivas, *They Call Me Mix*, 28.

79 Rivas, 28.

80 Ada Volkmer, "Up up with liberation," *Se Ve Se Escucha/Seen and Heard*, episode 9, podcast, https://soundcloud.com.

81 Volkmer, "Up up with liberation."

82 This course was likely either "The Heart of It: Creating Children's Books That Matter" or "Make Books Now! Indie Publisher Training and Action Program."

83 Volkmer, "Up up with liberation."

84 See the "About" page on Breena Nuñez: Cartoonist and Educator, at www
    .breenache.com.

85 Breena Nuñez (@breenache), Instagram post, November 12, 2018, www.instagram
    .com.

86 Rivas, *They Call Me Mix*, 30.

87 Rivas, 31.

88 Rivas, 32.

89 Rivas, 32.

90 Rivas, 32.

91 Rivas, 32.

92 See Anderson and Travers, *Transgender Athletes in Competitive Sport*.

93 Kaia Findlay and Anita Rao, "Parenting beyond the Gender Binary," *Embodied
    Radio Show*, WUNC 91.5 North Carolina Public Radio, published March 25, 2022,
    originally aired June 11, 2021, www.wunc.org.

94 Findlay and Rao, "Parenting beyond the Gender Binary."

95 Findlay and Rao.

96 For discussions of autism and gender from feminist and disability scholars, see
    Bumiller, "Quirky Citizens"; Strang et al., "Both Sex- and Gender-Related Factors
    Should Be Considered in Autism Research and Clinical Practice."

97 Margie Fishman, "Part 1. A Child's Journey to 'Truegender,'" *News Journal*, origi-
    nally published May 4, 2017, updated November 30, 2021, www.delawareonline.com.

98 Fishman, "Part 1. A Child's Journey to 'Truegender.'"

99 Diana Tourjée, "Youth, Interrupted: Trinity," *VICE*, interview for Broadly Video,
    www.vice.com; also see Diana Tourjée, "'Do You Want a Happy Little Girl or a
    Dead Little Boy?': My Choice as a Mother," *VICE*, www.vice.com.

100 Tourjée, "Youth, Interrupted."

101 Tourjée.

102 Tourjée.

103 Tourjée.

104 Fishman, "Part 1. A Child's Journey to 'Truegender.'"

105 Tourjée, "Youth, Interrupted."

106 Fishman, "Part 1. A Child's Journey to 'Truegender.'"

107 Margie Fishman, "Part 2. Transgender Teen Pushes Boundaries to Be 'Legal,'"
    News Journal, originally published May 5, 2017, updated May 7, 2017, www
    .delawareonline.com.

108 Mother and daughter document and publicly share their lived experiences on
    social media, especially through DeShanna Neal's Facebook account.

109 Michelle Brown, "DeShanna Neal: An Accidental Activist Just Fighting for
    Her Daughter," *Collections by Michelle Brown*, interview, July 22, 2021, https:
    //soundcloud.com.

110 "My Rainbow," *The Tiny Activist Blog*, December 20, 2020, https://thetinyactivist
    .com.

111 Neal and Neal, *My Rainbow*.

112 "Brightly Storytime LIVE: A Celebration of Black Love," Brightly Storytime, YouTube, February 27, 2022, www.youtube.com/watch?v=EO8tvfTr6ow.

113 See Banks, *Hair Matters*; Spellers, "The Kink Factor."

114 "Brightly Storytime LIVE."

115 "Brightly Storytime LIVE."

116 Peter Porker can also be spotted on video (Tourjée, "Youth, Interrupted") and is mentioned in Margie Fishman's Part 2 interview. T. Neal's parents (DeShanna and Chris) are both science fiction and comic enthusiasts who not only named the pig after Marvel's character Peter Porker but also named their children after superheroes and SciFi characters. The name Trinity was originally their "baby's middle name, in a nod to the fierce female hacker from 'The Matrix' who escapes simulated reality. The idea came to DeShanna in a dream. The expectant mother was surrounded by blue wallpaper on all sides until the paper ripped into shards, exposing a patch of pink" (Fishman, "Part 1" and "Part 2").

117 Kit Yan, "Bio," Kit Yan's personal website, quoted 2023, https://kityanpoet.com.

118 "Kit Yan and Melissa Li Master Class," Playwright Horizons, May 10, 2021, www .playwrightshorizons.org.

119 Kit Yan, "Artist Statement," Kit Yan's personal website, quoted 2020, https: //kityanpoet.com.

120 Kit Yan, "I AM: Trans People Speak, Kit Yan," GLAAD, YouTube, November 14, 2012, www.youtube.com/watch?v=88AEMSTEOGA.

121 Kit Yan, "Third Gender," *Drive Away Home*, Good Asian Drivers, 2009, https: //open.spotify.com.

122 Yan.

123 "Kit Yan and Melissa Li Master Class."

124 Yan, "I AM."

125 See "Edwin's Poem" in Yan, *Queer Heartache*, 30–33.

126 Fishman, "Part 2. Transgender Teen Pushes Boundaries to Be 'Legal.'"

127 "Kit Yan and Melissa Li Master Class."

128 Bill Chappell, "A Texas Lawmaker Is Targeting 850 Books That He Says Could Make Students Feel Uneasy," *NPR*, October 28, 2021, www.npr.org.

129 Tourjée, "Youth, Interrupted."

130 Tourjée.

131 I will instead offer a few titles published in or prior to 2020 here and encourage readers to seek them out: Emmanuel Romero and Drew Stephens' *Prinsesa: The Boy Who Dreamed of Being a Princess* (2013); Tobi Hill-Meyer's *A Princess of Great Daring!* (2015); and Juan A. Ríos Vega's *Carlos, the Fairy Boy/Carlos, el niño hada* (2020). Picture books by parents of color of gender expansive children include Cheryl Kilodavis's *My Princess Boy* (2009) and Laurin Mayeno's *One of a Kind, Like Me/Único como yo* (2016).

4. SHOWING AND TELLING

Epigraph: M. Johnson, *Large Fears*, dedication page; E. J. Martínez, *On Making Sense*, 96; Anthony, quoted in "HBO 'Behind the Scenes' with *La Serenata*" (2020).

1 Anya Kamentz and Cory Turner, "The Birds and the Bees: How to Talk to Children about Sex," Podcast Life Kit, excerpts adapted and published on NRP.org, December 17, 2019, www.npr.org. Most of this literature is directed at adults in the form of manuals or guidebooks aimed at teaching them how to discuss sexuality in general with children; see Doef, Bennett, and Lueks, *Can I Have Babies Too?*

2 For a children's picture book example, see Higginbotham, *Tell Me about Sex, Grandma*.

3 Foucault, *The History of Sexuality*, 29.

4 Foucault, 30.

5 The full quote reads: "Speaking about children's sex, inducing educators, physicians, administrators, and parents to speak of it, or speaking to them about it, causing children themselves to talk about it, and enclosing them in a web of discourses which sometimes address them, sometimes speak about them, or impose canonical bits of knowledge on them, or use them as a basis for constructing a science that is beyond their grasp—all this together enables us to link an intensification of the interventions of power to a multiplication of discourse." Foucault, *The History of Sexuality*, 29–30.

6 Exceptions include Okami, Olmstead, and Abramson, "Sexual Experiences in Early Childhood"; Volbert, "Sexual Knowledge of Preschool Children."

7 Curran, Chiarolli, and Pallotta-Chiarolli, "The C Words," 161.

8 Curran, Chiarolli, and Pallotta-Chiarolli, 161.

9 Maria Pallotta-Chiarolli discusses "queerly raising" in "My Moving Days"; for a more detailed account of Pallotta-Chiarolli's parenting and theories on children's sexuality see *Border Sexualities, Border Families in Schools*.

10 Quoted in Curran, Chiarolli, and Pallotta-Chiarolli, "The C Words," 157. Also, see Robinson, "'Queerying' Gender, Heteronormativity in Early Childhood Education"; Robinson, "In the Name of 'Childhood Innocence.'" For discussions of children's sexuality in relation to discourses around pedophilia, see Kincaid, *Child-Loving*; Angelides, *The Fear of Child Sexuality*.

11 Sedgwick, "How to Bring Your Kids Up Gay."

12 I want to reiterate Stockton's theory of *Growing Sideways* and the queer potential of all children.

13 See Fields, "Children Having Children'"; Bernstein, *Racial Innocence*.

14 See Somerville, *Queering the Color Line*.

15 For a discussion of children's sexuality as it relates to adult asexuality, see chapter 3, "Growing into Asexuality," in Przybylo, *Asexual Erotics*.

16 Katherine James is a pseudonym for "a woman who works as support personnel in the music industry in Los Angeles" interviewed by Denise Moore ("Halfway Home").

17 Lorde, *Zami: A New Spelling of My Name*, 36–37.

18 Lorde, 38.
19 Lorde, 39.
20 Lorde, 40.
21 Lorde, 42.
22 Rivera, "Queens in Exile, the Forgotten Ones."
23 Acosta, "The Boy in Fear Who Became a Latino/a LGBT Advocate in Philadelphia," 109–111.
24 Jewell, "Interview with Stephanie Byrd."
25 Allegra, "Lavender Sheep in the Fold"; Clarke, "I Guess I Never Will."
26 Gomez, "I Lost It at the Movies."
27 Rice-González, *Chulito*, 167–168.
28 C. Womack, *Drowning in Fire*.
29 "In Conversation with Myles E. Johnson," *Lumina Journal*, October 18, 2018, https://luminajournal.com.
30 "In Conversation with Myles E. Johnson."
31 "In Conversation with Myles E. Johnson."
32 "In Conversation with Myles E. Johnson."
33 "In Conversation with Myles E. Johnson."
34 Kendrick Daye, "About," Kendrick Daye's personal website, www.kendrickdaye.com.
35 Myles E. Johnson and Kendrick Daye, "Story," Kickstarter Campaign, www.kickstarter.com/projects/2042756481/large-fears.
36 Johnson and Daye.
37 Johnson and Daye.
38 "Mars was named by the ancient Romans for their god of war because its reddish color was reminiscent of blood"; see "Mars: The Red Planet," NASA Solar System Exploration, updated July 8, 2021, https://solarsystem.nasa.gov.
39 See "Phobos: In Depth" and "Deimos: In Depth" at https://solarsystem.nasa.gov.
40 See Kidd, "Maurice Sendak and Picturebook Psychology," in *Freud in Oz*.
41 "In Conversation with Myles E. Johnson."
42 "In Conversation with Myles E. Johnson."
43 See Dery, ed., *Flame Wars*; A. Nelson, "Afrofuturism"; A. Nelson, "Introduction."
44 Y. Womack, *Afrofuturism*, 9.
45 His mother was of Puerto Rican descent and his father was Haitian; he spoke French, Spanish, and English.
46 Quoted from the back cover of Steptoe, *Radiant Child*. Within queer of color critique, scholars such as José Esteban Muñoz have also taken up his artwork and its political implications; see *Disidentifications*, especially chapter 1, "Famous and Dandy like B. 'n' Andy: Race, Pop, and Basquiat." For other readings on Basquiat and his motifs, see hooks, *Art on My Mind*; Thompson, "Royalty, Heroism, and the Streets"; Saggese, *The Jean-Michel Basquiat Reader*.
47 Charline Jao, "Stop Calling Diversity an Agenda: Meg Rosoff and Large Fears," *The Mary Sue*, October 13, 2015, www.themarysue.com.

48 Jao.

49 Debbie Reese elaborated on this in her Arbuthnot Honor Lecture on August 2019 titled "An Indigenous Critique of Whiteness in Children's Literature." She also includes a discussion of #diversityjeti.

50 Edith Campbell, "Sunday Morning Reads," *Crazy Quilt Edi Blog*, October 11, 2015, https://campbele.wordpress.com.

51 As I mentioned in chapter 1, there are many challenges or limitations to bestowing the label of "literary firsts." Although I have taken great lengths in my research, there may be other titles I was simply unable to find. I would not be too surprised, for example, if I may have missed a picture book, especially one self-published or published by a small independent press. I look forward to continuing my quest of discovering new queer children's literature and welcome additional recommendations. That said, I also limited my scope to the parameters of my research goals such that for example, middle-grade or YA books are not included here.

52 E. J. Martínez, *When We Love Someone We Sing to Them*, 13–16.

53 E. J. Martínez, 34.

54 E. J. Martínez, 34.

55 E. J. Martínez, 4.

56 E. J. Martínez, 10–11.

57 "New Children's Book, Movie Put a Song in Professor's Heart," *Around the O* (University of Oregon), December 10, 2018, https://around.uoregon.edu.

58 E. J. Martínez, *When We Love Someone We Sing to Them*, 34.

59 E. J. Martínez, 34.

60 E. J. Martínez, 39.

61 See Mathiowetz and Turner, *Flower Worlds*.

62 E. J. Martínez, *When We Love Someone We Sing to Them*, 39.

63 E. J. Martínez, 20.

64 E. J. Martínez, 22.

65 E. J. Martínez, 24.

66 E. J. Martínez, 26.

67 E. J. Martínez, 26.

68 E. J. Martínez, 26.

69 Andrés's parent or caregiver is not given a name or pronouns.

70 Although the mother is not depicted in the first spread, we can surmise the father is singing to her as he explains to his son how he sends "love through song" and "soft music kisses." E. J. Martínez, *When We Love Someone We Sing to Them*, 2–3.

71 E. J. Martínez, 34.

72 E. J. Martínez, 34.

73 Rachael McDonald, "UO Prof Pens Children's Book about the Mexican Serenade Tradition with an LGBTQ Twist," interview on *Ahora si* with Jill Torres and Carolina Arredondo Sanchez Lira, KLCC NPR, September 16, 2019, www.klcc.org.

74 McDonald.

75 McDonald.

76 McDonald.

77 McDonald.

78 Ernesto Javier Martínez, email correspondence, June 16, 2022. Also see E. J. Martínez, "Jotería Storytelling Project (JSP)," *AJAAS Newsletter* 1, no 1 (2017): n.p.

79 Maya Gonzalez, "A Note from the Artist/How This Book Came to Be," in E. J. Martínez, *When We Love Someone We Sing to Them.*

80 E. J. Martínez, *When We Love Someone We Sing to Them*, 34.

81 McDonald, "UO Prof Pens Children's Book."

82 McDonald.

83 La Fountain-Stokes, "Trans/Bolero/Drag/Migration."

84 See Morad, "Queer Bolero." Boleros were introduced to Mexico from Cuba; for a brief history, see Pedelty, "The Bolero."

85 As with all other translations, unless otherwise noted, these are my own. However, as translation scholars have emphasized, poetry and songs are uniquely challenging given they are written in verse. In Spanish, one can note the unique rhymes and figurative language, which is not conveyed within the English translation above.

86 Lyrics in Spanish provided at the back of the picture book (E. J. Martínez, *When We Love Someone We Sing to Them*, 38) as well as by the Femeniños Project: www.femeniños.com.

87 E. J. Martínez, 38.

88 McDonald, "UO Prof Pens Children's Book."

89 "The Sesame Workshop Writers' Room is a summer-long writing intensive program for underrepresented writers interested in children's media," Sesame Workshop Writers' Room, https://sesamewritersroom.org.

90 This is anchored in Maya Gonzalez and Reflection Press' guiding principles on children's literature; see "Why Children's Books Are a Radical Act," Maya Gonzalez: Artist, Author, Educator, Activist, October 13, 2016, www.mayagonzalez.com.

91 McDonald, "UO Prof Pens Children's Book."

92 McDonald.

93 In using "possible worlds" here, I am also considering Maria Lugones's multiple definitions for "a possible world" or "worlds." See Lugones, "Playfulness, 'World'-Travelling, and Loving Perception."

5. AUTOFANTASTIC (MIS)READINGS

Epigraph: N. Hurley, *Circulating Queerness*, xi; Fawaz and Smalls, "Queers Read This! LGBTQ Literature Now," 171.

1 The title, *De los gustos y otras cosas*, may also be translated more directly as "Of one's likes and other things."

2 Moya, *The Social Imperative*, 25.

3 Muñoz, *Cruising Utopia*, 22.

4 Cohen, "Punks, Bulldaggers, and Welfare Queens," 31.

5 The space is now known as Somos Voces and functions as a bookstore and community center. The name Voces en Tinta now describes the editorial press created by the former owner of the bookstore, Bertha de la Maza.

6 "La historia que a ti y a mí nos han contado está mal construida: a mí me dijeron que los niños éramos de una manera y las niñas éramos de otra; que las personas blancas éramos de una manera y las indígenas de otra; y así, un montón de burradas."

7 "Y a ti, ¿qué te han contado?"

8 "Poder escribir ahora las historias de mejor manera es muy importante y me gusta que este libro sea un ejemplo de cómo hay que contarlas. . . . Un mundo sin estas historias es un mundo incompleto. . . . Aquí comienza la historia de una editorial que habla de un mundo al revés."

9 "Sobre Nostras" [About Us], Las Reinas Chulas, http://lasreinaschulas.com. For additional scholarship on their performances, see Baker, "Staging *Narcocorridos*"; Gutierrez, "El derecho de re-hacer"; Alzate, "'Fiesten' una pastorela cabaretera multitudinaria de Las Reinas Chulas."

10 "Ediciones Chulas tiene como misión ofrecer textos que funcionen como herramientas para lograr sensibilizar, divertir y llevar a la reflexión desde el humor y el placer, con una postura crítica ante la realidad y los discursos dominantes, pero sobre todo, comprometida con el pleno ejercicio de los derechos humanos." See "Presentación de las ediciones Chulas (Boletín)," Las Reinas Chulas, November 15, 2013, http://lasreinaschulas.com.

11 The second book was announced at this event but presented officially at the FIL Guadalajara (co-edited with La Revista Emeequis). The two authors were accompanied by Luz Elena Aranda, representing the publisher, and Carmen López-Portillo Romano, who moderated. See "Presentación de las ediciones Chulas (Boletín)."

12 "Presentación de las ediciones Chulas (Boletín)."

13 Ana Francis Mor, personal interview, 2019.

14 Mor.

15 Mor. A direct translation would be "Let everyone adjust their own coat," which implies "to each their own."

16 Marcela Arévalo Contreras, personal interview, 2019.

17 "Resulta que el otro día platicaba con mamá acerca de aquella niña que en mi mente siempre está."

18 What may have been an artistic "error" appears to bleed through from one page to the next, giving the illusion of a cloud or thought bubble.

19 "Es que ¡en serio! sus pestañas le llegan hasta la luna y cuando me mira siento un sabor como de tuna."

20 "Y así seguimos hablando de las cosas que nos gustan de dragones y de monstruos que, por cierto, no me asustan."

21 "Gracias por escribir este libro. A mi no me gustan las zapatillas ni los vestidos pero mi abuela dice que si no me los pongo me va a sacar de la escuela porque no quiere una nieta lesbiana."

22 "Nadie tiene derecho a decirte cómo debes ser. Nunca lo olvides."

23 User "Arlequinas" @las_arlequinas replying to @sandralorenzano on May 13, 2018: "Una niña que platica con mamá de la niña que en su mente siempre está. Lindo para los peques." The post was in reply to Sandra Lorenzano, "Opinón: ¿Me dejan contarles una de amor?," *Sin Embargo*, May 13, 2018, www.sinembargo .mx. Although I have yet to confirm this, this twitter user/account regularly posts about Las Reinas Chulas leading me to speculate that they are either associated with them, their venue, or a fan who regularly frequents their shows.

24 Raquel Castro, "País de maravillas: De los gustos y otras cosas," *La Jornada Aguas-calientes*, April 8, 2014, 13.

25 Adolfo Córdova, "Los días felices: Diversidad sexual y libros para niños, niñas, niñes y jóvenes," *Linternas y bosques: Literatura infantil y juvenil*, June 28, 2019, modified January 28, 2020, https://linternasybosques.wordpress.com.

26 Although all the other picture book titles I engage with throughout *Coloring into Existence* are by queer or trans of color authors, I made an exception by including Marcela Arévalo Contreras, a heterosexual author, in order to include *De los gustos y otras cosas* as an example of my own autofantastic reading practice.

27 I began exploring Anzaldúa's picture books as examples of autofantasía within "Contested Children's Literature: Que(e)ries into Chicana and Central American Autofantasías," *Signs: Journal of Women in Culture and Society* 41, no. 1 (2015): 199–224. Portions of my analysis of Anzaldúa overlap between this article and this chapter.

28 Moraga and Anzaldúa, *This Bridge Called My Back*; see also Keating "Appendix 2: Timeline," in *The Gloria Anzaldúa Reader*, 326.

29 Anzaldúa, "Ghost Trap/Trampa de Espanto," 157. Anzaldúa drafted stories for children that have not yet been published. Some included Prietita as their child protagonist and were directed at children, while others read more like short stories of Prietita as a child and Anzaldúa's reflections of her childhood. She shared five of these stories with Harriet Rohmer of Children's Book Press in 1989. See Harriet Rohmer, "Personal letter to Anzaldúa," 1989, Gloria Evangelina Anzaldúa Papers, 1942–2004 (box 9, folder 4), Nettie Benson Latin American Collection, University of Texas at Austin.

30 Anzaldúa, "Writing: A Way of Life," 244.

31 The US Immigration and Customs Enforcement (ICE) was created in 2003; it was preceded by the US Immigration and Naturalization Service.

32 Vásquez, "La Gloriosa Travesura de la Musa Que Cruza," 65.

33 Anzaldúa, "Spirituality, Sexuality, and the Body," 94.

34 The United Nations Convention on the Rights of the Child was adopted by the UN General Assembly in 1989. The US signed in 1995, but never ratified the treaty.

35 For additional scholarship on *Prietita and the Ghost Woman*, see Esquibel, *With Her Machete in Her Hand*; Perez, "A New Generation of Cultural/Critical Readers"; Ferrari, "Gloria Anzaldúa's Decolonizing Aesthetics"; Garcia, "Latina

Feminist Agency"; Rhodes, "Processes of Transformation"; S. Rodríguez, "Conocimiento Narratives."

36 Anzaldúa, *Light in the Dark*, 177.

37 Interview by Irene Lara, published as Chapter 4, "Daughter of Coatlicue: An Interview with Gloria Anzaldúa," in Keating, *EntreMundos/AmongWorlds*, 55.

38 As Edith M. Vásquez suggests, in Anzaldúa's children's books, "children's behavior prevails as humanitarian, diplomatic, and instinctually responsive to the borderlands' dangers. Anzaldúa shapes children's behaviors into a manifesto for human rights. Childish *travesuras*, or antics, constitute a mode of oppositional poetics and politics" (Vásquez, "La Gloriosa Travesura de la Musa Que Cruza," 74).

39 Anzaldúa, *Borderlands/La Frontera*, 19.

40 Anzaldúa, "La Prieta," 209.

41 Anzaldúa, "To(o) Queer the Writer—Loca, escritora y chicana," 172.

42 For additional discussions of masculinity and boyhood within children's literature, see Serrato, "Transforming Boys, Transforming Masculinity, Transforming Culture"; Alamillo, Mercado-López, and Herrera, *Voices of Resistance*, especially chapters five and seven; Stephens, *Ways of Being Male*.

43 Anzaldúa, "Writing," 245.

44 Anzaldúa, "Toward a Mestiza Rhetoric," 259.

45 Anzaldúa, *Light in the Dark*, 39. For a detailed account of Keating's process and decision-making while editing, see "Editor's Introduction," ix–xxxvii.

46 Anzaldúa, *Light in the Dark*, 40.

47 Moraga and Anzaldúa, *This Bridge Called My Back*. Also see the history of queer of color critique, which owes its existence to queer women of color scholarship (Ferguson, "Queer of Color Critique") and Kimberlé W. Crenshaw's intersectionality ("Demarginalizing the Intersection of Race and Sex"; "Mapping the Margins").

48 Anzaldúa described in a letter: "I just returned from two gigs where the campus bookstores were selling Amigos del otro lado [Friends] like hotcakes. They lined up for hours during my autograph sessions." [Personal letter to Laura Atkins], Gloria Evangelina Anzaldúa Papers, 1942–2004 (box 9, folder 4), Nettie Benson Latin American Collection, University of Texas at Austin.

49 Jacqueline Woodson, "What Reading Slowly Taught Me about Writing," TED Talk video, April 2019, 10:47, www.ted.com.

50 Sullivan, *Jacqueline Woodson*, 16.

51 Woodson, "Too Good," in *Brown Girl Dreaming*, 269.

52 Woodson, "Poem on Paper," in *Brown Girl Dreaming*, 275.

53 Woodson originally published *Brown Girl Dreaming* in 2014. The 2016 version published by Penguin includes additional poems. Direct quotes are cited from the 2014 version.

54 Carole Boston Weatherford, "Transcript from an Interview with Jacqueline Woodson," *Reading Rockets*, www.readingrockets.org.

55 Popular texts include Jacqueline L. Tobin and Raymond G. Dobard's *Hidden in Plain View: The Secret Story of Quilts and the Underground Railroad* (Anchor Books, 2000); and Barbara Brackman, *Facts and Fabrications: Unraveling the History of Quilts and Slavery* (C&T Publishing Inc, 2010).

56 Weatherford, "Transcript from an Interview with Jacqueline Woodson."

57 Genealogically, Georgiana Scott Irby (1913–2001) is also Woodson's maternal grandmother who "Had herself two girls at once, named them Caroline and Ann." Although not twins, they were born close together (Caroline "Kay" Irby in 1941 and Mary Ann Irby in 1942). See "Irby Family Tree" in Woodson, *Brown Girl Dreaming*.

58 Jacqueline Woodson, "Picture Books: Show Way," Jacqueline Woodson's personal website, www.jacquelinewoodson.com.

59 Woodson, "Picture Books: Show Way."

60 Stover, *Jacqueline Woodson*, 17–18.

61 *Last Summer with Maizon* was published in 1990 by Delacorte Press; however, several biographies incorrectly list 1991.

62 Jacqueline Woodson, "Picture Books: This Is the Rope," Jaqueline Woodson's personal website, www.jacquelinewoodson.com.

63 In *Brown Girl Dreaming* Woodson writes: "On the day he is buried, my sister and I wear white dresses" (277).

64 Terry Gross, "Jacqueline Woodson on Growing Up, Coming Out, and Saying Hi to Strangers," *NPR*, 2014, www.npr.org.

65 Gross.

66 Jacqueline Woodson initially felt sad when her baby brother was born (see "New York Baby," *Brown Girl Dreaming*, 135).

67 Jacqueline Woodson, "Picture Books: Pecan Pie Baby," Jacqueline Woodson's personal website, www.jacquelinewoodson.com.

68 Woodson.

69 They were introduced by Toshi Reagon, Woodson's best friend and former partner. Woodson describes how they met in "Before Her," an autobiographical short story published as part of Amazon's "The One" series.

70 This could also apply to *Each Kindness* (2012).

71 See Nyong'o, *Afro-Fabulations*.

72 *Brown Girl Dreaming*, 13–14.

73 See Emily Eakin, "'I Grew Up in a Southern Family—There Was a Lot of Talking': Jacqueline Woodson on Her Two New Best Sellers," *New York Times*, September 7, 2018, www.nytimes.com.

74 He served as part of USCT (United States Colored Troops) within the 5th Regiment Infantry US Colored Troops (formerly the 127th Ohio Volunteer Infantry Regiment).

75 *Brown Girl Dreaming*, 14.

76 See Thomas, *The Dark Fantastic*; especially chapter 2, "Lamentations of a Mockingjay."

77 "Jacqueline Woodson," in *Contemporary Authors: New Revision Series*, vol. 87 (Boston: Gale Group, 2000), 433–437. Quoted in Stover, *Jacqueline Woodson*, xii.

78 Sullivan, *Jacqueline Woodson*, 38.

79 Stover, *Jacqueline Woodson*, 152–153.

80 Woodson, "Jacqueline Woodson," 16–18.

81 Sullivan, *Jacqueline Woodson*, 39.

82 Sullivan, 39.

83 Sullivan, 39.

84 Sullivan, 39.

85 Sullivan, 39.

86 "Jacqueline Woodson: By the Book," *New York Times*, August 25, 2016, www.nytimes.com.

87 "Jacqueline Woodson: By the Book."

88 Syrus Marcus Ware, "About," Syrus Marcus Ware's website, www.syrusmarcusware.com. Also see "On Creating Spaces for Joy: An Interview with Syrus Marcus Ware," *The Creative Independent*, https://thecreativeindependent.com; "Disabled: Not a Burden, Not Disposable," Transgender Law Center, YouTube, April 22, 2020, www.youtube.com/watch?v=jA8PkucFrCk.

89 Ware is an active member and co-founder of Black Lives Matter Toronto; see "Love and Living," Creative Time Summit, September 28–30, 2017, https://creativetime.org.

90 Ware and Dias, "Revolution and Resurgence," 35–36.

91 "Artist Syrus Marcus Ware Wouldn't Trade Being Black, Trans and Queer for Anything," *Black News: For Us by Us*, February 24, 2018, www.akh99.com.

92 Ware, "All Power to All People?," 171.

93 Ware, *Love is in the Hair*, 10.

94 Ware, 10.

95 Ware, 12.

96 The illustration is of a large brick building—Mount Sinai West Hospital (formally Roosevelt Hospital)—on 1000 Tenth Avenue, even though the sign reads "St. Luke's." In tiny letters on the bottom right corner, one can make out "St. Luke's—Roosevelt Hospital Center," which at the time included St. Luke's Hospital and Roosevelt Hospital (in 2015, it was renamed Mount Sinai West Hospital). See "History of Mount Sinai West," Mount Sinai, www.mountsinai.org.

97 Ware, *Love is in the Hair*, 18.

98 Ware, 20.

99 Ware, 22.

100 Ware, 20.

101 "Interview with Syrus Marcus Ware," *Everyday Abolition/Abolition Every Day*, February 23, 2013, https://everydayabolition.com.

102 "Interview with Syrus Marcus Ware."

103 "Interview with Syrus Marcus Ware." Ware adds, "I think that money actually is quite evil. So I think that being able to barter and trade means I know that I have a variety of resources I can share . . .—but I must say, it's very tricky being a parent and worrying about 'having enough.'"

104 Also, Syrus Marcus Ware's portraits of local Black Lives Matter activists have been featured in an art exhibit titled "Baby, Don't Worry, You Know That We Got You" (2017), www.syrusmarcusware.com.

105 Riggs, *Tongues Untied*.

106 The BLM Toronto protest of 2016 Pride Parade was followed by backlash and hate mail; see "Black Lives Matter Flooded with Hate Mail Following Toronto Pride Parade Sit-In," *CBC*, July 5, 2016, www.cbc.ca. For a list of demands, see "Black Lives Matter Tweets List of Demands That Were Agreed Upon by Pride Toronto," *Toronto News*, July 4, 2016, www.toronto.com.

107 "Artist Syrus Marcus Ware Wouldn't Trade Being Black, Trans and Queer for Anything."

108 "Artist Syrus Marcus Ware Wouldn't Trade Being Black, Trans and Queer for Anything."

109 Ware, "All Power to All People?," 170.

110 Ware, 177.

111 Samantha Sarra, "Meet the Fathers: Queer Men Increasingly Considering Parenting," *Xtra**, June 18, 2008, https://xtramagazine.com.

112 Sarra.

113 Ware, "Confessions of a Black Pregnant Dad," 65.

114 Sarra, "Meet the Fathers."

115 Ware, "Confessions of a Black Pregnant Dad," 65.

116 Ware, 65.

117 Ware, 64.

118 Ware, 64.

119 The prior spread asked Carter to dream up a favorite memory. We might ask ourselves if a memory can only be of the past or if memories can also include desired futures? Both are possible within science fiction and fantasy. Or simply, rather than a memory, Carter is dreaming of the morning when she will be able to meet her baby sibling.

120 Ware and Marshall, "Disabilities and Deaf Culture," 54.

121 April Hubbard, "Disability Identity," *In Focus*, season 1, episode 6, June 9, 2022, www.ami.ca.

122 Syrus Marcus Ware, "Work in Culture," Syrus Marcus Ware channel, YouTube, May 13, 2016, www.youtube.com.

123 See Yousef Kadoura, Kalya Besse, and Kristina McMullin, "Crip Times Episode 1: The Syrus Marcus Ware Episode," *Crip Times: A Podcast Series*, November 16, 2020, https://bodiesintranslation.ca.

124 Ware, "Work in Culture."

125 Ware.

126 Ware.

127 The Mama and kiddo are depicted in multiple outfits suggesting that they either changed clothing multiple times that evening or their dialogue spans across multiple evenings.

128 Kadoura also acted in Ware's film project, Antarctica. See Yousef Kadoura's website, "About Yousef," www.yousefkadoura.com.

129 Hubbard, "Disability Identity."

130 Hubbard.

131 It might also be helpful to put Ware in conversation with other disability and/or trans scholars such as Snorton (*Black on Both Sides*), Siebers (*Disability Aesthetics*), or Spade (*Normal Life*).

132 For example, see Sedgwick's 1997 edited volume *Novel Gazing: Queer Readings in Fiction*; Norton's 1999 discussion of transreading in "Transchildren and the Discipline of Children's Literature"; Thomas's discussion of interpretive agency in *The Dark Fantastic*; Barker and Murray, *The Cambridge Companion to Literature and Disability*. Also, see Gonzalez and Smith-Gonzalez's "Playing with Pronouns" strategies within *They, She, He Me: Free to Be!*

133 By bottom up, I mean in relation to power dynamics and systemic inequality. For example, I do not mean to suggest that I am endorsing reading practices that erase marginalized characters or further normalize or impose privilege.

CODA

Epigraph: Baldwin, quoted in Standley and Pratt, *Conversations with James Baldwin*, 98; M. Gonzalez, "Welcome," in *Coloring the Revolution #1*, n.p.

1 Anzaldúa, *Light in the Dark*, 69.

2 Brant, "Giveaway," 945.

3 Boggs and Brody, introduction to *Little Man, Little Man*, xv. Also, see Boggs, "Baldwin and Yoran Cazac's 'Child's Story for Adults.'" Baldwin and Cazac originally published *Little Man, Little Man: A Story of Childhood* in Great Britain with Michael Joseph Ltd. in 1976. This 2018 version is a reprint by Duke University Press; in addition to the introduction, it also includes a foreword by Tejan Karefa-Smart and an afterword by Aisha Karefa-Smart.

4 Beauford Delaney was a Black gay artist primarily known for his abstract expressionists' paintings. Baldwin considered him a close friend and mentor who taught him how to "see," writing about their relationships in publications such as "On the Painter Beauford Delaney," and *The Price of the Ticket*. Their relationship was also displayed in the exhibition titled "Beauford Delaney and James Baldwin: Through the Unusual Door" at the Knoxville Museum of Art in 2020 (Feb. 7 through Oct. 25).

5 Karefa-Smart, "Little Man, Little Man," xiii.

6 Boggs and Brody, introduction to *Little Man, Little Man*, xv.

7   Baldwin, "A Talk to Teachers," 326–27. Baldwin originally delivered this speech on October 16, 1963 as "The Negro Child—His Self-Image," published in the *Saturday Review*, December 21, 1963.

8   Baldwin, *Little Man, Little Man*, 31.

9   This is similar to other works by Baldwin where women and girls are made tangential to their male counterparts; see Harris, *Black Women in the Fiction of James Baldwin*; even though Harris does not engage with *Little Man, Little Man*, her claims could also apply to female characters such as Blinky, TJ's mother, Miss Lee, and Miss Beanpole.

10   Baldwin, *Little Man, Little Man*, 57.

11   For an overview of Apollo Theater's historical significance, see Carlin and Conwill, *Ain't Nothing Like the Real Thing*.

12   Baldwin, "A Talk to Teachers," 330.

13   Baldwin, 332.

14   Baldwin, *The Evidence of Things Not Seen*, 5–6.

15   Gonzalez, *The Interrupting Chupacabra* [PDF booklet]; see page 1 of the PDF handout and the last page (back cover) when compiled and folded in half. The document is composed of six PDF pages, which when folded in half, create a twelve-page sample book. However, the cover and copyright pages are not numbered within the story. Page 1 of the story corresponds to the sample book's title page.

16   Gonzalez, page 2 of the PDF and page 1 of the story.

17   Gonzalez, page 2 of the PDF and the unnumbered copyright, bio, and dedication page of the story.

18   Gonzalez, page 3 of the PDF and pages 2–3 of the story.

19   Gonzalez, page 5 of the PDF and pages 6–7 of the story.

20   Here, one might also consider ephemera in relation to queer phenomenology; see Ahmed, *Queer Phenomenology*, especially chapter 1, "Orientations toward Objects."

21   An earlier version of these comments was published within that year's conference proceedings; see Millán, "Autofantasías."

22   D. Johnson, *The Lavender Scare*.

23   See Chavez, *Queer Migration Politics*.

24   Gonzalez also recommended collage as a useful illustration style in her videos.

25   This also made me recall a conversation with Karleen Pendleton Jiménez regarding earrings on Alex in *Tomboy*.

26   Isabel Millán, "Chabelita's Heart: 'Create Your Own Bow Tie' with Isabel Millán," YouTube, March 9, 2022, www.youtube.com/watch?v=4ZUqtsLidXM.

27   Ware, "All That We Touch, We Change," 112.

BIBLIOGRAPHY

Abate, Michelle Ann. *Tomboys: A Literary and Cultural History*. Philadelphia: Temple University Press, 2008.

Abate, Michelle Ann, and Kenneth Kidd, eds. *Over the Rainbow: Queer Children's and Young Adult Literature*. Ann Arbor: University of Michigan Press, 2011.

"About the Front Cover." In "Lesbian Mothering." Special issue, *Journal of the Association for Research on Mothering* 1, no. 2 (Fall/Winter 1999): 6–7.

Abrams, Meyer Howard. *The Mirror and the Lamp: Romantic Theory and the Critical Tradition*. Oxford: Oxford University Press, 1953.

Acey, Katherine T. "Letter from the Executive Director." *Threads: Astraea Lesbian Foundation for Justice*, Summer 2005, 2.

Acosta, David. "The Boy in Fear Who Became a Latino/a LGBT Advocate in Philadelphia." In *Queer Brown Voices: Personal Narratives of Latina/o LGBT Activism*, edited by Uriel Quesada, Letitia Gomez, and Salvador Vidal-Ortiz, 109–11. Austin: University of Texas Press, 2015.

Acton, Janice, Donna Bobier, and Liz Martin. "Women's Press: The First Five Years." *Other Woman* 5, no. 1 (January–February 1977): 3, 20, 22.

Adams, Rachel. *Continental Divides: Remapping the Cultures of North America*. Chicago: University of Chicago Press, 2009.

Adeyoha, Angel. *The Zero Dads Club*. Illustrated by Aubrey Williams. Toronto: Flamingo Rampant Press, 2015.

Adeyoha, Koja, and Angel Adeyoha. *47,000 Beads*. Illustrated by Holly McGillis. Toronto: Flamingo Rampant Press, 2017.

Ahmed, Sara. *Living a Feminist Life*. Durham, NC: Duke University Press, 2017.

———. *Queer Phenomenology: Orientations, Objects, Others*. Durham, NC: Duke University Press, 2006.

———. *Willful Subjects*. Durham, NC: Duke University Press, 2014.

Alamillo, Laura, Larissa M. Mercado-López, and Cristina Herrera, eds. *Voices of Resistance: Interdisciplinary Approaches to Chican@ Children's Literature*. New York: Rowman and Littlefield, 2018.

Alarcón, Francisco X. *Laughing Tomatoes and Other Spring Poems/Jitomates risueños y otros poemas de primavera*. Illustrated by Maya Christina Gonzalez. San Francisco: Children's Book Press, 1997.

Alcoff, Linda Martin. *Visible Identities: Race, Gender, and the Self*. Oxford: Oxford University Press, 2006.

Aldama, Frederick Luis, ed. *Comics Studies Here and Now*. New York: Routledge, 2018.

———. "Magical Realism." In *The Routledge Companion to Latino/a Literature*, edited by Suzanne Bost and Frances R. Aparicio, 334–41. New York: Routledge, 2012.

Allain, Carol, and Rosamund Elwin, eds. *Getting Wet: Tales of Lesbian Seductions*. Toronto: Women's Press, 1992.

Allegra, Donna. "Lavender Sheep in the Fold." In *Does Your Mama Know? An Anthology of Black Lesbian Coming Out Stories*, edited by Lisa C. Moore, 149–59. New Orleans: Redbone Press, 1998.

Alzate, Gastón A. "'Fiesten' una pastorela cabaretera multitudinaria de Las Reinas Chulas." *Letras Femeninas* 37, no. 1 (2011): 71–86.

Anderson, Eric, and Ann Travers, eds. *Transgender Athletes in Competitive Sport*. New York: Routledge, 2017.

Anderson, Mark. *Black and Indigenous: Garifuna Activism and Consumer Culture in Honduras*. Minneapolis: University of Minnesota Press, 2009.

Angelides, Steven. *The Fear of Child Sexuality: Young People, Sex, and Agency*. Chicago: University of Chicago Press, 2019.

Angelou, Maya. *Life Doesn't Frighten Me*. Illustrated by Jean-Michel Basquiat. Edited by Sara Jane Boyers. New York: Stewart, Tabori, and Chang, 1993.

Anzaldúa, Gloria. *Borderlands/La Frontera: The New Mestiza*. San Francisco: Aunt Lute, 1987.

———. *Friends from the Other Side/Amigos del otro lado*. Illustrated by Consuelo Méndez. San Francisco: Children's Book Press, 1993.

———. "Ghost Trap/Trampa de Espanto." In *The Gloria Anzaldúa Reader*, edited by AnaLouise Keating, 157–62. Durham, NC: Duke University Press, 2009.

———. "La Prieta." In *This Bridge Call My Back*, edited by Gloria Anzaldúa and Cherríe Moraga, 198–209. Watertown, MA: Persephone Press, 1981.

———. *Light in the Dark/Luz en lo Oscuro: Rewriting Identity, Spirituality, Reality*. Edited by AnaLouise Keating. Durham, NC: Duke University Press, 2015.

———. "The New Mestiza Nation: A Multicultural Movement." In *The Gloria Anzaldúa Reader*, edited by AnaLouise Keating, 203–16. Durham, NC: Duke University Press, 2009.

———. "now let us shift . . . the path of conocimiento . . . inner work, public acts." In *this bridge we call home: radical visions for transformation*, edited by Gloria E. Anzaldúa and AnaLouise Keating, 540–77. New York: Routledge, 2002.

———. *Prietita and the Ghost Woman/Prietita y la Llorona*. Illustrated by Maya Christina Gonzalez. San Francisco: Children's Book Press, 1995.

———. "Spirituality, Sexuality, and the Body: An Interview with Linda Smuckler." In *The Gloria Anzaldúa Reader*, edited by AnaLouise Keating, 74–94. Durham, NC: Duke University Press, 2009.

———. "To(o) Queer the Writer—Loca, escritora y chicana." In *The Gloria Anzaldúa Reader*, edited by AnaLouise Keating, 163–75. Durham, NC: Duke University Press, 2009.

———. "Toward a Mestiza Rhetoric: Gloria Anzaldúa on Composition, Postcoloniality, and the Spiritual." In *Gloria Anzaldúa: Interviews/Entrevistas*, edited by AnaLouise Keating, 251–80. New York: Routledge, 2000.

——. "Writing: A Way of Life. An Interview with María Henríquez Betancor." In *Gloria E. Anzaldúa: Interviews/Entrevistas*, edited by AnaLouise Keating, 235–50. New York: Routledge, 2000.

Anzaldúa, Gloria, and Terri de la Peña. "Interview: On the Borderlands with Gloria Anzaldúa." *Off Our Backs* 21, no. 7 (1991): 1–4.

Apter, Andrew. "M. G. Smith on the Isle of Lesbos: Kinship and Sexuality in Carriacou." *New West Indian Guide* 87 (2013): 273–93.

Arévalo Contreras, Marcela. *De los gustos y otras cosas*. Illustrated by Ilyana Martínez Crowther. Mexico City: Ediciones Chulas, 2013.

——. *Los abuelos son de Marte*. Illustrated by Ilyana Martínez Crowther. Mexico City: Editorial Axial-Colofón, 2008.

Ariès, Philippe. *Centuries of Childhood: A Social History of Family Life*. Translated by Robert Baldick. New York: Vintage, 1962.

Arkles, Gabriel. "No One Is Disposable: Going beyond the Trans Military Inclusion Debate." *Seattle Journal for Social Justice* 13, no. 2 (2014): 459–514.

Avilés, Elena. "Chillante Pedagogy, 'She' Worlds, and Testimonio as Text/Image: Toward a Chicana Feminist Pedagogy in the Works of Maya Christina Gonzalez." In *Voices of Resistance: Essays on Chican@ Children's Literature*, edited by Laura Alamillo, Larissa M. Mercado-López, and Cristina Herrera, 123–36. Lanham, MD: Rowman and Littlefield, 2017.

——. "Reading Latinx and LGBTQ+ Perspectives: Maya Christina Gonzalez and Equity Minded Models at Play." *Bilingual Review/La Revista Bilingüe* 33, no. 4 (2017): 34–44.

Azcona, Estevan César. "Chicano Movement Music." In *Encyclopedia of Latino Popular Culture*, vol. 1, edited by Cordelia Chavez Candelaria, Arturo J. Aldama, Peter J. Garcia, and Alma Alvarez-Smith, 143–47. Westport, CT: Greenwood Press, 2004.

Baker, Christina. "Staging *Narcocorridos*: Las Reinas Chulas' Dissident Audio-Visual Performance." *Latin American Theatre Review* 48, no. 1 (2014): 93–113.

Baldwin, James. *The Evidence of Things Not Seen*. New York: Henry Holt, 1985.

——. *Little Man, Little Man: A Story of Childhood*. Illustrated by Yoran Cazac. Edited by Nicholas Boggs and Jennifer DeVere Brody. Durham, NC: Duke University Press, 2018. Originally published in Great Britain by Michael Joseph Ltd., 1976.

——. "On the Painter Beauford Delaney." *Transition*, no. 18 (1965): 45.

——. *The Price of the Ticket: Collected Nonfiction, 1948–1985*. New York: St. Martin's Press, 1985.

——. "A Talk to Teachers." In *The Price of the Ticket, Collected Non-Fiction, 1948–1985*, 325–32. New York: St. Martin's Press, 1985.

Banks, Ingrid. *Hair Matters: Beauty, Power, and Black Women's Consciousness*. New York: New York University Press, 2000.

Barker, Clare, and Stuart Murray, eds. *The Cambridge Companion to Literature and Disability*. Cambridge: Cambridge University Press, 2018.

Barthes, Roland. "The Death of the Author." In *Image, Music, Text*, translated by Stephen Heath, 142–48. New York: Hill and Wang, 1977.

Becker, Susan J. "Child Sexual Abuse Allegations against a Lesbian or Gay Parent in a Custody or Visitation Dispute: Battling the Overt and Insidious Bias of Experts and Judges." *Denver Law Review* 74, no. 1 (1996): 75–158.

Beek, Titia F., Peggy T. Cohen-Kettenis, and Baudewijntje P. C. Kreukels. "Gender Incongruence/Gender Dysphoria and Its Classification History." *International Review of Psychiatry* 28, no.1 (2016): 5–12.

Belausteguigoitia, Marisa, and Lucía Melgar, eds. *Fronteras, violencia, justicia: Nuevos discursos.* Mexico City: Universidad Nacional Autónoma de México, 2007.

Bell, Elizabeth, Lynda Haas, and Laura Sells, eds. *From Mouse to Mermaid: The Politics of Film, Gender, and Culture.* Bloomington: Indiana University Press, 1995.

Bennett, Herman L. *Colonial Blackness: A History of Afro-Mexico.* Bloomington: Indiana University Press, 2009.

Bergman, S. Bear. *The Adventures of Tulip, Birthday Wish Fairy.* Illustrated by Susy Malik. Toronto: Flamingo Rampant Press, 2012.

———. *Backwards Day.* Illustrated by K. D. Diamond. Toronto: Flamingo Rampant Press, 2012.

———. *Is That for a Boy or a Girl?* Illustrated by Rachel Dougherty. Toronto: Flamingo Rampant Press, 2015.

Bernstein, Robin. *Racial Innocence: Performing American Childhood from Slavery to Civil Rights.* New York: New York University Press, 2011.

Berta-Ávila, Margarita, Anita Tijerina Revilla, and Julie López Figueroa. *Marching Students: Chicana and Chicano Activism in Education, 1968 to the Present.* Reno: University of Nevada Press, 2011.

Boggs, Nicholas. "Baldwin and Yoran Cazac's 'Child's Story for Adults.'" In *The Cambridge Companion to James Baldwin,* edited by Michele Elam, 118–32. New York: Cambridge University Press, 2015.

Boggs, Nicholas, and Jennifer DeVere Brody. Introduction to *Little Man, Little Man: A Story of Childhood,* by James Baldwin, xv–xxii. Durham, NC: Duke University Press, 2018.

Bohlmann, Markus P. J., and Sean Moreland, eds. *Monstrous Children and Childish Monsters: Essays on Cinema's Holy Terrors.* Jefferson, NC: McFarland, 2015.

Bost, Suzanne. *Shared Selves: Latinx Memoir and Ethical Alternatives to Humanism.* Urbana: University of Illinois Press, 2019.

Brady, Mary Pat. "Children's Literature." In *The Routledge Companion to Latino/a Literature,* edited by Suzanne Bost and Frances R. Aparicio, 375–82. New York: Routledge, 2012.

———. *Extinct Lands, Temporal Geographies: Chicana Literature and the Urgency of Space.* Durham, NC: Duke University Press, 2002.

———. *Scales of Captivity: Racial Capitalism and the Latinx Child.* Durham, NC: Duke University Press, 2022.

Brant, Beth. "Giveaway: Native Lesbian Writers." *Signs: Journal of Women in Culture and Society* 18, no. 4 (1993): 944–47.

Bridges, Ruby. *Through My Eyes.* Edited by Margo Lundell. New York: Scholastic, 1999.

Bruhm, Steven, and Natasha Hurley, eds. *Curiouser: On the Queerness of Children.* Minneapolis: University of Minnesota Press, 2004.

Bumiller, Kristin. "Quirky Citizens: Autism, Gender, and Reimagining Disability." *Signs* 33, no. 4 (2008): 967–91.

Canclini, Néstor García. *Consumers and Citizens: Globalization and Multicultural Conflicts.* Translated by Gorge Yúdice. Minneapolis: University of Minnesota Press, 2001.

Candelario, Ginetta E. B. *Black behind the Ears: Dominican Racial Identity from Museums to Beauty Shops.* Durham, NC: Duke University Press, 2007.

Cantú, Lionel, Jr. *The Sexuality of Migration: Border Crossings and Mexican Immigrant Men.* Edited by Nancy Naples and Salvador Vidal-Ortiz. New York: New York University Press, 2009.

Capuzza, Jamie C. "'T' Is for 'Transgender': An Analysis of Children's Picture Books Featuring Transgender Protagonists and Narrators." *Journal of Children and Media* 14, no. 3 (2020): 324–42.

Cardoza, Melissa. *Tengo una tía que no es monjita.* Illustrated by Margarita Sada. Guadalajara: Ediciones Patlatonalli, 2004.

———. *13 colores de la resistencia hondureña/13 Colors of the Honduran Resistance.* Translated by Matt Ginsberg-Jaeckle. Chicago: El BeiSmAn Press, 2016.

Carlin, Richard, and Kinshasha Holman Conwill, eds. *Ain't Nothing Like the Real Thing: How the Apollo Theater Shaped American Entertainment.* Washington, DC: Smithsonian Books, 2010.

Cart, Michael, and Christine A. Jenkins. *The Heart Has Its Reasons: Young Adult Literature with Gay/Lesbian/Queer Content, 1969–2004.* Lanham, MD: Scarecrow Press, 2006.

Carter, Julie. "Vancouver, Canada: Gay and Lesbian Educators of British Columbia." *Journal of Gay and Lesbian Issues in Education* 1, no. 1 (2003): 100–103.

Caserio, Robert L, Lee Edelman, Jack Halberstam, José Esteban Muñoz, and Tim Dean. "The Antisocial Thesis in Queer Theory." *PMLA* 121, no. 3 (2006): 819–28.

Cellini, Benvenuto. *Memoirs of Benvenuto Cellini: A Florentine Artist.* Translated by Thomas Roscoe. London: H. Colburn, 1822. Originally published in 1728.

Chamberlain et al. v. The Board of Trustees of School District No. 36 (Surrey) and Others, 1998 CanLII 6723 (BC SC), Canada.

Chamberlain et al. v. Surrey School District No. 36, 1999 BCCA 516, Canada.

Chamberlain v. Surrey School District No. 36, 2000 BCCA 519, Canada.

Chamberlain v. Surrey School District No. 36, 2002 SCC 86 [2002] 4 SCR 710–833, Canada.

Chambers-Letson, Joshua. *After the Party: A Manifesto for Queer of Color Life.* New York: New York University Press, 2018.

Chan, Kwok-bun. "Inner Hybridity in the City: Toward a Critique of Multiculturalism." *Global Economic Review* 32, no. 2 (2003): 91–105.

Chavez, Karma R. *Queer Migration Politics: Activist Rhetoric and Coalitional Possibilities.* Urbana: University of Illinois Press, 2013.

Chew, Selfa. "Mexicanidades de la Diáspora Asiática: Considerations of Gender, Race, and Class in the Treatment of Japanese Mexicans during WWII." *Chicana/Latina Studies* 14, no. 1 (2014): 56–87.

Cisneros, Sandra. *Hair/Pelitos*. Illustrated by Terry Ybáñez. Decorah, IA: Dragonfly Books, 1997.

Clark, Beverly Lyon. *Kiddie Lit: The Cultural Construction of Children's Literature in America*. Baltimore: John Hopkins University Press, 2003.

———. *Regendering the School Story: Sassy Sissies and Tattling Tomboys*. New York: Routledge, 1996.

Clarke, Cheril N., and Monica Bey-Clarke. *Keesha's South African Adventure*. Illustrated by Julia Selyutina. Sicklerville, NJ: My Family! Products, 2016.

Clarke, Tonda. "I Guess I Never Will." In *Does Your Mama Know? An Anthology of Black Lesbian Coming Out Stories*, edited by Lisa C. Moore, 117–22. New Orleans: Redbone Press, 1998.

Coats, Karen. *Looking Glasses and Neverlands: Lacan, Desire, and Subjectivity in Children's Literature*. Iowa City: University of Iowa Press, 2004.

———. "Visual Conceptual Metaphors in Picturebooks: Implications for Social Justice." *Children's Literature Association Quarterly* 44, no. 4 (Winter 2019): 364–80.

Cohen, Cathy J. "Punks, Bulldaggers, and Welfare Queens: The Radical Potential of Queer Politics?" *GLQ* 3 (1997): 437–65.

Collins, Patricia Hill. *Black Sexual Politics: African Americans, Gender, and the New Racism*. New York: Routledge, 2004.

Combahee River Collective. "The Combahee River Collective: A Black Feminist Statement." In *Capitalist Patriarchy and the Case for Socialist Feminism*, edited by Zillah Eisenstein. New York: Monthly Review Press, 1978. Statement originally dated April 1977.

Cotera, Maria Eugenia, and Maria Josefina Saldana-Portillo. "Indigenous but Not Indian? Chicana/os and the Politics of Indigeneity." In *The World of Indigenous North America*, edited by Robert Warrior, 549–68. New York: Routledge, 2014.

Crenshaw, Kimberlé W. "Demarginalizing the Intersection of Race and Sex: A Black Feminist Critique of Antidiscrimination Doctrine, Feminist Theory and Antiracist Politics." *University of Chicago Legal Forum* 1989: 139–67.

———. "Mapping the Margins: Intersectionality, Identity Politics, and Violence against Women of Color." *Stanford Law Review* 43, no. 6 (1991): 1241–99.

Crisp, Thomas. "Setting the Record 'Straight': An Interview with Jane Severance." *Children's Literature Association Quarterly* 35, no. 1 (2010): 87–96.

Curb, Rosemary, and Nancy Manaham, eds. *Lesbian Nuns: Breaking the Silence*. Tallahassee, FL: Naiad Press, 1985.

Curran, Greg, Steph Chiarolli, and Maria Pallotta-Chiarolli. "'The C Words': Clitorises, Childhood and Challenging Compulsory Heterosexuality Discourses with Pre-service Primary Teachers." *Sex Education* 9, no. 2 (2009): 155–68.

de la Peña, Terri. *Faults*. Los Angeles: Alyson Books, 1999.

de la tierra, tatiana. "Coming Out and Creating Queer Awareness in the Classroom: An Approach from the U.S.-Mexican Border." In *Lesbian and Gay Studies and the Teaching of English: Positions, Pedagogies, and Cultural Politics*, edited by William J. Spurlin, 168–90. Urbana, IL: National Council of Teachers of English, 2000.

———. *For the Hard Ones: A Lesbian Phenomenology/Para las duras: Una fenomenología lesbiana*. San Diego: Calaca Press, 2002.

———. *Xía y las mil sirenas*. Illustrated by Anna Cooke. Guadalajara: Patlatonalli, 2009.

Delgado, Grace Peña. *Making the Chinese Mexican: Global Migration, Localism, and Exclusion in the U.S.-Mexico Borderlands*. Stanford, CA: Stanford University Press, 2012.

Deliman, Amanda. "Picturebooks and Critical Inquiry: Tools to (Re)Imagine a More Inclusive World." *Bookbird: A Journal of International Children's Literature* 59, no. 3 (2021): 46–57.

DePalma, Renee. "Gay Penguins, Sissy Ducklings . . . and Beyond? Exploring Gender and Sexuality Diversity through Children's Literature." *Discourse: Studies in the Cultural Politics of Education* 37, no. 6 (2016): 828–45.

dePaola, Tomie. *Oliver Button Is a Sissy*. New York: Harcourt Brace Jovanovich, 1979.

Dery, Mark. "Black to the Future: Interviews with Samuel R. Delany, Greg Tate, and Tricia Rose." *South Atlanta Quarterly* 92, no. 4 (1993): 735–78.

———, ed. *Flame Wars: The Discourse of Cyberculture*. Durham, NC: Duke University Press, 1994.

Doef, Sanderijin van der, Clare Bennett, and Arris Lueks. *Can I Have Babies Too? Sexuality and Relationships Education for Children from Infancy up to Age 11*. London: Jessica Kingsley, 2021.

Douglass, Frederick. "The Color Line." *North American Review* 132, no. 295 (1881): 567–77.

Driskill, Qwo-Li, Chris Finley, Brian Joseph Gilley, and Scott Lauria Morgensen, eds. *Queer Indigenous Studies: Critical Interventions in Theory, Politics, and Literature*. Tucson: University of Arizona Press, 2011.

Du Bois, W. E. B. "To the Nations of the World (1900)." In *W. E. B. Du Bois: International Thought*, edited by Adom Getachew and Jennifer Pitts, 18–21. Cambridge: Cambridge University Press, 2022.

Dupriez, Bernard. *A Dictionary of Literary Devices: Gradus, A–Z*. Translated by Albert W. Halsall. Toronto: University of Toronto Press, 1991. Originally published as *Gradus: Les procédés littéraires (Dictionnaire)*. Paris: Union générale d'éditions, 1984.

Dyer, Hannah. *The Queer Aesthetics of Childhood: Asymmetries of Innocence and the Cultural Politics of Child Development*. New Brunswick, NJ: Rutgers University Press, 2019.

Dykstra, Laurel A. "Trans-Friendly Preschool." *Journal of Gay and Lesbian Issues in Education* 3, no. 1 (2005): 7–13.

Echeverría, Bolívar. "*Queer*, manierista, *bizarre*, barroco." In "Raras rarezas." Special issue, *Debate Feminista* 16 (October 1997): 3–8.

Edelman, Lee. *No Future: Queer Theory and the Death Drive*. Durham, NC: Duke University Press, 2004.

Elwin, Rosamund, ed. *Countering the Myths: Lesbians Write about the Men in Their Lives*. Toronto: Women's Press, 1996.

———. "Introduction: Tongues on Fire: Speakin' Zami Desire." In *Tongues on Fire: Caribbean Lesbian Lives and Stories*, 7–10. Toronto: Women's Press, 1997.

———, ed. *Tongues on Fire: Caribbean Lesbian Lives and Stories*. Toronto: Women's Press, 1997.

Elwin, Rosamund, and Michele Paulse. *Asha's Mums*. Illustrated by Dawn Lee. Toronto: Women's Press, 1990.

———. *The Moonlight Hide-and-Seek Club in the Pollution Solution*. Illustrated by Cheryl Henhawke. Toronto: Women's Press, 1992.

Elwin, Rosamund, and Karen X. Tulchinsky, eds. *Tangled Sheets: Stories and Poems of Lesbian Lust*. Toronto: Women's Press, 1995.

Epstein, B. J. "We're Here, We're (Not?) Queer: GLBTQ Characters in Children's Books." *Journal of GLBT Family Studies* 8 no. 3 (2012): 287–300.

Escudero, Kevin A. "Organizing While Undocumented: The Law as a 'Double Edged Sword' in the Movement to Pass the DREAM Act." *Crit: A Critical Legal Studies Journal* 6, no. 2 (2013): 31–52.

Eshun, Kodwo. *More Brilliant than the Sun: Adventures in Sonic Fiction*. London: Quartet Books, 1998.

Esposito, Jennifer. "We're Here, We're Queer, but We're Just Like Heterosexuals: A Cultural Studies Analysis of Lesbian Themed Children's Books." *Journal of Educational Foundations* 23, no. 3–4 (2009): 61–78.

Esquibel, Catrióna Rueda. *With Her Machete in Her Hand: Reading Chicana Lesbians*. Austin: University of Texas Press, 2006.

Evans, Amie M., and Trebor Healey, eds. *Queer and Catholic*. New York: Routledge, 2008.

Faherty, Vincent E. "Is the Mouse Sensitive? A Study of Race, Gender, and Social Vulnerability in Disney Animated Films." *Studies in Media & Information Literacy Education* 1, no. 3 (2001): 1–8.

Fawaz, Ramzi, and Shanté Paradigm Smalls. "Queers Read This! LGBTQ Literature Now." *GLQ: A Journal of Lesbian and Gay Studies* 24, nos. 2–3 (2018): 169–87.

Feaver, William. *When We Were Young: Two Centuries of Children's Book Illustrations*. New York: Holt, 1977.

Ferfolja, Tania. "LGBT Equity and School Policy: Perspectives from Canada and Australia." In *World Education Research Yearbook 2015*, edited by Lori Diane Hill and Felice J. Levine, 94–113. New York: Routledge, 2015.

Ferguson, Roderick A. *Aberrations in Black: Toward a Queer of Color Critique*. Minneapolis: University of Minnesota Press, 2004.

———. "Queer of Color Critique." In *Oxford Research Encyclopedia of Literature*. Oxford: Oxford University Press, 2018.

Fernandez, Joseph A. *Children of the Rainbow: First Grade* [Curriculum]. New York: New York City Public Schools, 1991.

Ferrari, Martina. "Gloria Anzaldúa's Decolonizing Aesthetics: On Silence and Bearing Witness." *Journal of Speculative Philosophy* 34 no. 3 (2020): 323–38.

Fields, Jessica. "'Children Having Children': Race, Innocence, and Sexuality Education." *Social Problems* 52, no. 4 (2005): 549–71.

Fishzon, Anna, and Emma Lieber, eds. *The Queerness of Childhood: Essays from the Other Side of the Looking Glass*. New York: Palgrave Macmillan, 2022.

Flores, Gabriel. "Teachers Working Cooperatively with Parents and Caregivers When Implementing LGBT Themes in the Elementary Classroom." *American Journal of Sexuality Education* 9, no. 1 (2014): 114–20.

Ford, Elizabeth A. "H/Z: Why Lesléa Newman Makes Heather into Zoe." *Children's Literature Association Quarterly* 23, no. 3 (1998): 128–33.

Ford, Richard Thompson. *Dress Codes: How the Laws of Fashion Made History*. New York: Simon and Schuster, 2021.

Foucault, Michel. *The History of Sexuality*. New York: Vintage Books, 1988.

Francis Mor, Ana. *Manual de la buena lesbiana, 2*. Mexico City: Ediciones Chulas,

Franco, Jean. *Plotting Women: Gender and Representation in Mexico*. New York: Columbia University Press, 1989.

Fregoso, Rosa Linda. *MeXicana Encounters: The Making of Social Identities on the Borderlands*. Berkeley: University of California Press, 2003.

Garcia, Elizabeth, "Latina Feminist Agency: Manifestations of a New Mestiza Consciousness in Gloria Anzaldúa's Children's Books." *Children's Literature Association Quarterly* 46, no. 2. (2001): 111–24.

Gay, Carol. "ChLA: 1973–1983." In *Festschrift: A Ten Year Retrospective*, edited by Perry Nodelman and Jill P May, 4–8. West Lafayette, IN: Children's Literature Association, 1983.

Genette, Gérard. *Paratexts: Thresholds of Interpretation*. Translated by Jane E. Lewin. Cambridge: Cambridge University Press, 1997. Originally published as *Seuils*. Paris: Editions du Seuil, 1987.

George, Marie-Amélie. "The Custody Crucible: The Development of Scientific Authority about Gay and Lesbian Parents." *Law and History Review* 34, no. 2 (2016): 487–529.

Gill-Peterson, Jules. *Histories of the Transgender Child*. Minneapolis: University of Minnesota Press, 2018.

Gill-Peterson, Jules, Rebekah Sheldon, and Kathryn Bond Stockton. "Introduction: What Is the Now, Even of Then." In "The Child Now." Special issue, *GLQ: A Journal of Lesbian and Gay Studies* 22, no. 4 (2016): 495–503.

Gomez, Jewelle. "I Lost It at the Movies." In *Does Your Mama Know? An Anthology of Black Lesbian Coming Out Stories*, edited by Lisa C. Moore, 170–75. New Orleans: Redbone Press, 1998.

Gómez-Quiñones, Juan, and Irene Vásquez. *Making Aztlán: Ideology and Culture of the Chicana and Chicano Movement, 1966–1977*. Albuquerque: University of New Mexico Press, 2014.

Gonzalez, Maya Christina. *Call Me Tree/Llámame árbol*. New York: Children's Book Press, 2014.

———. *Claiming Face: Self-Empowerment through Self-Portraiture*. San Francisco: Reflection Press, 2010.

———. *Coloring the Revolution #1*. San Francisco: Reflection Press, 2017.

———. *Gender Now Activity Book: School Edition*. San Francisco: Reflection Press, 2011.

———. *Gender Now Coloring Book: A Learning Adventure for Children and Adults*. San Francisco: Reflection Press, 2010.

———. *The Gender Wheel: A Story about Bodies and Gender for Every Body*. San Francisco: Reflection Press, 2017.

———. *The Gender Wheel: A Story about Bodies and Gender for Every Body [School Edition]*. San Francisco: Reflection Press, 2018.

———. *I Know the River Loves Me/Yo sé que el río me ama*. San Francisco: Children's Book Press, 2009.

———. *The Interrupting Chupacabra* [PDF booklet]. San Francisco: Reflection Press, 2015.

———. *Ma Llorona: A Ghost Story, a Love Story*. San Francisco: Reflection Press, 2017.

———. *My Colors, My World/Mis colores, mi mundo*. San Francisco: Children's Book Press, 2007.

Gonzalez, Maya, and Matthew Smith-Gonzalez. *They, She, He: Easy as ABC*. San Francisco: Reflection Press, 2019.

———. *They, She, He, Me: Free to Be!* Illustrated by Maya Christina Gonzalez. San Francisco: Reflection Press, 2017.

González, Rigoberto. *Antonio's Card/La tarjeta de Antonio*. Illustrated by Cecilia Concepción Álvarez. San Francisco: Children's Book Press, 2005.

———. *Autobiography of My Hungers*. Madison: University of Wisconsin Press, 2013.

———. *Butterfly Boy: Memories of a Chicano Mariposa*. Madison: University of Wisconsin Press, 2006.

———. *Soledad Sigh-Sighs/Soledad suspiros*. Illustrated by Rosa Ibarra. San Francisco: Children's Book Press, 2003.

———. *Unpeopled Eden*. New York: Four Way Books, 2013.

———. *What Drowns the Flowers in Your Mouth: A Memoir of Brotherhood*. Madison: University of Wisconsin Press, 2018.

Gordon, Lewis R., ed. *Existence in Black: An Anthology of Black Existential Philosophy*. New York: Routledge, 1997.

Gould, Lois. "X: A Fabulous Child's Story." *Ms.*, 1972. Illustrated by Jacqueline Chwast.

Grenby, M. O., and Andrea Immel. *The Cambridge Companion to Children's Literature*. Cambridge: Cambridge University Press, 2009.

Grimes, Nikki. *Kamala Harris: Rooted in Justice*. Illustrated by Laura Freeman. New York: Atheneum Books for Young Readers, 2020.

Guerrero, M. Luisa. *El viejo coche/The Old Car*. Barcelona: ONG por la No Discriminación, 2008.

Guignard, Florence Pasche. "A Gendered Bun in the Oven: The Gender-Reveal Party as a New Ritualization during Pregnancy." *Studies in Religion* 44, no. 4 (2015): 479–500.

Gutierrez, Laura G. "'El derecho de re-hacer': Signifyin(g) Blackness in Contemporary Mexican Political Cabaret." *Arizona Journal of Hispanic Cultural Studies* 16 (2012): 163–76.

Gutterman, Lauren Jae. *Her Neighbor's Wife: A History of Lesbian Desire within Marriage*. Philadelphia: University of Pennsylvania Press, 2019.

Halberstam, Jack. *Wild Things: The Disorder of Desire*. Durham, NC: Duke University Press, 2020.

Hall, K. Melchor Quick. *Naming a Transnational Black Feminist Framework: Writing in Darkness*. New York: Routledge, 2020.

Hamer, Naomi, Perry Nodelman, and Mavis Reimer, eds. *More Words about Pictures: Current Research on Picture Books and Visual/Verbal Texts for Young People*. New York: Routledge, 2017.

Hames-García, Michael, and Ernesto Javier Martínez, eds. *Gay Latino Studies: A Critical Reader*. Durham, NC: Duke University Press, 2011.

Hamilton, Virginia. *Zeely*. New York: Macmillan, 1967.

Harris, Trudier. *Black Women in the Fiction of James Baldwin*. Knoxville, TN: University of Tennessee Press, 1985.

Harvey, Robert. *The Art of the Comic Book: An Aesthetic History*. Jackson: University Press of Mississippi, 1996.

Hatfield, Charles. "Comic Art, Children's Literature, and the New Comic Studies." *The Lion and the Unicorn* 30, no. 3 (2006): 360–82.

Hatfield, Charles, and Craig Svonkin. "Why Comics Are and Are Not Picture Books: Introduction." *Children's Literature Association Quarterly* 37, no. 4 (Winter 2012): 429–35.

Hemphill, Essex. "If Freud Had Been a Neurotic Colored Woman: Reading Dr. Frances Cress Welsing." *Out/Look: National Lesbian and Gay Quarterly* 4, no. 1 (Summer 1991): 50–55.

Hernandez, Catherine. *I Promise*. Illustrated by Syrus Marcus Ware. Vancouver: Arsenal Pulp Press, 2019.

———. *M is for Mustache: A Pride ABC Book*. Illustrated by Marisa Firebaugh. Toronto: Flamingo Rampant, 2015.

Hernández, Ellie D. *Postnationalism in Chicana/o Literature and Culture*. Austin: University of Texas Press, 2009.

Herzog, Ricky. "Sissies, Dolls, and Dancing: Children's Literature and Gender Deviance in the Seventies." *The Lion and the Unicorn* 33, no. 1 (2009): 60–76.

Higginbotham, Anastasia. *Tell Me about Sex, Grandma*. New York: The Feminist Press at CUNY, 2017.

Hill-Meyer, Tobi. *A Princess of Great Daring!* Illustrated by Elenore Toczynski. Toronto: Flamingo Rampant Press, 2015.

Honychurch, Lennox. "Crossroads in the Caribbean: A Site of Encounters and Exchange on Dominica." *World Archaeology* 28, no. 3 (1997): 291–304.

hooks, bell. *Art on My Mind: Visual Politics*. New York: The New Press, 1995.

———. *Happy to Be Nappy*. Illustrated by Chris Raschka. New York: Hyperion Books for Children, 1999.

Hunt, Peter, ed. *Children's Literature: An Illustrated History*. Oxford: Oxford University Press, 1995.

———, ed. *International Companion Encyclopedia of Children's Literature*. New York: Routledge, 1996.

Hunter, Nan D., and Nancy D. Polikoff. "Custody Rights of Lesbian Mothers: Legal Theory and Litigation Strategy." *Buffalo Law Review* 25, no. 3 (1976): 691–733.

Hurley, Dorothy L. "Seeing White: Children of Color and the Disney Fairy Tale Princess." *Journal of Negro Education* 74, no. 3 (2005): 221–32.

Hurley, Natasha. *Circulating Queerness: Before the Gay and Lesbian Novel*. Minneapolis: University of Minnesota Press, 2018.

Ito, Kinko. "A History of Manga in the Context of Japanese Culture and Society." *Journal of Popular Culture* 38, no. 3 (2005): 456–75.

Jackson, Shannon. "Performing Show and Tell: Disciplines of Visual Culture and Performance Studies." *Journal of Visual Culture* 4, no. 2 (2005): 163–77.

Jaspers, Karl. *Philosophy of Existence*. Translated by Richard F. Grabau. Philadelphia: University of Pennsylvania Press, 1971. Originally published as *Existenzphilosophie*. Berlin: de Gruyter, 1938.

Jenkins, Christine A. "Young Adult Novels with Gay/Lesbian Characters and Themes, 1969–92: A Historical Reading of Content, Gender, and Narrative Distance." In *Over the Rainbow: Queer Children's and Young Adult Literature*, edited by Michelle Ann Abate and Kenneth Kidd, 147–63. Ann Arbor: University of Michigan Press, 2011.

Jewell, Terri. "Interview with Stephanie Byrd." In *Does Your Mama Know? An Anthology of Black Lesbian Coming Out Stories*, edited by Lisa C. Moore, 129–38. New Orleans: Redbone Press, 1998.

Johnson, David K. *The Lavender Scare: The Cold War Persecution of Gays and Lesbians in the Federal Government*. Chicago: University of Chicago Press, 2004.

Johnson, Myles E. *Large Fears*. Illustrated by Kendrick Daye. Self-published, 2015.

Johnson, Sarita [Sarita Johnson-Calvo]. *A Beach Party with Alexis*. Boston: Alyson Wonderland, 1993. Originally self-published in 1991.

——— [Sarita Johnson-Hunt]. *A Day with Alexis*. Self-published, n.d.

———. "Occupation: Ornament (or) How to Be Used at Your Own Expense." *Black Lesbian Newsletter* 2, no. 2 (April/May 1983).

Jones, Katharine. "Getting Rid of Children's Literature." *The Lion and the Unicorn* 30, no. 3 (2006): 287–315.

Jordan, MaryKate. *Losing Uncle Tim*. Illustrated by Judith Friedman. Park Ridge, IL: Albert Whitman, 1989.

Kanhai, Rosanne, ed. *Bindi: The Multifaceted Lives of Indo-Caribbean Women*. Kingston: University Press of the West Indies, 2011.

Karefa-Smart, Tejan. "Little Man, Little Man: We the Children." Foreword to *Little Man, Little Man: A Story of Childhood*, by James Baldwin, edited by Nicholas Boggs and Jennifer DeVere Brody, xi–xiii. Durham, NC: Duke University Press, 2018.

Kau-Arteaga, Kanoa. *Colors of Aloha*. Illustrated by J. R. Keaolani Bogac-Moore. Toronto: Flamingo Rampant Press, 2019.

Keating, AnaLouise, ed. *EntreMundos/AmongWorlds: New Perspectives on Gloria E. Anzaldúa*. New York: Palgrave Macmillan, 2005.

———, ed. *The Gloria Anzaldúa Reader*. Durham, NC: Duke University Press, 2009.

Keeling, Kara. "'Ghetto Heaven': Set If Off and the Valorization of Black Lesbian Butch-Femme Sociality." *Black Scholar* 33, no. 1 (2003): 33–46.

Khaki, El-Farouk, and Troy Jackson. *Moondragon in the Mosque Garden*. Illustrated by Katie Commodore. Toronto: Flamingo Rampant Press, 2017.

Kidd, Kenneth. *Freud in Oz: At the Intersection of Psychoanalysis and Children's Literature*. Minneapolis: University of Minnesota Press, 2011.

———. "Queer Theory's Child and Children's Literature Studies." *PMLA* 126, no. 1 (2011): 1–23.

Kilodavis, Cheryl. *My Princess Boy*. Illustrated by Suzanne DeSimone. Seattle: KD Talent, 2009.

Kincaid, James. *Child-Loving: The Erotic Child and Victorian Culture*. New York: Routledge, 1992.

Kirby, Diana Gonzalez. "Reading with Uncle Sam: A Review of Children's Literature from the US Government, 1940–1990." *Behavioral and Social Sciences Librarian* 11, no. 2 (1992): 1–38.

Klein, Gillian. *Reading into Racism: Bias in Children's Literature and Learning Materials*. New York: Routledge, 1985.

Labelle, Sophie. *Rachel's Christmas Boat*. Toronto: Flamingo Rampant Press, 2017.

La Fountain-Stokes, Lawrence. "La política queer del espanglish." In "Fronteras, intersticios y umbrales." Special issue, *Debate Feminista* 33 (2006): 141–53.

———. "Trans/Bolero/Drag/Migration: Music, Cultural Translation, and Diasporic Puerto Rican Theatricalities." *Women's Studies Quarterly* 36, no. 4 (2008): 190–209.

Lambert, Aida. "We Are Black Too: Experiences of a Honduran Garifuna." In *The Afro-Latin@ Reader: History and Culture in the United States*, edited by Miriam Jiménez Román and Juan Flores, 431–33. Durham, NC: Duke University Press, 2010.

Lampert, Jo. *Children's Fiction about 9/11: Ethnic, National and Heroic Identities*. New York: Routledge, 2010.

Lane, Kimberly, Yaschica Williams, Andrea N. Hunt, and Amber Paulk. "The Framing of Race: Trayvon Martin and the Black Lives Matter Movement." *Journal of Black Studies* 51, no. 8 (2020): 790–812.

Larkin, Lesley. "Authentic Mothers, Authentic Daughters and Sons: Ultrasound Imaging and the Construction of Fetal Sex and Gender." *Canadian Review of American Studies* 36, no. 3 (2006): 273–92.

Larrick, Nancy. "The All-White World of Children's Books." *Saturday Review*, September 11, 1965: 63–85.

Leaf, Munro. *The Story of Ferdinand*. Illustrated by Robert Lawson. New York: The Viking Press, 1936.

Lerer, Seth. *Children's Literature: A Reader's History from Aesop to Harry Potter*. Chicago: University of Chicago Press, 2008.

Lesbian Writing and Publishing Collective, ed. *Dykeversions: Lesbian Short Fiction*. Toronto: Women's Press, 1986.

———. *Dykewords: An Anthology of Lesbian Writing*. Toronto: Women's Press, 1990.

Lester, Jasmine Z. "Homonormativity in Children's Literature: An Intersectional Analysis of Queer-Themed Picture Books." *Journal of LGBT Youth* 11, no. 3 (2014): 244–75.

Levander, Caroline, and Robert Levine, eds. *Hemispheric American Studies*. New Brunswick: Rutgers University Press, 2008.

Lewis, Davis. *Reading Contemporary Picturebooks: Picturing Text*. New York: Routledge, 2001.

Livingstone, Leon. "Autobiografia y autofantasia en la Generacion del 98: Teoria y practica del querer ser." In *Homenaje a Juan Lopez Morillas: De Cadalso a Aleixandre*, edited by José Amor y Vázquez and A. David Kossoff, 293–302. Madrid: Editorial Castalia, 1982.

Lopez, Christina Garcia. *Calling the Soul Back: Embodied Spirituality in Chicanx Narrative*. Tucson: University of Arizona Press, 2019.

López Oro, Paul Joseph. "A Love Letter to Indigenous Blackness: Garifuna Women in New York City Working to Preserve Life, Culture, and History across Borders and Generations Are Part of a Powerful Lineage of Resistance to Anti-Blackness." *NACLA Report on the Americas* 53, no. 3 (2021): 248–54.

Lorde, Audre. *Sister Outsider: Essays and Speeches*. Berkeley, CA: Crossing Press, 1984.

———. *Zami: A New Spelling of My Name*. Watertown, MA: Persephone Press, 1982.

Lugones, Maria. "Playfulness, 'World'-Travelling, and Loving Perception." *Hypatia* 2, no. 2 (1987): 3–19.

MacCann, Donnarae. *White Supremacy in Children's Literature: Characterizations of African Americans, 1830–1900*. New York: Routledge, 2001. Originally published in 1998.

Mack, Bruce. "Jesse's Dream Skirt." *Magnus: A Socialist Journal of Gay Liberation*, no. 2 (1977). Illustrated by Larry Hermsen. Published under the pseudonym "Morning Star."

———. *Jesse's Dream Skirt*. Illustrated by Marian Buchanan. Chapel Hill, NC: Lollipop Power, 1979.

Martínez, Elizabeth. *De Colores Means All of Us: Latina Views for a Multi-Colored Century*. Cambridge, MA: South End Press, 1998.

Martínez, Ernesto Javier. *On Making Sense: Queer Race Narratives of Intelligibility*. Stanford, CA: Stanford University Press, 2013.

———. *When We Love Someone We Sing to Them/Cuando amamos cantamos*. Illustrated by Maya C. Gonzalez. San Francisco: Reflection Press, 2018.

Mason, Derritt. *Queer Anxieties of Young Adult Literature and Culture*. Jackson: University Press of Mississippi, 2021.

Mathiowetz, Michael D., and Andrew D. Turner. *Flower Worlds: Religion, Aesthetics, and Ideology in Mesoamerica and the American Southwest*. Tucson: University of Arizona Press.

Mayeno, Laurin. *One of a Kind, Like Me/Único como yo*. Illustrated by Robert Liu-Trujillo. Oakland, CA: Blood Orange Press, 2016.

Mayo, Cris. *Disputing the Subject of Sex: Sexuality and Public School Controversies*. Lanham, MD: Rowman and Littlefield, 2004.

McCaskell, Tim. "Fighting Homophobia in Toronto Schools." In *Unleashing the Popular: Talking about Sexual Orientation and Gender Diversity in Education*, edited by Isabel Killoran and Karleen Pendleton Jiménez, 78–82. Olney, UK: Association for Childhood Education International, 2007.

———. *Queer Progress: From Homophobia to Homonationalism*. Toronto: Between the Lines, 2016.

———. *Race to Equity: Disrupting Educational Inequity*. Toronto: Between the Lines, 2005.

Mercer, Kobena. "Black Hair/Style Politics." *New Formations* 3 (1987): 33–54.

Mickenberg, Julia L. *Learning from the Left: Children's Literature, the Cold War, and Radical Politics in the United States*. New York: Oxford University Press, 2006.

Mickenberg, Julia L., and Philip Nel, eds. *Tales for Little Rebels: A Collection of Radical Children's Literature*. New York: New York University Press, 2008.

Mignolo, Walter D. *Local Histories/Global Designs: Coloniality, Subaltern Knowledges, and Border Thinking*. Princeton, NJ: Princeton University Press, 2000.

Millán, Isabel. "Apples Begone: Queer and Trans of Color Aesthetics of Joy in ABC Books." In *Reading LGBTQ+ Children's Picture Books*, edited by Jennifer Miller and Sara Austin. Jackson: University Press of Mississippi, expected 2024.

———. "Autofantasías: Reinventing Self & Inspiring Travesuras in Children's Cultural Productions." In *El Mundo Zurdo 6, Conference Proceedings*, edited by Sara A. Ramírez, Larissa M. Mercado-López, and Sonia Saldívar-Hull, 27–44. San Francisco: Aunt Lute Books, 2018.

———. *Chabelita's Heart/El corazón de Chabelita*. San Francisco: Reflection Press, 2022.

———. "Contested Children's Literature: Que(e)ries into Chicana and Central American *Autofantasías*." *Signs: Journal of Women in Culture and Society* 41, no. 1 (2015): 199–224.

Miller, Jennifer. "For the Little Queers: Imagining Queerness in 'New' Queer Children's Literature." *Journal of Homosexuality* 66, no. 12 (2019): 1645–70.

———. "A Little Queer: Ambivalence and the Work of Gender Play in Children's Literature." In *Heroes, Heroines, and Everything in Between: Challenging Gender and Sexuality Stereotypes in Children's Entertainment Media*, edited by CarrieLynn D. Reinhard and Christopher J. Olson, 35–50. Lanham, MD: Lexington Books, 2017.

———. *The Transformative Potential of LGBTQ+ Children's Picture Books*. Jackson: University Press of Mississippi, 2022.

Miller, Jennifer, and Sara Austin, eds. *Reading LGBTQ+ Children's Picture Books*. Jackson: University Press of Mississippi, expected 2024.

Miller, Miriam Youngerman. "Illustrations of the 'Canterbury Tales' for Children: A Mirror of Chaucer's World?" *Chaucer Review* 27, no. 3 (1993): 293–304.

Mitchell, Claudia. "'What's Out There?' Gay and Lesbian Literature for Children and Young Adults." In *Lesbian and Gay Studies and the Teaching of English: Positions, Pedagogies, and Cultural Politics*, edited by William J. Spurlin, 112–30. Urbana, IL: National Council of Teachers of English, 2000.

Mitchell, Penni. *About Canada: Women's Rights*. Black Point, NS: Fernwood, 2015.

Mogrovejo Aquise, Norma. "The Latin American Lesbian Movement: Its Shaping and Its Search for Autonomy." In *Provocations: A Transnational Reader in the History of Feminist Thought*, edited by Susan Bordo, M. Cristina Alcalde, and Ellen Rosenman, 312–20. Oakland: University of California Press, 2015.

———. *Un amor que se atrevió a decir su nombre: La lucha de las lesbianas y su relación con los movimientos homosexual y feminista en América Latina*. Mexico City: CDAHL, 2000.

Mondragón Rocha, Lorena. *Mi mami ya no tiene frío*. Illustrated by Dirce Hernández. Guadalajara: Ediciones Patlatonalli, 2012.

Moore, Denise. "Halfway Home: Interview with Katherine James." In *Does Your Mama Know? An Anthology of Black Lesbian Coming Out Stories*, edited by Lisa C. Moore, 105–15. New Orleans: Redbone Press, 1998.

Moore, Lisa C., ed. *Does Your Mama Know? An Anthology of Black Lesbian Coming Out Stories*. New Orleans: Redbone Press, 1998.

Morad, Moshe. "Queer Bolero: Bolero Music as an Emotional and Psychological Space for Gay Men in Cuba." *Psychology Research* 5, no. 10 (2015): 565–84.

Moraga, Cherríe, and Gloria Anzaldúa, eds., *This Bridge Called My Back: Writings by Radical Women of Color*. Watertown, MA: Persephone, 1981.

Morton, Gillian. "Racism in the Arts." *Rebel Girls' Rag: A Forum of Women's Resistance* 4, no. 2 (February 1990): 6.

Moya, Paula M. L. *The Social Imperative: Race, Close Reading, and Contemporary Literary Criticism*. Stanford, CA: Stanford University Press, 2015.

Mozetič, Brane. *Mi primer amor*. Illustrated by Maja Kastelic. Barcelona: Ediciones Bellaterra, 2016. Originally published in Slovene as *Prva ljubezen* in 2014.

Muñoz, José Esteban. *Cruising Utopia: The Then and There of Queer Futurity*. New York: New York University Press, 2009.

———. *Disidentifications: Queers of Color and the Performance of Politics*. Minneapolis: University of Minnesota Press, 1999.

Naidoo, Jamie Campbell. *Rainbow Family Collections: Selecting and Using Children's Books with Lesbian, Gay, Bisexual, Transgender, and Queer Content*. Santa Barbara, CA: Libraries Unlimited, 2012.

Naidoo, Jamie Campbell, and Kaitlyn Lynch. "Global Rainbow Families: Examining Visual Depictions of Same-Sex Couples in International Picturebooks." *Bookbird: A Journal of International Children's Literature* 58, no. 4 (2020): 31–51.

Neal, Trinity and DeShanna Neal. *My Rainbow*. Illustrated by Art Twink. New York: Kokila, 2020.

Nel, Philip. *Was the Cat in the Hat Black? The Hidden Racism of Children's Literature, and the Need for Diverse Books*. Oxford: Oxford University Press, 2017.

Nel, Philip, and Lissa Paul, eds. *Keywords for Children's Literature*. New York: New York University Press, 2011.

Nelson, Alondra. "Afrofuturism: Past-Future Visions." *Color Lines* 3, no. 1 (2000): 34–47.

———. "Introduction: Future Texts." *Social Text* 71, vol. 20, no. 2 (2002): 1–15.

Nelson, Claudia. "Writing the Reader: The Literary Child in and beyond the Book." *Children's Literature Associated Quarterly* 31, no. 3 (2006): 222–36.

Newman, Lesléa. *Belinda's Bouquet*. Illustrated by Michael Willhoite. Boston: Alyson Books, 1989.

———. *Gloria Goes to Gay Pride*. Illustrated by Russell Crocker. Boston: Alyson, 1991.

———. *Heather Has Two Mommies*. Illustrated by Diana Souza. Northampton, MA: In Other Words, 1989; Boston: Alyson Wonderland, 1990. Illustrated by Laura Cornell. Somerville, MA: Candlewick Press, 2015.

———. *Paula tiene dos mamás*. Illustrated by Mabel Piérola. Translated by Silvia Donoso. Barcelona: Edicions Bellaterra, 2003.

Ng'weno, Bettina, and Lok Siu. "Comparative Raciality: Erasure and Hypervisibility of Asian and Afro Mexicans." In *Global Raciality: Empire, PostColoniality, DeColoniality*, edited by Paola Bacchetta, Sunaina Maira, and Howard Winant, 62–82. New York: Routledge, 2019.

Niedzwiecki, Thaba. "Print Politics: Conflict and Community-Building at Toronto's Women's Press." Master's thesis, University of Guelph, 1997.

Nikolajeva, Maria, ed. *Aspects and Issues in the History of Children's Literature*. London: Greenwood Press, 1995.

Nodelman, Perry. Introduction to *More Words about Pictures: Current Research on Picture Books and Visual/Verbal Texts for Young People*, edited by Naomi Hamer, Perry Nodelman, and Mavis Reimer, 1–17. New York: Routledge, 2017.

———. "Picture Book Guy Looks at Comics: Structural Differences in Two Kinds of Visual Narrative." *Children's Literature Association Quarterly* 37, no. 4 (2012): 436–44.

———. *Words about Pictures: The Narrative Art of Children's Picture Books*. Athens: University of Georgia Press, 1988.

Norton, Jody. "Transchildren and the Discipline of Children's Literature." *The Lion and the Unicorn* 23, no. 3 (1999): 415–36.

Nyong'o, Tavia. *Afro-Fabulations: The Queer Drama of Black Life*. New York: New York University Press, 2019.

Oikawa, Mona, Dionne Falconer, Rosamund Elwin, and Ann Decter, eds. *Out Rage: Dykes and Bis Resist Homophobia*. Toronto: Women's Press, 1993.

Okami, Paul, Richard Olmstead, and Paul R. Abramson. "Sexual Experiences in Early Childhood: 18-Year Longitudinal Data from the UCLA Family Lifestyles Project." *Journal of Sex Research* 34, no. 4 (1997): 339–47.

Opie, Iona. "Playground Rhymes and the Oral Tradition." In *International Companion Encyclopedia of Children's Literature*, edited by Peter Hunt, 173–86. London: Routledge, 1996.

Pallotta-Chiarolli, María. *Border Sexualities, Border Families in Schools.* Lanham, MD: Rowman and Littlefield, 2010.

———. "'My Moving Days': A Child's Negotiation of Multiple Lifeworlds in Relation to Gender, Ethnicity, and Sexuality." In *Queering Elementary Education: Advancing the Dialogue about Sexualities and Schooling*, edited by William J. Letts IV and James T. Sears, 71–81. Lanham, MD: Rowman and Littlefield, 1999.

Pan-African Association. "To the Nations of the World, ca. 1900." W. E. B. Du Bois Papers. (MS 312) Series 1A General Correspondence, Special Collections and University Archives, University of Massachusetts Amherst Libraries. https://credo.library.umass.edu.

Paoletti, Jo B. "The Gendering of Infants' and Toddlers' Clothing in America." In *The Material Culture of Gender, the Gender of Material Culture*, edited by Katherine A. Martinez and Kenneth L. Ames, 27–35. Hanover, NH: University Press of New England, 1997.

———. *Pink and Blue: Telling the Boys from the Girls in America.* Bloomington: Indiana University Press, 2012.

Paulse, Michele. "Commingled." In *Miscegenation Blues: Voices of Mixed Race Women*, edited by Carol Camper, 43–44. Toronto: Sister Vision Press, 1994.

———. "'Everyone Had Their Differences but There Was Always Comradeship': Tramway Road, Sea Point, 1920s to 1961." In *Lost Communities, Living Memories: Remembering Forced Removals in Cape Town*, edited by Sean Field, 44–61. Claremont, South Africa: David Philip, 2001.

———. "Keynotes." In *Dykeversions: Lesbian Short Fiction*, edited by Lesbian Writing and Publishing Collective, 65–69. Toronto: Women's Press, 1986.

Paulse, Michele, Nila Gupta, Ellen Quigley, and Maureen FitzGerald. "Notes about Racism in the Process." In *Dykeversions: Lesbian Short Fiction*, edited by Lesbian Writing and Publishing Collective, 11–15. Toronto: Women's Press, 1986.

Pedelty, Mark. "The Bolero: The Birth, Life, and Decline of Mexican Modernity." *Latin American Music Review/Revista de Música Latinoamericana* 20, no. 1 (1999): 30–58.

Peña Muñoz, Manuel. *Historia de la literatura infantil en América Latina.* Madrid: Fundación SM, 2009.

Pendleton Jiménez, Karleen. *Are You a Boy or a Girl? A Zine for Progressive Children.* Toronto: BK, 1999.

———. *Are You a Boy or a Girl?* Toronto: Green Dragon Press, 2000.

———. *Are You a Boy or a Girl?* 20th anniversary ed. Toronto: Two Ladies Press, 2022.

———. *The Street Belongs to Us.* Vancouver: Arsenal Pulp Press, 2021.

———. "'Tell Them You're Mexican,' and Other Motherly Advice." In *Mother of Invention: How Our Mothers Influenced Us as Feminist Academics and Activists*, edited by Vanessa Reimer. Bradford, ON: Demeter Press, 2013.

Perez, Domino R. "A New Generation of Cultural/Critical Readers." In *There Was a Woman: La Llorona from Folklore to Popular Culture*, 179–93. Austin: University of Texas Press, 2008.

Perry, Imani. *Vexy Thing: On Gender and Liberation*. Durham, NC: Duke University Press, 2018.

Philip, Marlene Nourbese. "Journal Entries against Reaction: Damned If We Do and Damned If We Don't." In *Moving beyond Boundaries*, vol. 1, *International Dimensions of Black Women's Writing*, edited by Carole Boyce Davies and 'Molara Ogundipe-Leslie, 95–102. New York: New York University Press, 1995.

Piepzna-Samarasinha, Leah Lakshmi. *Bridge of Flowers*. Illustrated by Syrus Marcus Ware. Toronto: Flamingo Rampant Press, 2019.

———. *Care Work: Dreaming Disability Justice*. Vancouver: Arsenal Pulp Press, 2018.

———. *Dirty River: A Queer Femme of Color Dreaming Her Way Home*. Vancouver: Arsenal Pulp Press, 2015.

———. *Tonguebreaker: Poems and Performance Texts*. Vancouver: Arsenal Pulp Press, 2019.

Przybylo, Ela. *Asexual Erotics: Intimate Readings of Compulsory Sexuality*. Columbus: Ohio State University Press, 2019.

Pugh, Tison. *Innocence, Heterosexuality, and the Queerness of Children's Literature*. New York: Routledge, 2011.

Ramírez, Catherine S. "Afrofuturism/Chicanafuturism: Fictive Kin." *Aztlán: A Journal of Chicano Studies* 33, no. 1 (2008): 185–94.

———. "Cyborg Feminism: The Science Fiction of Octavia E. Butler and Gloria Anzaldúa." In *Reload: Rethinking Women + Cyberculture*, edited by Mary Flanagan and Austin Booth, 374–402. Cambridge, MA: MIT Press, 2002.

———. "Deus Ex Machina: Tradition, Technology, and the Chicanafuturist Art of Marion C. Martinez." *Aztlán: A Journal of Chicano Studies* 29, no. 2 (2002): 55–92.

Rankin, Sandy, and R. C. Neighbors. "Introduction: Horizons of Possibility: What We Point to When We Say Science Fiction for Children." In *The Galaxy Is Rated G: Essays on Children's Science Fiction Film and Television*, edited by R. C. Neighbors and Sandy Rankin, 1–14. Jefferson, NC: McFarland, 2011.

Reisberg, Mira. "Maya Gonzalez: Portrait of the Artist as a Radical Children's Book Illustrator." *Visual Culture and Gender* 3 (2008): 53–67.

Rey, Mario. *Historia y muestra de la literatura infantil Mexicana*. Mexico City: SM de Ediciones, 2000.

Reynolds, Kimberley. *Children's Literature: A Very Short Introduction*. Oxford: Oxford University Press, 2011.

Rhodes, Cristina. "Processes of Transformation: Theorizing Activism and Change through Gloria Anzaldúa's Picture Books." *Children's Literature in Education* 52 (2021): 464–77.

Rice-González, Charles. *Chulito*. New York: Mangus Books, 2011.

Riggs, Marlon. *Tongues Untied*. San Francisco: Frameline, 1989.

Rivas, Lourdes. *They Call Me Mix/Me llaman Maestre*. Illustrated by Breena Nuñez. Self-published, 2018.

Rivera, Sylvia. "Queens in Exile, the Forgotten Ones." In *GenderQueer: Voices from Beyond the Sexual Binary*, edited by Joan Nestle, Clare Howell, and Riki Wilchins, 67–85. Los Angeles: Alyson Books, 2002.

Rivero, Yeidy M. *Turning Out Blackness: Race and Nation in the History of Puerto Rican Television*. Durham, NC: Duke University Press, 2005.

Rivers, Daniel Winunwe. "'In the Best Interest of the Child': Lesbian and Gay Parenting Custody Cases, 1967–1985." *Journal of Social History* 43, no. 4 (2010): 917–43.

———. *Radical Relations: Lesbian Mothers, Gay Fathers, and Their Children in the United States since World War II*. Chapel Hill: University of North Carolina Press, 2013.

Robinson, Kerry H. "In the Name of 'Childhood Innocence': A Discursive Exploration of the Moral Panic Associated with Childhood and Sexuality." *Cultural Studies Review* 14, no. 2 (2008): 113–29.

———. "'Queerying' Gender, Heteronormativity in Early Childhood Education." *Australian Journal of Early Childhood* 30, no. 2 (2005): 9–28.

Robson, Ruthann. "Making Mothers: Lesbian Legal Theory and the Judicial Construction of Lesbian Mothers." *Women's Rights Law Reporter* 22, no. 1 (2000): 15–35.

Rodríguez, Juana María. *Queer Latinidad: Identity Practices, Discursive Spaces*. New York: New York University Press, 2003.

———. *Sexual Futures, Queer Gestures, and Other Latina Longings*. New York: New York University Press, 2014.

Rodríguez, Sonia Alejandra. "Conocimiento Narratives: Creative Acts and Healing in Latinx Children's and Young Adult Literature." *Children's Literature* 47 (2019): 9–29.

Rodríguez Matus, Juan. *Las tres Sofías*. Illustrated by Anna Cooke. Guadalajara: Ediciones Patlatonalli, 2008.

Roffiel, Rosamaría. *Amora*. Mexico City: Planeta, 1989.

———. *El secreto de las familias*. Illustrated by Tlalli Ávila Loera. Mexico City: Prensa Editorial LeSVOZ, 2021.

Romero, Emmanuel, and Drew Stephens. *Prinsesa: The Boy Who Dreamed of Being a Princess*. Illustrated by Marconi Calindas. Self-published, 2013.

Rothberg, Michael. "W. E. B. Du Bois in Warsaw: Holocaust Memory and the Color Line, 1949–1952." *Yale Journal of Criticism* 14, no. 1 (2001): 169–89.

Rough, Bonnie J. *Beyond Birds and Bees: Bringing Home a New Message to Our Kids about Sex, Love, and Equality*. New York: Seal Press, 2018.

Russell, Vanessa. "Equity Undone: The Impact of the Conservative Ontario Government's Educational Reforms on the Triangle Program." *Journal of Gay & Lesbian Issues in Education* 3, no. 4 (2006): 45–57.

Russell-Brown, Katheryn. *She Was the First! The Trailblazing Life of Shirley Chisholm*. Illustrated by Eric Velasquez. New York: Lee & Low Books, 2020.

Saavedra, Yvette J. *Pasadena before the Roses: Race, Identity, and Land Use in Southern California, 1771–1890*. Tucson: University of Arizona Press, 2018.

Saggese, Jordana Moore, ed. *The Jean-Michel Basquiat Reader: Writings, Interviews, and Critical Responses*. Berkeley: University of California Press, 2021.

Saldívar, José David. *Border Matters: Remapping American Cultural Studies*. Berkeley: University of California Press, 1997.

Saldívar-Hull, Sonia. *Feminism on the Border: Chicana Gender Politics and Literature*. Berkeley: University of California Press, 2000.

Sánchez-Eppler, Karen. "Childhood." In *Keywords for Children's Literature*, edited by Philip Nel and Lissa Paul, 35–41. New York: New York University Press, 2011.

Scotto, Thomas. *Jerome by Heart*. Illustrated by Olivier Tallec. New York: Enchanted Lion Books, 2018. Originally published in France as *Jérôme par coeur* in 2009.

Sedgwick, Eve Kosofsky. "How to Bring Your Kids Up Gay." *Social Text* 29 (1991): 18–27.

———, ed. *Novel Gazing: Queer Readings in Fiction*. Durham, NC: Duke University Press, 1997.

Seif, Hinda. "'Coming Out of the Shadows' and 'Undocuqueer': Undocumented Immigrants Transforming Sexuality Discourse and Activism." *Journal of Language and Sexuality* 3, no. 1 (2014): 87–120.

Serafini, Frank. "Design Elements of PictureBooks: Interpreting Visual Images and Design Elements of Contemporary Picturebooks." *Connecticut Reading Association Journal* 1, no. 1 (2012): 3–9.

Serrato, Phillip. "Transforming Boys, Transforming Masculinity, Transforming Culture: Masculinity Anew in Latino and Latina Children's Literature." In *Invisible No More: Understanding the Disenfranchisement of Latino Men and Boys*, edited by Pedro Noguera, Aída Hurtado, and Edward Fergus, 153–65. New York: Routledge, 2012.

Severance, Jane. *Lots of Mommies*. Illustrated by Jan Jones. Chapel Hill, NC: Lollipop Power, 1983.

———. *When Megan Went Away*. Illustrated by Tea Schook. Chapel Hill, NC: Lollipop Power, 1979.

Shraya, Vivek. *The Boy and the Bindi*. Illustrated by Rajni Perera. Vancouver: Arsenal Pulp Press, 2016.

———. *God Loves Hair*. Vancouver: Arsenal Pulp Press, 2014. Originally self-published in 2010.

Shukla, Sandhya, and Heidi Tinsman. *Imagining Our Americas: Toward a Transnational Frame*. Durham, NC: Duke University Press, 2007.

Siebers, Tobin. *Disability Aesthetics*. Ann Arbor: University of Michigan Press, 2010.

Siemerling, Winfried, and Sarah Phillips Casteel, eds. *Canada and Its Americas: Transnational Navigations*. Kingston, ON: McGill-Queen's University Press, 2010.

Silvera, Makeda, Sharon Fernandez, Michele Paulse, and Stephanie Martin. "Racism Stops Women and Words." *Kinesis*, February 1986.

Silverberg, Cory, and Fiona Smyth. *You Know, Sex: Bodies, Gender, Puberty, and Other Things*. New York: Triangle Square, 2022.

Sipe, Lawrence R., and Caroline E. McGuire. "Picturebook Endpapers: Resources for Literary and Aesthetic Interpretation." *Children's Literature in Education* 37 (2006): 291–304.

skelton, j. wallace. *The Last Place You Look*. Illustrated by Justin Alves. Toronto: Flamingo Rampant Press, 2017.

———. *The Newspaper Pirates*. Illustrated by Ketch Wehr. Toronto: Flamingo Rampant Press, 2015.

———. "Not Exceptional or Punished: A Review of Five Picture Books That Celebrate Gender Diversity." *TSQ: Transgender Studies Quarterly* 2, no. 3 (2015): 495–99.

Smith, Barbara, ed. *Home Girls: A Black Feminist Anthology*. New York: Kitchen Table/ Woman of Color Press, 1983.

Smith, M. G. *Kinship and Community in Carriacou*. New Haven, CT: Yale University Press, 1962.

Smith, Sidonie, and Julia Watson. *Reading Autobiography: A Guide for Interpreting Life Narratives*. 2nd ed. Minneapolis: University of Minnesota Press, 2010.

Snider, Kathryn. "Race and Sexual Orientation: The (Im)possibility of These Intersections in Educational Policy." *Harvard Educational Review* 66, no. 2 (1996): 294–303.

Snorton, C. Riley. *Black on Both Sides: A Racial History of Trans Identity*. Minneapolis: University of Minnesota Press, 2017.

Somerville, Siobhan B. *Queering the Color Line: Race and the Invention of Homosexuality in American Culture*. Durham, NC: Duke University Press, 2000.

Sorell, Traci. *Classified: The Secret Career of Mary Golda Ross, Cherokee Aerospace Engineer*. Illustrated by Natasha Donovan. Minneapolis: Millbrook Press, 2021.

Soto, Sandra K. *Reading Chican@ Like a Queer: The De-Mastery of Desire*. Austin: University of Texas Press, 2010.

Spade, Dean. *Normal Life: Administrative Violence, Critical Trans Politics, and the Limits of Law*. Durham, NC: Duke University Press, 2015.

Spear, Thomas C. "Introduction: Autobiographical Que(e)ries." *Auto/Biography Studies* 15, no. 1 (2000): 1–4.

Spellers, Regina E. "The Kink Factor: A Womanist Discourse Analysis of African American Mother/Daughter Perspectives on Negotiating Black Hair/Body Politics." In *Understanding African American Rhetoric: Classical Origins to Contemporary Innovations*, edited by Ronald L. Jackson II and Elaine B. Richardson, 223–43. New York: Routledge, 2003.

Standley, Fred L., and Louis H. Pratt, eds. *Conversations with James Baldwin*. Jackson: University Press of Mississippi, 1989.

Steiner, Charlotte. *Tomboy's Doll*. New York: Lothrop, Lee, and Shepard, 1969.

Stephens, John, ed. *Ways of Being Male: Representing Masculinities in Children's Literature*. New York: Routledge, 2002.

Steptoe, Javaka. *Radiant Child: The Story of Young Artist Jean-Michel Basquiat*. New York: Little, Brown, 2016.

Stockton, Kathryn Bond. "Growing Sideways, or Versions of the Queer Child: The Ghost, the Homosexual, the Freudian, the Innocent, and the Interval of Animal." In *Curiouser: On the Queerness of Child*, edited by Steven Bruhm and Natasha Hurley, 277–315. Minneapolis: University of Minnesota Press, 2004.

———. *The Queer Child, or Growing Sideways in the Twentieth Century*. Durham, NC: Duke University Press, 2009.

Stover, Lois Thomas. *Jacqueline Woodson: "The Real Thing."* Lanham, MD: Scarecrow Press, 2003.

Strang, John F., Anna IR van der Miesen, Reid Caplan, Cat Hughes, Sharon daVanport, and Meng-Chuan Lai. "Both Sex- and Gender-Related Factors Should Be Considered in Autism Research and Clinical Practice." *Autism* 24, no. 3 (2020): 539–43.

Sullivan, Laura L. *Jacqueline Woodson: Spotlight on Children's Authors*. New York: Cavendish Square, 2015.

Swartz, Patti Capel. "Bridging Multicultural Education: Bringing Sexual Orientation into the Children's and Young Adult Literature Classrooms." *Radical Teacher* no. 66 (2003): 11–16.

Tafolla, Carmen, and Sharyll Teneyuca. *That's Not Fair! Emma Tenayuca's Struggle for Justice/¡No es justo! La lucha de Emma Tenayuca por la justicia*. Illustrated by Terry Ybánez. San Antonio, TX: Wings, 2008.

Taylor, Nathan. "U.S. Children's Picture Books and the Homonormative Subject." *Journal of LGBT Youth* 9, no. 2 (2012): 136–52.

Teves, Stephanie Nohelani. *Defiant Indigeneity: The Politics of Hawaiian Performance*. Chapel Hill: University of North Carolina Press, 2018.

Thom, Kai Cheng. *Fierce Femmes and Notorious Liars: A Dangerous Trans Girl's Confabulous Memoir*. Montreal: Metonymy Press, 2016.

———. *For Laika: The Dog Who Learned the Names of the Stars*. Illustrated by Kai Yun Ching. Vancouver: Arsenal Pulp Press, 2021.

———. *From the Stars in the Sky to the Fish in the Sea*. Illustrated by Wai-Yant Li and Kai Yun Ching. Vancouver: Arsenal Pulp Press, 2017.

———. *I Hope We Choose Love: A Trans Girl's Notes for the End of the World*. Vancouver: Arsenal Pulp Press, 2019.

Thomas, Ebony Elizabeth. *The Dark Fantastic: Race and the Imagination from Harry Potter to the Hunger Games*. New York: New York University Press, 2019.

Thompson, Robert Farris. "Royalty, Heroism, and the Streets: The Art of Jean-Michel Basquiat." In *The Hearing Eye: Jazz and Blues Influences in African American Visual Art*, edited by Graham Lock and David Murray, 253–81. Oxford: Oxford University Press, 2009.

Tillich, Paul. "Existential Philosophy." *Journal of the History of Ideas* 5, no. 1 (1944): 44–70.

Tofiño, Iñaki, and Sebastià Martín. *La fiesta de Blas*. Illustrated by Mabel Piérola. Barcelona: Ediciones Bellaterra, 2008. Originally published in Catalan as *La festa d'en Blai*.

Tosh, Jemma. *Psychology and Gender Dysphoria: Feminist and Transgender Perspectives*. New York: Routledge, 2016.

Towbin, Mia Adessa, Shelley A. Haddock, Toni Schindler Zimmerman, Lori K. Lund, and Litsa Renee Tanner. "Images of Gender, Race, Age, and Sexual Orientation in

Disney Feature-Length Animated Films." *Journal of Feminist Family Therapy* 15, no. 4 (2004): 19–44.

Trujillo, Carla. *What Night Brings*. Willimantic, CT: Curbstone Press, 2003.

Tunks, Karyn Wellhousen, and Jessica McGee. "Embracing William, Oliver Button, and Tough Boris: Learning Acceptance from Characters in Children's Literature." *Childhood Education* 82, no. 4 (2006): 213–18.

Urquijo-Ruiz, Rita E. "Tomboy." *Chicana/Latina Studies: The Journal of Mujeres Activas en Letras y Cambio Social* 8, nos. 1–2 (2009): 60–64.

Valentine, Johnny. *One Dad, Two Dads, Brown Dad, Blue Dads*. Illustrated by Melody Sarecky. Los Angeles: Alyson Wonderland, 1994.

Van Allsburg, Chris. *Bad Day at Riverbend*. Boston: Houghton Mifflin, 1995.

Vásquez, Edith M. "La Gloriosa Travesura de la Musa Que Cruza/The Misbehaving Glory(a) of the Border-Crossing Muse: Transgression in Anzaldúa's Children's Stories." In *EntreMundos/AmongWorlds: New Perspectives on Gloria Anzaldúa*, edited by AnaLouise Keating, 63–75. New York: Palgrave Macmillan, 2005.

Vázquez, David J. *Triangulations: Narrative Strategies for Navigating Latino Identity*. Minneapolis: University of Minnesota Press, 2011.

Vega, Juan A. Ríos. *Carlos, the Fairy Boy/Carlos, el niño hada*. San Francisco: Reflection Press, 2020.

Vinson, Ben, III, and Matthew Restall. *Black Mexico: Race and Society from Colonial to Modern Times*. Albuquerque: University of New Mexico Press, 2009.

Volbert, Renate. "Sexual Knowledge of Preschool Children." *Journal of Psychology and Human Sexuality* 12, nos. 1–2 (2000): 5–26.

Walters, Alexander. *My Life and Work*. New York: Fleming H. Revell, 1917.

Ware, Syrus Marcus. "All Power to All People? Black LGBTTI2QQ Activism, Remembrance, and Archiving in Toronto." *TSQ: Transgender Studies Quarterly* 4, no. 2 (2017): 170–80.

———. "All That We Touch, We Change." *Canadian Art Magazine*, Spring 2017, 112–15.

———. "Boldly Going Where Few Men Have Gone Before: One Trans Man's Experience." In *Who's Your Daddy? And Other Writings on Queer Parenting*, edited by Rachel Epstein, 65–72. Toronto: Sumach Press, 2009.

———. "Confessions of a Black Pregnant Dad." In *Birthing Justice: Black Women, Pregnancy, and Childbirth*, edited by Julia Chinyere Oparah and Alicia D. Bonaparte, 63–71. New York: Routledge, 2016. First published in 2015 by Paradigm.

———. *Love is in the Hair*. Toronto: Flamingo Rampant Press, 2015.

Ware, Syrus Marcus, and Giselle Dias. "Revolution and Resurgence: Dismantling the Prison Industrial Complex through Black and Indigenous Solidarity." In *Until We Are Free: Reflections on Black Lives Matter in Canada*, edited by Rodney Diverlus, Sandy Hudson, and Syrus Marcus Ware, 32–56. Regina, SK: University of Regina Press, 2020.

Ware, Syrus Marcus, and Zack Marshall. "Disabilities and Deaf Culture." In *Trans Bodies, Trans Selves: A Resource for the Transgender Community*, edited by Laura Erickson-Schroth, 54–61. Oxford: Oxford University Press, 2014.

Wargo, Jon M., and James Joshua Coleman. "Speculating the Queer (In)Human: A Critical, Reparative Reading of Contemporary LGBTQ+ Picturebooks." *Journal of Children's Literature* 47, no 1 (2021): 84–96.

Weheliye, Alexander G. *Habeas Viscus: Racializing Assemblages, Biopolitics, and Black Feminist Theories of the Human.* Durham, NC: Duke University Press, 2014.

W[hite], T[homas]. *A Little Book for Little Children: Wherein Are Set Down, in a Plain and Pleasant Way, Directions for Spelling, And Other Remarkable Matters.* London, 1702. www.bl.uk.

Willhoite, Michael. *Daddy's Roommate.* Boston: Alyson, 1991.

Winthrop, Elizabeth. *Tough Eddie.* Illustrated by Lillian Hoban. New York: Dutton, 1985.

Wolf, Alexander, and Emanuel K Schwartz. "Irrational Psychotherapy: An Appeal to Unreason (III)." *American Journal of Psychotherapy* 12, no. 4 (1958): 744–59.

Womack, Craig S. *Drowning in Fire.* Tucson: University of Arizona Press, 2001.

Womack, Ytasha L. *Afrofuturism: The World of Black Sci-Fi and Fantasy* Culture. Chicago: Lawrence Hill Books, 2013.

Wong, Lloyd, and Shiboa Guo, eds. *Revisiting Multiculturalism in Canada: Theories, Debates and Issues.* Rotterdam: Sense, 2015.

Woodson, Jacqueline. *After Tupac and D Foster.* New York: Puffin Books, 2008.

———. *Autobiography of a Family Photo: A Novel.* New York: Dutton, 1995.

———. "Before Her: The One." Seattle: Amazon, 2019.

———. *Brown Girl Dreaming.* New York: Nancy Paulsen Books, 2014.

———. *The Day You Begin.* Illustrated by Rafael López. New York: Nancy Paulsen Books, 2018.

———. *The Dear One.* New York: Delacorte Press, 1991.

———. *Each Kindness.* Illustrated by E. B. Lewis. New York: Nancy Paulsen Books, 2012.

———. *From the Notebooks of Melanin Sun.* New York: Blue Sky Press, 1995.

———. *The House You Pass on the Way.* New York: Delacorte Press, 1997.

———. *I Hadn't Meant to Tell You This.* New York: Delacorte Books for Young Readers, 1994.

———. "Jacqueline Woodson." In *The Letter Q: Queer Writers' Notes to Their Younger Selves,* edited by Sarah Moon, 16–18. New York: Scholastic, 2012.

———. *Last Summer with Maizon.* New York: Delacorte Press, 1990.

———. *Martin Luther King Jr. and His Birthday.* Illustrated by Floyd Cooper. Englewood Cliffs, NJ: Silver Press, 1990.

———. *The Other Side.* Illustrated by E. B. Lewis. New York: Putnam, 2001.

———. *Our Gracie Aunt.* Illustrated by Jon J. Muth. New York: Jump at the Sun, Hyperion Books for Children, 2002.

———. *Pecan Pie Baby.* Illustrated by Sophie Blackall. New York: Putnam, 2010.

———. *Show Way.* Illustrated by Hudson Talbott. New York: Putnam, 2005.

———. *Sweet, Sweet Memory.* Illustrated by Floyd Cooper. New York: Jump at the Sun, Hyperion Books for Children, 2000.

―――. *This Is the Rope: A Story of Great Migration*. Illustrated by James Ransome. New York: Nancy Paulsen Books, 2013.

―――. *Visiting Day*. Illustrated by James E. Ransome. New York: Scholastic Press, 2002.

―――. *We Had a Picnic This Sunday Past*. Illustrated by Diane Greenseid. New York: Scholastic; Hyperion, 1997.

Yan, Kit. *Casey's Ball*. Illustrated by Holly McGillis. Toronto: Flamingo Rampant Press, 2019.

―――. *Queer Heartache: Poems*. Los Angles: Trans-Genre Press, 2016.

Zipes, Jack. "The Twists and Turns of Radical Children's Literature." Foreword to *Tales for Little Rebels: A Collection of Radical Children's Literature*, edited by Julia L. Mickenberg and Philip Nel, vii–ix. New York: New York University Press, 2008.

Zipes, Jack, Lissa Paul, Lynne Vallone, Peter Hunt, and Gillian Avery, eds. *The Norton Anthology of Children's Literature*. New York: Norton, 2005.

Zolotow, Charlotte. *William's Doll*. Illustrated by William Pène Du Bois. New York: HarperCollins,1972.

INDEX

Page numbers in *italics* indicate Figures.

ABOUT THE AUTHOR

ISABEL MILLÁN is Assistant Professor in the Department of Women's, Gender, and Sexuality Studies at the University of Oregon whose research interests include children's literature, queer and trans of color theory, and border studies. Millán is the author and illustrator of the children's picture book *Chabelita's Heart/El corazón de Chabelita* (2022). Her scholarship has appeared in *Keywords for Comic Studies, Signs: Journal of Women in Culture and Society, Aztlán: A Journal of Chicano Studies*, and *The Routledge Companion to Latina/o Popular Culture*.